High-level Vision

High-level Vision
Object Recognition and Visual Cognition

Shimon Ullman

A Bradford Book

The MIT Press
Cambridge, Massachusetts
London, England

Third printing, 2000

This book was set in Computer Modern by the author and was printed and bound in the United States of America.

Library of Congress Cataloging-in-Publication Data

High-level vision / Shimon Ullman.
      p.   cm.
"A Bradford book."
Includes bibliographical references and index.
ISBN 0-262-21013-4 (hc: alk. paper).
1. Visual perception.   I. Title.
QP475.U44   1995
152.14—dc20   95-36691
                                                                         CIP

To Chana, Tomer, Yonatan

Contents

Preface

Our visual sense provides us with rich and detailed information about the environment: we use it effortlessly to find our way, recognize our friends and distinguish their moods, guide our movements, manipulate objects, and for a large variety of other tasks. As seeing agents, we are so used to the benefits of vision, and so unaware of how we actually use it, that it took a long time to appreciate the almost miraculous achievements of our visual system. If one tries to adopt a more objective and detached attitude, by considering the visual system as a device that records a band of electromagnetic radiation as an input, and then uses it to gain knowledge about surrounding objects that emit and reflect it, one cannot help but be struck by the richness of information this system provides.

Vision is a complex process that includes many interacting components involved, for example, with the analysis of color, depth, motion, shape, and texture of objects, and with the use of visual information for recognition, locomotion, and manipulation. I will deal here only with some of these aspects, in particular, problems related to visual object recognition, and the area of visual cognition, which has to do with the perception of shape properties and spatial relations.

The collection of processes involved in visual perception are often perceived as a hierarchy spanning the range from "low" via "intermediate" to "high-level" vision. Using this terminology, which is explained in detail below, the focus of the book is on tasks that belong to the domain of intermediate- and high-level vision, rather than low-level visual processes. The notions of "low" and "high-level" vision are used routinely, but there is no clear definition of the distinction between what is considered "high" as opposed to "low-level" vision. Roughly speaking, this means that I will be concerned more with the interpretation of what is seen in the image than with the more preliminary processing of the image, for example, the detection of lines and edges, or the extraction of motion, binocular disparity, or color.

Low-level vision is usually associated with the extraction of certain physical properties of the visible environment, such as depth, three-dimensional (3-D) shape, object boundaries, or surface material properties. A number of characteristics are typically asso-

ciated with low-level vision processes: they are spatially uniform
and parallel; that is, with allowance for the decrease in resolution
from the center of the visual field outwards, similar processing is
applied simultaneously across the visual field. For example, processes involved in edge detection, motion, or stereo vision, often
proceed in parallel across the visual field, or a large part of it.
Low-level visual processes are also considered "bottom-up" in nature. This means that they are determined by the data and are
relatively independent of the task at hand or knowledge associated
with specific objects. As far as we know edge detection or stereo,
for example, are performed in the same manner for images of different objects, and with no regard to whether the task has to do
with moving around, looking for a misplaced object, or enjoying
the landscape.

High-level vision, in contrast, is concerned with problems such
as the extraction of shape properties and spatial relations, and
with object recognition and classification. It is concerned primarily with the interpretation and use of the information in the image,
rather than the direct recovery of physical properties. High-level
visual processes are applied to a selected portion of the image,
rather than uniformly across the entire image, and they often depend upon the goal of the computation and knowledge related to
specific objects. Within the domain of higher-level vision, processes that do not depend on knowledge about specific objects
are sometimes called intermediate-level vision. We will see examples of these processes in discussing problems of visual cognition
and certain aspects of segmentation and selection. For example,
the extraction of shape properties and spatial relations is often
confined to selected elements in the scene and does not proceed
uniformly and in parallel across the image. At the same time, the
processing is largely independent of knowledge associated with
specific objects.

I will not discuss further aspects of the distinction between low-,
intermediate-, and high-level vision. These notions are used as a
rough delineation of the issues considered here: they include visual routines, segmentation and selection, and object recognition
and classification, but not problems such as stereo vision, color
or motion perception. The distinctions can serve a useful role,

but they should not be taken to imply that what is traditionally
called "high-level" necessarily comes later in the temporal succession of processing stages, or that the higher level stages can only
be performed after the lower level stages completed their task. In
fact, I suspect that certain aspects of object recognition that are
traditionally considered high-level do not necessarily come after
(in terms of processing stages) some processes that are considered
lower level, but are working in parallel with them, and interacting with them in both directions. Some of these aspects will be
considered in greater detail in the last chapter. Some of the distinctions between the processing stages may become clearer, and
may also have to be revised, following a better understanding of
the visual process in general and the so-called higher level aspects
in particular.

Scope of the Book

The first half of the book deals with the problem of object recognition, and the second with related issues, including classification,
segmentation, and with the general issue of visual cognition. The
first chapter introduces the problem of visual recognition, and discusses the reasons why the problem is so difficult. The difficulty
of the task may seem surprising, since recognition often appears
to us natural and effortless. It may also seem that all one must do
to recognize an object visually is to store a sufficient number of
instances of the object in question, and subsequently identify the
object by comparing it with the stored views. As it turned out,
the problem is in fact exceedingly difficult, and consequently we
do not yet have artificial systems that can perform the task adequately. Chapter 1 discusses the difficulties involved in performing
visual recognition.

Chapter 2 reviews the main approaches that have been developed over the years to deal with visual recognition. A great number of different methods have been attempted, but most of them
use variations of a small number of key ideas. The chapter classifies the past approaches into three main classes: the use of invari-

ant properties, the use of parts and structural descriptions, and
the alignment of pictorial descriptions.

The alignment approach is developed further in the next three
chapters. In this approach, recognition proceeds by explicitly compensating for the differences separating the object in view with a
previously stored model of the same object. Chapter 3 focuses
on a method, called 3-D alignment, that uses explicitly three-
dimensional internal models that are aligned with the image in
the course of the recognition process. As it turns out, objects with
smooth bounding surfaces and lacking distinctive features deserve
within this framework a somewhat extended treatment, and this is
the subject of chapter 4. Chapter 5 then presents a modification
of the alignment approach that does not employ explicit three-
dimensional object models. Instead, each object is represented in
terms of a small number of two-dimensional views. During the
recognition process, the object in view is matched against certain
combinations of the stored views. The chapter also considers extensions of the scheme, to deal, for example, with partial views
and with non-rigid transformations. The final section of chapter 5
summarizes briefly the main properties of the approach to recognition developed in the first half of the book. These properties
include the use of pictorial description and matching, the use of
alignment—applying transformations to bring the internal model
and the viewed object into close agreement—and the use of multiple corresponding views and view combinations. The general
approach is quite different from the view I had when I started to
consider the problem. At the time, the dominant approach to 3-
D recognition was based on symbolic structural descriptions, and
recognition was generally viewed as a symbolic, abstract, high-
level activity. The view that emerges from the work described in
this book as well as related studies is that significant aspects of
recognition can be accomplished by processes that are relatively
low-level and pictorial in nature.

These chapters contain some mathematical material, but most
of the more detailed material is summarized separately in several
appendices. When mathematical expressions and derivations appear in the text, they are accompanied by informal explanations
that summarize the main conclusions from the derivations.

In chapter 6 the focus shifts from the identification of individual objects to the problem of object classification. The problem here is to assign an object to a general class such as a "house," "dog," "face," rather than identify a particular house or an individual face. One intriguing aspect of this problem is that for biological systems classification is easier and more immediate than individual identification, whereas for artificial systems the opposite is true — for them classification is a difficult and challenging problem.

Chapters 7 and 8 deal with two specific processes that constitute important parts of the overall recognition process. The first has to do with the establishment of correspondence between the internal model and the viewed object. The second, examined in chapter 8, has to do with segmentation and the identification of image structures that are likely to form the image of a single object.

Chapter 9 discusses the domain of visual cognition—the visual extraction of shape properties and spatial relations. The discussion goes beyond the domain of recognition, since the visual analysis of shape and spatial relations is used in many other tasks, such as in planning and guiding object manipulation, planning and executing movements in the environment, selecting and following a path, or interpreting maps, charts, and diagrams.

Finally, chapter 10 uses computational considerations discussed throughout the book, combined with psychophysical and biological data, to propose a model for the general flow of information in the visual cortex. The model uses a process called "sequence seeking" which is a search for a sequence of transformations and mappings that link an image with a stored object representation. The chapter discusses computational aspects of the model and its possible implementation in cortical circuitry.

Acknowledgments

I benefited from scientific discussions and collaborations with a number of friends, co-workers, and students, and from the comments of colleagues on different parts of this work. Thanks go to T. Poggio, W. Richards, A. Yuille, E. Grimson, S. Edelman R. Basri, D. Huttenlocher, P. Joliceour, J. Mahoney, Y. Moses, A. Shashua, P. Lipson, I. Bachelder, A. Zeira, Y. Yolles, M. Bar, C. Koch, D. Mumford, C. Gilbert, K. Martin, J. Maunsell. I thank P. Sinha for his talent and patience in producing the cover design, and D. Cantor-Adams for her editorial help. Special thanks go to E. Hildreth and to L. Ullman who provided insightful and helpful comments on the manuscript, to P. O'Donnell, who was always willing to help with sound technical advice, and to T. Ehling, who was a patient and supporting editor—I thank them warmly.

I am grateful to H.L. Kundel and C.F. Nodine for their permission to reproduce the beautiful figures in (Kundel & Nodine 1983). I would also like to thank the following publishers and journals for their permission to reproduce figures in this book. *Radiology*, for the figures from (Kundel & Nodine 1983), *International Journal of Computer Vision*, Kluwer Academic Publishers Group, for figures from (Huttenlocher & Ullman 1990), *IEEE PAMI*, IEEE Publishing Services, for figures from (Ullman & Basri 1991), *Computer Vision, Graphics, and Image Processing*, Academic Press, Inc., for figures from (Basri & Ullman 1993), *Acta Psychologica*, Elsevier Science Publications, for the beautiful drawings in (Green & Courtis 1966), *Cognition*, Elsevier Sequoia S.A., for figures from (Ullman 1984) and (Ullman 1989), and *Cerebral Cortex*, for figures from (Ullman 1995).

The work described in this book was supported by several research grants, and I would like to thank the granting agencies for their support. Parts of the research were done at the Massachusetts Institute of Technology, in the department of Brain and Cognitive Sciences and in the Artificial Intelligence Laboratory. Support for the laboratory's artificial intelligence research was provided in part by an Office of Naval Research under several programs, including University Research Initiative grant under contract N00014-86-K-0685, and in part by the Advanced Research Projects Agency of the Department of Defense under Army contract number DACA76-85-C-0010 and under Office of Naval

Research contract N00014-85-K-0124. The work on segmentation and selection was supported by NSF Grant IRI-8900267. Parts of the work were conducted at the Weizmann Institute in Rehovot, Israel, with support from The Ministry of Science and Technology under grant 3164-1-89. Parts of the biologically-related work were supported by The Israel Science Foundation administered by the Israel Academy of Sciences and Humanities.

Special thanks go to Samy and Ruth Cohn for their continuing support over many years.

Shimon Ullman
Rehovot, Israel, 1995.

High-level Vision

1 Object Recognition

Object recognition is one of the most important, yet least understood, aspects of visual perception. For many biological vision systems, the recognition and classification of objects is a spontaneous, natural activity. Young children can recognize immediately and effortlessly a large variety of objects. Simple animals, such as the pigeon (with its pea-pod sized brain) exhibit remarkable recognition behavior. Even insects, such as the bee, use visual recognition for purposes such as navigation and finding its home, or identifying flower shapes (Gould 1985).

In contrast, the recognition of common objects is still way beyond the capabilities of artificial systems, or any recognition model proposed so far. The contrast between the brain and the computer in their capacity to perform visual recognition and classification makes the problem particularly fascinating. The brain generalizes spontaneously from visual examples without the need for explicit rules and laborious instruction. For example, a child can generalize from a limited number of views of a dog, say, to many different dogs, under a variety of viewing conditions. In contrast, computers can be programmed to recognize specific objects with fixed, well defined shapes, such as machine parts. It is considerably more difficult to capture in a computer recognition system the essence of a dog, a house, or a tree – the kind of classification that is natural and immediate for the human visual system.

The difficulties involved in visual recognition do not seem to result from the lack of sufficient progress in our understanding of the early processing stages. It does not seem, for instance, that further improvements in processes such as edge detection or stereo computation would be of fundamental importance for making progress in the area of visual object recognition. The problems are primarily conceptual in nature, and what appears necessary is a better understanding of the underlying issues, such as: what makes object recognition difficult? are there different types of object recognition and classification processes? how can the overall task be broken down into more manageable problems? how can different views of an object, including novel ones, be identified as representing a single object?

1.1   Shape-Based Recognition

Visual object recognition is not a single problem. One reason
for the diversity of approaches to the problem is that there are
several different paths leading to visual object recognition, based
on different sources of information. We often recognize an object
(a car, a familiar face, a printed character) visually on the basis
of its characteristic shape. We may also use visual, but non-shape
cues, such as color and texture. The recognition of a tree of a given
type is based in some cases more on texture properties, branching
pattern, and color, than on precise shape. Certain animals such
as a tiger or a giraffe can also be identified sometimes on the basis
of texture and color pattern rather than shape. Similarly, various
material types, as well as different scene types such as a "lake
scenery" or "mountainous terrain," can be recognized visually,
without relying on precise shape.

Objects can also be recognized visually primarily on the basis
of their location relative to other objects. For example, a door
knob may have a non-standard shape, and still be recognized immediately as a door knob on the basis of its location relative to
the door. Yet another possibility is to recognize objects visually
on the basis of their characteristic motion. For example, a fly in
the room may be perceived as a small dark blob, and still be recognized as a fly, on the basis of its characteristic erratic motion
(Cutting & Kozlowski 1977, Johansson 1973).

In all of the above examples, recognition can be said to be primarily visual, that is, the recognition process proceeds primarily
on the basis of the visual information. There are also situations in
which the recognition process uses sources that are not primarily
visual in nature. One example has to do with the use of prior
knowledge, expectations, and temporal continuity (Biederman *et
al.* 1982, Morton 1969, Palmer 1975, Potter 1975). For example,
one may recognize a white object on one's desk as being a familiar
telephone even when the visual image does not contain enough detail for clear object recognition (because the viewing was too brief,
or the illumination level too low). Finally, in some cases, visual
recognition employs processes that may be described as reasoning,
for example, recognizing a fence surrounding a field may be based

in part not on a specific visual form, but on reasoning about its potential use.

Here, we will be concerned primarily with the problem of shape-based recognition. Most common objects can be recognized in isolation, without the use of context or expectations. For the recognition of many objects, color, texture, and motion, play only a secondary role. Furthermore, as far as recognition is concerned, shape usually dominates over other cues: we can easily recognize, say, a pink elephant, despite the unusual color. Recognition by shape properties is probably the most common and important aspect of visual recognition and therefore "object recognition" is often taken to mean the visual recognition of objects based on their shape properties. There are some difficulties in defining the term "shape" unequivocally, but such a precise definition will not be required in the present discussion. Other types of visual object recognition, for example, on the basis of color or motion alone, rather than shape, will not be considered here.

1.2   What Is Recognition?

Although we are constantly engaged in the process of object recognition, it is not easy to define the term "object recognition" in a simple, precise and uncontroversial manner. This problem is raised here briefly not to suggest a full definition of the term, but to delineate the scope of the problem as examined in the next few chapters.

What do we mean, exactly, when we say that we "recognize an object" (visually)? The simplest answer might be: "naming an object in sight." However, this natural answer is not entirely unambiguous. In recognizing an object, we wish sometimes to identify an individual object, or a specific "token" (such as "my car"), while in other cases recognition means identifying the object as a member of a certain class, or a type, ("a truck"). Furthermore, an object may belong to a number of classes or categories simultaneously (e.g., my cat, a Siamese cat, a cat, an animal). Recognition would require in such cases a classification at the appropriate level, and what is considered appropriate may depend on the circumstances. An image often contains multiple objects, and each object may contain a number of recognizable parts. Again, the problem of appropriateness arises. In the image of a cat, one may also recognize an eye, a whisker, or a tail. If the question is, "what's in the image," different answers may be appropriate under different circumstances.

Finally, naming is not necessarily the end product of the recognition process; animals lacking the language faculty can still recognize objects visually. The important end product is the ability to retrieve information associated with an object, or a class of objects, that is not apparent in the image itself. An object's name is an example of such "invisible" information, but, of course, not the only example.

These and related issues pose pertinent problems for the theory of object recognition, but they will not be considered here in detail. For the purpose of the present discussion we will focus on the recognition of individual objects (classification will be discussed later, in chapter 6). We will assume initially that there exists a collection of individual objects that can change their location and orientation in space with respect to the viewer, as well as their sizes. We will later deal also with other changes that may affect the appearance of the object, such as changes in the illumination conditions. We are then given an image of an object, or a region in the image containing a single object or a partial view of it (that is, the object may be partially occluded). Given such a region (that will be called the "image of the object," or a "viewed object"), the problem is to identify, for example, to name, the object that gave rise to the image in question. We will also deal with the identification of an image region that may contain an object to be recognized—the problems of selection and segmentation.

1.3   Why Object Recognition Is Difficult

Why is visual recognition difficult? It may appear initially that the problem could perhaps be overcome by using a sufficiently large and efficient memory system. In performing recognition, we are trying to determine whether an image we currently see corresponds to an object we have seen in the past. It might be possible, therefore, to approach object recognition by storing a sufficient number of different views associated with each object, and then comparing the image of the currently viewed object with all the views stored in memory (Abu-Mostafa & Psaltis 1987). Several mechanisms, known as associative memories, have been proposed for implementing this "direct" approach to recognition. These mechanisms, usually embodied in neuron-like networks, can store a large number of patterns $(P_1, P_2, ..., P_n)$, and then, given an input pattern Q, they can retrieve the pattern P_i which is most similar to Q (Willshaw, Buneman & Longuet-Higgins 1969, Kohonen 1978, Hopfield 1982).

Have associative memories of this type solved the problem of object recognition? Discussions of associative memories sometimes suggest that they have. When the system has stored a representative view, or several views, of each object, a new view would automatically retrieve the stored representation which most closely resembles it. A major problem with the direct approach is that it relies on a simple and restricted notion of similarity to measure the distance between the input image and each of the images stored previously in memory. As we will see in the following discussion, the use of a simple image comparison is insufficient by itself to cope with the large variations between different images of a given object. A typical similarity measure used in associative memory models, for instance, is the so-called "Hamming distance." (This measure is defined for two binary vectors. Suppose that **u** and **v** are two binary vectors, i.e., strings of 1's and 0's. The Hamming distance between **u** and **v** is simply the number of coordinates in which they differ.) Another similarity measure that is used frequently for direct image comparison is the so-called L_2 norm between grey level images, which sums the squared differences between image intensity values at corresponding points.

It should be noted that a similarity measure, such as the Hamming distance, could be applied not to the images, but to a more abstract representation. For example, the image of a written character could be recoded as a vector specifying properties such as the existence of closed loops, the number of free ends, and the like. Objects could then be compared by comparing distances between abstract description vectors. In discussing the direct approach I consider, however, only the direct comparison of the images themselves, with little or no recoding.

The use of simple similarity measures of this type in recognition may be appropriate for some special applications and also for certain non-visual domains, such as olfaction (Freeman 1979). It also appears quite plausible that a large scale memory may in fact play an important part in object recognition, and in some simpler animals it may even play a dominant part. The pigeon, for example, can store a large number of arbitrary visual patterns and use them in recognition tasks. In one study, pigeons were trained to sort 320 slides of natural scenes into two arbitrary categories, positive and negative (Vaughan & Greene 1984). The pigeons learned the task rapidly, performed it with a high level of accuracy, and showed significant retention without additional practice after a period of over two years. Even the fly can remember and recognize patterns visually, and the evidence suggests that this is achieved by a direct comparison with previously stored patterns at particular retinal locations (Dill, Wolf & Heisenberg 1993).

For the general problem of visual object recognition this direct approach is insufficient, however, for two reasons. First, the space of all possible views of all the objects to be recognized is likely to be prohibitively large. The second, and more fundamental reason, is that the image to be recognized will often not be sufficiently similar to any image seen in the past. There are several main sources for this variability, and it seems to me that the success of any recognition scheme will depend on its ability to cope with these variations.

• *Viewing position:* The first reason for the variability between new and old images has to do with the effect of viewing position. Three-dimensional objects can be viewed from a variety of viewing positions (directions and distances), and these different views can give rise to widely different images. It is sometimes difficult to appreciate this effect of viewing direction, since two views of the same object separated by, say, 20-30 degrees usually appear perceptually quite similar. When the two 2-D projections are superimposed and compared it becomes apparent, however, how

a

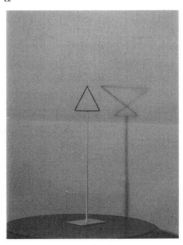

b

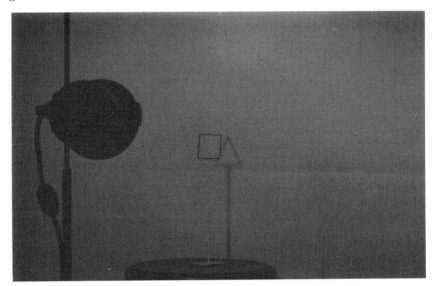

Figure 1.1
Different views of the same three-dimensional object, observed from different viewing directions. Views *a* and *b* are separated by 5° of rotation about the vertical axis. Note the triangular shadow of the square object in *b*.

different they can become with even a modest change in viewing direction, as we will see more quantitatively below.

An extreme illustration of the possible effect of small changes in viewing direction is shown in figure 1.1. The images in (*a*) and (*b*) show two views of the same three dimensional object, separated by a small rotation (5 degree about the vertical axis). Figure 1.1b actually shows the two views simultaneously—note the object's shadow on the wall. The image in (*c*) is another view of the same object that makes its 3-D structure clearer. This example is not confined to a wireframe object—a solid shape can also be constructed with a similar set of projections. The example uses specially constructed object, but the point it illustrates is a general one: changes in viewing direction often produce large differences in the object's appearance.

• *Photometric effects:* The second source of variability comes from photometric effects. These include the positions and distribution of light sources in the scene, their wavelengths, the effects of mutual illumination by other objects, and the distribution of shadows and specularities. Photometric effects of this type can change drastically the light intensity distribution in the image, but they usually do not affect our ability to recognize the objects in the image.

• *Object setting:* In natural scenes, objects are rarely seen in isolation: they are usually seen against some background, next to, or partially occluded by other objects. When the image contains a familiar object in a new setting, the new image, taken as a whole, will fail to match past images of the same object stored in memory.

• *Changing shape:* The fourth and final source is the effect of changing shape. Many objects, such as the human body, can maintain their identity while changing their 3-D shape. In order to identify such objects correctly, the recognition scheme must be able to deal with the effects induced by changes of shape. Changing objects, such as a pair of scissors, can sometimes be composed of rigid sub-parts. Other objects may undergo non-rigid distortions, for example, faces undergoing complex transformations due to facial expressions.

The effects of these sources of variation, in particular the effects of viewing position and illumination direction, were examined quantitatively in the domain of face images (Moses, Adini & Ullman 1994). It is worth while to review briefly the main results, to illustrate some of the difficulties introduced by the various sources of image variations. In the study, a number of different individuals were imaged from a number of viewing directions and under different illumination conditions. The general idea was to compare images of different individuals with images of the same individual but under different viewing conditions. In this manner it becomes possible to examine whether the differences induced by mere changes in the viewing conditions are large or small compared with the differences between distinct individuals. The images used were of twenty-six individuals (all males, with no glasses, beards, etc., and with the hairline covered), taken from five viewing directions (face-on, and rotations of 17 and 34 degrees around the vertical axis to the left and right), and under four different illumination conditions. The different images were taken by moving a robotic arm with a TV camera to different locations in space.

To compare the different images, one needs to define a measure of similarity between two-dimensional images. The study employed a number of simple and commonly used distance measures. For example, one of the measures used the average absolute difference between the image intensity levels of corresponding points. The face images were normalized in size, orientation, and position before this measure was computed. Another measure allowed some local distortions between the two images: the grey level value at a given point was compared not only to a single corresponding location in the second image, but to all the points within a given neighborhood (typically 5×5), and then the best-matching value within this neighborhood was selected. The computation of image differences also included compensation for changes in overall intensity level and linear intensity gradients, so that the difference measure became insensitive to these global parameters. This was obtained by the following method: Before comparing the two images, an overall intensity level $\mathbf{I}$ and an intensity gradient $\mathbf{g}$ were added to one of the images. $\mathbf{I}$ and $\mathbf{g}$ were determined by an optimization procedure so as to minimize the differences between the two images being compared.

Another type of difference measure used transformed versions of the images, obtained by applying to the images various linear filters, such as difference-of-gaussians, or DOG filters (Marr & Hildreth 1980), Gabor filters (Daugman 1989), and using directional derivatives of the grey level images. Filtering of this kind appears to take place in the early processing stages of the mammalian visual system, and it is also often used in artificial image processing systems. Finally, the study also compared the images by first obtaining an edge map from each image, and then comparing the resulting contour maps. The use of such edge maps is also a standard procedure in image processing, partly because they are less sensitive to illumination conditions than the original grey level images. For each of the different measures, comparisons were made between the full face images, but also between partial face images, such as the upper or lower parts.

The main result that emerged from these comparisons is that the differences induced by changes in the viewing conditions are large compared with the differences between different individuals. An example can be seen in table 1.1 from (Moses, Adini & Ullman 1994). The table compares the effects of changes in illumination and in viewing direction, with differences between individuals, for ten different faces (F_1 to F_{10}). Each face is compared to an image of the same face under a different illumination (first column, marked "IC" for Illumination Condition), to an image of the same face viewed from a different direction (17° change in direction, column marked "VP," for Viewing Position), and finally to all other ten faces viewed under the original viewing conditions. For example, for the first face, F_1, a change in illumination induced a difference measure of 59 units between the two images, and for a change in viewing direction the difference measure was 25 units. When this face image was compared with another face image, F_2, the difference measure was 21 units. This means that the changes induced by variations in the viewing conditions were larger than the difference between the two individuals. In fact, for eight out of the ten face images, the differences due to viewing conditions were the same or larger than the differences between distinct individuals.

FC	IC	VP	Pairs of Faces									
			F1	F2	F3	F4	F5	F6	F7	F8	F9	F10
F1	59	25		21	25	26	24	39	25	22	23	22
F2	56	23			16	18	27	25	16	14	16	15
F3	56	26				17	27	27	14	15	20	16
F4	58	27					26	26	18	18	20	20
F5	54	30						38	29	26	23	15
F6	50	25							26	28	25	24
F7	57	30								17	20	17
F8	51	23									18	17
F9	54	24										7
F10	53	21										

Table 1.1
Distances between face images. Column FC lists 10 different faces. Column IC: distances between images of the same face, but under different illumination. Column VP: distances between images of the same face taken from frontal and 17 degrees side view. Column Pairs of Faces: distances between all face pairs.

One conclusion from these comparisons is that it will not be possible to base a face identification scheme on simple image comparisons. Suppose, for example, that we attempt to identify the faces of just the limited set of twenty-five individuals in the study by comparing an input image to a set of twenty-five images, one for each face, stored in memory, and then selecting the stored image that most closely resembles the input image. How well will such a procedure perform? The results show that such a scheme will be highly inadequate: for each image in the face database, the wrong answer will often be selected. The simple comparison, even in combination with the pre-normalization used for size, orientation, and position, was clearly insufficient. These results apply to one of the distance measures used (the average absolute difference in image intensities), but similar results were obtained with all the difference measures used, including the comparison of edge maps.

How well do humans perform under the same conditions? Are they confused in a similar manner, or can they cope better with the effects of illumination and viewing directions? This question was examined psychophysically by training eight subjects on a single image of each one of the individuals in the database, and then testing their recognition performance using all the other images. In 12 sessions of experimental testing, recognition was highly accurate: over 97% of the stimuli were identified correctly. Clearly, humans can compensate well for variations in illumination and viewing direction, and generalize well from a single image to novel viewing conditions. At the same time, this performance cannot be based on simple image difference measures of the type examined in the study.

It is also interesting to note that the behavior of the simple image comparison schemes is qualitatively different from human perception. Applying simple image comparisons to the face images, changes in illumination had the largest effect, followed by changes in viewing position, then changes in facial expression. The opposite order holds for human perception: changes in illumination of the type used in the study are usually hardly noticeable, viewing position tends to have a larger effect, and changes in expression are perceptually often quite pronounced.

We see, in conclusion, that a single object can give rise to a large variety of different images. The recognition system must somehow deal with these variations, and it will not be enough to use for this purpose simple, straightforward image comparison. One can consider the variation problem in terms of a mapping M that maps a given object O_i to one of a large set of possible views $(V_{i_1}, \ldots, V_{i_{ki}})$. Given a view of the object, the problem is in a sense to invert M and recover the original object O_i The problem is that the mapping is one-to-many, since a single object gives rise to many distinct images, and we do not want to store them all. If this mapping is governed by some general principles, or has certain regularities, one can use these regularities in the recognition process in a manner that will generalize better to novel views than direct image comparison to stored views. The recognition methods that will be discussed all try to find and exploit such regularities.

In the next several chapters we will focus on the variations caused by changes in viewing position. Chapter 2 will review the main approaches to this problem. Chapters 3, 4, and 5 will develop a particular approach, called alignment. The alignment method in chapters 3 and 4 uses three-dimensional object models. The method in chapter 5 does not use explicitly 3-D models, but uses instead collections of two-dimensional images.

2 Approaches to Object Recognition

A large variety of methods have been proposed for the task of visual object recognition, some of them as models of human vision, others as possible schemes for machine vision. Some of the proposed schemes are general in nature, others were developed for specific application domains (see Binford 1981, Besl & Jain 1985 for reviews). In this chapter I will compare the basic approaches to recognition, and classify them into three main classes, based on the major principles they employ.

The different approaches to recognition can be classified in several ways: methods differ in the features they extract from the image, whether the process relies primarily on 2-D or 3-D information, and along many other dimensions. However, the most significant criterion to compare different approaches of recognition is according to how they approach the central issue of recognition, namely, variability across views.

All approaches to recognition assume, at least implicitly, that the set of views belonging to a given object is not arbitrary, but contains certain regularities that can be exploited by the recognition process. The efficient use of such regularities will allow the recognition system to outperform the direct approach significantly, in terms of efficiency and the capacity to generalize to novel views. To recognize, for instance, triangles of any shape, position, and size, it is clearly not necessary to store in memory a large number of representative shapes. All of the shapes in this set have certain properties in common, and these regularities can be used in the recognition process. By using the common properties that define a triangle, it will become possible to limit the number of stored representations, and it will be possible to recognize novel shapes that are not similar in any simple direct measure to triangles seen before.

For simple geometrical shapes, such as triangles, the set of transformations that a member in the family of views may undergo is well-defined and straightforward to characterize. The problem of defining the regularities across views becomes difficult, however, when we consider natural objects under various possible viewing conditions. For the family of views representing a 3-D object, the set of "allowable transformations" that the views may undergo cannot be defined easily, especially when the object can undergo non-rigid transformations. For example, what would be the regularities in the transformations linking the different possible views of a rabbit?

Approaches to visual object recognition differ in the type of regularities they propose to exploit. The proposal is not always made explicit, but any theory of object recognition that goes beyond the direct approach must make some assumptions regarding the expected regularities within a family of views that belong to the same object. The prevailing theories of object recognition are classified below on the basis of their approach to the regularity problem. Three main classes are distinguished: (i) invariant properties methods, (ii) parts decomposition methods, and (iii) alignment methods. Theories in the first class assume that certain simple properties remain invariant under the transformations that an object is allowed to make. This approach leads to the notions of invariances, feature spaces, clustering, and separation techniques. The second class relies on the decomposition of objects into parts. This leads into the notions of symbolic structural descriptions, feature hierarchies and syntactic pattern recognition. By and large, the first of these general approaches was the dominant one in the earlier days of pattern recognition and the second approach has become more popular in recent years, in both cognitive psychology and computer vision. It seems to me, however, that both of these approaches are insufficient for the general problem of shape-based visual recognition. A third approach, called the alignment method, will be presented and compared with the previous two.

The classification into invariant properties, part decomposition, and alignment methods, is a taxonomy of the underlying ideas, not of existing schemes. That is, a given scheme is not required to belong strictly to one of these classes, but may employ one or more of these ideas. A successful recognition scheme may in fact benefit from incorporating key ideas from all three classes. The point is that the variety of methods used seem to rely on a small number of basic ideas for dealing with the regularity problem, and it will be useful to examine and compare these ideas explicitly.

2.1   Invariant Properties and Feature Spaces

A common approach to object recognition has been to assume that objects have certain invariant properties that are common to all of their views (Pitts & McCulloch 1947). For example, in identifying different types of biological cells a "compactness measure," defined as the ratio between the cell's apparent area and its perimeter length squared, has been a useful characteristic. Cells that tend to be round and compact will have a high score on this measure, whereas long and narrow objects will have a low score. Furthermore, the measure will be unaffected by rotation, translation, and scaling in the image plane. Certain Fourier descriptors (coefficients in the Fourier transform) and object moments are additional examples of invariant measures that have been proposed. The idea is to define a number of such measures, and collectively they will then serve to identify each object unambiguously.

Formally, a property of this type can be defined as a function from the set of object views to the real numbers. It is important that these functions be relatively simple to compute. In recognizing, for example, different instances of the letter "A," one may define a function whose value is 1 if the viewed object is the letter "A," and 0 otherwise. This function would be an invariant of the letter A, but the problem of computing this invariance would be, of course, equivalent to the original problem of recognizing the letter. The invariant properties approach must therefore prescribe, together with the set of invariant properties proposed, effective procedures for extracting these properties. The invariant measures considered in this section are also assumed to depend on the image alone. A broader use of "invariants" in recognition (e.g., Mundy & Zisserman 1992) includes computations that depend on both the input image and stored internal models, or more than a single input image. Some of these schemes, such as the use of "affine invariants" are in fact close to the alignment approach, described in a later section.

In an invariant properties scheme the overall recognition process is thus broken down into the extraction of a number of different properties followed by a final decision based on these properties, where each of these stages is relatively simple to compute.

Object-1	Object-2
0 1 0 1 0 0	1 0 1 0 1 1
0 1 0 0 0 0	0 1 1 1 0 1
1 0 0 0 1 0	1 1 0 1 1 1
1 0 0 1 0 1	1 1 1 1 1 0

Table 2.1
Invariants in the domain of binary vectors. Which property distinguishes the "views" of Object-1 from those of Object-2?

2.1.1   An Example: The Domain of Binary Vectors

An example of the invariant properties approach is illustrated schematically in Table 2.1 for the simplified domain of binary vectors. This domain does not incorporate many of the complexities of real objects, but, in analogy to common discussions of associative memory models, it is often a useful domain to illustrate in a simple and schematic manner some underlying principle.

Suppose that the set of "images" consists simply of binary vectors, that is, strings of 0's and 1's, all six elements long. As in visual object recognition, we assume that a given object may give rise to different sequences. In lack of any regularity in the set of "views" belonging to a given object, there will not be a more efficient "object recognition" scheme in this domain than the direct approach. The set of 64 possible sequences may include, for example, eight different "objects," each one giving rise to eight different sequences. If no regularities can be found, recognition would require essentially storing all of the sequences in memory.

Table 2.1 shows a simpler case, in which only eight sequences are considered. Four of them (on the left) are classified as "object-1," the remaining four as "object-2." In this example, a simple property would suffice for distinguishing between the two objects: all the instances of object-1 are composed mostly of 0's: they include at most three 1's in them, while the sequences representing object-2 have four 1's or more. This simplified example illustrates in a schematic manner the principle of recognition by invariant properties. Rather than storing a large number of representative shapes, recognition proceeds by computing a small number of simple functions (properties) of the viewed objects. These properties are supposed to be common to all of the views representing a given object (or class of objects), and to distinguish this class of views from other classes. The properties are also often global, as in the above example: they are not associated with any restricted part of the object, but depend for their computation on the object as a whole.

2.1.2 Feature Spaces and Separating Functions

In some approaches, a property defined for a given object (or class of objects) is not expected to remain entirely invariant, only to lie within a restricted range. Properties of different objects may have partially overlapping ranges, but the hope is that by defining a number of different properties, it will become possible to define each object (or class) uniquely. This leads naturally to the concept of "feature spaces" which have been used extensively in pattern recognition. (A better term would have been "property spaces," but "feature spaces" is the accepted terminology.) If n different properties are measured, each viewed object is characterized by a vector of n real numbers. It then becomes possible to represent a given view by a point in an n-dimensional space, R^n. The set of all the views induced by a given object define in this manner a subspace of R^n (e.g., Tou & Gonzalez 1974). This representation could become useful for identifying and classifying objects, provided that the subspaces have simple shapes. For example, suppose that each class to be recognized is contained within a sphere in R^n, and the spheres for the different classes are non-overlapping. Each class can then be represented simply by the center point and the radius of its sphere. A viewed object, including a novel view, would then be classified by determining the sphere in which the point lies in R^n.

Another common method of carving up the space R^n is by a set of linear separating functions. In the case of $n = 3$, for example, the three-dimensional feature space is divided into subspaces using a set of 2-D planes. The main reason for using planar separating functions is to keep the computations involved manageable. When the shape of the subspaces does not permit the use of simple separation functions, the space can sometimes be "corrected," for example, by re-scaling different axes. In any case, if the properties are in fact almost invariant, each object will be represented by a compact "cloud" of points, with relatively little scatter.

A psychological theory that belongs to the general category of invariant properties theories (but without using the feature-space formulation) is Gibson's theory of high-order invariances (Gibson 1950, 1979). Gibson proposed the use of the cross-ratio of four colinear points as a projective invariant that could be used in perception (this was in fact originally proposed not by J.J. Gibson, but by E. Gibson, in Gibson, Owsley & Johnston (1978)), and postulated that additional invariant properties of objects may be reflected in so-called "higher order" invariances in the optic array. Such invariances may be based, for example, on spatial and temporal gradients of texture density. A set of invariances may be "picked up," according to this theory, by the visual system, and may be used to characterize objects and object classes.

How useful have invariant properties methods of the type discussed above been for approaching the problem of visual object recognition? The invariant properties approach, including the construction of feature spaces and their separation into sub-spaces, has probably been studied more extensively than any other method for object recognition. It has met with some success within certain limited domains: a number of industrial vision systems perform simple recognition of industrial parts based on the measurement of global properties such as area, elongation, perimeter length, and shape moments (see a review in Bolles & Cain 1982). For the general problem of visual object recognition, however, this approach on it own has significant limitations. In specific domains, such as the recognition of flat unoccluded parts, well-defined invariant properties may be sufficient to reliably characterize different objects (Mundy & Zisserman 1992). In more general visual recognition problems of complex objects the use of simple invariant properties of the type discussed here is insufficient. What simple invariances would distinguish, for example, a fox from a dog? To make such distinctions, it appears that a more precise description of shape, rather than a restricted set of basic invariances, would be necessary. Even with simpler, man-made objects, it is not clear how a set of invariances would suffice to capture the regularities in the different views of an object or a class of objects. For example, it would be difficult to recognize the set of all motorcycles using primarily global invariant properties such as apparent area, perimeter length, different moments, and the like.

In summary, the invariant properties approach offers one possible solution to the regularity problem of object recognition: the required many-to-one mapping is performed in an efficient manner (compared with the direct approach) by computing invariant properties rather than storing a comprehensive set of views. In some cases, simple invariant properties may be common to all the views of a given object. In other, less restricted cases, such invariances may not exist. In visual object recognition there is no particular reason to assume the existence of relatively simple properties that are preserved across the transformations that an object may undergo. It is not surprising, therefore, that despite considerable effort, invariant properties of general applicability for visual object recognition proved difficult to find. This does not mean, however, that invariant properties are not useful for object recognition. As we shall see later, they can be usefully combined with other methods for recognition, and can also play a useful role in indexing and classification—a problem examined in chapter 6.

There is also an interesting question regarding the universality of the invariant measures used for recognition. In the ideal use of invariants, one would like to have a fixed set of measures, say, $m_1 \cdots m_k$ that can be applied to the image of any given object. One would like the resulting measurements to be an invariant signature of the object. That is, the resulting measurements should be independent of the viewing position. At the same time, distinct objects should yield, of course, different sets of measurements.

As it turns out, such an ideal set of measurements is theoretically impossible. Suppose that we have a set of k measurements, $m_1 \cdots m_k$, that we will denote collectively by M. Ideally, we would like M to fulfill two conditions. First, for all 3-D objects we would like M to be invariant with respect to viewing position. That is, if v_1 and v_2 are two views of the same 3-D object, then $M(v_1) = M(v_2)$. Second, if the two views v_1 and v_2 come from two different objects, then M should distinguish between the objects, that is, $M(v_1)$ and $M(v_2)$ should be different. It can be shown, however, that if M fulfills the first of these conditions, then it must be simply a constant function; that is, it gives the same value for all views of all objects (Burns, Weiss & Riseman 1992, Clemens & Jacobs 1991, Moses & Ullman 1991). M is indeed invariant, since it does not depend on the viewing direction, but it has, of course, no use for recognition purposes. The result does not change substantially when the requirements on M are relaxed, and it is allowed to make, for each object, a substantial number of errors (Moses & Ullman 1991). Furthermore, even for a limited set of objects, the best measure M to use will depend on the particular objects to be recognized. If a given measure M is selected *a priori*, it is always possible to find a set of objects for which the measure M in question will not be optimal. It follows from this analysis that if a set of invariant measures is employed for recognition, there is no universal set of measures that is applicable to all sets of objects. Instead, the set of measures used should be tailored to the set of objects that need to be recognized. This issue is related to the use of class-specific processes in recognition, that is discussed in more detail in chapters 6 and 10.

2.2   Parts and Structural Descriptions

A second general approach to object recognition relies on the decomposition of objects into constituent parts. This approach clearly has some intuitive appeal. Many objects seem to contain natural parts: a face, for example, contains the eyes, nose, and mouth as distinct parts that can often be recognized on their own. These parts could be found first, and then the recognition of the entire object could use the identified parts.

The part decomposition approach assumes that each object can be decomposed into a small set of generic components. The components are "generic" in the sense that all objects can be described as different combinations of the same components. The decomposition must also be stable, that is, preserved across views. The recognition process locates the parts, classifies them into the different types of generic components and then describes the objects in terms of their constituent parts. As we shall see below, such parts can be, for example, some simple and standard geometric shapes, such as boxes or cylinders.

A potential advantage of this approach is that the many-to-one mapping implied by object recognition begins at the parts level. Instead of confronting directly the problem of variations in appearance at the level of the entire object, the problem is handled first at the level of simpler parts. Furthermore, the simpler parts constitute the building blocks for all other objects, and therefore the recognition of the individual parts provides an important ingredient for the recognition of the compound objects. This can result in substantial savings compared with the direct approach.

2.2.1   Parts in the Domain of Binary Vectors

The basic idea is illustrated schematically in Table 2.2 for the simplified case of binary vectors. The domain in this example consists again of binary vectors six components long. There are 64 different vectors, a table of 64 "images" can therefore be used to completely specify the association between images and objects. It is assumed, however, that the first three components of each vector define a "part," and the last three another part. Each part can be of type *part-1* or *part-2*. Table 2.2 shows how parts (vectors three-components long) are classified as either *part-1* or *part-2*. It can be seen that a many-to-one reduction is achieved already at the part level, since many different sub-sequences are all classified as different instances of the same part type, *part-1* or *part-2*.

The second part of Table 2.2 gives the final classification of objects in terms of their parts. An object composed of either the pair *(part-1, part-2)* or *(part-2, part-2)* is considered object-1, whereas *(part-1, part-1)*, *(part-2, part-1)* are instances of object-2. These rules are sufficient to classify unambiguously each of the possible sixty-four vectors. Consider, for instance, the "image" (1 1 1 0 1 0) in this domain. From Table 2.2 the image can be classified unambiguously as an instance of object-2. Because of the decomposition into parts, it is possible to avoid the storage of all sixty-four six-long vectors; two reduced tables are sufficient to cover all of the possibilities. Substantial saving is obtained because an object whose first part is, for instance, *part-1*, and

Part-1	Part-2
0 0 0	0 0 1
1 0 0	0 1 1
0 1 0	0 1 1
1 1 0	1 1 1

Object-1	Object-2
Part-1 Part-2	Part-1 Part-1
Part-2 Part-2	Part-2 Part-1

Classify the object: (1 1 1 0 1 0)

Table 2.2
Recognition by part decomposition in the domain of binary vectors. The first table gives the classification of the individual parts, and the second shows the composition of parts into complete objects.

the second is *part-2*, will be classified as object-1 regardless of the details of the internal structure of each of the parts, since these details were already examined at the part identification level.

The simplified example can be used to consider two issues that are relevant to the use of parts in recognition. First, we can ask whether the use of parts is always a good idea: can it always be applied and make the recognition problem simpler? The example illustrates that the degree of saving obtained depends on the structure of the sets of patterns in question: some sets of patterns may admit useful part structures, others may not. The last example was chosen in a manner that made part decomposition useful, but clearly examples can be given for which part decomposition will not offer a significant advantage. For instance, in the case illustrated in Table 2.1, where views were classified based on the frequency of the feature "1," part decomposition will not be helpful. This is a straightforward but important conclusion: the relative merits of the different approaches depend on the domain of objects to which they are applied.

Second, it is worth noting that part decomposition and the use of invariant properties are not mutually exclusive, but can be combined. In the example given in Table 2.2, each of the two parts has been defined using an exhaustive list of its different instances. It is also possible to consider a situation in which a part is defined, for instance, as composed mainly of $1's$, as in Table 2.1. For such a domain, the best approach will be in fact a mixture of the part decomposition and invariants approaches. A less abstract example along this line is to use a description such as "a bushy tail" in the recognition of a squirrel. The idea behind such descriptions is to combine the advantages of part decomposition with the use of invariant properties for classifying the constituent parts. We will return to this issue at the end of the next chapter, in discussing the matching of pictorial descriptions.

Following the initial classification of the individual components, there remains the problem of recognizing the object itself on the basis of the constituent components. In the language of the binary sequences example, the part classification stage results in a shorter sequence of part types, and a final classification must then be performed on the basis of the parts string. In the example above this final stage was achieved by a listing of the possibilities. In more realistic object recognition problems other methods are usually employed, as discussed below.

2.2.2   Feature Hierarchies and Syntactic Pattern Recognition

There have been two main approaches to this second stage, of combining the parts into a complete object. One approach is to try to repeat the decomposition process: certain parts are decomposed into simpler parts. Alternatively, some low-level parts can be identified first, and then groups of simple parts are identified as together forming higher-order parts. In this repeated part decomposition, the assumption is again that certain configurations can be classified independently of other parts and configurations, and that the internal structure of a configuration is immaterial as far as the recognition process is concerned.

An example of a simple part hierarchy is to detect straight line segments as the most basic parts and then detect higher-level parts such as corners and vertices, based on the already-detected line segments. These parts can be combined in turn into higher-level structures. For example, certain configurations of lines and vertices can be combined to define triangles. Such approaches are known as "feature hierarchies." The simple basic level parts are termed "features" (a term also used in many other contexts) and higher level structures are constructed hierarchically (Self-ridge 1959, Sutherland 1959, 1968, Barlow 1972, Milner 1974). This approach has been motivated in part by physiological find-ings (Hubel & Wiesel 1962, 1968) in the cat and monkey that can be interpreted as the extraction by the visual cortex of elementary features such as oriented edge fragments and line segments.

A close relative of the feature-hierarchy approach is the syn-tactic pattern recognition method (Fu 1974). Here, too, the first stage consists of identifying simple parts in the input image, fol-lowed by the grouping of elementary parts into higher-order ones. The emphasis in the syntactic approach is on the construction of higher order parts using methods borrowed from the syntactic analysis of formal languages.

2.2.3   Structural Descriptions

A second approach to the transition from parts to objects can be viewed as a mixture of part decomposition with the invari-ant properties approach, where the invariant properties are de-fined using relations among parts. The underlying assumption is that it would be easier to capture object invariances at the level where parts have been identified. For example, the total number of parts of a given type may be an invariant of the object. A triangle, for instance, always has three lines, three vertices, and no free line terminators. This is in fact how perceptrons, which are simple parallel pattern recognition devices, have been used to recognize triangles independent of shape, location and size (Min-sky & Papert 1969). Such schemes combine feature extraction with simple invariants (the existence and lack of certain features), without attempting to describe inter-part relationships. Similarly, in the "pandemonium" scheme (Selfridge 1959) a shape is classi-fied based on the existence of certain parts, or features, without describing spatial relations among different parts.

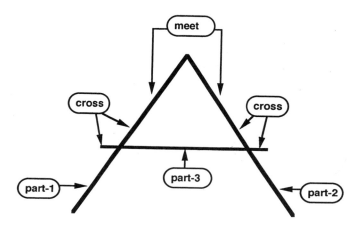

Figure 2.1
A structural description of the letter "A". The shape is described in terms of
its major parts and relations that hold between parts.

In other schemes, relations between constituent parts play a central role in capturing invariants that are common to all the object's
views. In the capital letter "A," for example, details of the shape
may vary, but the overall structure usually remains unchanged:
the figure is composed of three line segments, two of the parts
meet at a vertex, and so on, and these properties hold for most
variations of the letter (see figure 2.1). Here, again, part decomposition is obtained first, and in the next stage simple invariances
are defined in terms of the constituent parts. The invariances are
expressed in terms of relations between two or more parts, such
as "above," "to the left of," "longer than," "containing," and the
like. For 2-D applications, in which objects are restricted to move
parallel to the image plane, simple relations such as distances and
angles measured in the image would remain invariant (Bolles &
Cain 1982, Grimson & Lozano-Perez 1984, Faugeras 1984, 1993).

In the more general 3-D case, distances and angles in the image
change with changing viewing position. To deal with 3-D objects,
part decomposition schemes try to employ relations such as "connected together," "larger than," "inside of" and the like, that will

remain invariant over a wide range of different viewing positions (Biederman 1985, Marr & Nishihara 1978).

The use of spatial relations among parts and features allows the system to distinguish between configurations that have similar parts, but in different arrangements. The capacity to make such distinctions is fundamental to the human visual system, but apparently it is only rudimentary is some other visual systems. For example, pigeons have been shown to recognize successfully pictures containing, for instance, people, a particular person, trees, pigeons, fish, and letters in the alphabet. They fail to distinguish, however, a given figure from a scrambled version of the figure (Herrnstein 1984, Cerella 1986). This behavior is more consistent with recognition on the basis of a collection of local parts and features, rather than a direct comparison of complete figures. It also suggests that, in contrast to the human visual system, simpler systems may not possess developed mechanisms for extracting spatial relations among features and parts.

When augmented with descriptions of relations among parts, the object decomposition approach leads to the notion of structural descriptions. Recognition using such structural descriptions has become in recent years a popular approach to visual object recognition. Early computational examples of this approach include Grimsdale *et al.* (1959), Clows (1967), and Winston (1970). As psychological models, early examples of structural descriptions theories applied to human vision are Sutherland's (1968) theory, and Milner's (1974) model of visual shape recognition. The main basic-level parts used in these two theories are edges and line segments. In a second level, invariant properties and relations are defined using, for instance, the total number of parts (such as the number of line segments of a given orientation) and length ratios of line pairs.

Perhaps the best developed example of a structural description recognition scheme is Biederman's (1985) theory of recognition by components (RBC). According to this scheme, objects are described in terms of a small set of primitive parts called "geons." These primitives are similar to the generalized cylinders used by Binford (1971), Marr and Nishihara (1978), and Brooks (1981). They include simple 3-D shapes such as boxes, cylinders, and wedges. More complex objects are described by decomposing them into their constituent geons, together with a description of the spatial relations between components. The number of primitive geons is assumed to be small (less than 50), and objects are typically composed of a small number of parts (less than 10).

In any scheme that relies on decomposition into parts it is crucial to devise a reliable and stable procedure for identifying part boundaries. Otherwise, the same object may give, under slightly different viewing conditions, different descriptions in terms of its constituent parts. In Biederman's scheme certain "non-accidental" relationships between contours in the image are used to determine the part decomposition. These relations include, for example, the colinearity of points or lines, symmetry and skew symmetry, and parallelism of curve segments.

Another scheme employing part-decomposition is the "codon" scheme proposed by Hoffman and Richards (1986) for the description and recognition of contours. Contours are segmented at curvature minima (the "transversality rule"). The resulting parts are then described in terms of a small "vocabulary" of shape primitives termed "codons."

The RBC and the codon schemes are complementary in that they emphasize different aspects of the problem. One can approach the problem of producing part-based description from two different directions: either by starting at the image and examining how to extract useful parts, or by starting at the object level and examine what type of parts would be useful for object description. The codon scheme starts from the image side, and builds up simple contour parts based on local properties, such as segments of concavity, convexity, and inflection. The RBC model starts at the object side, concentrating on the issues of useful object parts, and the description of 3-D objects in terms of these parts.

Attempts have been made at combining these two levels of analysis into working systems that would actually recognize 3-D objects from their projections. The idea was to start the analysis from simple parts that can be identified in an image in a straightforward manner, and then progressively group them into more complex parts, and produce eventually a complete structural descriptions of 3-D objects.

An example is a scheme developed by Connell (1985). This scheme starts at the level of analyzing image contours. It first describes the contours in terms of constituent parts and their properties, using a representation scheme developed by Brady and his co-workers (Brady 1984). It then proceeds to generate higher-level constructs that eventually correspond to entire objects. The resulting description can become quite elaborate. Formally, the description has a graph structure in which the nodes represent components and labelled arcs represent relations between parts. Recognition can proceed later on by matching such graphs generated from the image with similar graph structures stored in memory.

Figure 2.2a shows an example of a contour image of an airplane, 2.2b shows the description generated by the system for a part of this figure (the right elevator). In schemes of this type that use simple parts the graph typically contains a large number of nodes, and the matching stage faces combinatorial problems (sub-graph isomorphism is NP-complete, Garey & Johnson 1979, see also Grimson 1990a for a discussion of the computational complexity involved in the matching).

The schemes mentioned above use primarily one-dimensional contour segments and 3-D volumes as their primitive shape parts. Other schemes use 2-D surface patches as their primitives (Dane & Bajcsy 1982, Potmesil 1983, Faugeras 1984, Brady *et al.* 1985, Faugeras & Hebert 1986). There are significant differences between the various structural description schemes that have been proposed, but they all share a basic underlying idea: regularities in the families of views corresponding to an object (or class of objects) can be best captured by part decomposition and the description of part configurations. Different schemes differ in the type of parts they use (such as contours, surface patches, or primitive volumes), but they all attempt to employ simple parts, so that the identification of a part would be significantly simpler than the recognition of a complex object. The entire object is then recognized in a second stage in terms of spatial relations among the already classified parts.

For a variety of objects, the recognition by the arrangement of simple parts appears to be natural. A table, for instance, is often

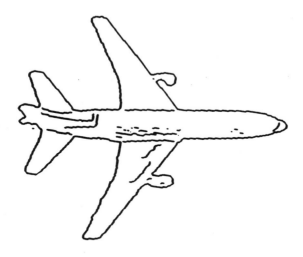

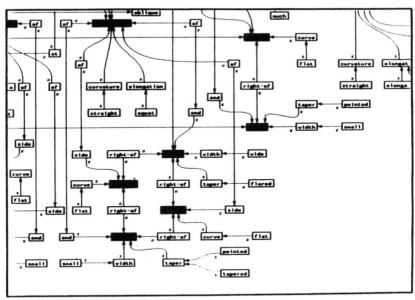

Figure 2.2
An example of a detailed structural description. *a*. A contour image of an airplane. *b*. A structural description of a part of this image (the right elevator). From Connell (1985).

composed of a flat surface supported from below by four legs. Such a description appears much more natural than trying to characterize table images in terms of simple properties such as total area and perimeter length as used in the invariant properties approach. It is also true that, as argued by Palmer (1977), Hoffman (1983) and Biederman (1985), human observers sometimes find it easy to identify the parts of an object even when the object is unfamiliar.

The identification of object parts, when parts are clearly distinguishable, has some clear advantages. At the same time, it appears that for the purpose of visual object recognition the use of structural descriptions as the main strategy has a number of serious limitations. The first problem is that the decomposition into generic parts often falls considerably short of characterizing the object in question. For example, a dog, a fox, a cat, and many other animals, have similar and perhaps identical decompositions into main parts. These animals are distinguishable not because each one has a different arrangement of parts, but because of differences in the detailed shape at particular locations (such as the snout). It may be argued, perhaps, that these animals are indistinguishable at some "basic level category" (Rosch *et al.* 1976, Biederman 1985): they are first recognized perhaps as four-legged animals, and only a second recognition stage distinguishes among them. As we shall see later, in the chapter on classification, preceding the identification stage by a more general classification stage may indeed offer important advantages to an object recognition system. However, the separation into two stages does not, by itself, solve the identification problem: an explanation of how the objects are eventually identified is still required, and this identification requires precise shape descriptions.

A second limitation of the structural description approach is that many objects do not decompose naturally into a union of clearly distinct parts. What, for example, are the decomposition of a shoe, a loaf of bread, or a sleeping cat? It would be difficult to decompose these objects into parts that are sufficient to characterize the objects and are at the same time generic, namely, common to many other objects as well. A possible approach, illustrated by the aircraft example in figure 2.2, is to include in the description very simple generic parts, such as edges and line segments. The use of such parts, however, causes, the resulting structural descriptions to be highly complex.

Finally, the identification in the image of the main parts of an object can be a difficult task. It may appear natural to decompose an animal figure into its head, torso, limbs, and so on, but identifying reliably these parts and their boundaries, for instance, in an image of a sleeping cat, can become a daunting task.

It seems, therefore, that for many objects the attempt to construct a structural description results in making strong commitments too early in the recognition process. The approach forces a categorization of shapes and relations into a small set of classes, and assumes that the details of the shapes and relations not captured by the structural description are immaterial for the purpose of recognition. These limitations do not mean that part decomposition and structural descriptions are not useful in recognition. They can play in fact a useful role, in particular in aspects of object classification (discussed in chapter 6), and in establishing a correspondence between the image and stored model (discussed in chapter 7). It is quite clear, however, that this approach by itself is insufficient, and is not well-suited for object identification.

The approach presented next—the alignment method—attempts to avoid the limitations discussed above. It preserves details of the viewed shape without enforcing a classification into predetermined categories of parts and spatial relations. The alignment approach is not incompatible with the notion of part decomposition. Aspects of both approaches can, in fact, be incorporated in a single scheme. However, to keep the distinction between the approaches clear, the alignment approach will be presented first in a simple and "pure" form. Combinations with other schemes will be considered in a subsequent section.

2.3   The Alignment Approach

The basic idea of the alignment approach is to compensate for the transformations separating the viewed object and the corresponding stored model, and then compare them. For example, the image and the stored model may be similar, except for a difference in size. Scaling one of them will remove this discrepancy and improve the match between them.

More generally, the alignment approach assumes that for each object model M_i stored in memory, there is a set of "allowed transformations" T_{ij} that the object may undergo, such as changes in scale, position, or orientation in space. Recognition can then be viewed as a search for a particular model and a particular transformation that will maximize some measure of fit F between the object and a model. If V is the viewed object to be recognized, the search is for a maximum in $F(V, (M_i, T_{ij}))$ over the possible object-models M_i and their transformations T_{ij}. In the alignment approach, transformations are explicitly applied to the incoming image or the stored model. Some of the allowed transformations can in general be applied to the incoming image. For example, a change in scale, position, or orientation in the image plane, can be applied to the viewed object. Other transformations use information associated with particular models. For example, the model can contain precise 3-D information that is difficult to obtain from a single image, and therefore 3-D transformations are better applied to the stored models. Similarly, the model can contain information about object-specific transformations, such as the distortions of a face image caused by facial expressions. Such changes can be compensated for by applying object-specific transformations to stored models.

To illustrate the approach, let us consider first a two-dimensional example, the more general problem of 3-D objects will be discussed in the next chapter. The example is from the domain of character recognition. It is used here in a simplified form; the full problem of character recognition, despite the 2-D nature, is in fact a complex and specialized one. Learning to recognize the letters in an alphabet is a difficult task that requires considerable training. The recognition of written material, especially cursive script, appears to require the use of some specialized skills that are not necessarily representative of object recognition in general, and will not be discussed here in detail.

Suppose that a character recognition system is required to recognize characters in the alphabet regardless of position, size, and orientation. A simple alignment scheme would proceed in the following manner. For each character, an instance of the character would be stored in memory. Given an input character, the system will first go through an alignment phase. The goal of this stage is to "undo" the shift, scale, and rotation transformations. This may be accomplished by applying compensating transformations to the character. For example, to "undo" a possible shift, the center of mass of the input can be computed, and the character then shifted, so that its center of mass always coincides with a fixed pre-determined location. In this manner, characters that differ in their position in the input image are "transformed back" to a canonical location. Similarly, scale can be compensated for by computing, for instance, the area of the character's convex hull. (The convex hull is the smallest convex envelope surrounding the character; see Preparata & Shamos 1985.)

Orientation changes are more complicated to compensate for. (They are often more problematic in human perception as well (Neisser 1967, Rock 1973).) Orientation can be determined for some letters on the basis of bilateral symmetry as in the case of (A, H, M) and others. Many characters have a line segment that, in the proper orientation, is oriented either vertically as in (B, D, E), or horizontally, as in (L, T, Z), and these can be used to determine a small number of likely orientations. The detection of bilateral symmetry and the orientation of the component line segments, together with the computation of center of mass and the convex hull area, would be performed during the alignment stage. After shift, scale, and orientation have been compensated for, the "normalized" input is matched (possibly in parallel) against the stored representations of the different characters. Since the transformations have already been removed, the matching stage itself is expected to be relatively straightforward. At this stage, an associative memory-like mechanism may suffice to compare the transformed input in parallel with the stored models. It should be noted, however, that even following the alignment the final matching cannot be as simple as, for instance, 2-D correlation between the contours. The difference between different characters, such as O and Q, may be a small but crucial contour element. Some parts of the model may therefore contribute more to the overall quality of the match than other parts.

The use of alignment for recognition has been usually restricted to changes in position, orientation, and scale in the 2-D image plane. The use of alignment for more general objects raises a number of difficulties that must be considered. For example, the set of transformations that must be compensated for in 3-D object recognition is not limited to simple image transformations. When an object moves and rotates in 3-D space, the transformations induced in the image are considerably more complex. Another difficulty is that the methods used for normalization typically rely on global properties such as the object's apparent area, perimeter length, or center of mass. Such measures do not perform well in the face of occlusion, when only a part of the object is visible.

The next chapters describe the application of recognition by alignment to complex 3-D objects. The method is introduced by an alignment scheme that manipulates explicitly internal 3-D models. The method is then extended to deal with complex objects bounded by smooth surfaces. A subsequent chapter then introduces a variation that does not employ explicit 3-D models, but uses instead small collections of 2-D views.

In all of these schemes, the recognition system is required to solve two related problems: to find the appropriate model M_i, and the best compensating transformation T_{ij}. The emphasis in the discussion will be on the selection of the appropriate compensating transformation. The problem of selecting the best model will be deferred to later chapters.

2.4   Which Is the Correct Approach?

Before turning to describe the alignment approach in detail, it may be useful to consider briefly the approaches discussed so far. Three different approaches have been introduced—the use of invariant measures, the use of parts and structural descriptions, and the alignment method. Is one of them the "correct" method, that should be preferred under all circumstances?

It seems to me that in fact there is no single best scheme that is appropriate for all cases. This was illustrated schematically for the simplified case of binary vectors in Tables 2.1 and 2.2. As the tables indicate, a given approach may be clearly superior for one set of conditions, but not for others. These different approaches cannot be classified as "correct" or "incorrect" in general, but, rather, should be evaluated according to their usefulness in dealing with different types of objects and object transformations. For real objects too, a recognition scheme must exploit well the regularities inherent in a given domain, and it may very well employ more than one single strategy.

In the discussion above, it was argued that the two most popular approaches, the invariant properties approach and the structural description approach, are insufficient by themselves for dealing with shape-based recognition. The alignment approach can provide an important, perhaps the main, missing ingredient. However, the alignment method on its own also suffers from certain deficiencies. As we shall see in more detail later on, aspects of the different methods can be usefully combined, together with the alignment approach, within a single recognition scheme.

3 The Alignment of Pictorial Descriptions

This chapter describes a particular version of the alignment approach and its application to the recognition of three-dimensional objects, seen from different viewing positions. This alignment method uses the fact that rigid objects do not change in an arbitrary manner: the set of transformations applied to them is lawful and restricted. In the method described in this chapter, the transformation is recovered explicitly and compensated for. A key point of this scheme is that the transformation can be determined uniquely on the basis of very limited information.

The general idea is the following. Given an input image and a candidate model, a correspondence is first established between them. This means that a small number of features (including pointwise features and lines) are identified as matching features in the image and the model. Based on the corresponding features, the transformation separating the model from the image is uniquely determined. The recovered transformation is then applied to the model. The image generated by the transformed model is then compared with the viewed object. Based on the degree of match, the candidate model is selected or rejected. To be accepted, the match must be sufficiently close, and also better than that of competing models.

The version of the alignment method described in this chapter deals with simple, rigid objects. It uses 3-D object models and relies on feature correspondence between the image and model. Subsequent chapters will discuss extensions that deal with more complex objects that use 2-D rather than 3-D models, and rely less on feature correspondence.

3.1 Using Corresponding Features to Recover the Transformation

To illustrate how the alignment is performed, assume initially that three dots, a red one, a green one, and a blue one, have been painted on every object in the collection the recognition system is required to recognize. The reason for this assumption is simply to make clear that we need a number of identifiable features that can be matched reliably in the image and the stored model. We will deal later with the problem of identifying such features in real images. The exact location of the points on the object's surface is immaterial. They must only be visible (i.e., not occluded), and must not be colinear. We will call these points, which are used in the alignment stage, the "anchor-points" of the object.

For each object O_i in the collection of objects to be recognized, an internal model, M_i, is constructed and stored. The model is based simply on a picture of the object from a particular viewpoint. This model will be used to recognize the object from a range of viewing directions around the original viewing direction. The picture used to construct the model is an orthographic projection of the object on the image plane. (See appendix E for the definitions of orthographic as well as other types of projection.) It includes the projection of the object's boundary, as well as internal contours, and the position of the three anchor-points. The model also contains three-dimensional information: we assume that the depth values of the points used in the model (the contours and the anchor-points) are known. The acquisition of this three-dimensional information is a part of the model learning stage, and it need not concern us here. It could be derived, for example, from binocular stereo (Grimson 1981, Julesz 1971) or the structure-from-motion processes (Ullman 1979).

The real projection of objects on the retina or a camera's image plane is, of course, perspective rather than orthographic (see appendix E) but an orthographic projection combined with an admissible scale change provides a good approximation, unless the projection center is very close to the viewed object. The deviation of perspective projection from its approximation by the combination of orthographic projection and scale change will be treated as any other distortion of the object.

We are now given a view V of an unknown object, and the problem is to decide, for a given model M_i, whether or not V matches M_i (that is, whether V is a possible view of M_i). To reach a decision, we can at first ignore the entire image of the object, and examine only the position of the three anchor-points. Let (P_1, P_2, P_3) be the 3-D coordinates of the three points in the model, and (p_1, p_2, p_3) their 2-D image coordinates.

The crucial point is that the model M_i and the view V can be aligned in a unique manner given only the coordinates (P_1, P_2, P_3) (known in the model) and p_1, p_2, p_3 (recovered from the image). In other words, the displacement D, the rotation in space R, and the scaling S, possibly relating M_i to V, are uniquely determined (up to a reflection about the image plane, which can be ignored for the present discussion) on the basis of the three corresponding points (appendix A). This transformation is now applied to M_i. Following the transformation, M_i and V should be in complete registration. Unlike the original situation, M_i and V following the transformations should be in close agreement as 2-D images. If V is not an instance of M_i, then M_i and V following the compensating transformations would still be out of register. The recognition process is decomposed in this manner into two stages: an initial alignment, followed by a matching stage. Following the alignment, the similarity between the object and model increases significantly, and a relatively straightforward matching metric can determine the appropriate model.

Figures 3.1, 3.2, and 3.3 show an example of using this method. The objects in this example, shown in figure 3.1 are flat rigid machine parts that were allowed to translate, rotate in space, and change scale (as their distance from the camera changes). These objects were simpler to deal with, primarily because they do not create problems of self-occlusion. It should be noted, however, that although the parts are flat, this is not a purely two-dimensional problem, since the objects are not restricted to move in the plane—they are allowed to move and rotate in 3-D space. The system used to recognize these objects, as well as more complex objects described below, was developed by D. Huttenlocher (Huttenlocher & Ullman 1990). Figure 3.2 shows the alignment of a model with the corresponding part in the image. The image contains one of the objects known to the system, resting at one edge on a block. This causes the object to be slanted, and foreshortened in one direction with respect to the model, as shown in figure 3.2b. Figure 3.2c shows the edges extracted from the image and used for alignment with the model. The figure also shows feature points extracted by the system and used in the alignment process. The final part of the figure shows the transformed model,

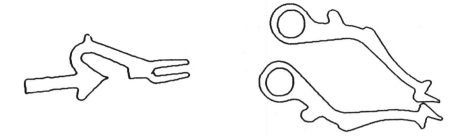

Figure 3.1
Alignment applied to flat objects. Examples of the objects recognized by the
system developed by D. Huttenlocher (Huttenlocher & Ullman 1990). The
parts were recognized from grey level images in cluttered scenes.

following alignment, superimposed on the same object in the edge
image. Figure 3.3 shows what happens when a match is attempted
with an incorrect model. Based on the extracted feature points,
an alignment transformation was applied to the candidate model.
Unlike the previous case, following the alignment, the discrepancy
between the model and the object is still large, and therefore the
model can be rejected as inappropriate.

The fact that three corresponding points are sufficient to "undo"
the rotation, translation and scale is shown in appendix A. These
transformations can be specified by six parameters: three for the
rotation in space, two for the translation (under orthographic projection, absolute depth remains undetermined), and one for the
scaling. Three points supply six equations (two for each point),
and therefore the number of constraints matches the number of
unknowns. This counting argument by itself is insufficient (a more
complete proof is therefore given in the appendix), but it suggests
why this small number of matching points may provide sufficient
information for recovering the transformation uniquely. The resulting transformation is unique, up to a mirror reflection of the
three points about the image plane, and translation in depth (that,
under orthographic projection, does not affect the image). The
three points are required to be non-colinear. When the points get
close to colinearity, the solution is still mathematically unique,

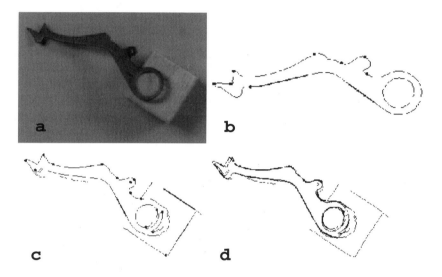

Figure 3.2
Matching an object with the correct model using alignment. *a*. A part-image:
the part is resting on a cube at one end. *b*. A part-model. The part in the
image is smaller in size and slanted, compared with the model. *c*. An edge
map of the image, together with feature points selected for alignment, marked
by black dots. *d*. The aligned model superimposed on the image. Following
the alignment, the model and image are in close agreement. Example from
Huttenlocher & Ullman (1990).

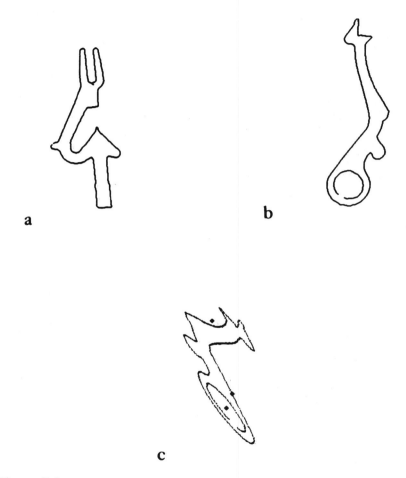

Figure 3.3
Attempting to match an object with an incorrect model using alignment. *a*.
A part-image. *b*. A part-model. *c*. The model transformed in an attempt to
align it with the image. The points used in the alignment are marked by black
dots. Following the alignment, the model and object are still in disagreement.
Example from Huttenlocher & Ullman (1990).

but the stability of the computation decreases. That is, the recovered transformation becomes more sensitive to small errors in the input data, the measured coordinates of the points. A mathematical analysis of the method's sensitivity can be found in (Shoham & Ullman 1988). The analysis shows how feature points can be selected so as to maximize the stability of the recovery process, essentially, by avoiding features that are neatly colinear.

It is worth noting that as shown in appendix A, the alignment stage does not require the extraction of 3-D information from the image: the 2-D coordinates of the points are sufficient. Three-dimensional information could be used, when available, to simplify the alignment stage somewhat, but the process can proceed in the absence of precise 3-D data.

The recognition system illustrated in this section did not use, of course, colored points painted on the object. Instead, it identified a small number of salient and stable points defined by the object's boundary. Such points included deep concavities, strong maxima in curvature, and the centers of closed or almost closed blobs. The anchor-points identified and used by the recognition program are marked in figure 3.2 and 3.3. Instead of the color of the points, the scheme used labeling of the points to determine uniquely the correspondence between image points and points in the model without the need for search. A label of a point includes a point-type, such as blob-center, concavity, or a sharp curvature maximum, and may include a rough description of location. It is desirable, although not strictly necessary, to obtain a unique correspondence between the object and model anchor-points based on their associated labels. If this correspondence is not unique, a number of transformations will have to be evaluated, for the different possible pairings of the anchor-points.

Following the alignment, a simple matching measure was sufficient in this domain to unambiguously select the appropriate model. The similarity measure used was the summed distance between all the points in the model and their nearest neighboring points in the image. That is, for each model point, the single nearest image point was found and the distance between this pair added to the overall sum. For more general recognition problems such a matching criterion may not be sufficient. More general considerations regarding the final matching and model selection are discussed in the final section of this chapter.

Before considering more complex examples, it will be useful to compare briefly the three main approaches described so far to visual object recognition. The different approaches were described and compared in the last chapter in general terms. We can now use a concrete example, and consider what it would mean to actually apply each of the approaches to this example. As diagrammed schematically in figure 3.4, each of the methods could in principle be applied to the recognition of the objects in figure 3.1, but it can be seen that the methods are in fact quite different. The invariant features approach will attempt to identify some relatively simple measures such as compactness, area, length, or object moments and identify the objects on the basis of these measurements. The results of these measurements are represented in the figure by a binary vector. The structural description approach will decompose the object into a small number, perhaps three of four major parts, and produce a description in terms of a set of generic shape primitives and spatial relations. The alignment approach will use a pictorial model of the object, and will compare the model and image following a compensation for the separating transformation.

3.2   The Use of Multiple Models for 3-D Objects

The alignment of solid 3-D objects is somewhat more complicated compared with that of the flat objects in the previous examples. The main difference is caused by self-occlusion: different aspects of the object are visible from different viewing positions, and therefore some of the contours, and also the features used for alignment (the "alignment key"), will not be visible from all viewing directions.

There are two possible approaches to the problem of aligning 3-D models. One is to maintain a single 3-D model for each object, and use the 3-D transformations recovered in the alignment stage to transform the model into alignment with the viewed object. The required transformation will be complicated from a computational standpoint. The computation will require, for instance,

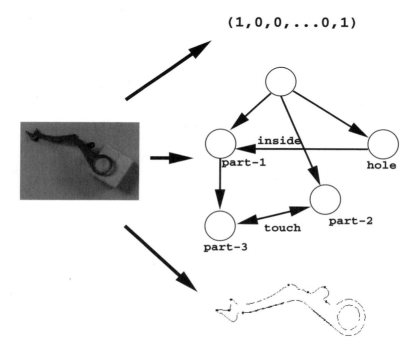

Figure 3.4
Three different approaches to recognition. The first method extracts a set of invariant measures. The second produces a structural description. The third aligns the image and stored object-model.

a process of "hidden line elimination," i.e., the computation of which object features are visible from a given viewing position (Lowe 1985, 1987). In addition, a problem arises since the alignment features visible from some viewing angles may be occluded from others, making it difficult to use a single model to represent the object from all viewing directions.

An alternative possibility is to store a number of models and a number of alignment keys associated with them, representing the object from sufficiently different viewing positions (c.f. Koenderink & van Doorn 1979). Each model will now be responsible for a range of orientations for which the alignment key is visible. The matching will proceed on the basis of the contours associated with this model, without resorting to complex processes such as hidden line elimination. Note that this process is not very sensitive: it does not require that all of the contours in the selected model will in fact be visible in the image; it is enough to have a high quality match with a sufficiently large subset of model contours. The required computations in this multiple-model scheme will be simplified, but at the expense of storing more models. For a system such as the brain, which appears to have a capacity to store a large number of patterns and retrieve them in a parallel manner (Willshaw et al. 1969, Kohonen 1978, Hopfield 1982), this is probably a useful tradeoff.

In the first of these alternatives the model is truly object centered and view independent (Marr & Nishihara 1978). In the second, the representation is view dependent, since a number of different models of the same object from different viewing positions will be used (Perrett et al. 1985, Rock & Di Vita 1987). It is expected, however, to be view-insensitive, since the differences between views are partially compensated by the alignment process.

As far as the human visual system is concerned, there are indications that observers can identify under certain situations views that correspond to the same 3-D object from new and widely disparate viewing positions (Shepard & Metzler 1971, Shepard & Cooper 1982). This may be taken as evidence in support of the single-model hypothesis. However, the process involved in these "mental rotation" judgements appears to be slow, and may be restricted to relatively simple shapes. It is still unclear, therefore, whether this process is an integral part of ordinary object recognition, or a special process that is used for limited purposes only. (See also Palmer (1978) on the large differences between recognition and simultaneous comparison.)

Figures 3.5, 3.6, and 3.7 show examples of recognition by alignment applied to 3-D solid objects. The examples are from the system developed by D. Huttenlocher and described in (Huttenlocher & Ullman 1990). The scheme used a number of models for each 3-D object, each one representing the object from a different viewing direction. The recognition process then proceeded in a similar manner to the process described above for flat objects.

Each individual model consisted of a set of contours, together with their 3-D coordinates. The recognition process started with a grey level image of an office scene containing one or more of the objects to be recognized. Edges were extracted from the image, using standard edge detection techniques (Canny 1986). Feature points used for alignment were corners and significant inflection points along the object's contours. The system also used connectivity information between adjacent features: in matching triplets of features from the image and the model, pairs of connected features were used together. The system matched two pairs of connected features (a total of four pointwise features, compared with the minimum necessary of three). The alignment transformation was then derived and applied to the model. The system illustrated that a small set of models was sufficient in this case to match each solid object from any view direction.

In performing recognition by alignment using this approach, the correspondence stage emerges as the most difficult and time consuming part. In solving the correspondence problem, that is, matching image and model features, two approaches can be taken. The first is to try many different pairings, and then select the one that yields the best match between the image and transformed model. The Huttenlocher system used connected feature-pairs rather than single features as the basic elements for the match, and two feature-pairs of this type are required for alignment. If there are m feature-pairs in the model and n in the image, then a full evaluation of all the possibilities requires on the order of $m^2 n^2$

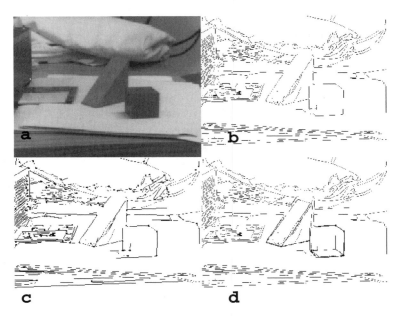

Figure 3.5
Recognition by alignment of solid 3-D objects. The objects were 3-D solids—a
cube, a pyramid, and a more complex polyhedron. Each example contains four
panels. *a*. Original grey level image. *b*. An edge map. *c*. Features extracted for
alignment. *d*. Recovered instances: the model following alignment projected
onto the image.

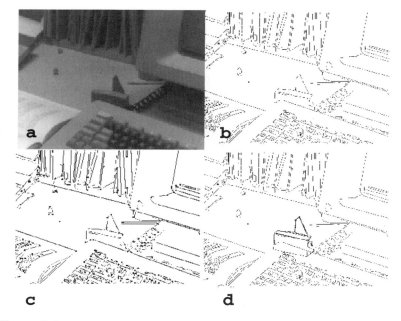

Figure 3.6
a. Original grey level image. *b*. An edge map. *c*. Features extracted for alignment. *d*. Recovered instances: the model following alignment projected onto the image.

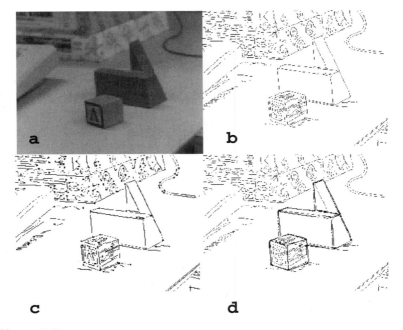

Figure 3.7
a. Original grey level image. *b*. An edge map. *c*. Features extracted for alignment. *d*. Recovered instances: the model following alignment projected onto the image. Examples from (Huttenlocher & Ullman 1990).

trials. The complexity of this computation also interacts with the image segmentation stage. If a single object can be somehow segmented from the rest of the image, then it becomes possible to consider only those image features that belong to the object. If segmentation is not performed, then at the correspondence stage it is still unknown which of the features in fact belong to the object, and all the features need to be considered. The number n of object features then depends on the number of feature points in the image (or a part of it that is being considered) rather than the number of feature points in the object itself.

Several recognition systems, for example the system developed by Grimson and Lozano-Perez (1987), use this search approach. The Huttenlocher system also evaluated a large number of possible matches. Each possible match is followed by what is known as a verification stage: a transformation is computed and applied to the model, and the transformed model is matched against the image. Techniques have been developed to speed up this verification stage. A common one is to first use a coarse verification, for example, by checking first only a limited number of model points. A wrong match can be rejected quickly based on coarse verification, and the number of matches that need to be verified in detail can be substantially reduced. As can be expected, the performance of such a search approach depends on the image segmentation stage (Grimson 1990b). The segmentation stage need not be perfect: it may distinguish only a part of the object, and it may mix some object and background features. However, some segmentation is usually required to make the search approach feasible in practice. This issue of scene segmentation is taken up in more detail in chapter 8.

An alternative to the correspondence-search approach is to try to obtain a unique image-to-model correspondence. One way of reducing the number of possible matches to consider is, as mentioned above, to label the different feature points, such as a corner, inflection, blob-center, and the like. Another method of reducing the number of possible matches is to perform a stage of rough alignment. The idea is first to compensate for large differences between the model and the viewed object in size, position and orientation in the image plane. Such differences can often be roughly compensated for without a detailed point-to-point match. This rough alignment brings corresponding feature points closer together, and therefore the search for corresponding feature points can become more limited. This issue of performing efficient image-to-model correspondence, and alternatives of performing alignment without a prior feature correspondence stage, is discussed in more detail in chapter 7.

Before leaving this topic, it is worth pointing out that correspondence can be established not only between pointwise features, but also between linear features that are sometimes easier to identify and match. A linear feature is a straight line whose endpoints cannot be identified reliably. If the endpoints can be identified, then the line segment is simply equivalent to a pair of pointwise features. But even without the endpoint, the line can still be thought of as supplying two constraints, given, for example, by its orientation and distance from the origin. In this respect, it is similar to a single pointwise feature that supplies two constraints, given, for instance, by its x and y coordinates. Can points and linear features be used in any mixture? At least in the case where the features are coplanar, features can be interchanged; that is, except for some degenerate cases, the aligning transformation can be recovered from three corresponding points, or two lines and a point, a point and two lines, or three (intersecting) lines (Shoham & Ullman 1988).

Alignment processes similar to the method described above were used successfully in a number of object recognition systems. It seems, in fact, that in terms of implemented systems that can actually perform 3-D object recognition (in limited domains), the alignment approach, in several variations, has become the dominant method. In terms of the three main approaches I have listed, it appears that there has been a discernible move from an emphasis on methods that use invariant measures and feature spaces, to structural descriptions, to alignment methods. It should be mentioned again, however, that the different approaches are not mutually exclusive, and, as we shall see later, can be combined.

One of the earliest alignment schemes to be developed and used for recognizing 3-D objects in space is Lowe's Scerpo system (Lowe 1985, 1986). The alignment in this system is not performed in a separate stage, but is intertwined with the recognition process (see also Faugeras & Hebert 1986). This system is used mainly to recognize polyhedral objects. The alignment procedure used in the system relies on perspective rather than orthographic projection, which makes the alignment somewhat more complicated. It is implemented as an iterative scheme, based on Newton's method. In terms of performing image-to-model correspondence, Scerpo does not attempt to "label" the alignment features,but relies on a search that evaluates different possible matches between image and model features.

Other systems also use at least some aspects of the alignment approach. In particular, they recover the transformation separating the model and viewed object, and use it during the matching phase. Among these systems are the early work of Roberts (1965), the Ransac system of Fischler and Bolles (1981), and also the work of Chien & Aggarwal, Linainmaa, Harwood, and Davis (1985), Thomson and Mundy (1987), and Lamdan, Schwartz, and Wolfson (1988).

3.3   Aligning Pictorial Descriptions

3.3.1   Adding Abstract Descriptions

The last few sections have discussed the alignment approach in a "pure" form. The object models consisted of unarticulated contours, without defined parts, as in the structural description approach, and without abstract descriptions, as in the invariant properties approach. It is possible, however, to combine the main advantages of the part decomposition and invariant properties approaches with the alignment approach. The resulting scheme may be more suitable for recognizing objects that cannot be handled easily by a "pure" method alone.

Consider for instance the rooster sketch in figure 3.8. An internal model for this figure in a structural description method will contain a number of parts with their associated shape descriptions, together with a symbolic description of the spatial relations among the parts. A pure alignment method would keep a replica of the figure as an internal model. In evaluating the match between

Figure 3.8
The use of an abstract label in a pictorial description. The exact details of
the part are replaced by an abstract description.

this model and a new viewed object, which is another possible
instance of a rooster figure, the method will first try to align the
model and the viewed object as precisely as possible. Clearly, the
details of the rooster's crown have no particular importance in
the normal process of recognizing such a figure. In a part decomposition approach, the details of the constituent parts are often
ignored and replaced by a more abstract description. The same
kind of abstraction can be used in the alignment approach. One
can imagine a "label" stating "wiggly line" being overlaid over
the crown contour. This description is "abstract" in the sense
that it is less specific than the original image itself: many different images will map onto the single label ("wiggly," in this case).
This abstract label is associated with a given location in the figure
and it is shifted along with it in the course of the alignment process. When the aligned figure is then matched against the rooster
model, the detailed internal contours of the crown in the aligned
object and the model may not be in good agreement, but they will
both have the same label in corresponding locations. The abstract
label is added to the more detailed image rather than replacing
it, since both may be required eventually for the matching with a
stored model. Labels of this type may describe properties of 2-D
contours, but may also be 3-D in nature, such as locally convex
or concave surface patches. This use of abstract labels has prop-

erties in common with structural description schemes, because it describes parts of the object. Similar to the invariant properties approach, an abstract property that is expected to remain adequate for different views of the object is used to characterize the part in question.

There are two differences in the manner that abstract descriptions are used in the alignment scheme compared with the structural description approach. First, in the alignment method abstract descriptions do not replace lower-level descriptions—they are added to them. A match may eventually occur at a low level (the actual contours may be in close agreement), or it may occur at a higher level (the corresponding abstract descriptions may match without a good match at the lower level). In the pure structural description method, without alignment, the low-level components such as boundary contours cannot be expected to match. The scheme must rely instead entirely on the correct categorization of parts; namely, that different views of the same part will end up with the same abstract description. Unlike the part decomposition scheme, in the alignment scheme the part decomposition is not required to be complete. Abstract labels may be associated with some locations, while other pieces of the object may remain unarticulated, not broken into parts, and not assigned to any category, or described by any abstract descriptors. Because of the alignment stage, which is not used in the structural description approach, these unarticulated parts are expected to produce (following the alignment) a good match with the stored model.

The second difference is that in the alignment method the description may be called "pictorial." It is much closer to the image compared with structural descriptions. In structural descriptions, spatial relations, like part shapes, are described using a limited set of categories such as "above," "in between," "near," and the like. The position of part A may be described as "above B and near it, and to the left of C." This description is abstract in the sense that many different configurations in the input would fit a given category such as "above" or "left of." In the alignment approach, in contrast, spatial relations are not categorized. Instead, the actual position of parts and labels is preserved. The resulting description consequently has an image-like structure in which labels are associated with particular locations. Unlike part decomposition schemes, descriptive labels are associated with specific locations, without requiring a precise delineation of part boundaries. In the context of face recognition, for example, it is natural in such a scheme to associate descriptions with locations such as the cheeks or forehead in a face image. These are well-defined locations, but not precisely delineated parts in the sense used in part decomposition schemes.

The use of pictorial labels of this general type is not entirely new. In fact, one can view edge detection and representation as a simple example of abstract pictorial descriptions. At the raw input level, the light intensity distribution around an object boundary would change with the illumination conditions. The operation of edge detection replaces the intensity distribution around an intensity edge with a more abstract label (the presence of an edge). The label is pictorial: it is associated with a location, and transforms with it during alignment.

The combined scheme, using alignment as well as abstract descriptions, can be described as the *"alignment of pictorial descriptions."* This name implies three components. First, it is an alignment method. Second, it also uses abstract descriptions. Third, these descriptions are used pictorially: they are associated with specific locations, rather than being described by spatial relation categories. Such descriptions can be rotated, scaled, stretched, and so on, prior to the matching stage. The entire object recognition process is, in the alignment approach, less symbolic, more pictorial, and closer to the lower-level visual processes than the structural description approach.

3.4   Transforming the Image or the Models?

In matching a viewed object to a potential model using the alignment method, one of them (at least) must be transformed to compensate for the transformations between the two. It is possible to transform either the viewed object, or the stored model, or both. Applying the alignment transformations to the viewed object only has one important advantage: the transformation is applied only once. All the models remain unchanged. This can be accomplished provided that the various models are stored in memory in a common "canonical" form. Consider, for example, the case in which the viewed object is aligned to the model on the basis of three anchor-points. For simplicity assume that each model has exactly three anchor-points. An alignment transformation applied to the viewed object must bring the three points into alignment with the corresponding points in all of the potentially relevant models simultaneously. This implies that all of these models must be stored in a canonical form, in which the three anchor-points are already in register. A canonical form may be defined in an analogous manner also for alignment based on dominant orientation rather than anchor-points. In either case, however, the use of canonical forms for the models also has its drawbacks. One complication arises if it is desired to recognize the same object using different alignment keys. Such a redundancy is useful, for example, for dealing with occlusion. In a canonical form scheme, each model will have to be represented by multiple copies, one for each different alignment key (Lamdan, Schwartz, and Wolfson 1988).

An alternative would be to apply an alignment transformation separately to each of the potentially relevant models. In this case, the models need not be stored in any canonical form, since each one is transformed individually to align it with the viewed object. This also has the advantage that different transformations may be applied to different models. For example, the model of an object may include 3-D information that is not available from a single view of the object. This 3-D information could be used in transforming the model and predicting how it will appear from a different viewpoint. The model may also specify, for instance, that a certain point in the object can serve as a joint, where parts can change their relative orientation. For this model, but not for other ones, an attempt to align the model with the object may include bending around this known point. Such individual transformations add flexibility to the matching process, but at the cost of increased computational effort.

Two additional considerations are relevant to the question of transforming the viewed object or the stored models. First, it is

not necessary to adopt an extreme approach; a combination of the
two is also possible. For example, oriented objects may be stored
in a canonical orientation. The viewed object is then rotated once
to bring its own orientation into alignment with the canonical
orientation of the models. Following this common stage, an additional transformation, such as change of scale, may be applied to
each model individually. More generally, the mixed approach is to
apply to the viewed object all the alignment transformations that
are common to all of the relevant models, yet allow the application
of additional transformations to the different models. The combination of model-based and image-based transformations will be
discussed again in chapter 10.

Second, it may be possible to keep the object-specific transformations simple in nature, for example, some scaling or stretching along one direction, instead of performing the full veridical
transformation dictated by the object's 3-D shape. When the discrepancy between a particular view of an object and its models
already stored in memory becomes too large to be overcome using
these restricted transformations, an additional model of the object
can be added to the model library. The object-specific transformations may therefore be kept sufficiently restricted, so that the
computational load required for applying the transformations to
many objects in parallel may be kept within reasonable bounds.
The tradeoff here is between memory requirement and complexity
of computation: the computation becomes simpler, the storage
requirement increases, and the capacity of the system to perform
generalizations to new views will also be degraded.

3.5   Before and After Alignment

The last several sections outlined the notion of aligning pictorial
descriptions and its use in object recognition. The discussion focused on the alignment stage itself. We have not discussed the processing stages that extract the information from the image prior
to the alignment stage, or the matching that takes place following
it. To put the alignment stage in perspective, this section will list
briefly some of the other steps that are involved in the recognition

process, and describe the problems that they raise. Some of these issues will be discussed in more detail in later chapters.

Selection. By "Selection" (sometimes called "cuing") we mean identifying in the image a location that is likely to contain an object of interest (without delineating the object to be recognized). A human observer rarely scans the entire scene in a systematic manner. Very often, objects of interest somehow attract our attention, and subsequent processing seems to be concentrated at these locations. Lowe (1987) has proposed a scheme in which feature configurations that have the least probability of arising by coincidence are examined first. (A similar notion was suggested by Witkin & Tenenbaum 1983.) In human vision the initial selection appears to be based on simpler criteria. The human visual system seems unable to extract relational properties among features in the early, pre-attentive, parallel stage (Treisman & Gelade 1980). Selection may be based instead on some measure of saliency defined by local differences in contrast, color, size, orientation, and so on (Engel 1974, Sagi & Julesz 1985).

Segmentation. By "segmentation" in this context I mean the delineation of a sub-part of the image to which subsequent recognition processes will be applied. Segmentation schemes have been investigated extensively in the field of image processing, but their goals are usually more ambitious than what is required for recognition by alignment. For example, they often attempt to segment the entire image, as opposed to just the region of interest. For recognition by alignment, the main requirement from the segmentation stage is that the alignment key will be selected from a region that is likely to correspond to a single object. The exact delineation of the entire object is not of major importance at this stage. Selection and segmentation are discussed in more detail in chapter 8.

Image description. The next stage involves the extraction of information that will be used for matching the viewed object with stored object-models. Most recognition schemes propose that the viewed object be described for this purpose in some fashion, using

1-D contours (Baker 1977), 2-D surface patches (Dane & Bajcsy 1982, Potmesil 1983, Faugeras 1984, Brady *et al.* 1985), or 3-D volumetric descriptions (Marr & Nishihara 1978, Biederman 1985).

An interesting question at this stage is to what extent the description of the viewed object should rely on detailed 3-D information. Some recognition schemes (see Besl & Jain 1985) assume the availability of a detailed and precise depth map of the visible surfaces. Such information is not always available in the image, and from human vision it appears that recognition can often proceed in the absence of detailed 3-D information (Bülthoff & Edelman 1992). It is desirable, therefore, that the recognition process should not depend critically on detailed 3-D information, although such information may be used when available.

If detailed 3-D information is not required, it appears that descriptions based on object contours are better suited for the recognition task than surface-based and volumetric descriptions. At the same time, it is important not to identify object contours with intensity edges. Many intensity edges in the image are irrelevant to the purpose of recognition, and recognition can proceed in the absence of intensity edges altogether. For example, objects can be recognized in random dot stereograms. In this case object contours are defined by discontinuities in depth and surface orientation, but not by intensity changes.

In any case, the main point is that even in the alignment approach that is more pictorial in nature than alternative schemes, the comparison of the viewed object and stored models is not performed between raw images, but follows processing stages that produce more abstract patterns. One part of the processing, therefore, is the creation of these internal descriptions that are manipulated and compared during the recognition process.

Extracting an alignment key.   The alignment key is the information used to bring the viewed object and internal models into alignment. As discussed above, a number of different alignment procedures may be used, depending on some properties of the viewed object. For example, if it has a clearly defined orientation, then this orientation may be used for alignment. If the object is unoriented, the alignment key may be composed of salient points.

We will also see alternative versions of the alignment scheme (in chapters 7 and 10) that do not require the extraction of an alignment key.

Alignment. This stage brings the object into register with potentially matching objects. As suggested above, it may be possible to break down the alignment stage into two steps. In the first, the viewed object is brought into correspondence with a large number of models stored in memory in some canonical form. The second stage is composed of individual alignments: different models align themselves individually to the viewed object. A number of problems remain regarding the parallel execution of this stage. Can a large number of models be aligned simultaneously? If not, how can the load required by individual alignments be reduced? These issues will be taken up again in subsequent chapters.

Indexing. Following alignment, the degree of match between the viewed object and a stored model can be assessed. An important problem arises when the number of stored object models becomes large. Will it become necessary to perform alignment and matching for each one of them individually? A number of recognition schemes precede the final match with a stage termed "indexing." The goal of this stage is to use some simple criteria to "filter out" unlikely models, and obtain a smaller set of likely candidates (Lowe 1985, Grimson 1990a). In other schemes this stage also includes rank-ordering of the models, so that matching with the more likely ones is attempted first. This use of indexing is closely related to the notion of classification. During classification, an object is assigned to a general class (such as "a house," "a car," "a face"), or a small number of possible classes. At subsequent stages the viewed object can be compared with individual models within this class only. The notion of classification, and its relation to identification, is further discussed in chapter 6.

Matching. Following the alignment stage, the correct model and the viewed object are expected to be in better agreement, but usually differences between them will still exist. A measure of the degree of match is therefore required to decide which of the models resembles the viewed object most closely. Issues related to the matching will be considered in subsequent chapters; here I will only mention three general requirements for this measure. First, the contributions of different parts of the object to the match quality may carry different weights. Some parts may be small in size, but still be crucial for defining the object. Other parts may carry little weight and even no weight at all. In some cases it is also expected that the distinction between highly similar objects may require an additional separate stage. Two objects that differ only in small details would not be distinguished immediately, but would trigger a specialized routine to distinguish between them.

Second, in aligning pictorial descriptions, a match may be obtained at different levels, such as the underlying object contours, or the level of more abstract descriptors. The contributions of the different levels will have to be combined in an appropriate manner. The matching score is likely to increase with the set of features (contours and labels) in common to the object and the model, and decrease as a function of the features that appear in the one but not in the other (see Tversky 1977).

Finally, the decision regarding the best matching model will be affected by factors other than similarity of shape. The degree of match may have to take into account, for instance, the amount of distortion that was required to bring the viewed object and model into registration. The selection of the appropriate model may also be biased, for example, by prior expectation and by proximity to other objects in the scene.

4 The Alignment of Smooth Bounding Contours

Objects with smooth bounding surfaces present a special difficulty to alignment-based approaches. The alignment approach described in the previous chapter proceeds by recovering the alignment transformation, and then using it to predict the appearance of the model following the application of the required transformation. It is this prediction stage that makes objects with smooth bounding surfaces more difficult to handle—the prediction becomes considerably more complex than predicting the appearance of objects with sharp bounding contours.

The problem of predicting the new appearance of a smooth object following a rotation is illustrated in figure 4.1. In this figure and the discussion that follows we will make use of the following terminology. Given an object O and a viewpoint v, the *rim* is the set of all the points on the object's surface, whose normal is perpendicular to the visual axis (Koenderink & Van Doorn 1981). The importance of the rim points on the object is that (assuming orthographic projection, see appendix E) they generate the bounding contours of the object in the image. This set is therefore also called the *contour generator* (Marr 1977). A *silhouette* is an image generated by the orthographic projection of the rim. The distinction, then, is that the rim is a set of points on the object, and the silhouette is the image generated by the rim points. In the analysis below we assume that every point along the silhouette is generated by a single rim point. This is just a technical point, that excludes special situations in which two rim points on the object happen to be exactly aligned, and project to a single point in the image. An edge map of an object usually contains the silhouette, which is generated by its rim, and also contains other edges as well, such as internal edges generated by changes in reflectance properties, or color, of different regions on the object.

Figure 4.1 shows a bird's eye view of two rotating objects, a cube (a & b) and an ellipsoid (c & d). For both objects, points P and Q lie on the object's rim, and therefore their projections lie in the image on its silhouette. When the cube rotates from position

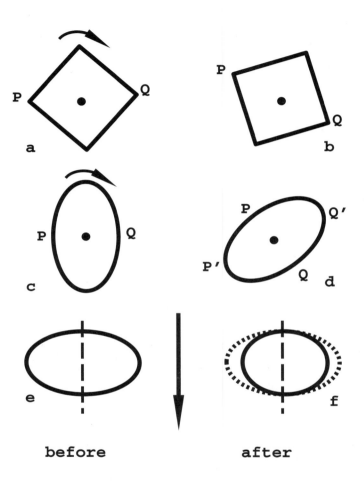

Figure 4.1
Changes in the rim during rotation. (a) A bird's eye view of a cube. (b) The
cube after rotation. Before and after the rotation points **P**, **Q** lie on the rim.
(c) A bird's eye view of a rotating ellipsoid. (d) The ellipsoid after rotation.
The rim points **P**, **Q** in (c) are replaced by **P′**, **Q′** in (d). The imgage is now
generated by a new set of points. (e) An ellipsoid in a frontal view. (f) The
rotated ellipsoid (outer contour), superimposed on the appearance of the rim,
as a planar object, after rotation by the same amount (inner contour). The
vertical arrow indicates the direction of projection. After (Basri & Ullman,
1993).

(a) to (b), P and Q, remain on the rim. Their new 3-D position is easily determined: it is simply given by the position of the points following a known rotation. Therefore, the new silhouette can be predicted in a straightforward manner. In contrast, when the ellipsoid rotates from position (c) to (d), the new 3-D position of P and Q is no longer relevant, since these points no longer lie on the object's rim. The silhouette is now generated by a new set of points, including P', Q' in (d). The problem, then, is to predict the newe silhouette, generated by the new set of rim points. Figures 4.1 (e & f) provide another illustration of the same problem. They depict the ellipsoid in a frontal view before and after the rotation, compared to its appearance if the rim, as a planar space curve, had been rotated by the same amount. As can be seen from the figure, the problem is that a rim generated by a sharp edge is stable on the object as long as the edge is visible. In contrast, a rim that is generated by a smooth surface changes continuously with the viewpoint. The conclusion is that the prediction problem for smooth objects is in general significantly more complicated than that of objects with sharp edges.

This chapter will describe a simple solution to the prediction problem, using a scheme called the "curvature method" (Basri & Ullman 1993). Objects with either sharp edges or smooth bounding surfaces are treated by this method on equal footing: sharp edges are simply obtained as a special case, where the relevant radius of curvature of the bounding surfaces becomes diminishingly small. For smooth bounding contours the method produces an approximate rather than an exact solution, but in the limiting case of sharp edges it becomes exact.

How to Predict the New Appearance

Many existing schemes restrict themselves to polyhedral objects and do not treat objects with smooth curved surfaces (Lowe 1987, Huttenlocher & Ullman 1987, Thompson & Mundy 1987). As for smooth boundaries, two main approaches have been attempted. The first approach describes an object as a composition of either volumetric or surface primitives that have simple geometrical structures (Marr & Nishihara 1978, Brown 1981, Dane & Bajcsy 1982, Potmesil 1983, Brady *et al.* 1985, Faugeras & Hebert 1986). When the object changes, by changing orientation in space, the transformation is applied to each primitive. Since the primitives have simple geometrical structures, their silhouette can be predicted. For example, the scheme may use shape primitives such as cones, spheres, and cylinders, and the prediction problem is then limited to transformations applied to these particular 3-D shapes. The silhouette of each primitive is determined, and the extreme points of the collection of the primitives' silhouettes are taken to be the object's overall silhouette. The second approach approximates the object's surface by a set of 3-D wires (Baker 1977). The transformation is applied to each wire, and the extreme wires are then taken to be the object silhouette.

The decomposition approach works well for simple objects, but usually not for complex ones. The wire approach is often costly from a computational standpoint due to the large number of wires required and the need to perform "hidden line elimination." In addition, these approaches usually enable the prediction of the bounding contours only. Internal contours and surface markings, that may have a significant role in shape-based recognition, are often not treated.

This chapter presents a different approach to the prediction problem. Let me first introduce the main idea and results in general terms, the details and results of testing the method are then described in the next few sections. The general approach is an extension of the alignment scheme described in the previous chapter. As before, a 3-D object is represented by a number of views, taken from different viewing directions. Each view contains some supplementary information that makes it possible to predict how the image will distort with changes in viewing direction. For the objects considered so far, the supplementary information consisted of the depth values of contour points. To deal with objects with smooth bounding contours, information related to curvature is added to the object representation. We will see below that by using the 3-D surface curvature of each point along the silhouette, it becomes possible to make an accurate estimation of the silhouette after the transformations. A single object-model handles a range of viewing directions, and several models of this kind are sufficient for predicting the object's appearance from any given viewpoint.

4.1   The Curvature Method

The method is based on representing surface curvature of points along the silhouette. The basic idea is shown in figure 4.2. We will choose a coordinate system so that the X and Y will be the axes of the image plane, and the Z-axis will be the line of sight. We will consider an object O rotating by a rotation R about the vertical axis Y, and analyze the distortion of its bounding contour. Let us start with a point p on its rim. The figure shows a section of the object through p, viewed from above, that is, perpendicular to Y, the axis of rotation. The main addition is to use the value of r, the curvature radius of p in this section. Roughly speaking, the value of r is obtained by fitting a small circle to the contour around p. We will also think of r as a vector of length r parallel to the X-axis. This means, for example, that $p - r$ is the point p displaced by a distance of r to the right. When the object rotates by R, point p ceases to be a rim point, and it is replaced by a new point p' approximated by

$$p' \approx R(p - r) + r. \tag{4.1.1}$$

This equation has a simple intuitive meaning. The point $O = p - r$ is the center of the circle of curvature of p (p, r are vectors). To predict the new rim point we first apply R to O. We obtain $O' = R(p - r)$, which is the new position of O following the rotation. The new rim point is then simply $p' = O' + r$, as can be seen in the figure. This approximation holds as long as the circle of curvature provides a good approximation to the section at p.

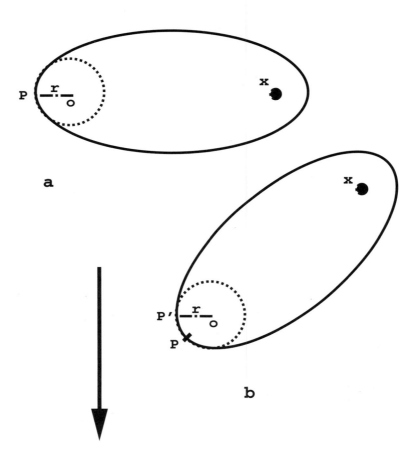

Figure 4.2
The curvature method. (a) A horizontal section of an ellipsoid. p is a point
on the rim, r is the radius of curvature at p, O is the center of the curvature
circle, and x is the rotation axis. The arrow shows the direction of projection.
(b) The ellipsoid rotated. p' is the new rim point, and it is approximated by
the formula: $p' \approx R(p - r) + r$.

It is worth noting that "sharp" boundaries, such as the cube edges in figure 4.1, or markings on the surface itself, do not require a special treatment. They are included in equation (4.1.1) as the special case $r = 0$.

So far we have considered rotations about the vertical Y axis. We shall next consider the effect on the silhouette of a rotation about an arbitrary axis in space. The problem is that the relevant radius of curvature depends on the axis of rotation. The question then is how many different radii of curvature we must store in order to solve the problem for rotations around an arbitrary axis in 3-D. As it turns out, we still need only a single parameter.

To analyze the situation, we will make use of the fact that any 3-D rotation can be decomposed into the sum of two successive rotations: a rotation about some axis V in the image plane, followed by a second rotation about the Z-axis. This decomposition is convenient because the effect of rotating the object about the line of sight Z is, of course, easy to predict. The problem, therefore, is to predict the appearance of the object following a rotation about an axis V lying in the image plane.

In general, the vector of curvature radius r used in equation (4.1.1) would depend on the rotation axis. Let r_x, r_y be the radii of curvature at p for rotations about the Y and X axes respectively. It turns out that the radius of curvature for a rotation about any axis can be determined conveniently from r_x, r_y, alone. This is summarized in the following statement:

Statement 1:   Let p be a rim point, and let V_α be an axis lying within the image plane and forming an angle α with the X-axis. The curvature radius at p for rotations about V_α is given by

$$r_\alpha = r_y \cos \alpha - r_x \sin \alpha. \qquad (4.1.2)$$

(A proof is given in appendix B.)

From this proposition and equation (4.1.1) we can predict the position of p', the new rim point, for a rotation about an arbitrary axis within the image plane, and consequently any 3-D axis as well, using the two parameters r_x, r_y at p. However, r_x and r_y are in fact related, and, as summarized by the next statement, a single parameter is sufficient.

Statement 2:   Let $\mathbf{r} = (r_x, r_y)$ be the curvature vector at p, and let $\mathbf{t}$ be the tangent vector to the silhouette at p. Then $\mathbf{r}$ is perpendicular to $\mathbf{t}$, that is, $\mathbf{r} \cdot \mathbf{t} = 0$.

(A proof is given in appendix B.)

It follows from the two propositions above that a single value is sufficient to determine the radius of curvature for a rotation about any axis in the image plane. This number is the magnitude of the curvature vector, $\| \mathbf{r} \|$ (also called, the *radial curvature* at p (Koenderink 1984, Brady *et al.* 1985), see also Giblin & Weiss 1987). We only need this magnitude, since the direction of $\mathbf{r}$ is known—it is perpendicular to the $\mathbf{t}$, the tangent to the curve. All other parameters can therefore be derived in a simple manner, as follows. Let θ be the angle between the tangent vector to the silhouette, $\mathbf{t}$, and the X-axis, then

$$
\begin{aligned}
r_x &= \| \mathbf{r} \| \sin \theta \\
r_y &= \| \mathbf{r} \| \cos \theta \\
r_\alpha &= \| \mathbf{r} \| \cos(\theta + \alpha).
\end{aligned}
\tag{4.1.3}
$$

The scheme is therefore the following. An object model M is a 2-D (orthographic) projection of its visible contours (including its sharp and smooth boundaries, as well as internal markings), as observed from a particular viewing direction. To represent the entire object, several different views would be required, but as will be seen in the examples below, this number is usually small. Each point along the silhouette has associated with it, along with its spatial coordinates, the radial curvature $\| \mathbf{r} \|$. Given a transformation T of the object in space, the translation, scaling and rotation about the line of sight are applied to M in a straightforward manner. The effect of rotation about an arbitrary axis in the image plane is computed as follows. First, for each point on the model, the radius of curvature r with respect to the rotation axis is determined by the expression for r_α in equation (4.1.3). Once r is known, the new position of the point in the image is determined using equation (4.1.1), where r is replaced by a vector of size r perpendicular to the rotation.

In this approach an object is represented using a number of viewer-centered descriptions, rather than a single object-centered representation. Each description covers a range of possible viewing angles, and to represent the entire object a number of descriptions are required. This representation is somewhat similar to the so-called "aspect graph" (Koenderink & Van Doorn 1979), in which an object representation is composed of a number of "aspects," each corresponding to a qualitatively different 2-D view of a 3-D object. Because the scheme provides an approximation rather than an exact prediction of the new view, the number of views depends on properties of the object's shape and on its similarity to other objects. As shown in the examples below, this number is small for moderately complex objects. Using symmetries, the cars used in these examples required four models to cover all common views, which included all vertical rotations and elevation of $\pm 30°$. Because of the orthographic projection approximation, if the object is to be recognized over a large range of viewing distances, additional models will be required. The computations required in this scheme during the prediction stage are simple, for example, no hidden line elimination is necessary.

4.2   Accuracy of the Curvature Method

The appearance of objects with sharp boundaries, for which the relevant radius of curvature vanishes, is predicted exactly by the curvature method. The prediction is also precise for the special case of spherical and cylindrical objects. The appearance of smooth objects with arbitrary structures is, however, only approximated by this method. In this section, the accuracy of the method is examined analytically, by deriving and evaluating a number of expressions for the magnitude of the error of the method, defined as the difference between the predicted and true image of an object, under various conditions. The discussion is somewhat technical in nature. The main reason for considering here the error issue in more detail compared with the previous chapter is that, unlike the case of sharp object boundaries, the method for smooth objects provides an approximation rather than an exact prediction. It is of interest to know, therefore, whether this approximation will be reasonable under a wide range of conditions. The problem is studied by a combination of methods: analytic studies of relatively simple shapes (in this section), and experimental testing using complex objects (in the next). The main conclusion from these two sections is that the method can tolerate substantial rotations with good accuracy, and consequently the number of models required to cover a given object from all directions is usually small. Readers who are less interested in the more technical error analysis can skip directly to the next section, were the method of model construction, and the results of applying the method to real 3-D objects are described.

In order to study the properties of the curvature method, we applied this method to ellipsoids and analyzed the errors obtained. We first compute the errors obtained when a canonical ellipsoid rotates around the vertical (Y) axis. In appendix C we then compute the errors obtained when the same ellipsoid rotates arbitrarily in 3-D space, and show that the errors obtained in the two cases are similar. The error depends on the shape of the ellipsoid, in other words, on the relative length of its axes, and it increases as the ellipsoid becomes "deep" (elongated in the Z-direction). We show that the errors are usually small, and that, in general, a small number of models is required to predict the appearance of an ellipsoid from all possible views. Additional details of this analysis are described in (Basri & Ullman 1993).

Let us first describe the error function used to compare the actual and predicted images. Consider an ellipsoid rotating about some axis V in the image plane. Let $p_1 = (x_1, y_1)$ be the projected location of some rim point. Following rotation, the rim changes, and the point p_1 is replaced by a new point, $p_2 = (x_2, y_2)$, such that the vector $p_2 - p_1$ is perpendicular to the axis V. Denote the approximated location of p_2 according to the curvature method by $\hat{p}_2 = (\hat{x}_2, \hat{y}_2)$. The observed error is measured by $\| \hat{p}_2 - p_2 \|$. Clearly, if we scale the ellipsoid the observed error would scale as well. We will prefer, however, to consider a normalized value for the error, that is independent of scale. This normalization of the error is obtained as follows. Consider the planar section through p_1 that is perpendicular to the rotation axis V. This section forms an ellipse, and let $p_0 = (x_0, y_0)$ be the center of this ellipse. The relative error is now defined by

$$E = \frac{\| \hat{p}_2 - p_2 \|}{\| p_1 - p_0 \|}.$$

E reflects the observed error relative to the projected size of the ellipsoid. Notice that E is independent of translation and scale of the ellipsoid.

Rotation around the Vertical Axis The surface of a canonical ellipsoid can be described by the formula:

$$\frac{x^2}{a^2} + \frac{y^2}{b^2} + \frac{z^2}{c^2} = 1.$$

Let $p_1 = (x_1, y_1)$ be a point on its silhouette. When the ellipsoid rotates about the vertical (Y) axis by an angle θ, p_1 disappears and is replaced by a new contour point $p_2 = (x_2, y_2)$ with an identical y-value, $y_2 = y_1$. Let $\hat{p}_2 = (\hat{x}_2, \hat{y}_2)$ be the approximated position of p_2 according to the curvature method. The horizontal section of the ellipsoid through p_1 is an ellipse centered around $p_0 = (0, y_0)$. Notice that the points p_1, p_2, $\hat{p}_2$, and p_0 all lie on the same horizontal section, implying that $y_1 = y_2 = \hat{y}_2 = y_0$. The relative error is therefore reduced to

$$E = \left| \frac{\hat{x}_2 - x_2}{x_1} \right|.$$

The error E is then given by:

$$E(\frac{c^2}{a^2}, \theta) = \cos\theta + \frac{c^2}{a^2}(1 - \cos\theta) - \sqrt{\cos^2\theta + \frac{c^2}{a^2}\sin^2\theta}. \qquad (4.2.4)$$

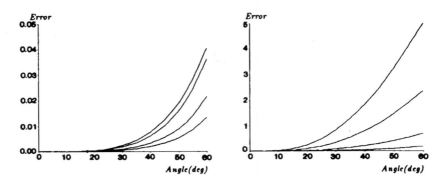

Figure 4.3
The error of the curvature method as a function of θ, the angle of rotation. (a)
$\frac{c^2}{a^2} = \frac{1}{16}, \frac{1}{9}, \frac{1}{4}$ and $\frac{1}{2}$. (b) $\frac{c^2}{a^2} = 2, 4, 9$ and 16. (The parameters correspond
the curves at increasing heights.)

(The derivation is given in appendix C.)

The expression obtained for the error depends on two parameters: the aspect ratio of the ellipsoid, $\frac{c^2}{a^2}$, and the angle of rotation, θ, and it is invariant under a uniform scaling of the ellipsoid.

Properties of the Error   The prediction error obtained by the curvature method for a canonical ellipsoid rotating about the Y-axis vanishes in a number of special cases:

- $\theta = 0$ (that is, no rotation).
- $\frac{c^2}{a^2} = 1$ (that is, $c = a$, the cross section is a circle).
- $\frac{c^2}{a^2} = 0$ (that is, $c = 0$, a planar object).

As a function of θ, the angle of rotation, the error function is symmetric, that is, similar errors are obtained both for positive and negative rotations. The absolute value of the error increases monotonically with the absolute value of θ. Figure 4.3 shows the error as a function of θ for several ellipses.

As a function of $\frac{c^2}{a^2}$, the relative size of the axes of the ellipsoid, the error behaves differently in each of the two ranges: (1) when $c \leq a$, and (2) when $c > a$. In the first case the ellipsoid's width

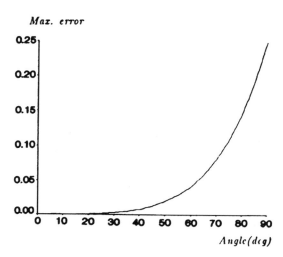

Figure 4.4
The maximal value of the error for canonical ellipsoids with $c \leq a$ as a function of θ, the angle of rotation.

is larger than its depth. In this case the error remains small even for fairly large values of θ. The maximal error is obtained when

$$\frac{c^2}{a^2} = \frac{3}{4} - \frac{1}{2(1 + \cos\theta)} \tag{4.2.5}$$

and it assumes the following values

- 0.24% at 30° ($\frac{c^2}{a^2} = 0.482$).
- 1.26% at 45° ($\frac{c^2}{a^2} = 0.457$).
- 4.14% at 60° ($\frac{c^2}{a^2} = 0.417$).

Figure 4.4 shows the maximal error as a function of θ. For each rotation, the ellipsoid yielding the largest error was determined, and the resulting error plotted in the graph.

When the ellipsoid becomes elongated in depth, that is, $c > a$, the error assumes larger values, and it becomes unbounded when θ increases to 90°. A model for such an ellipsoid would therefore cover only a restricted range of rotations. Larger rotations should be treated by additional models. Figure 4.5 shows the error as a function of $\frac{c^2}{a^2}$ for several values of θ. For a given rotation, the

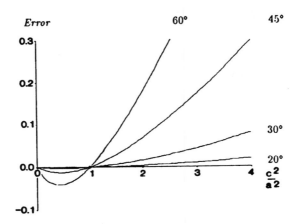

Figure 4.5
The error as a function of the aspect ratio, $\frac{c^2}{a^2}$, of the ellipsoid for $\theta = 20°$, 30°, 45°, and 60°. (The parameters correspond the curves at increasing magnitude.)

error increases with $\frac{c^2}{a^2}$. The errors for the previous case of wide ellipsoids, i.e., $c < a$, are plotted in this graph as negative values.

The error in the predicted appearance determines the number of views required to model an object. The analysis above shows that the error is smaller for "flat" ellipsoids, when $c < a$, and it becomes larger when $a < c$. Following a rotation of 90° about the Y-axis, the two axes, a and c, change their roles. Therefore, an ellipsoid with $c < a$ changes after a 90° rotation to an ellipsoid with $c > a$. An ellipsoid with a high aspect ratio, $\frac{c^2}{a^2}$, changes to an ellipsoid with a low aspect ratio. Consequently, the more restricted range of rotations covered by a model for an ellipsoid with a large aspect ratio, is balanced by the larger range of rotations covered by a model for the same ellipsoid after a 90° rotation. The result will be that a small number of models will be sufficient for representing the ellipsoid from all possible views.

Table 4.1 shows the number of models required to cover the entire range of rotations about the Y-axis for several ellipsoids. Because of symmetry considerations, only rotations up to 90° need

$\frac{c^2}{a^2}$	1%	2%	3%	4%	5%	6%
2	3	3	2	2	2	2
4	3	3	3	3	2	2
9	4	3	3	3	3	2
16	4	3	3	3	3	2
49	4	3	3	3	2	2
100	4	3	3	2	2	2

Table 4.1
The number of models required as a function of allowed error.

be considered. We see from the table that the number of views is small and does not exceed four, even for extreme aspect ratios and allowed error limited to 1%.

In determining the number of required views, each ellipsoid was initially represented by two models, one taken at its canonical position, the other following a 90° rotation. If the two models did not cover the entire range of rotations, additional models were added at intermediate positions. In this case the value of the error is somewhat different from the canonical case. An expression describing this value is given in appendix C. The appendix also contains an analysis of the error for rotations around an arbitrary axis in 3-D space. The analysis gives bounds for the case of ellipsoids. Complex realistic objects are more difficult to analyze. We therefore turn to empirical testing, by applying the method to complex 3-D objects.

4.3   Empirical Testing

The alignment scheme using the curvature method was implemented by R. Basri (Basri & Ullman 1993) and tested on images of 3-D objects. To apply the scheme, models of the viewed objects must be acquired. We first describe how object models were acquired in practice, and then present the results of applying the recognition scheme using these models.

One of the points that this section illustrates is technical in nature. The radius of curvature that is used by the curvature method is a parameter that involves changes in the direction of the object's surface normal. It can be considered a second-order quantity, in the sense that it involves the rate of change of the surface normal, defined in turn by the first derivatives of the surface. The estimation of quantities that involve high-order derivative tends to be noisy, and therefore a natural question is whether schemes that depend on curvature estimation can be used in practice. The sections below illustrate that even a simple approximation to the surface curvature can be sufficient for the purpose of the curvature method.

4.3.1   Model Construction

For our purpose, an object model must contain the spatial coordinates as well as the radii of curvature of the object's visible contours. The required 3-D information can be obtained during a learning period using various 3-D cues, such as stereo information and shading.

To estimate the radii of curvature we have not used explicit 3-D reconstruction of the object. Instead, the curvature was estimated using three edge pictures of each object. It is not surprising that three images are required for this estimate. In general, from two nearby samples of the value of a given function one can obtain an estimate of the derivative, or local rate of change of the function in question. Three samples are required to estimate curvature, or change in the derivative. This is because two points are required to define a line, and three points are required to determine a circle. In principle, then, three pictures are used to define the local circles of curvature at each point.

The curvatures were estimated from the three images using the following procedure. Consider three silhouette pictures (denoted by A, B and C) taken from three different viewpoints along a circle in space perpendicular to the Y-axis (figure 4.6). Suppose that α is the rotation angle between pictures A and B, and β is

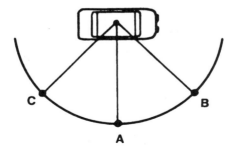

Figure 4.6
Constructing a model using three edge pictures, a bird's eye view. Points A, B and C are the three camera locations along a circle in space perpendicular to the Y-axis.

the rotation angle between pictures A and C. (Typical values for these rotations in the empirical testing was $30°$ each.) Let p_1, p_2 and p_3 be three corresponding points in A, B and C respectively. Since the camera was rotated about the Y-axis between successive pictures, all three points share the same y coordinate, so that $p_1 = (x_1, y, z_1)$, $p_2 = (x_2, y, z_2)$, and $p_3 = (x_3, y, z_3)$. According to the curvature method, expressed in equation (4.1.1)

$$x_2 = (x_1 - r_x)\cos\alpha + z_1 \sin\alpha + r_x. \tag{4.3.6}$$

$$x_3 = (x_1 - r_x)\cos\beta + z_1 \sin\beta + r_x. \tag{4.3.7}$$

These are two linear equations with two unknown parameters z_1 and r_x, and therefore the values of z_1 and r_x can be determined. We can express these values explicitly:

$$z_1 = \frac{x_1(\cos\alpha - \cos\beta) - x_2(1 - \cos\beta) + x_3(1 - \cos\alpha)}{(1 - \cos\alpha)\sin\beta - \sin\alpha(1 - \cos\beta)} \tag{4.3.8}$$

$$r_x = \frac{x_1 \sin(\alpha - \beta) + x_2 \sin\beta - x_3 \sin\alpha}{(1 - \cos\alpha)\sin\beta - \sin\alpha(1 - \cos\beta)}. \tag{4.3.9}$$

In the range $-\frac{\pi}{2} < \alpha, \beta < \frac{\pi}{2}$, $\alpha \neq \beta$, the denominator does not vanish, and the two values are well-defined.

For most contour points this procedure supplies all the information we need, since equation (4.1.3) establishes that in general r_x and the tangent to the contour are sufficient to estimate the curvature radius in all other directions. The exceptions are points where the tangent to the contour lies in the horizontal direction. In this case the curvature vector is vertical, and its magnitude cannot be estimated from this set of images. To estimate the value of r_y at these points a similar procedure can be applied to three edge pictures obtained by a rotation about the X-axis. For contour points whose tangent direction is not close to the horizontal this estimation of r_y is in principle redundant, but it can still be used to improve the estimate of the curvature. In this manner five pictures can be used to create a complete model, three for a rotation about the X-axis, and three for a rotation about the Y-axis, with the central picture common to both sets. The final model consists of an edge map of the central picture, together with the depth coordinates and the estimated magnitude of the curvature vector (r_x, r_y) at each point.

Note that the model construction requires the establishment of correspondence between images. This appears to be a general issue; we will see in subsequent chapters that alternative versions of the alignment scheme also require the establishment of correspondence for model construction. Identifying corresponding points in the pictures becomes easier when the model is constructed under controlled conditions. When the rotation is about the Y-axis, the corresponding points must lie on the same horizontal line. Each contour point therefore usually has a small number of candidate corresponding points to be considered. The issue of correspondence in model construction will be discussed in more detail in chapter 7.

The main conclusion from the discussion so far is that the model required by the curvature method can be constructed from a small number of corresponding pictures. The curvature method itself is used in fact in the procedure to derive the required parameters.

For a practical use of the method, the procedure for estimating the 3-D parameters can be simplified in a number of ways. By setting $\beta = -\alpha$ the equations above can be simplified. The values of the unknown parameters, z_1 and r_x, are now given by:

$$z_1 = \frac{x_2 - x_3}{2 \sin \alpha} \qquad (4.3.10)$$

$$r_x = \frac{x_2 + x_3 - 2x_1 \cos \alpha}{2(1 - \cos \alpha)}. \qquad (4.3.11)$$

If the angle α is known, the model parameters are derived immediately. If α is not known, but assuming that it is small, we can use a convenient small-angle approximation. To do this, we define new quantities $\hat{z}$, $\hat{r}_x$ as follows:

$$\hat{z} = z\alpha \approx \frac{x_2 - x_3}{2} \qquad (4.3.12)$$

$$\hat{r}_x = (r_x - x_1)\alpha^2 \approx x_2 + x_3 - 2x_1. \qquad (4.3.13)$$

This approximation uses $(\sin \alpha) \to \alpha$ and $(\cos \alpha) \to 1 - \frac{\alpha^2}{2}$. The idea is to use these modified parameters consistently instead of the original ones. When using these modified parameters, we would like the alignment procedure to provide, instead of a rotation angle θ used by the usual alignment method, the ratio $\frac{\theta}{\alpha}$. We use:

$$x' \approx x + z\theta + (r_x - x)\frac{\theta^2}{2} = x + \hat{z}(\frac{\theta}{\alpha}) + \frac{\hat{r}_x}{2}(\frac{\theta}{\alpha})^2. \qquad (4.3.14)$$

The equation shows that instead of using the original parameters and the rotation angle θ, we can use the modified parameters together with the ratio $\frac{\theta}{\alpha}$. This ratio $\frac{\theta}{\alpha}$ can in fact be determined during the alignment process. Suppose, for instance, that the alignment transformation is determined by three corresponding points. In this case a set of six equations determined by the corresponding points determines the transformation—rotation in 3-D space, translation and scale, as described in the preceding chapter. If the three points lie on the object's contour, we can substitute two of the six equations, those describing rotations about the X and Y axes, by equation (4.3.14). We will end up with a new set of six equations with six unknown parameters to solve. In this modified set of parameters, the angle of rotation θ is replaced by the ratio $\frac{\theta}{\alpha}$.

The result is a simplified scheme for model construction as well as for performing the alignment, assuming small angles of rotation. The range of rotations covered by a single model using this small-angle approximation will depend on the object's shape and on the similarity to other models. The results shown in the next section (section 4.3.2) regarding the accuracy of the method also hold for this approximation.

We have seen that object models can be derived for the purpose of the curvature method, based on a small number of corresponding pictures. This model construction involves the estimation of surface curvature. The estimation of curvature radii from several images was shown to be in general sensitive to camera calibration (Vaillant & Faugeras 1989, Blake & Cipolla 1990). How does this sensitivity affect the curvature method?

Before turning to the curvature method, it is worth noting that, in general, the estimation of the curvature can be improved in at least two ways. First, the method presented in this section requires three images. Additional images can be used to improve the estimation. Second, other sources of information about 3-D structure such as stereo and shading can also be used to achieve a robust estimation of the curvature radii.

For the curvature method, however, an improved estimation of the curvature does not appear to be necessary. As it turns out, the curvature method, unlike some other methods that use surface curvature, is relatively insensitive to calibration. The curvature radii are used here to predict the appearance of objects from different viewpoints. Instabilities in the computation are therefore significant only as long as they propagate into the predictions obtained by the method. Equation (4.3.14) above implies that calibration errors, namely, errors in estimating the angle α, can be largely compensated in the prediction stage by changing the angle of rotation θ appropriately. As can be seen from Eq. (4.3.14), the prediction results depend on the ratio $\frac{\theta}{\alpha}$ rather than on the exact value of α. It appears from the simulations and application to real images that the final predicted appearance is in fact quite accurate in practice.

In the next section, we consider the application of the method to images of real 3-D objects. Before describing these results, we illustrate the results of the curvature method applied to simple 3-D shapes, to examine the improvement obtained by using curvature data over 3-D alignment that uses 3-D depth data, but without curvature information.

For this purpose, models of different ellipsoids were constructed from three images obtained by a rotation of $\pm 60°$ and $\pm 30°$ about the vertical axis. These models were then tested by rotating them by $30°$ and $60°$ respectively to obtain both predictions for interpolation as well as extrapolation. The results are shown in figure 4.7. It can be seen that even when the curvature is estimated from only three images, the curvature method provides significantly better predictions of the appearance of the ellipsoids than when the curvature is not used.

4.3.2 Applying the Curvature Method to Real Images

A prototype system for object recognition using alignment, that predicts the appearance of objects using the curvature method, was implemented by R. Basri. Pictures comprised of 512×512 points (pixels) were obtained with a TV camera. Edge maps of the pictures were created using the Canny edge detector (Canny 1986). Toy models of two cars, a VW and a Saab, were assembled on a mechanical device, to enable controlled rotations about the vertical and the horizontal axes. The system first constructs object models comprising of depth values and curvature radii as described in section 4.3.1.

Models can be constructed in this system using either three images using rotations about the Y-axis, or five images using ro-

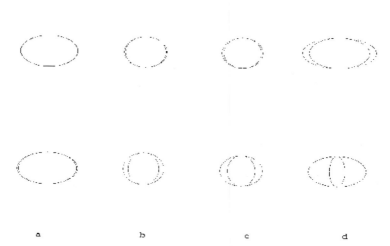

a   b   c   d

Figure 4.7
Matching models of ellipsoids with their images. The curvature values in
these models were estimated from three images of the ellipsoids obtained by
rotating the ellipsoid about the vertical axis by angles $\pm\alpha$. The models were
then rotated about the vertical axis by an angle θ, and the results were overlaid
with the accurate image. Upper pictures: using the curvature method. Lower
pictures: same experiments but the curvature is not used. (a) $\frac{c^2}{a^2} = 0.5$,
$\alpha = 60°$, $\theta = 30°$. (b) $\frac{c^2}{a^2} = 0.5$, $\alpha = 30°$, $\theta = 60°$. (c) $\frac{c^2}{a^2} = 2$, $\alpha = 60°$,
$\theta = 30°$. (d) $\frac{c^2}{a^2} = 2$, $\alpha = 30°$, $\theta = 60°$.

tations about both the Y and X axes. The internal model can then be used to predict the appearance of the object following 3-D rotation, translation and scaling, using the curvature method described in section 4.1.

Models of the two cars, the VW and the Saab, were created (figure 4.8). These two particular cars were selected for testing because they provide examples of complex objects bound by smooth surfaces. Furthermore, the two are quite similar in shape. To distinguish between them, the recognition system must be able to make precise shape discriminations. It is interesting to note in this regard that for human observers the task is not particularly challenging; reliable discrimination can be obtained after a brief training.

For each car model, three pictures were taken, with α and β (the angles between successive pictures, see section 4.3.1) taken to be $\pm 30°$ about the Y-axis. For each car, the procedure resulted in a single model, comprising of the edge map of the central image, together with the estimated depth and curvature along the edges. It was found that a single model of this type yields accurate predictions of the appearance of the object within the entire $60°$ of rotation about the Y-axis.

Figure 4.9 shows four pictures, two of each car, rotated by $\pm 15°$. In each case, the image of the rotated car is superimposed on the original, unrotated version. In can be seen that such rotations already create substantial deformations of the images, that the recognition process must deal with.

Figure 4.10 shows the results of aligning the models with the images. An approximation to the transformation (rotation, translation and scale) separating the model and the viewed object can be supplied by different alignment routines, such as using three corresponding points. The internal model is then transformed, using the alignment transformation, according to the curvature method described above. The figure shows the result of superimposing the transformed model over the image. For each car, a single internal model is used to try to match the images taken

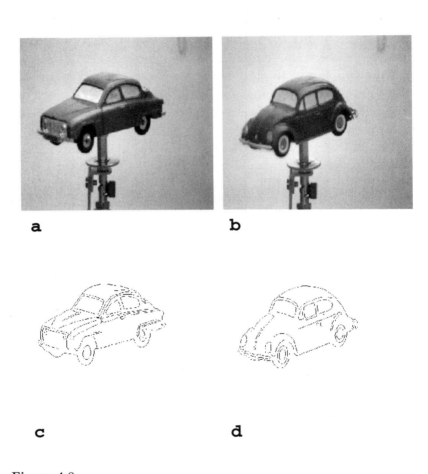

Figure 4.8
Models of two similar toy cars. (a) A picture of the model Saab car. (b) A picture of the model VW car. (c) An edge map of the Saab. (d) An edge map of the VW. The edge map representations were used is the recognition process.

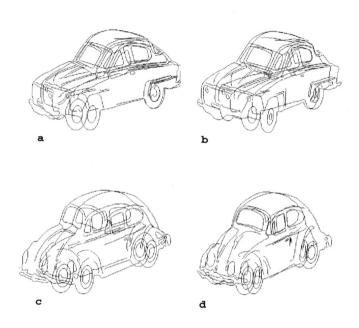

Figure 4.9
A rotation in space causes a deformation of the car images with respect to the original images. In each case, the image following a small rotation is superimposed over the original unrotated image. (a) A deformation of the Saab car image following a rotation of $-15°$. (b) A deformation of the Saab car image following a rotation of $+15°$. (c) A deformation of the VW car image following a rotation of $-15°$. (d) A deformation of the VW car image following a rotation of $+15°$. The recognition scheme is required to cope with these, and also much larger distortions.

from different viewing directions. It can be seen that by using this
alignment procedure, a single model gives an accurate fit to the
object seen from the different viewing positions.

Figure 4.11 shows the result of matching the two cars with the
incorrect models. In each case, the model was manipulated to obtain the best match between the model and the image. The discrepancy between the image and the aligned model is significantly
higher than in figure 4.10. A simple distance metric between the
image contours and the aligned model was therefore sufficient to
select the correct model. Figure 4.12 shows the result of matching
the two cars when the curvature information is not used. It can
be seen that, while internal contours align perfectly, the occluding
contours no longer match as well as they did when the curvature
was used. The deviations are not large, but they make the accurate distinction between two similar objects considerably more
difficult. It is worth noting that accurate predictions were obtained despite the fact that the objects have complex 3-D shapes,
and that we used crude approximations to the radii of curvature,
using three pictures.

The curvature method described above is not restricted to contours originating from elliptic surface patches. It can handle contours originating from hyperbolic patches—as long as the patches
are visible. When, however, a patch is self occluded, a new aspect of the object is observed, and an additional model should be
used. (In an elliptic surface patch the two main curvatures have
the same sign, they are both concave or convex, like the surface
of an egg. In a hyperbolic patch, the curvature in one direction is
positive, and in the orthogonal direction negative, as in the inside
of a torus.) The treatment of hyperbolic patches is demonstrated
in figure 4.13. Models of three tori with different radii were pre-
pared analytically. The models were matched to an image that
contained the tori in various positions and orientations. It can be
seen that although the points of the inner circles of the tori come
from hyperbolic patches, their prediction is still accurate.

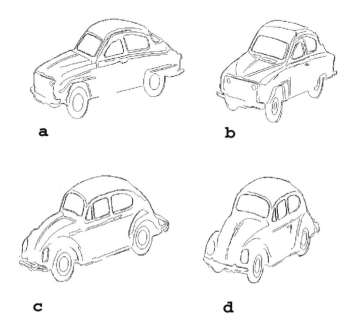

a   b

c   d

Figure 4.10
An alignment of the correct models with the their images. Following alignment, the models match their images well over a wide range of rotations in
space. (a) Alignment of the Saab model with the first Saab image. (b) Alignment of the same Saab model with the second Saab image. (c) Alignment
of the VW model with the first VW image. (d) Alignment of the same VW
model with the second VW image.

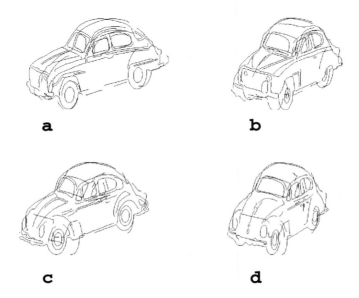

Figure 4.11
Matching the images with incorrect models. (a) Matching the first Saab image
to the VW model. (b) Matching the second Saab image to the same VW
model. (c) Matching the first VW image to the Saab model. (d) Matching
the second VW image to the same Saab model. A considerable discrepancy
remains between the image and the inappropriate model.

a

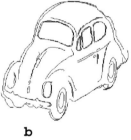

b

Figure 4.12
Matching the images with models that do not contain curvature information.
(a) Matching a Saab image to a Saab model. (b) Matching a VW image to a
VW model. The matching is less accurate then the match obtained with the
curvature scheme.

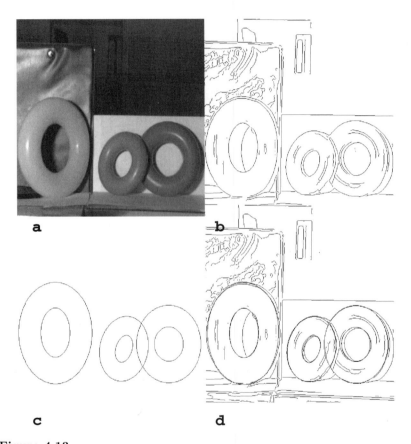

a   **b**

c   **d**

Figure 4.13
Alignment of doughnut-shape models with their images. (a) A picture of three
tori. (b) A contour image of the tori. (c) A prediction of the appearance of
the three tori, based on the curvature scheme. (d) Matching the prediction
to the actual image. These smooth, curved objects are matched well by the
curvature method.

In summary, the curvature method can be used for predicting the new appearance of an object with smooth surfaces following a similarity transformation (3-D rotation, translation and scaling). The method uses the 3-D surface curvature along the object contours. It turns out that a single parameter, the magnitude of the curvature vectors at these points, is sufficient for predicting the object's new appearance for a rotation about any given axis. Three pictures are in principle sufficient for approximating the radii of curvature for most contour points, and five can be used to estimate the components r_x, r_y independently.

The implemented scheme was found to give accurate results for large transformations. To cover all views of a given object, the object is represented in this scheme not by a single internal model, but by a number of models, each covering a range of potential viewpoints. The results show that only a small number of such models are required to predict the new appearance of an object from all viewpoints.

The curvature method can be used on its own right, as described in this chapter. It can also be used indirectly, as a part of a scheme that does not use 3-D information explicitly, but relies instead on the use of small collections of 2-D images. This method, the linear combination of images, is described in the next chapter.

5 Recognition by the Combination of Views

The alignment method described so far uses explicit three dimensional object models. During the recognition process, a candidate 3-D object is manipulated in an attempt to compensate for the transformation separating the model and the viewed object to be recognized.

This chapter presents a different approach, in which each model is represented by the combination of 2-D views of the object. It is still an alignment approach, since recognition is obtained by applying transformations and compensating for the differences between the viewed object and stored models. However, instead of using explicit 3-D models the new scheme stores and manipulates 2-D views. This approach has several advantages. First, it handles rigid 3-D transformations, but is not restricted to such transformations. Second, there is no need in this scheme to explicitly recover and represent the 3-D structure of objects. Third, the computations involved are often simpler than in previous schemes.

The first part of this chapter develops the basic idea: we show that the variety of views depicting the same object under different transformations can often be expressed as linear combinations of a small number of views. The intuition behind this approach can be explained in simple terms. Suppose that we have stored two views, V_1 and V_2, of the same three-dimensional object, taken from somewhat different viewing directions. We are then given a novel view, V, of the same object, but from some intermediate viewing direction, in between V_1 and V_2. Intuitively, we can expect the new view to be somewhat similar to V_1 and somewhat like V_2, and, in some sense, to be in between the two views. It turns out that this intuition can be made precise, and V is in fact a simple combination of the already existing views, V_1, V_2. More specifically, if $\mathcal{M} = \{M_1, ..., M_k\}$ is the set of pictures representing a given object, and P is the 2-D view of an object to be recognized, then P is considered an instance of M if it can be expressed as a sum $P = \sum \alpha_i M_i$ of the existing models for some constants α_i. We will see what this combination of models means, and will show that this approach handles correctly 3-D transformations of objects with sharp as well as smooth boundaries. The second part of the chapter illustrates how this view-combination property can be used in the recognition process. We will also consider possible extensions, such as the non-linear combination of models, and handling some non-rigid transformations.

The chapter describes a number of specific schemes, but also supports a more general view: that significant aspects of recognition can be accomplished by relatively low-level processes that use combinations or interpolation of pictorial representations.

5.1 Modeling Objects by the Combination of Images

The modeling of objects using linear combinations of views is based on the following observation. For many continuous transformations of interest in recognition, such as 3-D rotation, translation and scaling, it turns out that all the possible views of the transforming object can be expressed simply as the linear combination of other views of the same object. The coefficients of these linear combinations often follow certain functional restrictions.

The images we will consider are 2-D edge maps produced in the image by the (orthographic) projection of the bounding contours and other visible contours on 3-D objects. As in the alignment of 3-D models, for convenience of the presentation the discussion below will be divided into two cases: objects with sharp edges, and objects with smooth boundary contours. The difference between these two cases, discussed in the previous chapter (figure 4.1), is that for an object with sharp edges, the rim is stable on the object as long as the edge is visible. In contrast, the rim generated by smooth bounding surfaces is not fixed on the object, but changes continuously with the viewpoint. The two cases are not unrelated—sharp edges are a special case of the smooth bounding contours, when the relevant radius of curvature becomes small. In both cases, a small number of images M_i, with known correspondence, will constitute the object's model.

5.2 Objects with Sharp Edges

In the discussion below we examine the case of objects with sharp edges undergoing different transformations followed by an orthographic projection. In each case we show how the image of an object obtained by the transformation in question can be expressed as the linear combination of a small number of pictures. The coefficients of this combination are different for the x- and y-coordinates. That is, the intermediate view of the object is given by two linear combinations, one for the x-coordinates and the other for the y-coordinates. In addition, certain functional restrictions may hold among the different coefficients.

To introduce the scheme we first apply it to the restricted case of rotation about the vertical axis, that is simpler and more intuitive than the general case. Under vertical rotation, only the horizontal x-coordinates are changed from view to view. A straightforward derivation shows that any novel image is then given by a simple averaging of the x-coordinates in two stored views. A similar property also holds for more general transformations, that are examined next.

5.2.1 3-D Rotation around the Vertical Axis

Let P_1 and P_2 be two images of an object O rotating in depth around the vertical axis (Y-axis). P_2 is obtained from P_1 following a rotation by an angle α, ($\alpha \neq k\pi$). Let $\hat{P}$ be a third image of the same object obtained from P_1 by a rotation of an angle θ around the vertical axis. We wish to show how $\hat{P}$ can be obtained by combining the two images, P_1 and P_2. For this purpose, let us follow the position of a single point, p, in the three images. We assume for the analysis simple orthographic projection, which means that a point x, y, z, in space, simply loses the third dimension, and becomes a 2-D point x, y, in the image. The projections of a point $p = (x, y, z)$ of the object O in the three images are given by:

$$
\begin{aligned}
p_1 &= (x_1, y_1) &= (x, y) & \quad \textit{in view } P_1 \\
p_2 &= (x_2, y_2) &= (x \cos \alpha + z \sin \alpha, \, y) & \quad \textit{in view } P_2 \\
\hat{p} &= (\hat{x}, \hat{y}) &= (x \cos \theta + z \sin \theta, \, y) & \quad \textit{in view } \hat{P}
\end{aligned}
$$

Since the rotation takes place around the vertical y-axis the y-coordinates remain unchanged. The next goal is to express the new coordinate $\hat{x}$ in terms of the old ones, x_1 and x_2. The relation is quite simple. It turns out that two scalars a and b exist, such that for every point p on the object O:

$$
\hat{x} = ax_1 + bx_2
$$

This means that the new coordinates, $\hat{x}$, are just the linear combination of the old coordinates, x_1 and x_2. The coefficients a and b are the same for all the points, and they satisfy the relation:

$$
a^2 + b^2 + 2ab \cos \alpha = 1.
$$

To establish the claim, the scalars a and b are given explicitly. Let us take a and b to be:

$$
\begin{aligned}
a &= \frac{\sin(\alpha - \theta)}{\sin \alpha} \\
b &= \frac{\sin \theta}{\sin \alpha}.
\end{aligned}
$$

These values for a and b are now used to combine the two images:

$$
\begin{aligned}
ax_1 + bx_2 &= \frac{\sin(\alpha - \theta)}{\sin \alpha} x + \frac{\sin \theta}{\sin \alpha} (x \cos \alpha + z \sin \alpha) = \\
x \cos \theta + z \sin \theta &= \hat{x}. \tag{5.2.1}
\end{aligned}
$$

Therefore, an image of an object rotating around the vertical axis is always a linear combination of two model images. This means that the position of any object point in the novel view is a weighted sum of its positions in the original two views. Two global coefficients, a and b, were needed in this case to perform the combination. It is also straightforward to verify that the coefficients a and b satisfy the constraint given above.

The displacement pattern between the two images is a complex one: different points move by different amounts, depending on their spatial position. For a rotating object, points close to the axis of rotation move less than points further away from the axis, and points near the object boundary are displaced less in the image than points at the center. If the object is transparent, points can even move in opposite directions within the same image region. However, these complexities are already captured by the two images; any novel image will be a simple combination of the original two. By changing a and b, one image can be warped continuously towards the second, and intermediate views will correspond to the object observed from different directions. It is worth noting that the new view $\hat{P}$ is not restricted to be an intermediate view (that is, the rotation angle θ may be larger than α). Finally, it should be noted that we do not deal at this stage with occlusion. We assume here that the same set of points is visible in the different views. The issue of occlusion and self-occlusion will be discussed later.

5.2.2   Linear Transformations in 3-D Space

The linear combination property is not limited to the simple situation discussed above, it also generalizes to transformations in 3-D space. In this section we consider general linear transformations in space, and show that any novel view can be generated by a simple combination of three fixed views.

Let O be a set of object points. Let P_1, P_2 and P_3 be three images of O, obtained by applying 3×3 matrices R, S and T, respectively, to the object O. These matrices represent three transformations applied to the object. In particular, R can be the identity matrix—this will give us O without any changes. The transformations S, T, can be two rotations, producing the second and third views. Using these three fixed views, we want to predict the appearance of the object under novel conditions.

Let $\hat{P}$ be a new image of the same object obtained by applying a new 3×3 matrix, U, to O. We wish to show how the new image $\hat{P}$ can be represented as a combination of the three original images P_1, P_2, P_3. More specifically, we wish to show that the new x-coordinates are simply the linear combination of the old x-coordinates, and similarly for the y-coordinates. The linear combination means that the following relationship holds:

$$\hat{x} = a_1 x_1 + a_2 x_2 + a_3 x_3 \qquad (5.2.2)$$
$$\hat{y} = b_1 y_1 + b_2 y_2 + b_3 y_3 \qquad (5.2.3)$$

for some constants a_1, a_2, a_3 and b_1, b_2, b_3. These relations summarize the linear combination property, that is, the image coordinates of the points in the novel view are given by a simple combination of their positions in the three stored views. The proof of the claim is straightforward.

Let $\mathbf{r}_1$, $\mathbf{s}_1$, $\mathbf{t}_1$ and $\mathbf{u}_1$ be the first row vectors of R, S, T and U, respectively, and let $\mathbf{r}_2$, $\mathbf{s}_2$, $\mathbf{t}_2$ and $\mathbf{u}_2$ be the second row vectors of R, S, T and U respectively. The positions of a point $p \in O$ in the four images are then given by:

$$
\begin{array}{rclcl}
p_1 & = & (x_1, y_1) & = & (\mathbf{r}_1 p,\ \mathbf{r}_2 p) \\
p_2 & = & (x_2, y_2) & = & (\mathbf{s}_1 p,\ \mathbf{s}_2 p) \\
p_3 & = & (x_3, y_3) & = & (\mathbf{t}_1 p,\ \mathbf{t}_2 p) \\
\hat{p} & = & (\hat{x}, \hat{y}) & = & (\mathbf{u}_1 p,\ \mathbf{u}_2 p).
\end{array}
$$

We will assume that the sets $\{\mathbf{r}_1, \mathbf{s}_1, \mathbf{t}_1\}$ and $\{\mathbf{r}_2, \mathbf{s}_2, \mathbf{t}_2\}$ are, in general, both linearly independent (this assumption is justified below). If $\{\mathbf{r}_1, \mathbf{s}_1, \mathbf{t}_1\}$ are linearly independent, then they span $\mathcal{R}^3$. Consequently, there exist scalars a_1, a_2 and a_3 such that:

$$\mathbf{u}_1 = a_1 \mathbf{r}_1 + a_2 \mathbf{s}_1 + a_3 \mathbf{t}_1$$

Since $\hat{x} = \mathbf{u}_1 p$, it follows that

$$\hat{x} = a_1 \mathbf{r}_1 p + a_2 \mathbf{s}_1 p + a_3 \mathbf{t}_1 p.$$

Therefore,

$$\hat{x} = a_1 x_1 + a_2 x_2 + a_3 x_3. \qquad (5.2.4)$$

In a similar way we obtain that

$$\hat{y} = b_1 y_1 + b_2 y_2 + b_3 y_3. \qquad (5.2.5)$$

Therefore, an image of an object undergoing a linear transformation in 3-D space is a linear combination of three model images.

5.2.3   Rotation in 3-D Space

The section above dealt with general linear transformations of the object. We now turn our attention to the case of rigid transformations, and, in particular, the effect of rotation in 3-D space. Rotation is a non-linear subgroup of the linear transformations. Therefore, an image of a rotating object is still a linear combination of three model views. However, not every point in this linear space represents a pure rotation of the object. Indeed, we can show that only points that satisfy the following three constraints represent images of a rotating object. The constraints are:

$$\| a_1 \mathbf{r}_1 + a_2 \mathbf{s}_1 + a_3 \mathbf{t}_1 \| = 1$$
$$\| b_1 \mathbf{r}_2 + b_2 \mathbf{s}_2 + b_3 \mathbf{t}_2 \| = 1$$
$$(a_1 \mathbf{r}_1 + a_2 \mathbf{s}_1 + a_3 \mathbf{t}_1)(b_1 \mathbf{r}_2 + b_2 \mathbf{s}_2 + b_3 \mathbf{t}_2) = 0. \qquad (5.2.6)$$

These constraints reflect the fact that U is a rotation matrix. Therefore:

$$\| \mathbf{u}_1 \| = 1$$
$$\| \mathbf{u}_2 \| = 1$$
$$\mathbf{u}_1 \cdot \mathbf{u}_2 = 0.$$

The required terms are obtained directly by substituting $\mathbf{u}_1$ and $\mathbf{u}_2$ with the appropriate linear combinations. It also follows immediately that if the constraints are met, then the new view represents a possible rotation of the object. That is, the linear combination condition together with the constraints provide necessary and sufficient conditions for the novel view to be a possible projection of the same 3-D object.

These functional constraints are second-degree polynomials in the coefficients, and therefore span a nonlinear manifold within the linear subspace. In order to check whether a specific set of coefficients represents a rigid rotation, one direct possibility is to use the values of the matrices R, S and T. These can be retrieved by applying methods of "structure from motion" to the model views. It is known that in case of rigid transformations, four corresponding points in three views are sufficient for this purpose (Ullman 1979). An algorithm that can be used to recover the rotation matrices using mainly linear equations has been proposed by Huang & Lee (1989). (The same method can be extended to deal with scale changes, in addition to the rotation.)

The view-combination approach relies on 2-D rather than explicit 3-D information, and therefore it would be preferable to avoid the explicit recovery of the transformation matrices. In fact, in many cases the explicit computation of the transformation matrices will not be necessary. First, if the set of allowable object transformations includes the entire set of linear 3-D transformations (including non-rigid stretch and shear), then no additional test of the coefficients is required. Second, if the transformations are constrained to be rigid, but the test of the coefficients is not performed, then the penalty may be some "false positive" misidentifications: If the image of one object happens to be identical to the projection of a (non-rigid) linear transformation applied to another object, then the two will be confuseable. If the objects contain a sufficient number of points (five or more), the likelihood of such an ambiguity becomes negligible. In either case, we can ignore the difference between the rigid and the linear case: if the object can be expressed by the linear combination of the views constituting the model, we can accept it as an instance of the model in question. Finally, it is worth noting that it is also possible to determine the coefficient of the constraint equations above without computing the rotation matrices, by using a number of additional views, as will be explained further below.

Regarding the independence condition mentioned above, for many triplets of rotation matrices R, S and T both $\{\mathbf{r}_1, \mathbf{s}_1, \mathbf{t}_1\}$ and $\{\mathbf{r}_2, \mathbf{s}_2, \mathbf{t}_2\}$ will in fact be linearly independent. It will therefore be possible to select a non-degenerate triplet of views (P_1,

P_2 and P_3), in terms of which intermediate views are expressible as linear combinations. It is interesting to note, however, that in the special case where R is the identity matrix, S is a pure rotation about the X-axis, and T about the Y-axis, the independence condition does not hold.

Rigid Transformations and Scaling in 3-D Space   We have considered above the case of rigid rotation in 3-D space. We can now add translations in 3-D space as well as possible changes of size, and the novel views will still be the linear combinations of three 2-D views of the object. More specifically, let O be a set of object points, and let P_1, P_2 and P_3 be three images of O, obtained by applying the 3×3 rotation matrices R, S and T to O, respectively. Let $\hat{P}$ be a fourth image of the same object obtained by applying a 3×3 rotation matrix U to O, scaling by a scale factor s, and translating by a vector (t_x, t_y). Let $\mathbf{r}_1$, $\mathbf{s}_1$, $\mathbf{t}_1$ and $\mathbf{u}_1$ be again the first row vectors of R, S, T and U, and $\mathbf{r}_2$, $\mathbf{s}_2$, $\mathbf{t}_2$ and $\mathbf{u}_2$ the second row vectors of R, S, T and U, respectively. For any point $p \in O$, its positions in the original three images are given by:

$$
\begin{aligned}
p_1 &= (x_1, y_1) = (\mathbf{r}_1 p,\ \mathbf{r}_2 p) \\
p_2 &= (x_2, y_2) = (\mathbf{s}_1 p,\ \mathbf{s}_2 p) \\
p_3 &= (x_3, y_3) = (\mathbf{t}_1 p,\ \mathbf{t}_2 p)
\end{aligned}
$$

and the novel view is given by:

$$
\hat{p} = (\hat{x}, \hat{y}) = (s\mathbf{u}_1 p + t_x,\ s\mathbf{u}_2 p + t_y).
$$

The new view is still a simple combination of the old views. If we assume, as before, that the sets $\{\mathbf{r}_1, \mathbf{s}_1, \mathbf{t}_1\}$ and $\{\mathbf{r}_2, \mathbf{s}_2, \mathbf{t}_2\}$ are linearly independent, then there exist scalars a_1, a_2, a_3, a_4, and b_1, b_2, b_3, b_4, such that for every point $p \in O$:

$$
\hat{x} = a_1 x_1 + a_2 x_2 + a_3 x_3 + a_4 \tag{5.2.7}
$$
$$
\hat{y} = b_1 y_1 + b_2 y_2 + b_3 y_3 + b_4 \tag{5.2.8}
$$

with the coefficient satisfying the two constraints:

$$\| a_1 \mathbf{r}_1 + a_2 \mathbf{s}_1 + a_3 \mathbf{t}_1 \| = \| b_1 \mathbf{r}_2 + b_2 \mathbf{s}_2 + b_3 \mathbf{t}_2 \|$$

$$(a_1 \mathbf{r}_1 + a_2 \mathbf{s}_1 + a_3 \mathbf{t}_1)(b_1 \mathbf{r}_2 + b_2 \mathbf{s}_2 + b_3 \mathbf{t}_2) = 0.$$

We can view each of the above equations as the linear combination of three views, and a fourth, degenerate image, that is just a constant vector. Instead of a constant vector, one can take a fourth view generated internally by shifting one of the three images. In either case, the new view is formally a combination of four images, but only three views are really required. The fourth one is a "virtual" view that is generated internally without requiring a new view. The derivation is almost identical to the one in the given above and will not be detailed. As for the constraints on the coefficients, since U is a rotation matrix:

$$\| \mathbf{u}_1 \| = 1$$
$$\| \mathbf{u}_2 \| = 1$$
$$\mathbf{u}_1 \mathbf{u}_2 = 0.$$

It follows that

$$\| s\mathbf{u}_1 \| = \| s\mathbf{u}_2 \|$$
$$(s\mathbf{u}_1) \cdot (s\mathbf{u}_2) = 0$$

and the constraints are obtained directly by substituting the appropriate linear combinations for $s\mathbf{u}_1$ and $s\mathbf{u}_2$.

5.3   Using Two Views Only

In the scheme described above, any image of a given object (within a certain range of rotations) is expressed as the linear combination of three fixed views of the object. For general linear transformations, it is also possible to use instead just two views of the object. (This observation was also made independently by T. Poggio.) This two-views formulation uses a mixture of x and y-coordinates, unlike the three-views formulation, where the x-coordinates in the novel view depends only on the x-coordinates in the stored view, and similarly for the y-coordinates. This combination is somewhat less intuitive than the combination of three views, but the use of only two rather than three views is sometimes more convenient, and it is also useful in analyzing mathematical properties of the view-combination method. The section below first describes the mathematical expressions used in the combination of two views, and then compares the combination of two and three views.

Let O again be a rigid object (a collection of 3-D points). P_1 is a 2-D image of O, and P_2 the image of O following a rotation by R (a 3×3 matrix). We will denote by $\mathbf{r}_1$, $\mathbf{r}_2$, $\mathbf{r}_3$, the three rows of R, and by $\mathbf{e}_1$, $\mathbf{e}_2$, $\mathbf{e}_3$, the three rows of the identity matrix. For a given 3-D point $\mathbf{p}$ in O, its coordinates (x_1, y_1) in the first image view are $x_1 = \mathbf{e}_1\mathbf{p}$, $y_1 = \mathbf{e}_2\mathbf{p}$. Its coordinates (x_2, y_2) in the second view are given by: $x_2 = \mathbf{r}_1\mathbf{p}$, $y_2 = \mathbf{r}_2\mathbf{p}$.

Consider now any other view obtained by applying another 3×3 matrix $\mathbf{U}$ to the points of O. The coordinates $(\hat{x}, \hat{y})$ of $\mathbf{p}$ in this new view will be:

$$\hat{x} = \mathbf{u}_1\mathbf{p}, \quad \hat{y} = \mathbf{u}_2\mathbf{p}$$

(where $\mathbf{u}_1$, $\mathbf{u}_2$, are the first and second rows of $\mathbf{U}$, respectively). Assuming that $\mathbf{e}_1$, $\mathbf{e}_2$ and $\mathbf{r}_1$ span $\mathcal{R}^3$ (see below), then:

$$\mathbf{u}_1 = a_1\mathbf{e}_1 + a_2\mathbf{e}_2 + a_3\mathbf{r}_1$$

for some scalars a_1, a_2, a_3. Therefore:

$$\hat{x} = \mathbf{u}_1\mathbf{p} = (a_1\mathbf{e}_1 + a_2\mathbf{e}_2 + a_3\mathbf{r}_1)\mathbf{p} = a_1x_1 + a_2y_1 + a_3x_2.$$

This equality holds for every point $\mathbf{p}$ in O. Let now $\mathbf{x}_1$ be the vector of all the x-coordinates of the points in the first view, $\mathbf{x}_2$ in the second, and $\hat{\mathbf{x}}$ in the novel view; $\mathbf{y}_1$ is the vector of y-coordinates in the first view. Then:

$$\hat{\mathbf{x}} = a_1\mathbf{x}_1 + a_2\mathbf{y}_1 + a_3\mathbf{x}_2. \qquad (5.3.9)$$

Here $\mathbf{x}_1$, $\mathbf{y}_1$ and $\mathbf{x}_2$ are used as a basis for all of the views. For any other view of the same object, its vector $\hat{\mathbf{x}}$ of x-coordinates is the linear combination of these basis vectors. The y-coordinates can be expressed in a similar manner:

$$\hat{\mathbf{y}} = b_1\mathbf{x}_1 + b_2\mathbf{y}_1 + b_3\mathbf{x}_2 \qquad (5.3.10)$$

The vector $\hat{\mathbf{y}}$ of y-coordinates in the new view is therefore also the linear combination of the same three basis vectors. In this version the basis vectors are the same for the x and y-coordinates, and they are obtained from two rather then three views. One can view the situation as follows. Within an n-dimensional space, the vectors $\mathbf{x}_1$, $\mathbf{y}_1$, $\mathbf{x}_2$ span a three-dimensional subspace. For all the views of the object in question, the vectors of both the x and y-coordinates must reside within this three-dimensional subspace. Instead of using $(\mathbf{e}_1, \mathbf{e}_2, \mathbf{r}_1)$ as the basis for $\mathcal{R}^3$ we could also use $(\mathbf{e}_1, \mathbf{e}_2, \mathbf{r}_2)$. One of these bases spans $\mathcal{R}^3$, unless the rotation R is a pure rotation around the line of sight.

The use of two views described above is applicable to general linear transformations of the object, and, without additional constraints, it is impossible to distinguish rigid from linear but non-rigid transformations of the object. To impose rigidity (with possible scaling), the coefficients $(a_1, a_2, a_3, b_1, b_2, b_3)$ must meet two simple constraints. Since $\mathbf{U}$ is now a rotation matrix (with possible scaling),

$$\mathbf{u}_1 \cdot \mathbf{u}_2 \;=\; 0$$
$$\| \mathbf{u}_1 \| \;=\; \| \mathbf{u}_2 \| .$$

In terms of the coefficients a_i, b_i, $\mathbf{u}_1 \mathbf{u}_2 = 0$ implies:

$$a_1 b_1 + a_2 b_2 + a_3 b_3 + (a_1 b_3 + a_3 b_1) r_{11} + (a_2 b_3 + a_3 b_2) r_{12} = 0.$$

The second constraint implies:

$$a_1{}^2 + a_2{}^2 + a_3{}^2 - b_1{}^2 - b_2{}^2 - b_3{}^2 =$$

$$2(b_1 b_3 - a_1 a_3) r_{11} + 2(b_2 b_3 - a_2 a_3) r_{12}.$$

A third view can therefore be used to recover, using two linear equations, the values of r_{11} and r_{12}. (r_{11} and r_{12} can in fact be determined to within a scale factor from the first two views, only one additional equation is required.) The full scheme for rigid objects is then the following. Given an image, determine whether the vectors $\hat{\mathbf{x}}$, $\hat{\mathbf{y}}$, are linear combinations of $\mathbf{x}_1$, $\mathbf{y}_1$ and $\mathbf{x}_2$. Only two views are required for this stage. Using the values of r_{11} and r_{12}, test whether the coefficients a_i, b_i, $(i = 1, 2, 3)$ satisfy the two constraints above.

It is of interest to compare this use of two views to structure-from-motion (SFM) techniques for recovering 3-D structure from orthographic projections. It is well known that three distinct views are required; two are insufficient (Ullman 1979). Given only two views and an infinitesmal rotation (the velocity field), the 3-D structure can be recovered to within depth-scaling (Ullman 1983). It is also straightforward to establish that if the two views are separated by a general affine transformation of the 3-D object (rather than a rigid one, see appendix E), then the structure of the object can be recovered to within an affine transformation (Koenderink & Van Doorn, 1991).

Our use of two views above for the purpose of recognition is thus related to known results regarding the recovery of structure from motion. Two views are sufficient to determine the object's structure to within an affine transformation, and three are required to recover the full 3-D structure of a rigidly moving object. Similarly, the linear combination scheme uses in the match two (for general linear transformation) or three views (for rigid rotation and scaling). The matching does not require the full 3-D model. Instead, linear combinations of the 2-D views are used directly.

Finally, it can also be observed that an extension of the scheme above can be used to recover structure from motion. It was shown how the scheme can be used to recover r_{11} and r_{12}. In a similar manner, r_{21} and r_{22} can also be recovered. Consequently, it becomes possible to recover 3-D structure and motion in space based on three orthographic views, using linear equations. (For alternative methods that use primarily linear equations see Longuet-Higgins 1981, Huang & Lee 1989.)

5.4   Using a Single View: Symmetric Objects and Virtual Views

We have seen how the number of views in the view-combination method can be reduced from three to two. Under some conditions we can take a step further, and perform image combination based on a single view. This extension was developed by Vetter, Poggio and Bülthoff (1994) for the class of bilaterally symmetric objects. One intuitive way of looking at this special case of symmetric objects is by considering the two symmetric halves of the object as two distinct views of a single part. Under the assumptions discussed in the previous section (orthographic projections, affine object transformations), two views are sufficient to recognize the object in question.

A similar way is to use the symmetry to generate additional "virtual" views that can then be used in the recognition process. Given a single view of the object, it is possible to generate new 2-D views of the same object. These views could have been generated by rotating the object in space, but they are generated instead by a simple transformation of the image itself. The transformation assumes that the symmetry of the object is known, that is, we know the correspondence between symmetric points on the object. If (x, y) and (x', y') are a symmetric pair of points, then an example of a transformation that generates a virtual view is obtained by replacing each symmetric pair by the new coordinates $(-x', y')$, $(-x, y)$. After obtaining a new virtual view, generated internally from the single original view, the view-combination method of two views discussed above can be applied directly. Vetter, Poggio and Bülthoff (1994), as well as Liu, Knill and Kersten (1995), have shown that for human observers the recognition of symmetric 3-D objects from a single training view is indeed better than for non-symmetric objects. For the symmetric objects, the experiments showed a broader generalization, that is, observers recognized the symmetric test objects correctly over a wider range of rotations. Furthermore, recognition rates were highest for the training view as well as an additional virtual view, supporting the suggestion that the visual system used the objects' symmetry in the recognition process.

This treatment of symmetric objects is an example of a more general method of using common class properties for the recognition of an individual member of the class in question. In this case, properties of symmetric objects in general are used for the recognition of an individual symmetric object. In the more general case, other class properties, such as the typical 3-D shape of objects in the class and typical distortions they undergo, can be used for the recognition of individual class members. We will return to the use of class properties in the recognition process in chapter 6, in discussing the topic of object classification.

General Constraints from a Single View   A single 2-D view of a general object is of course insufficient to determine the object uniquely: the depth values are unknown, and therefore the observed image is compatible with infinitely many 3-D objects. If the image V consists of discrete points x_i, y_i, then we can generate different 3-D objects, all consistent with the projected image, by selecting different values for the depth coordinates z_i. Suppose that we have seen the object once only, so that the single image V contains all the information we have regarding the object. Can the single view be used in attempting to recognize the object in a novel view? Although the object is under-determined, the single view places constraints on subsequent views of the object. Given a new view V', the main constraint is that every point in V must lie on a known line in V' (Koenderink & Van Doorn-1991). This can be used to reject a new view V' as incompatible with the object represented by V. To see this constraint in more detail, we can go back to the linear combination of two views (section 5.3) above. As before, we assume an orthographic projection, and that between views the object undergoes a linear transformation. We have used three vectors, $\mathbf{x}_1, \mathbf{y}_1, \mathbf{x}_2$ as a basis to express the x and y-coordinates in novel views. The same basis can also be used to express the y-coordinates in the second view, namely:

$$\mathbf{y}_2 = a_1 \mathbf{x}_1 + a_2 \mathbf{y}_1 + a_3 \mathbf{x}_2. \qquad (5.4.11)$$

This means that for a given point x_i, y_i in V, the corresponding point x_i', y_i' in V' is restricted to lie on the line given by $y_i' = a_1 x_i + a_2 y_i + a_3 x_i'$. The coefficients a_1, a_2, a_3 are determined by three corresponding points in the two views, and a fourth point is used as the common origin in both views.

In principle, this can be used for limited recognition from a single view in the following manner. The first view, V, is used as a model. Given a novel view V' we first establish correspondence between four pairs of points in the two views. We then derive for each point x_i, y_i in V its constraint line in V'. In practice, due to limited accuracy, there will be a constraint region rather than a line. If the points in V' fail to lie within their respective constraint regions, then we can reject V' as possibly representing the object seen before.

There are two main limitations to this use of a single view as an object model. First, the scheme does not discriminate between objects that have a similar 2-D view but a different 3-D structure. This will cause problems in the identification of similar objects, such as similar faces. Second, the scheme relies on point correspondence between the two views. Identifying feature points and matching them in different views is a difficult problem, and therefore schemes that minimize this requirement are usually preferable. (This issue is discussed im more detail in chapter 7). Under conditions that make point correspondence practical, the single-view constraint may still be used, especially to reject some inappropriate objects from further consideration.

5.5   The Use of Depth Values

The view-combination scheme does not require depth information in the viewed object: a 2-D image, devoid of 3-D information, can be matched against the stored model. What happens, however, when 3-D information is available, for example, from binocular vision—can it be usefully employed in the recognition process?

From the linear combination scheme it also follows that the depth values of points in a novel image are the linear combination of the depth values of the corresponding points in the stored views. That is, if $\hat{\mathbf{z}}$ is the vector of depth values in the novel image, then:

$$\hat{\mathbf{z}} = a_1\mathbf{z}_1 + a_2\mathbf{z}_2 + a_3\mathbf{z}_3.$$

In this case the use of 3-information relies on the use of stored depth values associated with the stored model views. So far we have not used explicit depth information in the stored views: the view-combination scheme proceeded instead by using only simple 2-D views. These 2-D views can be used directly, however, without requiring additional 3-D information, to evaluate the depth information obtained from the image. Following the same line of reasoning used in the combination of two views, it is straightforward to establish that

$$\hat{\mathbf{z}} = c_1\mathbf{x}_1 + c_2\mathbf{y}_1 + c_3\mathbf{x}_2. \tag{5.5.12}$$

The depth values in the novel view are obtained here by a simple combination of the image coordinates of the stored views. If the image to be recognized contains depth information, then the depth at three points in the image can be used to determine the coefficients of this combination. From this, the depth values at any other location can be predicted and compared with the measured values in the image. This use of 3-D information illustrates that although depth information in the viewed object is not required, it can be utilized in the recognition process. Three-dimensional information can also be used in a more qualitative manner, using abstract labels as discussed in chapter 3. The abstract labels associated with different locations in the stored pictorial representations may include 3-D properties, such as a convex, concave, or wrinkled region. These local descriptions of 3-D properties will then be compared with similar descriptions in the corresponding locations in the viewed object following alignment.

Psychophysical studies indicate that 3-D information can be used to improve recognition performance, but this effect is modest and depends on the viewing direction. For example, Edelman and Bülthoff (1992) compared recognition performance using a fixed set of objects while manipulating the 3-D information available to the viewer, by adding binocular stereo, shading and texture cues. The use of these cues, in particular, binocular stereo, had a modest effect on recognition performance. At the same time, the generalization to novel views was closely similar under the 2-D and 3-D conditions. The availability of strong 3-D cues did not change the measured dependence of performance on the viewing direction. These psychophysical results are compatible with the use of 3-D information described above. They suggest that the availability of 3-D information during recognition is of secondary importance, that it can be used to improve recognition performance, and its use appears to be similar, as in the scheme above, to the use of the available 2-D information.

5.6   Summary of the Basic Scheme

An object with sharp contours, undergoing rigid transformations and scaling in 3-D space followed by an orthographic projection, can be expressed as the linear combination of three images of the same object. In this scheme, the model of a 3-D object consists of a number of 2-D views, taken from different viewing positions. The views are in correspondence, in the sense that it is known which are the corresponding points in the different views. Two views are sufficient to represent general linear transformations of the object; three views are required to represent rigid transformations in 3-D space. The views can be tested for rigidity of the transformation by using the coefficients of the image combinations, but for practical purposes the test can often be omitted.

The linear combination scheme assumes that the same object points are visible in the different views. When the views are sufficiently different, this will no longer hold, due to self-occlusion.

To represent an object from all possible viewing directions (such as both "front" and "back"), a number of different models of this type will be required. This notion is similar to the use of different object aspects suggested by Koenderink and Van Doorn (1979). Other aspects of occlusion are examined in the final discussion.

The view combination scheme described above was implemented and applied first to artificially created images. Figure 5.1 shows examples of object models and their linear combinations. The figure shows how 3-D similarity transformations can be represented by the linear combinations of two-dimensional images. The figure shows two objects, a cube and a pyramid. Several views of each object are shown; these were taken to be the initial object models. We then see in the figure some new views of the cube and the pyramid. The main point is that these new views were not generated by manipulating 3-D object models, but by linear combinations of the original 2-D views. The linear combination of a more complex object is shown in figure 5.2. The images M1 and M2 are two views of the same individual from different viewing directions. The image marked N is a novel view, from an intermediate viewing direction. This view is approximated by the image labeled LC2, obtained by a linear combination of the original views. The combinations LC1 and LC3 are extrapolated views, beyond the range of viewing directions spanned by the two original images. This example uses some extensions of the basic scheme including the removal of hidden surfaces and the combination of grey-level images discussed lated in this chapter and in section 7.6.

The figures also illustrate the possible use of the view combination approach for applications related to graphics rather than recognition. Novel object views can be generated and presented by combining a small number of stored object views instead of manipulating 3-D object models. For the rendering of objects, however, additional care must be taken to deal with occlusion and visibility issues. For the purpose of recognition, the exclusion of all the occluded features from the predicted view is usually not

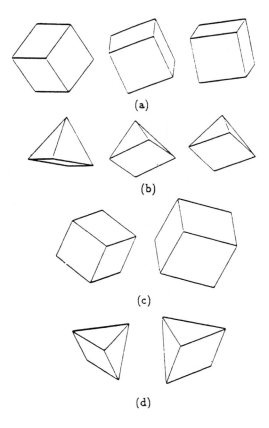

Figure 5.1
Generating novel object views by linear combinations. (a) Three model pictures of a cube. (b) Three model pictures of a pyramid. (c) Two linear combinations of the cube model: the new views were obtained by image combination rather than the rotation of a 3-D model. The left picture was obtained using the following parameters. The x coefficients: $(0.343, -2.618, 2.989, 0)$, the y coefficients: $(0.630, -2.533, 2.658, 0)$, corresponding to a rotation of the cube by $10°$, $20°$ and $45°$ around the X-, Y- and Z-axes respectively. The right picture was obtained using: x coefficients $(0.455, 3.392, -3.241, 0.25)$, y coefficients $(0.542, 3.753, -3.343, -0.15)$. These coefficients correspond to a rotation of the cube by $20°$, $10°$ and $-45°$ around the X-, Y- and Z-axes respectively, followed by a scaling of 1.2, and a translation of $(25, -15)$ pixels. (d) Two linear combinations of the pyramid model taken with the same parameters as the pictures in (c). After (Ullman & Basri 1991).

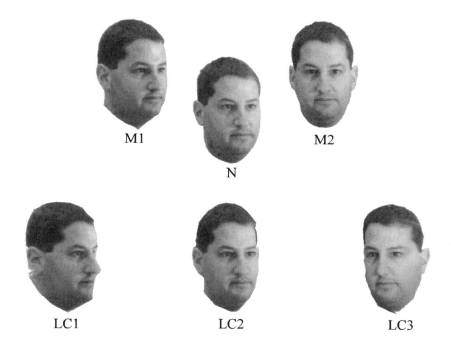

Figure 5.2
Novel views obtained by the combination of grey-level images. $M1$ and $M2$ are two views of the same individual, observed from different viewing directions. N is a novel, intermediate view. This novel view is approximated by $LC2$, which is a obtained from the original images by the linear combination method. $LC1$ and $LC3$ are additional view-combinations. They correspond to viewing directions outside the range spanned by the original two images. Figure produced by A. Zeira.

crucial, but for the purpose of object rendering, the visibility of each feature must be determined exactly.

5.7 Objects with Smooth Boundaries

The case of objects with smooth boundaries is similar to the case of objects with sharp edges as long as we deal with translation, scaling and image rotation. The difference arises when the object rotates in 3-D space. The preceding chapter provided a method for predicting the appearance of such objects following 3-D rotations. In this method, called "the curvature method," a model is represented by a set of 2-D contours. Each point $p = (x, y)$ along the contours is labeled with its depth value z, and a curvature value r. The curvature value is the length of a curvature vector at p, $r = \| (r_x, r_y) \|$. (r_x is the surface's radius of curvature at p in a planar section in the X direction, r_y in the Y direction, and the curvature vector is normal to the contour at p.) This representation was then used to predict the appearance of the object following rotations in space. Suppose that the object rotates about the axis V_ϕ, a line lying in the image plane and forming an angle ϕ with the positive X direction. For this axis we use the curvature value $\mathbf{r}_\phi$, a vector of length $r_\phi = r_y \cos \phi - r_x \sin \phi$ and perpendicular to V_ϕ. When the object is rotated around V_ϕ, we approximate the new position of the point p in the image by:

$$p' = R(p - \mathbf{r}_\phi) + \mathbf{r}_\phi \qquad (5.7.13)$$

where R is the rotation matrix.

This expression is precise for circular arcs, and gives a good approximation for other surfaces, provided that the angle of rotation is not too large. The depth and the curvature values can be estimated, as discussed in the preceding chapter, by using a small number (three to five) of pictures.

In this section we show how the curvature method can also be replaced by linear combinations of a small number of pictures. The main point is that exactly the same approximation used by the

curvature method can also be embedded in the linear combination
scheme. The result is a linear combination scheme that can deal
with smooth as well as sharp object contours. The main difference
is in the number of images required: three images are required to
represent rotations around a fixed axis, and five images for general
rotations in 3-D space.

The final conclusion of this section is that for objects with
smooth bounding surfaces, the x and y-coordinates following rotation in space are the linear combination of five fixed images. In
mathematical notation:

$$\hat{x} = \sum_{i=1}^{5} a_i x_i$$

$$\hat{y} = \sum_{i=1}^{5} b_i y_i.$$

The implication is that by combining 2-D views in the appropriate manner it becomes possible to account for variations in
viewing direction. This implication will be examined in detail in
subsequent sections.

5.7.1   General Rotation in 3-D Space

In this section we first derive an expression for the image deformation of an object with smooth boundaries under general 3-D
rotation. We then use this expression to show that the deformed
image can be expressed as the linear combination of five views.

Computing the Transformed Image   By using the curvature
method we can predict the appearance of an object undergoing a
general rotation in 3-D space as follows. A rotation in 3-D space
can be decomposed into the following three successive rotations:
a rotation around the Z-axis, a subsequent rotation around the
X-axis, and a final rotation around the Z-axis, by angles α, β
and γ respectively. This mathematical decomposition is convenient for the analysis, since the Z-axis coincides with the line of
sight, so that a rotation around the Z-axis is simply an image

rotation. Therefore, only the second rotation deforms the object, and the curvature method must be applied to it. Suppose that the curvature vector at a given point $p = (x, y)$ before the first Z-rotation is (r_x, r_y). Following the rotation by α it becomes $r'_x = r_x \cos\alpha - r_y \sin\alpha$ and $r'_y = r_x \sin\alpha + r_y \cos\alpha$. The second rotation is around the X-axis, and therefore the appropriate r_ϕ to be used in equation (1) becomes $r'_y = r_x \sin\alpha + r_y \cos\alpha$. The complete rotation (all three rotations) therefore takes a point $p = (x, y)$ through the following sequence of transformations:

First stage: rotation around the line-of-sight by α. The new coordinates are:

new x-coordinate: $x \cos\alpha - y \sin\alpha$
new y-coordinate: $x \sin\alpha + y \cos\alpha$

Second stage: rotation around the X-axis by β. Since the rotation is around the X-axis, only the y-values are affected. This is where the curvature method comes in, and the resulting coordinates are:

new x-coordinate: $x \cos\alpha - y \sin\alpha$
new y-coordinate: $(x \sin\alpha + y \cos\alpha) \cos\beta - z \sin\beta + (r_x \sin\alpha + r_y \cos\alpha)(1 - \cos\beta)$

Final stage: rotation around the line-of-sight by γ. This is a simple rotation around the line of sight (the Z-axis), and the final coordinates are:

final x-coordinate: $(x \cos\alpha - y \sin\alpha) \cos\gamma - ((x \sin\alpha + y \cos\alpha) \cos\beta - z \sin\beta + (r_x \sin\alpha + r_y \cos\alpha)(1 - \cos\beta)) \sin\gamma$
final y-coordinate: $(x \cos\alpha - y \sin\alpha) \sin\gamma + ((x \sin\alpha + y \cos\alpha) \cos\beta - z \sin\beta + (r_x \sin\alpha + r_y \cos\alpha)(1 - \cos\beta)) \cos\gamma$

This expression is an explicit derivation that takes us through the sequence of changes and produces the final coordinates of a point on the object's contour. This can also be expressed more compactly by using an extension of the rotation matrix. Let α, β and γ be the angles of the Z-X-Z rotations, as before. Together, they define a rotation in space. Like any rotation in space, this rotation can be represented by a 3×3 matrix, and $R = \{r_{ij}\}$ will denote this rotation matrix.

We now construct a new matrix $R' = \{r'_{ij}\}$ of size 2×5 as follows:

$$\begin{pmatrix} r_{11} & r_{12} & r_{13} & -\sin\alpha(1-\cos\beta)\sin\gamma & -\cos\alpha(1-\cos\beta)\sin\gamma \\ r_{21} & r_{22} & r_{23} & \sin\alpha(1-\cos\beta)\cos\gamma & \cos\alpha(1-\cos\beta)\cos\gamma \end{pmatrix}$$

The matrix is somewhat unusual, but it can be used to represent compactly what happens to the contour points following the rotation. Let $p = (x, y)$ be a contour point with depth z and curvature vector (r_x, r_y). Let us represent all these parameters by a single vector with five coordinates: $\tilde{p} = (x, y, z, r_x, r_y)$. Then, the new appearance of $\mathbf{p}$ after a rotation R is applied to the object is described by:

$$p' = R'\tilde{p} \tag{5.7.14}$$

This is true because this last equation is equivalent to the previous equation for p', with the appropriate values for r_ϕ. We next use this formulation to show how novel images can be expressed as combinations of old ones.

Expressing the Transformed Image as a Linear Combination The situation now becomes similar to the simpler case of objects with sharp boundaries. As before, let O be a set of contour points of an object rotating in 3-D space. Let P_1, P_2, P_3, P_4 and P_5 be five images of O, obtained by applying rotation matrices $R_1, ..., R_5$ respectively. $\hat{P}$ is a novel view of the same object obtained by applying a rotation matrix $\hat{R}$ to O. The goal, as before, is to express the new image in terms of the old ones. Let $R'_1, ..., R'_5, \hat{R}'$ be the corresponding 2×5 matrices, representing the transformations applied to the contour points according to the curvature method. Finally, let $\mathbf{r}_1, ..., \mathbf{r}_5, \hat{\mathbf{r}}$ denote the first row vectors of $R'_1, ..., R'_5, \hat{R}'$, and $\mathbf{s}_1, ..., \mathbf{s}_5, \hat{\mathbf{s}}$ the second row vectors $R'_1, ..., R'_5, \hat{R}'$ respectively. The positions of a point $p = (x, y) \in O$, $\tilde{p} = (x, y, z, r_x, r_y)$, in the six pictures is then given by:

$$p_i = (x_i, y_i) = (\mathbf{r}_i \tilde{p}, \mathbf{s}_i \tilde{p}) \in P_i, \ 1 \le i \le 5$$
$$\hat{p} = (\hat{x}, \hat{y}) = (\hat{\mathbf{r}} \tilde{p}, \hat{\mathbf{s}} \tilde{p}) \in \hat{P}.$$

If both sets $\{\mathbf{r}_1, ..., \mathbf{r}_5\}$ and $\{\mathbf{s}_1, ..., \mathbf{s}_5\}$ are linearly independent vectors, then there exist scalars $a_1, ..., a_5$ and $b_1, ..., b_5$ such that every point p in the object O can be expressed as:

$$\hat{x} = \sum_{i=1}^{5} a_i x_i$$

$$\hat{y} = \sum_{i=1}^{5} b_i y_i. \tag{5.7.15}$$

The situation is quite similar to the previous case. The vectors $\{\mathbf{r}_1, ..., \mathbf{r}_5\}$ are linearly independent and therefore they span $\mathcal{R}^5$. We can then express $\hat{\mathbf{r}}$ in terms of the basis vectors, that is, scalars $a_1, ..., a_5$ exist such that:

$$\hat{\mathbf{r}} = \sum_{i=1}^{5} a_i \mathbf{r}_i.$$

Since the new coordinates are given by $\hat{x} = \hat{\mathbf{r}} \tilde{p}$, it follows that $\hat{x} = \sum_{i=1}^{5} a_i \mathbf{r}_i \tilde{p}$, and similarly $\hat{x} = \sum_{i=1}^{5} a_i x_i$. In a similar manner we obtain that:

$$\hat{y} = \sum_{i=1}^{5} b_i y_i.$$

The final result is simple: as before, the coordinates of the points in the novel view are simple combinations of the corresponding points in the original images.

As before, in the case of pure rotation (rather than more general linear transformations), the coefficients of this linear combination satisfy additional constraints. These constraints, which are second degree polynomials, are given in (Ullman & Basri 1991). The coefficients of these polynomials can be found (by linear equations) using additional views. Again, one may or may not actually test for these additional constraints. Assuming that different objects in memory differ by more than just a linear transformation, if the test is omitted, the probability of a false-positive misidentification is slightly increased.

As in the case of sharp boundaries, it is possible to use mixed x- and y-coordinates to reduce the number of basic views for general linear transformations. For example, one can use five basis vectors $(\mathbf{x}_1, \mathbf{x}_2, \mathbf{x}_3, \mathbf{y}_1, \mathbf{y}_2)$ taken from three distinct views as the basis for the x- and y-coordinates in all other views.

The analysis above shows that an object with smooth boundaries, represented by the curvature scheme, can be represented as a linear combination of 2-D views. The discussion so far focused on changes in viewing direction, that is, an object undergoing rotation in 3-D space. As before, the method can be easily extended to handle also translation and scaling. As in the case of sharp object boundaries, scaling is included in the scheme without any changes. Translation can be handled by adding a single internal model. This does not require an additional image, since the additional image can be either a shifted version of one of the previously stored models, or just a constant vector. The linear combination scheme for objects with smooth bounding contours is thus a direct extension of the scheme for objects with sharp boundaries, and in both cases, object views are expressed as the linear combination of a small number of pictures.

We conclude that an object with smooth boundaries undergoing rigid transformations and scaling in 3-D space followed by an orthographic projection, can be expressed (within the approximation of the curvature method) as the linear combination of 2-D views of the object. Five images are used to represent rotations in 3-D space. A shifted image, or, alternatively, a constant vector, can be added to deal with translations. In fact, although the coordinates are expressed in terms of five basis vectors, only three distinct views are needed for a general linear transformation. The scaling does not require any additional image since it is represented by a scaling of the coefficients.

The scheme for objects with sharp boundaries can be viewed as a special case of the more general one, when r, the radius of curvature, vanishes. In practice, we found that it is possible to use the scheme for sharp boundaries also for general objects, provided that r is not too large (and at the price of increasing the number of models). In figure 5.2, for example, only two face images were used to generate the novel views. The distinction between objects with smooth or sharp boundaries is therefore useful for the purpose of analyzing the scheme, but it does not affect the application of the method. The scheme itself is uniform, and does not distinguish between different types of objects. Recognition is obtained by combining a number of views, and the number of views used will depend on the required accuracy.

These results show that the set of different views of the same 3-D object has in fact a simple structure. The implication for the purpose of recognition is that novel views, from new viewing directions, can be approximated by combinations of a small number of stored views. This raises the possibility of compensating for viewing directions by schemes that are based directly on 2-D pictorial representations, by processes that combine, or interpolate between, existing representations. Such pictorial representations are not necessarily 2-D images in the simplest sense (such as edge representations); they will include, for example, more abstract pictorial representations of the type discussed in connection with 3-D alignment methods. The next section discusses in more detail possible schemes for performing recognition based on image combinations.

5.8   Recognition by Image Combinations

We have seen in the previous sections that the set of possible views of an object can be expressed as the combinations of a small number of views. In this section we use this property to perform visual recognition from novel viewing directions.

A stored object model is given in the image combination scheme as a set of k corresponding 2-D images $\{M_1, ..., M_k\}$. We are now given P, a novel object view, and we wish to determine whether

P is a possible view of the stored model. We saw in the preceding analysis that if the new view is in fact a possible instance of the model, than there is a set of coefficients $\{a_1, ..., a_k\}$ (with some possible restrictions on these coefficients) such that:

$$P = a_1 M_1 + ... + a_k M_k. \tag{5.8.16}$$

One way to proceed with the recognition process is to explicitly recover the coefficients of the image combination. If we manage to determine the set of coefficients $a_1 \cdots a_k$, we can use the model images to generate a combined image and compare it with the input pattern P. For this purpose, we will consider next the problem of determining the unknown coefficients of the image combination. In practice, we may not be able to obtain a strict equality between the input pattern and the combined image. We will attempt, therefore, to minimize the difference between P and $a_1 M_1 + ... + a_k M_k$. In the following subsections we will discuss three alternative methods for approaching this problem: establishing a correspondence between image and model features, performing a search, and using a mapping between any image of an object and a canonical shape of the object in question.

5.8.1 Minimal Alignment: Using a Small Number of Corresponding Features

The coefficients of the linear combination that align the model to the image can be determined by using a small number of features, identified in both the model and the image to be recognized. This is similar to the use of corresponding features in the 3-D alignment approach discussed earlier (and also in Fischler & Bolles 1981, Huttenlocher & Ullman 1987, Lowe 1985, Shoham & Ullman 1988, Ullman 1989). It was shown that three corresponding points or lines are usually sufficient to determine the transformation that aligns a 3-D model to a 2-D view, assuming the object can undergo only rigid transformations and uniform scaling. The corresponding features (lines and points) were used to recover the 3-D transformation separating the viewed object from the stored model, and the transformation was then applied to an internal 3-D object model.

The linear combination scheme can also use a small set of corresponding features, that are used in this case to determine the coefficients of the combination, rather than recover the 3-D transformation. The coefficients of the image combination required to align the model views with the image can be derived by simply solving a set of linear equations supplied by the corresponding features. This method requires k points to align a model of k pictures to a given image. Therefore, four points are required to determine the transformation for objects with sharp edges, and six points for objects with smooth boundaries (only three and five, respectively, if translation is compensated for). I will discuss below the technical details of extracting the coefficients from the corresponding features, and then summarize how they are used to perform the actual recognition.

Deriving the Coefficients from Linear Equations   The coefficients of the image combination are determined by solving the following equations. We assume that a small number of corresponding points (the "alignment key") have been identified in the image and the model. Let X be the matrix of the x-coordinates of the alignment points in the model. That is, x_{ij} is the x-coordinate of the j'th point in the i'th model picture. $\mathbf{p}_x$ is the vector of x-coordinates of the alignment points in the image, and $\mathbf{a}$ is the vector of unknown alignment parameters we wish to recover. The linear system to be solved is then simply $X\mathbf{a} = \mathbf{p}_x$. The alignment parameters are given by $\mathbf{a} = X^{-1}\mathbf{p}_x$ if an exact solution exists. We may use an overdetermined system (by using additional points), in which case $\mathbf{a} = X^+\mathbf{p}_x$ (where X^+ denotes the pseudo-inverse of X).

A convenient property of the scheme is that the matrix X^+ used to derive the unknown coefficients does not depend on the image and can therefore be pre-computed and stored for a given model.

Future recovery of the coefficients simply requires a multiplication of $\mathbf{p}_x$ by the stored matrix.

Similarly, we solve for $Y\mathbf{b} = \mathbf{p}_y$ to extract the alignment parameters $\mathbf{b}$ in the y-direction from Y (the matrix of y-coordinates in the model), and $\mathbf{p}_y$ (the corresponding y-coordinates in the image). Once a correspondence has been established, the recovery of the coefficient is simple and straightforward. The stability of the computation in the face of noise will depend on the so-called condition number of the matrices XX^T and YY^T. These matrices depend on the model images only, and this raises the possibility of selecting the model images in a manner that will increase the stability of the computation during matching.

It is also worth noting that the computation can proceed in a similar fashion on the basis of correspondence between straight line segments rather than between points. In this case, due to the "aperture problem" (Marr & Ullman 1981), only the perpendicular component (to the contour) of the displacement can be measured. This component can be used, however, in the equations above. In this case each contour segment contributes a single equation (as opposed to a point correspondence, that gives two equations). This possibility, together with other aspects of the correspondence problem, are discussed in more detail in chapter 7.

Using the Coefficients for Recognition   The method above can be used to determine the coefficients of the linear combination of the stored views. A recognition system that uses feature correspondence in this manner will proceed along the following main processing stages. A rough alignment stage will compensate for gross changes in scale, position, and orientation. This is a useful stage that helps, as we shall see later on, in establishing the correspondence between the image and the stored models. Correspondence will then be established between a small number of image and model features (either pointwise or linear). The coefficients of the view-combination will be recovered using the simple procedure above. Using the recovered coefficients, an internal combined image will be generated and compared with the viewed object. The matching function used to compare the internal model and the viewed image will be discussed later on; it may also include some penalty for performing large transformations.

This linear combination scheme, using feature correspondence to determine the alignment coefficients was implemented by R. Basri, and applied to images of 3-D objects. Figures 5.3 and 5.4 show the application of the LC (linear combination) method to complex objects with smooth bounding contours. The rotation was about the vertical axis, and three 2-D views were used for each model. The models were created by taking three images and producing their edge maps. The edge maps were incomplete, since only edges that appeared in all three images were maintained. Under better illumination conditions it is possible to produce better, more complete images, but the partial images serve to illustrate the point that the high prediction accuracy makes it feasible to obtain reliable recognition from incomplete data. Since the rotation was around the vertical axis, a simple correspondence scheme was used to match points along the same horizontal line. The resulting matching accuracy was sufficient for unambiguous discrimination in the presence of unavoidable noise in image formation, edge detection, and correspondence. The figure shows a good agreement between the actual image and the appropriate image combination produced internally. The two objects in the figure have complex 3-D shapes, and are quite similar, but they were easily discriminable by the LC method within the entire 60° rotation range.

The general scheme above focuses on the comparison of a viewed object with a single object model, but it leaves open a number of general questions. One issue is the problem of model selection. Here we assume that a candidate model has been selected, and the scheme evaluates the agreement between this selected model and the viewed object. If many object models are stored in memory, do we have to examine all of them in this manner, or can we somehow focus on a smaller number of potential models? This

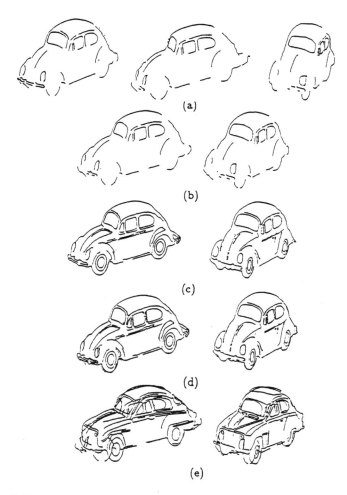

Figure 5.3
(a) Three model pictures of a VW car for rotations around the vertical axis.
The second and the third pictures were obtained from the first by rotations
of $\pm 30°$ around the Y-axis. Only a subset of the edges were used in the
model. (b) Two linear combinations of the VW model. The x-coefficients are
$(0.556, 0.463, -0.018)$ and $(0.582, -0.065, 0.483)$. These are artificial images,
created by combinations of the first three views, rather than actual views. (c)
Real images of a VW car. (d) Matching the linear combinations to the real
images. Each contour image is a superposition of an actual image with one
of the linear combinations. The agreement is good within the entire range of
$\pm 30°$. (e) Matching the VW model to pictures of the Saab car. After (Ullman
& Basri 1991).

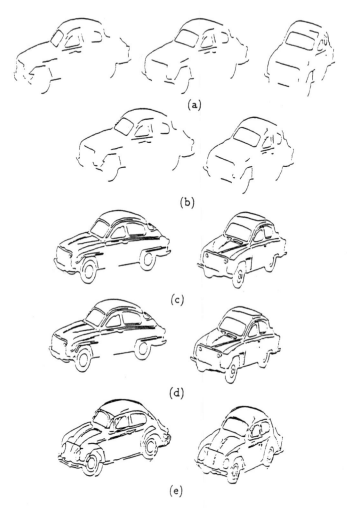

Figure 5.4
(a) Three model pictures of a Saab car, taken with approximately the same
3-D transformations as the VW model pictures. (b) Two linear combinations of the Saab model. The x-coefficients are $(0.601, 0.471, -0.072)$ and
$(0.754, -0.129, 0.375)$, corresponding to a rotation of the original model by
$\pm 15°$. (c) New real images of a Saab car. (d) Matching the linear combinations to the real images. (e) Matching the Saab model to pictures of the VW
car. After (Ullman & Basri 1991).

issue, sometimes called the model indexing problem, will be taken up later, in chapter 6. We also assumed above that the image of the viewed object is available to the recognition process. This raises the problem of image segmentation, since usually the image of the object in question will be part of a larger scene. This issue will be taken up again in chapter 8.

Finally, correspondence emerges as a key issue in this scheme. We will examine in chapter 7 possible schemes for establishing correspondence. We will also consider alternatives that do not rely on a separate correspondence stage. An example of such a "correspondence-less" scheme is discussed in the next section.

5.8.2   Searching for the Coefficients

An alternative method to determine the best linear combination is to perform a search in the space of possible coefficients. In this method, we first choose some initial values for the set $\{a_1, ..., a_k\}$ of coefficients, and then apply a linear combination to the model using these values. We repeat this process using a different set of coefficients, and finally choose the coefficient values that produced the best match of the model to the image.

A similar search approach can be used not only for the view combination method, but for other alignment schemes as well. In general, the set of possible alignment transformations $\{T_\alpha\}$ is parametrized by a parameter vector α, and a search is performed in the parameter space to determine the best value of α. A search can be applied, for example, to the 3-D alignment scheme described above. The deformable template method (Yuille, Cohen, & Hallinan, 1989) is another example of this approach—an alignment scheme where the aligning transformation is determined by search.

A problematic aspect of the search approach is that it may become time-consuming, requiring multiple evaluations of different possibilities before selecting the best combination. We can reduce the search-space by first performing a rough alignment of the model to the image. The identification of general features in

both the image and the model, such as a dominant orientation, the
center of gravity, and a measurement of the overall size of the imaged object, can be used for compensating roughly for image rotation, translation and scaling. Assuming that the initial alignment
process compensates for these transformations up to a bounded
error, and that the rotations in 3-D space covered by the model
are also restricted, then we can restrict the search for the best
coefficients to a limited domain. Instead of just employing a blind
search, the search can be guided by an optimization procedure.
To this end, one can define an error measure that measures the
discrepancy between the model and the viewed image, and then
use minimization techniques to reduce this error. Minimization-
guided search, using for example gradient descent, increases the
efficiency of the search, but it also runs the risk of obtaining a
local optimum rather than reaching the truly best solution. The
preliminary stage of rough alignment should be helpful in this respect, since the search for the unknown parameters will start in
the vicinity of the correct solution. In addition, one can employ
search procedures that are capable of escaping local minima. We
will discuss this search possibility in more detail in chapter 10.

5.8.3   Linear Mappings—Producing a Canonical View

The linear combination scheme is based on the fact that a 3-D
object can be modeled by the combination of a small number of
pictures. In this section we shall see how this property can be
used to construct a scheme that maps each view of the object to
a predefined canonical view that serves to identify the object. In
this method we do not recover explicitly the coefficients $(a_1, ..., a_k)$
of the linear combination. Instead, we assume that a full correspondence has been established between the viewed object and
the stored model, and then we use a scheme called "linear mapping" to test whether the viewed object is a linear combination
of the model views. The term "linear mapping" comes from the
fact that the scheme is a mapping between views—it takes a 2-D
view as an input and produces a new 2-D view as the output—

and it is linear in the mathematical sense. The special property of this scheme is that all the different views of a given object, taken from different viewing directions, produce a single, fixed view of the object in question. To use this method, we therefore apply the "linear mapping" to the input picture, and test whether the resulting transformed picture is sufficiently close to one of the canonical views of objects stored in memory. We will first see below how this mapping is constructed, and then how it can be used in a recognition process, including a brief discussion of the advantages and limitations of this method in comparison with alternative schemes.

For the purpose of the linear mapping method, it is convenient to consider an image as represented by a vector of numbers, and the recognition process then uses a matrix L that can be applied to such image vectors and produce new images. Suppose that a 2-D pattern P is represented by a vector $\mathbf{p}$ of its coordinates, in both the x and y directions, for example, by the sequence $(x_1, y_1, x_2, y_2, ..., x_n, y_n)$. Let us consider $\mathbf{p_1}$ and $\mathbf{p_2}$, two different patterns representing the same object, that is, two vectors that correspond to two different views of the same object. We can now construct a matrix L that maps both $\mathbf{p_1}$ and $\mathbf{p_2}$ to the same output vector $\mathbf{q}$. That is, $L\mathbf{p_1} = L\mathbf{p_2} = \mathbf{q}$. If such a mapping is constructed, then any linear combination $a\mathbf{p_1} + b\mathbf{p_2}$ will automatically be mapped to the same output vector $\mathbf{q}$, multiplied by the scalar $a + b$. In particular, we can select as the common output q one of the object's views, say, $\mathbf{p_1}$. In this case, any view of the object will be mapped by L to a single fixed view that will serve as the "canonical view" for the object in question.

We have seen already that different views of the same object can usually be expressed as linear combinations $\sum a_i \mathbf{p_i}$ of a small number of representative views, P_i. If the mapping matrix L is constructed in such a manner that all the views P_i of the same object are mapped to a common output picture $\mathbf{q}$, then any combined view, $\hat{\mathbf{p}} = \sum a_i \mathbf{p_i}$, will be mapped by L to the same $\mathbf{q}$ (up to a scale), since $L\hat{\mathbf{p}} = (\sum a_i)\mathbf{q}$.

L can be constructed as follows. Let $\{\mathbf{p}_1, ..., \mathbf{p}_k\}$ be k linearly independent vectors representing the model pictures (we can assume that they are all linearly independent since a picture that is not is obviously redundant). We next complete this set by additional vectors $\{\mathbf{p}_{k+1}, ..., \mathbf{p}_n\}$, such that $\{\mathbf{p}_1, ..., \mathbf{p}_n\}$ are all linearly independent. Using these vectors, we define the following two matrices:

$$P = (\mathbf{p}_1, ..., \mathbf{p}_k, \mathbf{p}_{k+1}, ..., \mathbf{p}_n)$$
$$Q = (\mathbf{q}, ..., \mathbf{q}, \mathbf{p}_{k+1}, ..., \mathbf{p}_n).$$

P is a set of input vectors, and Q is a corresponding set of the desired outputs for the input vectors. We can see how Q was selected: for all the views of the object in question, the required output is $\mathbf{q}$, the canonical representation of this object. All the other input patters are simply unaltered by the application of L.

We require, therefore, that:

$$LP = Q$$

and consequently L is given by:

$$L = QP^{-1}.$$

Note that since P is composed of n linearly independent vectors, the inverse matrix P^{-1} exists, and L is well-defined by this formula. By this construction we obtain a matrix L that maps any linear combination of the set of vectors $\{\mathbf{p}_1, ..., \mathbf{p}_k\}$ to a scaled pattern $\alpha \mathbf{q}$. Furthermore, any vector orthogonal to $\{\mathbf{p}_1, ..., \mathbf{p}_k\}$ will be mapped to itself. Therefore, if $\hat{\mathbf{p}}$ is a linear combination of $\{\mathbf{p}_1, ..., \mathbf{p}_k\}$ with an additional orthogonal noise component, it would be mapped by L to $\mathbf{q}$ combined with the same amount of noise. The use of this matrix L can be considered as a form of computing an invariance for the purpose of recognition, since all the images of the same objects produce the same output. It is different, however, from the use of invariant properties discussed in chapter 2, where the computed invariant properties were independent of a particular object model. In contrast, the invariant here is constructed for a particular object, using several views of the object in question.

In constructing the matrix L, one may use more than just k vectors $\mathbf{p}_i$, particularly if the input data is noisy. In this case a problem arises of estimating the best k-dimensional linear subspace spanned by a larger collection of vectors. This problem is a fairly standard one, and can be approached by principal component analysis, as discussed in (Ullman & Basri 1991).

In our implementation we have used $L\mathbf{p}_i = 0$ for all the view vectors $\mathbf{p}_i$ of a given object, rather than using one of the object's views. The reason is that if a new view of the object $\hat{\mathbf{p}}$ is given by $\sum a_i \mathbf{p}_i$ with $\sum a_i = 0$, then $L\hat{\mathbf{p}} = 0$. This means that the linear mapping L may send a legal view to the zero vector, and it is therefore convenient to choose the zero vector as the common output for all the object's views. If it is desirable to obtain at the output level a canonical view of the object such as $\mathbf{p}_1$ rather than the zero vector, then one can use as the final output the vector $\mathbf{p}_1 - L\hat{\mathbf{p}}$. This will ensure that the different views are mapped again to a fixed view, $\mathbf{p_1}$.

The decision regarding whether or not $\hat{\mathbf{p}}$ is a view of the object represented by L can be based on comparing $\| L\hat{\mathbf{p}} \|$ with $\| \hat{\mathbf{p}} \|$. If $\hat{\mathbf{p}}$ is indeed a view of the object, then this ratio will be small (exactly 0 in the noise-free condition). If the view is "pure noise" (in the space orthogonal to the span of $(\mathbf{p}_1, ... \mathbf{p}_k)$), then this ratio will be equal to 1. We therefore obtain a good separation between the views that belong to the object and views that do not.

Figure 5.5 shows the application of the linear mapping to two models of simple geometrical structures, a cube (a) and a pyramid (b). For each model we have constructed a matrix that maps any linear combination of the model pictures to the first model-picture, that serves as its 'canonical view'. Consider the cube images in 5.5a first. The left column depicts two different views of the cube. Applying the cube matrix to these views yields in both cases the canonical view, as shown in the middle column. When the input to the cube matrix was a pyramid rather than a cube, the output was

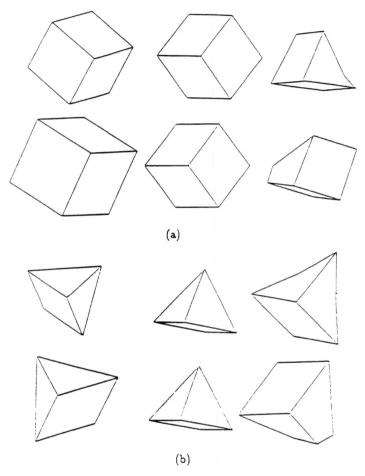

Figure 5.5
An illustration of the linear mapping method. (a) Applying cube and pyramid
matrices to cube images. (b) Applying pyramid and cube matrices to pyramid
images. Left column of pictures: the input images. Middle column: the result
of applying the appropriate mapping to the images, these results are identical
to the first model pictures (which serve as canonical views). Right column:
the result of applying the incorrect matrices to the images. The resulting
pictures are not similar to the canonical views.

different from the canonical view (right column). In this manner, different views of the cubes can be identified by comparing the output to the canonical cube. Figure 5.5b shows similar results obtained for the pyramid.

The appealing aspect of the linear mapping method is its simplicity. The main step in the recognition process consists of simply applying a matrix operation to the object representation. There are, however, two disadvantages that, outside some special application, make this route less practical than the alternative schemes. The first disadvantage is the need for full correspondence. By arranging the pattern as an ordered vector of coordinates we essentially assume full correspondence between the input patterns and a stored pattern. The second disadvantage is a related problem—it is difficult in this scheme to deal with occlusion. When the object is partially occluded, some parts of the pattern vector will be missing, and a question arises, how to apply the recognition matrix to a partial object vector.

5.8.4   Evaluating the Final Match

The different methods discussed above for performing alignment all share a common general structure. To compensate for possible variations between the stored model and the viewed object, the alignment approach allows the models (or the viewed object) to undergo certain compensating transformations during the matching stage. If T is the set of allowable transformations, the matching stage requires the selection of a model $M_i \in \mathcal{M}$ and a transformation $T_\alpha \in T$, such that the viewed object P and the transformed model $T_\alpha M_i$ will be as close as possible. That is, we attempt to minimize a distance measure $d(M, T_\alpha, P)$. T_α is the alignment transformation—it is supposed to bring the model M and the viewed object P into an optimal agreement.

Key problems that arise in any alignment scheme are how to represent the set of different models $\mathcal{M}$, what is the set of allowable transformations T, and, for a given model $M_i \in \mathcal{M}$, how to determine the transformation $T_\alpha \in T$ so as to minimize the difference between P and $T_\alpha M_i$. For example, in the curvature method, a model is represented by a set of 2-D contours, with associated depth and curvature values at each contour point. The set of allowed transformations includes 3-D rotation, translation and scaling, followed by an orthographic projection. The transformation is determined by identifying at least three corresponding features (points or lines) in the image and the object. In the linear combination method, a model is represented by a small set of corresponding 2-D views (or pictorial descriptions), and the set of allowable transformation can include, for example, the set of linear transformations in 3-D.

Another problem concerns the final distance measure. The distance measure d used for matching the image and the transformed model will depend on the type of alignment scheme used. Typically, it contains two contributions:

$$d(M, T_\alpha, P) = d_1(T_\alpha M, P) + d_2(T_\alpha).$$

The first term $d_1(T_\alpha M, P)$ measures the residual distance between the picture P and the transformed model $T_\alpha M$ following the alignment, and $d_2(T_\alpha)$ penalizes for the transformation T_α that was required to bring M into a close agreement with P. For example, it may be possible to bring M into a close agreement with P by stretching it considerably. In this case $d_1(T_\alpha M, P)$ will be small, but, if large stretches of the object are unlikely, $d_2(T_\alpha)$ will be large. The different types of alignment schemes will differ in the relative emphasis they place on d_1 and d_2.

In the minimal alignment scheme, T_α is determined by a small number of corresponding features in the model and the image. Methods using this approach assume that the set of possible transformations is restricted (usually to rigid 3-D transformations with possible scaling, or a Lie transformation group, (Brockett 1989)), so that the correct transformation can be recovered using a small number of constraints. This general approach has been used by Faugeras & Hebert (1986), Fischler & Bolles (1981), Huttenlocher & Ullman (1987), Shoham & Ullman (1988), Thompson & Mundy

(1987), Ullman (1986, 1989). In these schemes the term d_2 above is usually ignored, since there is no reason to penalize for a rigid 3-D aligning transformation, and the match is therefore evaluated by d_1 only.

In an alignment search scheme, a search is conducted in the space of possible transformations. The set of possible transformations $\{T_\alpha\}$ is parametrized by a parameter vector α, and a search is performed in the parameter space to determine the best value of α. A search can be applied to 3-D alignment, as well as to the linear combination method. The deformable template method (Yuille, Cohen, & Hallinan, 1989) is another example for this approach. Since the set of allowed transformations is usually restricted, the distance measure must penalize for the residual error, and it may also penalize for unlikely transformations.

In full alignment schemes, a full correspondence is established between the model and the image. This correspondence defines a distortion transformation that takes M into P. The set of transformations is not restricted in this approach to rigid transformations. Complex non-rigid distortions can be included as well. In contrast with minimal alignment, in the distance measure d above, the first term $d_1(T_\alpha M, P)$ does not play then an important role, since the full correspondence forces $T_\alpha M$ and P to be in close agreement. The match is therefore evaluated by the plausibility of the required transformation T_α.

5.8.5   Prototypical view and differences

In the view-combination scheme, the novel view is described as the linear combination of a small number of object views. The combined view can also be described as the combination of a single prototypical view with a number of difference image, depicting the deviation of particular views from the prototype. In these terms, the novel view is expressed as $c\mathbf{p} + \Sigma_i a_i \mathbf{V_i}$. Here $\mathbf{p}$ is a prototypical view, that can be obtained, for example, by the average of a number of object views. The $\mathbf{V_i}$'s are difference images, that is, each $\mathbf{V_i}$ is the difference between a particular view and the prototypical view. The two formulations are similar, but it is sometimes more convenient to treat the generation of intermediate models in terms of transformations applied to a prototypical view rather than the combination of views. As before, a single prototypical view will cover a limited range of viewing directions, and therefore a number of prototypical views of this type will be required.

5.9 Extensions to the View-Combination Scheme

The image combination scheme discussed so far is restricted in a number of ways. It will be of interest to extend it in several directions, such as: non-orthographic image views, nonlinear image combinations, dealing effectively with occlusion, and dealing with large libraries of objects. The discussion here will be limited to brief comments on these issues, some of them are explored further in subsequent chapters.

5.9.1 Non-Orthographic Projections

The scheme as presented assumes rigid transformations and an orthographic projection. Under these conditions, all the views of a given object are embedded in a low-dimensional linear subspace of a much larger space. What happens if the projection is perspective rather than orthographic, or if the transformations are not entirely rigid?

The effect of perspectivity appears to be quite limited. We have applied the linear combination scheme to objects with ratio of distance-to-camera to object-size down to 4:1, with only minor effects on the results (less then 3% deviation from the orthographic projection for rotations up to 45°).

Instead of using the convenient approximation of orthographic projection it is also possible to perform image combination directly using perspective views. The linear combination scheme provides a method for predicting a new view of an object based on a model constructed from two or more corresponding views. Shashua (1994) developed a similar method for perspective views.

Suppose that q_1, q_2, q_3 are vectors of the image coordinates of corresponding points in three different views of the same object. In the linear combination scheme we have seen how the coordinates of the third view can be expressed, under orthographic projection, in terms of the coordinates of the first two views. Mathematically, this took the form of two linear expressions, one for the x and the other for the y-coordinates. Shashua (1994) showed how more general expressions can be derived for the perspective case. The linear expressions are replaced in this case by two polynomials in the image coordinates, of the form $P(q_1, q_2, q_3) = 0$. These "view polynomials" are of the third degree. However, when two of the views are kept constant, and P is viewed as a polynomial in the third view only, then it becomes a linear expression in the coordinates of this view.

As in the linear combination case, the view polynomials contain coefficients that can be derived from a small set of corresponding points in the two views. Using these results, perspective views can be treated directly in a manner analogous to the linear combination scheme. As before, an object model is constructed from two corresponding views. (Additional views are required to cover the object from all viewing directions.) Given a novel view, a correspondence is established between a number of image and model features. Using the view polynomials, a predicted view is derived and compared with the input. As in the linear combination scheme, other variations of the method can be used, such as a search for the coefficients. The direct use of perspective views increases the accuracy of the reconstruction, but a larger set of corresponding features (seven or more) is required.

An intermediate case between orthographic and perspective projections was examined by Basri (1994). In this intermediate case, termed "paraperspective projection" (Aloimonos 1990), the projection is obtained by parallel rays. However, unlike the orthographic case, the projection rays are not required to be perpendicular to the image plane, but may intersect it at any angle. In addition, a scaling of the image is also allowed. (See appendix E for the different projection models.) Basri showed that the set of paraperspective images on an object under rigid transformations is identical to the set of orthographic projections of the same object under affine transformations. This result agrees with the empirical testing of the linear combination method under realistic perspective conditions, and together they suggest that the simple orthographic affine method provides a good approximation to the perspective case.

5.9.2 Nonlinear Image Combinations

As for non-rigid transformations and other possible distortions, an interesting general extension to consider is the case where the set of views is no longer a linear subspace, but still occupies a low-dimensional manifold within a much higher dimensional space. This manifold resembles locally a linear subspace, but it is no longer "globally straight." By analogy, one can visualize the simple linear combinations case in terms of a 3-D space, in which all the orthographic views of a rigid object are restricted to some 2-D plane. In the more general case, the plane will bend, to become a curved 2-D manifold within the 3-D space.

This issue of dealing effectively with lower-dimensional subspaces appears to be a general case of interest for recognition as well as for other learning tasks. The general reason can be explained by the following consideration. For recognition to be feasible, the set of views $\{V\}$ corresponding to a given object cannot be arbitrary, but must obey some constraints, that can be expressed in general in the form $F(V_i) = 0$. Under general conditions, these restrictions will define locally a manifold embedded in the larger space (as implied by the implicit function theorem). Algorithms that can learn to classify efficiently sets that form low-dimensional manifolds embedded in high-dimensional spaces will therefore be of general value.

An example of an algorithm that attempts to capitalize on the reduced dimensionality and the smooth structure of the sets that are being recognized, was developed by M. Kositsky (1994). The algorithm performs a covering of the relevant sets by unions of ellipsoids. By setting the dimensions and orientations of the ellipses, it becomes possible to cover low-dimensional manifolds embedded in high-dimensional spaces.

5.9.3   The RBF Method

An elegant approach that can use general, nonlinear combination of images, is the radial basis functions (RBF) method, developed by Poggio and his collaborators (Poggio 1990, Poggio & Edelman 1990, Poggio & Girosi 1990). This method uses nonlinear interpolation between 2-D images for the purpose of recognizing 3-D objects, as well as for other tasks that involve learning from examples.

The basic idea is to draw an analogy between learning from examples and the mathematical problem of approximation by smooth surfaces. As a simple illustration, suppose that we are trying to learn the shape of an unknown terrain. We are given a number of examples—in this case, the terrain elevation at a number of locations. We are then required to "generalize"—to estimate the terrain elevation at unknown locations. An obvious approach to this problem is to construct a smooth surface that passes through the known points. The problem of constructing such a surface is called an interpolation problem. In a variation of this problem, called approximation, the surface is required to pass near, but not exactly through, the known data points. Clearly, there are many different surfaces that can go through a given set of points. The problem is solved, therefore, by preferring a surface that passes through the data points and, at the same time, is as smooth as possible.

It turns out that a good solution to various problems of this kind can be obtained by the superposition of basis functions (such as gaussians) centered on the known data points. In the terrain example above, one places at each data point a gaussian function. The height of the gaussians is adjusted so that the surface elevation at each of the data points matches the known, measured height at this point. In a mathematical formula, the surface elevation at a point x is given by:

$$\Sigma_i a_i G(\parallel x - x_i \parallel) \tag{5.9.17}$$

where G is a gaussian function, and a_i is the amplitude of the $i'th$ gaussian. To determine the values of the amplitudes a_i we use the constraint that for each of the known points, x_k, this formula should give the measured elevation, h_k. That is:

$$\Sigma_i a_i G(\parallel x_k - x_i \parallel) = h_k. \tag{5.9.18}$$

This gives a set of linear equations from which the a_i can be derived. A similar procedure can also be used for approximation (rather then interpolation) problems. Extensions were also derived, for example, for cases where the number of basis functions used is smaller than the number of observed data points, or where the centers of the basis function do not coincide with the locations of the observed data points.

In using this approach, the recognition of 3-D objects from their 2-D images is considered an interpolation (or approximation) problem in a high-dimensional space. During a learning phase, we are given a number of input-output pairs: images together with the desired responses (such as a name, or a value specific to a given object). We then wish to generalize the response to images not seen during the learning stage. This is done in the RBF approach using approximation methods. The observed images are considered as points in some high-dimensional space. Using the RBF method, a smooth surface can be fit to the examples, and then used to produce an output for a novel input image.

To take full advantage of the results mentioned above (that the set of views of a given object spans a very low-dimensional subspace in the space of possible views) it will be of interest to consider extensions that allow the basis functions to be long-and-narrow rather than radial. To follow the local orientation of the lower dimension manifold, this will have to be performed locally, that is, the basis functions will end up pointing in different directions in different parts of the space.

The RBF and linear combination schemes are similar in that they rely on a limited number of 2-D patterns, and recognize novel views as combinations of stored patterns. In both, the stored views are assumed to be in correspondence, and some form of correspondence is also required between the models and the viewed object. One difference between the methods is that the linear combination method produces as compensated, or predicted internal model, that is typically not generated by the RBF method. The methods also emphasize slightly different general constraints. The emphasis in the RBF method is on the smoothness of the data set. In attempting to generalize from sparse data to novel inputs, the scheme assumes that the data form a smooth continuous surface in an appropriate representation space. Generalization is therefore obtained by fitting a smooth surface to the data points, or the "examples" used during a learning phase. This method is not limited to linear combinations of images, nonlinear combinations are also possible. In the linear combination scheme the emphasis is on the reduced dimensionality as well as the simplicity (linearity, or near-linearity) of the solution space. It will be of interest to explore further schemes that integrate in a useful manner complementary properties of these related schemes.

5.9.4   Non-rigid Objects

The modeling of objects by combinations of stored pictures is not limited to rigid objects only. The method can also be used to deal with several types of non-rigid transformations, such as articulations and non-rigid stretching. Distortions such as stretching and shearing are included in the scheme, because the method can handle affine rather than strictly rigid object transformations. Some mechanisms should probably be incorporated in the view-combination scheme to restrict the extent of the transformations accepted by the scheme as legal object changes. The unmodified scheme will treat even large stretches and shears as possible object transformations, but when these transformations become too large, they should detract from the quality of the overall match.

In the case of an articulated object, such as a pair of scissors, the object is composed of a number of rigid parts linked together by joints that constrain the relative movement of the parts. We saw that the x- and y-coordinates of a rigid part are constrained to a 4-D subspace. Two rigid parts reside within an 8-D subspace, but, because of the constraints at the joints, they usually occupy a smaller subspace (for example, 6-D for a planar joint). It is also possible to recognize first one of the rigid parts as an object in its own right, and then use this partial recognition to guide subsequent stages in the recognition process, as discussed further in chapter 6. The treatment of some characteristic non-rigid distortions of a certain class of objects, such as facial expressions, is discussed further in chapters 6 and 10. Finally, the recognition of some highly non-rigid objects, such as a crumpled sweater, is obtained mainly by non-shape methods, including the use of color, texture, and perhaps the use of abstract labels of the type discussion in chapter 3.

5.9.5   Occlusion

In the view-combination scheme we assumed that the same set of points is visible in the different views. What happens if some of the object's points are occluded either by self-occlusion or by other objects?

As we mentioned already, self-occlusion is handled by representing an object not by a single model, but by a number of models covering its different "aspects" (Koenderink & Van Doorn 1979) or "characteristic views" (Freeman & Chakravarty 1980).

As for occlusion by other objects, this problem is handled in a different manner by different versions of the alignment scheme. In the minimal correspondence version, a small number of corresponding features are used to recover the coefficients of the linear combination. In this scheme, occlusion does not present a major difficulty. We assume that the visible part of the object is sufficient for obtaining correspondence and thus for recovering the required coefficients. After computing the linear combination, a good match will be obtained between the transformed model and the visible part of the object, and recognition can then proceed on the basis of this match. Alignment search will behave in a similar manner: when the correct parameters are reached, a good match will be obtained between the model and the unoccluded part of the object. We have to make sure, however, that the matching function used by the scheme is sensitive to good partial matches. That is, an accurate match of a part of the object should be more significant than a mediocre match over a large portion of the object.

In the linear mapping version, an object's view is represented by a vector $\mathbf{v}_i$ of its coordinates. Due to occlusion, some of the coordinates will remain unknown. A method of evaluating the match in this case in an optimal manner is suggested by Ullman and Basri (1991), and will not be detailed here. In this scheme, the occlusion problem is more severe than the minimal correspondence and the search versions.

Scene clutter also affects the computation by making the correspondence more difficult. That is, model features (points or lines) may be incorrectly matched with spurious data in the image. This effect of clutter on model-to-image correspondence is discussed, for example, in Grimson (1990a,b). Additional aspects of these problems are discussed further in chapter 8, that deals with the issue of segmentation.

5.9.6   Hidden surface removal

Images constructed by extrapolating from two or more views can contain features that are occluded from view and will not in fact be visible from the new viewing direction. As long as the proportion of such hidden features is small, this will have only a minor effect on the match between the model and the novel image. It is also possible, however, to eliminate hidden features from the combined view. The problem arises when two features in the combined view share the same image coordinates, and therefore one of them will be occluded by the other. To determine the visibility of the features, their depth-ordering should be determined. Depth-ordering can be recovered in the following manner. From two orthographic views it is straightforward to recover, using the linear combination method, a quantity ("affine depth") w, that is related to the actual depth z by an affine transformation:

$$z = ax + by + cw. \tag{5.9.19}$$

Therefore, two object features sharing the same image coordinates will be separated in depth by: $\Delta z = c\Delta w$. Assuming that we know the sign of the constant c (this can be obtained, but will not be discussed here), Δz is determined directly by Δw, which is easily computable. This technique was applied to the extrapolated face images in figure 5.2.

5.9.7 Multiple Models

We have considered above primarily the problem of matching a viewed object with a single model. If there are many candidate models, a question arises regarding the scaling of the task complexity with the number of models.

In the view-combination scheme, the main problem is in the stage of performing the correspondence, since the subsequent testing of a candidate model is relatively straightforward. The linear mapping scheme is particularly attractive in this regard: once the correspondence is known, the testing of a model requires only a multiplication of a matrix by a vector. With respect to the correspondence stage, the question that arises is how to perform efficiently correspondence with multiple models. One general idea is to use pre-alignment to a prototype in the following manner. Suppose that $M_1, ..., M_k$ is a family of related models. A single model M will be used for representing this set for the purpose of alignment. The correspondence T_i between each M_i in the set and M is pre-computed. Given an observed object P, a single

correspondence $T : M \rightarrow P$ is computed. The individual transformations $M_i \rightarrow P$ are computed by the compositions $T \circ T_i$.
This method and other issues related to the problem of multiple
models are taken up in chapter 6, that discusses the problem of
classification.

5.10   Psychophysical and Physiological Evidence

Since object recognition involves a wide range of processes, psychological testing of the mechanisms participating in recognition
is not a straightforward task. The comparison of results obtained
from different experiments shows that they depend, among other
factors, on the nature of the task being performed and the type
of objects being recognized. The recognition system often uses
in a given experimental situation the appropriate strategy for the
task at hand. For example, if one of the objects presented has
a unique distinctive feature, such as a unique color, marking, or
appendage, this feature will often be used to distinguish it from
other objects (Eley 1982, Murray *et al.* 1993). Similarly, the distinction between a small number of highly different objects, (for
example, one object might be a wireframe and another a solid
shape) will produce different results compared with the recognition of a larger number of generally similar objects. This second
condition is more relevant to the purpose of the present discussion,
since the current focus is on object identification rather than on
crude discrimination.

One aspect of 3-D object recognition that has been examined
in detail by a number of different studies is the dependence of
recognition performance on the viewing direction. In such studies
an object is presented at a single orientation, and recognition is
subsequently tested when the object is presented at a novel 3-D
orientation. In many studies of this type it was found that recognition performance decreased with the departure from the original,
trained orientation: the error rates typically increased, as well
as the response time for correct recognition (Bülthoff & Edelman

1992, Corballis 1988, Edelman & Bülthoff 1992, Jolicoeur 1985, 1990, Rock & Di Vita 1987, Tarr & Pinker 1989, 1991). The dependence on viewing direction is present even when the object is seen in both the training and subsequent testing under conditions that facilitate the recovery of 3-D shape, using stereo, shading, and motion (Edelman & Bülthoff 1992). These findings provide evidence against theories based on structural descriptions as well as 3-D alignment. In structural description schemes, the precise view has no particular importance, since it is replaced during the processing by a symbolic structural description. As long as the new view gives rise to the same structural description, no significant effect of viewing direction is expected. In 3-D alignment, a single view that allows accurate recovery of 3-D information should be sufficient for generalization over a wide range. The findings are more consistent with theories, such as the image combination scheme, that use multiple 2-D views in the recognition process. It should be noted, however, that not all the studies in this area show the 3-D orientation effect. For example, Biederman and Gerhardstein (1993) found complete invariance of their test objects to viewing position. The objects in this study were designed to have a clear decomposition into a small number of simple parts, and this design may have contributed to the difference between this and other studies. In any case, the full nature of the viewing position dependency is still a matter of controversy, and further studies will be required to clarify the issue.

Recognition improves after training with additional object views (Poggio & Edelman 1990, Tarr & Pinker 1989); a similar finding was also observed in monkeys trained for object recognition (Logothetis et al. 1994). An interesting example of this improvement was reported by Bülthoff and Edelman (1992). In their study, they presented subjects with multiple views of the same object; however, the views were all obtained by rotations of the object about a fixed axis in the image plane, such as the horizontal or the vertical axis. The generalization to novel views proved to be better for views obtained by further rotations about the same axis,

compared with rotations about the orthogonal axis. This is difficult to reconcile with any theory except for the image combination
approach. In this approach, combination of images obtained from
rotations about, say, the vertical axis, produce new images that
are also constrained to rotations about the same axis.

Liu, Knill, and Kersten (1995) performed an elegant study that
compared recognition performance of human observers with what
they termed "2D ideal observer." The ideal observer compares a
novel object view with all the previously seen views of the same object. The comparison is performed with each of the stored views
separately, as opposed to the use of view combinations. They
found that humans performed better than the ideal observer in
generalizing to new views, demonstrating that independent comparisons to stored views are insufficient to account for human
recognition performance. The same conclusion was reached by
the study by Moses, Adini and Ullman (1994) described in the
first chapter.

Several studies have explored the effects on recognition of transformations other than 3-D rotation. Changing size was found in
some studies to have an effect on recognition time (Bundesen &
Larsen 1975, Larsen 1985, Cave & Kosslyn 1989), but other studies found complete size invariance (Biederman & Cooper 1992).
Palmer (1978) examined the effect of local image distortions using
both sequential and simultaneous shape comparisons, using 2-D
line figures. In simultaneous comparison two shapes are presented
side by side, and in sequential presentation only a single shape is
presented at a time. Simultaneous comparison was found to be
profoundly influenced by structural or configurational effects such
as the existence of closed loops or symmetric parts. In sequential
presentation that, akin to recognition, relies on a comparison of a
shape in view with a stored memory, configurational effects all but
disappeared: performance appeared to be governed by the simple
pictorial similarity.

Biological Aspects From the physiological standpoint, we have only a partial view of the mechanisms in the visual system involved in shape analysis and object recognition. From single cell recordings in the primarily visual cortex we know something about how the process of shape analysis in the visual system begins. Studies starting with the work of Hubel and Wiesel (1962, 1968) have shown that at the early processing stages in the primary visual cortex (V1), the image is represented in terms of simple local features such as oriented edges and lines. V1 also shows some degree of internal separation and specialization for different aspects of the stimulus. For example, color information appears to be processed by only a subset of the cells in this area. Separation of function exists to some degree in subsequent processing stages, and, in particular, it seems possible that some visual areas are more directly concerned with shape-related processing than others. A rough division has been suggested between the so-called dorsal stream of processing leading from V1 to parietal cortex, and the more ventral occipitotemporal stream going to inferotemporal cortex, where shape processing, leading for instance to object recognition, seems to take place (Ungerleider & Mishkin 1982). It also appears that within the ventral stream some populations of cells may be more involved in shape and object processing than others. For example, some cells (e.g., in area IT) respond to specific shapes irrespective of color and maintain shape-specific response across large changes of color variations (Gross 1992), while other populations may be more directly involved in color processing.

The notion that IT cortex is involved with object recognition is also supported by brain lesion studies. Damage to IT can cause deficits in object recognition, and, in particular, in the precise identification of individual objects as compared with broad classification (Damasio, Damasio & Tranel 1990).

Single cells recordings in IT revealed some cells responding to complex shapes. A particular population of such cells, in the STS region of IT, responds selectively to face images (Perret, Rolls, & Caan 1982, Perret *et al.* 1985, Rolls 1984, Young & Yamane 1992);

other cells in a nearby region have been reported to respond to
hand images. Some of the face-selective cells appear to respond to
complete face images, others to face parts. Many show considerable invariance along several dimensions, such as size, position,
orientation in the image plane, and color. In terms of 3-D viewing
angle, some cells show a selective response to an individual face
over considerable changes in viewing direction. At the same time,
the response is not entirely "object-centered": the selectivity does
not cover the full range from profile to full-face. The response is
typically optimal for a particular orientation and decreases gradually for other orientations. In addition to cells responding to
complex and meaningful stimuli, other cells in IT have been reported to respond to more elementary shapes and shapes that do
not correspond to familiar objects (Fujita *et al.* 1992).

Shape-selective cells in IT respond in a graded fashion, and will
respond not only to a single shape, but to similar shapes as well.
The shape of a specific face, for instance, may still be represented
by such cells in the population response of a number of cells. This
may be a general principle of encoding, that object shapes are
represented by the combined activity of cells either broadly tuned
to different shapes, or tuned to different parts of the entire shape.

Relatively little is known about shape processing along the way
from V1 to anterior IT. The initial studies in V1 regarding simple, complex, and end-stopped cells, have raised the possibility
of a processing hierarchy, were higher processing stages extract
increasingly elaborate shape features. There is at present little
evidence from single cell recordings to support a systematic hierarchy of shape features, although the notion cannot be ruled out.
Area V2, which is placed one step higher than V1 in cortical hierarchy, appears to be involved in some aspects of form processing:
some of the units in this area are sensitive to subjective contours,
others show sensitivity to a colinear arrangement of dots moving
coherently with respect to the background (Peterhans & von der
Heydt 1991), but these are not necessarily higher order elements
in a feature hierarchy compared with the processing in V1; these

processes may be involved in image segmentation processes discussed in chapter 8.

An aspect worth noting is that multiple stages along the chain of visual processing can be described as performing some abstraction of the input pattern. For example, already in V1 some units respond to the presence of an edge or bar at a particular orientation but irrespective of the sign of contrast. For example, the cell responds in a similar manner to both a dark and a light edge (Schiller, Finlay & Volman 1976.) In area MT some units respond to the presence of an edge or bar of a particular orientation regardless of whether the edges arise from luminance contrast or from dynamic texture boundary (Albright 1992). Such responses are more abstract in the sense that they signal the presence of a boundary irrespective of the specific conditions that define the boundary, such as increase or decrease in contrast, or discontinuity in texture. This abstraction is similar to the notion of pictorial representations discussed in the previous chapter: the units respond not to a specific image but to a more abstract pictorial arrangement. Cells along the hierarchy from V1 to V4 also show an increasing degree of tolerance for the position and size of their preferred stimuli.

The pattern of responses in IT appears to be consistent with the general notion of multiple pictorial representations. An object appears to be represented in IT by multiple units, tuned to different views of the object. The response of a face-specific unit, for example, appears to be governed by the stimulus' overall similarity to the unit's preferred 2-D pattern (Young & Yamane 1992), rather than by preferred 3-D shapes (such as a cube, cone, or cylinder, regardless of 3-D orientation), or abstract invariances (such as perimeter-to-area ratio, the cross ratio of colinear points, and the like).

There is some evidence that appears to be broadly compatible with a transformational, or alignment, view of shape processing in some of the higher visual areas. For example, damage to area V4 and posterior IT (Schiller & Lee 1991, Weiskrantz 1990, Schiller

1995), appears to affect especially the ability to compensate for transformations such as size, orientation, or illumination changes, rather than the ability to recognize non-transformed shapes. For example, in the experiments carried out by Weiskrantz, monkeys were trained to recognize a set of test objects, and were then tested with the original objects as well as objects similar to the test objects except for changes in scale, orientation in the image plane, and illumination. Lesions to area AIT (the anterior part of IT) caused a general deterioration in recognition capacity. Lesions to PIT (the posterior part of IT) and some prestriate areas had a more specific effect on the ability to recognize the transformed versions. Such results do not fit well with schemes that rely on the construction of invariant representations of the image, such as object-centered structural descriptions. The results suggest that shape analysis in intermediate areas may be concerned, at least in part, not with the creation of increasingly elaborate shape description, but with alignment and compensation processes.

The psychological and biological evidence is suggestive, but, not surprisingly, still insufficient to determine conclusively the nature of the processes and mechanisms responsible for visual object recognition. On the whole, it appears that the evidence does not support approaches to object recognition based primarily on invariant properties, structural descriptions, or 3-D alignment. As we shall see in the next chapter, however, the use of parts and invariant properties may play a more significant role in processes related to coarse object classification (see also Farah 1990, Kosslyn 1994).

The combination of computational and empirical considerations make recognition by combination of pictorial representations an attractive and likely possibility. The available psychophysical and physiological evidence appears on the whole to support such a scheme. The computational studies described in this chapter show that significant aspects of object recognition can be approached by using combinations of a small number of object views. In examining the human recognition system it is worth keeping in

mind, however, the distinction between the mathematical formulation of particular algorithms and the more general properties
of the approach. The image combination computation described
in this chapter illustrates the approach; however, as noted in an
earlier section, variations and extensions of the scheme are possible. My suggestion does not concern a specific algorithm, but
the more general approach, namely, that recognition by multiple
pictorial representations and their combinations constitutes a major component of 3-D object recognition. According to this view,
the brain will store for each object a small number of pictorial
descriptions, and the recognition process will involve the manipulation and some combination of these views. Unlike some of the
prevailing approaches that view object recognition as a symbolic
high-level activity, in this new approach the emphasis is on processes that are simpler, more direct, and pictorial in nature.

5.11   Interim Conclusions: Recognition by Multiple Views

The focus of the discussion so far has been on the identification
of individual 3-D objects. In the following chapters the emphasis will shift to related problems, including object classification,
image-to-model correspondence, segmentation, the use of visual
routines, and biological modeling. It will be useful, therefore, to
summarize here briefly the main characteristics of the approach
proposed up to this point in general, and the view combination
scheme discussed in the last chapter in particular.

Recognition Using Multiple Views   In the view-combination
approach developed in the last chapter, an object is represented
for the purpose of recognition by a number of its views, rather
than, for instance, a single 3-D representation. This approach is
therefore sometimes described as "recognition by multiple views."
It should be noted, however, that the views comprising the representation of a single object are not merely a collection of inde-

pendent 2-D object views. In the direct approach to recognition, objects are also represented by multiple views, but recognition is based in that approach simply on the best-matching individual view. In contrast, in the multiple views approach (including the view-combination and the RBF scheme) a number of object views are used collectively in the recognition process. A related property of the view-combination and similar schemes is that the representation by multiple views also includes a known correspondence between individual views. As was shown in the last chapter, a set of corresponding 2-D views provide a powerful and useful representation for the purpose of recognition. Without using explicit 3-D information, this representation contains detailed information about the object's structure, and this information is stored in a convenient form for the purpose of the recognition process. The correspondence also induces on the object views the useful structure of a vector space. In this space, notions such as averaging, combination, linear subspaces, the formation of a basis and the like can be applied to images in a meaningful manner, and this has been used in the computations above.

The object views used in this approach are not limited to simple images of the object. The use of abstract labels allows the scheme to incorporate in addition more abstract pictorial representations, and the stored views are also called "pictorial descriptions."

Image-to-Model Correspondence   Another aspect of the proposed approach is the role of image-to-model correspondence as a part of the recognition process. This aspect is related to the use of pictorial representations: when the model is stored in a pictorial form, a mapping between the model and novel object views becomes possible, unlike, for example, the modeling of an object by a set of invariant properties. This issue of image-to-model correspondence and its role in recognition will be discussed in more detail in chapter 7.

3-D *vs*. 2-D Information   In the view-combination approach, the model can be considered as three-dimensional and the viewed object as two-dimensional. Although the object representation is based on 2-D views, it contains implicitly 3-D information. Three corresponding views of the same object can be used in principle to reconstruct the object's 3-D shape (Ullman 1979). In the view-combination scheme this information is built into the recognition process without explicit 3-D modeling. As far as the viewed object is concerned, the view-combination approach does not require the extraction of 3-D information. There are possible methods of using 3-D information extracted from the image to facilitate the recognition process, but the process can proceed, as illustrated in the last several chapters, even lacking such 3-D information. The use of 3-D information in the model only is advantageous in recognition, because detailed 3-D information may be difficult to obtain reliably from a single image. It is therefore undesirable to base the recognition process on detailed 3-D information extracted from the viewed object. In contrast, during the model construction process, there is an opportunity to gather useful 3-D information from multiple views and over extended periods, and subsequently use this information in the recognition process.

Compensating Transformations The view combination approach uses explicitly compensating transformations to bring the internal model and the viewed object into close agreement. The stored model views are combined and manipulated to generate a new internal view that is as close as possible to the input view. Other schemes discussed in the last chapter also use compensating transformations, but in a more partial manner. For example, in the RBF scheme the input view is usually compensated for size, position, and orientation by normalizing the input view, but compensating for variations in 3-D viewing direction does not involve the explicit application of compensating transformations.

Combining Bottom-up with Top-Down Processing The internal object models in many recognition schemes play only a passive role in the recognition process. Processing is applied to the input view to generate a new representation that is relatively independent of the viewing conditions. This derived representation is then matched against stored internal models. In the view-combination approach the stored representations can play a much more active role. They can be used to generate internally intermediate representations, to be compared with the input image. We will return to the issue of combining bottom-up with top-down processing in the last chapter of the book.

Many issues remain open for further study. Some of them concern variations and elaborations of the approach; for example, the use of perspective rather than orthographic views, the role of grey level information, image contours, and other image features, and the use of pictorial abstractions. Other problems concern general issues that were not treated by the recognition approaches discussed so far, such as dealing with multiple objects, object classification, or the recognition of non-rigid objects. In the next few chapters we will turn to examine some of these general issues, starting with the problems of object classification and dealing with multiple objects.

6 Classification

6.1 Classification and Identification

Objects can be recognized at different levels of specificity. Sometimes they are assigned to a general class, such as a "house," "dog," "face"—classes that contain a variety of objects, of many different shapes. Objects can also be identified as unique individuals, such as my own house, or a particular friend's face. Classes of objects can also have different levels of generalization, such as a "golden retriever," "dog," or "quadruped."

The recognition schemes considered so far are aimed primarily at object identification. As we have seen, the alignment method, including the image combination scheme, can distinguish well between individual objects, such as two cars that have closely similar shapes. It will have a much harder time, however, classifying a new car, whose shape is not yet represented in the system.

The task of individual identification may appear initially more demanding than the more general levels of classification, since it requires finer, more accurate distinctions. But identification also has some advantages that make the task more tractable: it is concerned with specific shapes undergoing well-defined transformations, and therefore the changes are easier to specify and compensate for. This is why artificial recognition systems are usually more suitable for identification than for classification. It is easier, using current methods, to recognize known shapes, even complex ones, under well-defined changes in viewing and illumination conditions, than to capture the common characteristics of a class of objects. Although some attempts have been made to address the classification problem, recognizing novel images at the class level—a house, a car, a dog, a chair—is still an open and difficult problem.

Biological systems exhibit a very different behavior. For biological visual systems classification is a natural task, often performed spontaneously and effortlessly. Young children learn to recognize objects such as a dog, a house, a car, with little effort, but the recognition of specific individuals is more difficult. A simple animal such as the pigeon can recognize object classes, such as a person, a tree, a fish, but the generalization of a known object to novel viewing conditions appears to be poor (Cerella 1986). For biological systems, then, classification is easier than identification, while the opposite holds true for artificial systems. This is a fascinating contrast, and perhaps a better understanding of visual classification and identification will provide us with some clues regarding the differences in the way information is being processed and stored by biological and artificial systems.

One may ask in this context whether identification and recognition are in fact two distinct processes, or whether there is an entire range, from the very broad to the very specific. This is difficult to determine, but also not crucial for the current discussion. Individual identification and broad classification are rather different from a computational standpoint, and, as discussed below, there are also distinctions between these tasks from the biological and psychological perspectives. The important computational issue is to understand these tasks and study methods for accomplishing them. It will then also become more clear whether identification and classification are better thought of as two distinct processes, or as two endpoints in a spectrum of generalization levels.

6.2   The Role of Object Classification

Why is object classification at different levels of specificity useful? Recognizing an object at a specific level, such as a "golden retriever," is more informative than merely recognizing it as a "dog." Does this imply that the system should always attempt to recognize objects at the most specific level? As we shall see, object classification at different generalization levels is quite useful for two main reasons. First, classification is useful in its own right, particularly in dealing with novel objects. Second, it is a useful intermediate stage on the way to more specific identification.

6.2.1 Recognizing Novel Objects

Classifying objects at more general levels can serve a number of useful roles. Recognition in general allows us to use the observed image of an object to access additional information associated with the object in question, but not apparent in the image itself. Classification serves an important function in inferring likely properties of both known and novel objects, based on properties common to other objects in the same class. It is clearly useful to recognize, for instance, a tiger, and take an appropriate action, even when individual identification is not possible. Similarly, it is clearly useful to be able to classify a novel object as a car, or a person, and so on, even if we have not seen the particular individual before. The ability to recognize objects at different levels of generality is therefore an important aspect of a recognition system.

6.2.2 Classification on the Way to Identification

A second useful role of classification is as an intermediate stage on the way to more specific identification. Classification can aid identification in a number of ways.

First, classification can restrict the space of relevant object models. The recognition schemes discussed in previous chapters often assume that a candidate object model has been selected, and the task of the recognition system is to either accept or reject the candidate model. When the number of object models is small, it may be possible to consider them all, either in parallel or sequentially, in search of the best matching model. When the number of object models is large, it becomes desirable to perform a fast filtering stage that will allow the system to focus on the more likely object models. (This stage is sometimes called "indexing" in computer vision.) Classification can therefore increase the efficiency of the recognition process, by directing subsequent processing stages to the appropriate class of models. If the image can be classified, for example, as representing a face, without identifying the individual face, then subsequent processing stages can be directed to specific face models, rather than to models of other 3-D objects.

Additional saving can be obtained by applying some of the stages in the recognition process, such as image-to-model correspondence, or recovering the alignment transformation, to some prototypical member, or a representative of the class in question, rather than to each individual separately. We will see below some specific examples of using this approach.

Classification can also allow the recognition system to use class-specific information in the recognition process. In the alignment approach, recognition involves the application of compensation processes that reconcile the differences between the viewed object and the corresponding stored model. Some of the transformations that an object may undergo are specific to a particular class of objects. For example, faces can be distorted by facial expressions that are specific to this class of objects. Following classification, information regarding the pertinent set of transformations can be used for the recognition of specific individuals within the class.

Finally, classification can help to generalize from limited object-specific information. For example, suppose that we have seen a single image of a novel face. Will we be able to generalize and identify this face when seen from a different direction, under different illumination, and with a different facial expression? We have seen already that generalization is possible if we have sufficient information about the face in question, for example, in the form of several corresponding views. But even if this information is not available, it is still possible to use more general knowledge about faces to fill in the missing information and to generalize from a single view to novel conditions. For example, many faces have a generally similar 3-D shape, and this can be used to deal with the expected effects of viewing direction and illumination. Similarly, knowledge about common facial expressions can be used in the recognition of an individual face. In this manner, it will become possible to identify the smiling face of a person even if we have not seen this particular person smiling in the past.

We conclude that classification is a useful intermediate stage on the way to more specific identification. It restricts the space of relevant models, allows substantial saving in terms of the correspondence and alignment processes required, allows the use of class-specific information, and makes it possible to generalize from restricted object-specific information. The role of classification is discussed further in the next two sections. We first examine the use of class-level processing in identification and its use for generalization. We will then see how, by employing class prototypes, considerable saving can be obtained in performing correspondence and alignment with multiple objects.

6.3   Class-based Processing

On the way from classification to identification, the system can use specific information, associated with the class in question, to aid the recognition process. The role played by such class-based processing is probably much more significant than what is currently used in recognition systems.

We have addressed several aspects of the use of class-based processing in a study by Y. Moses (1993, Moses, Edelman & Ullman 1993a,b) of face identification. The study used both upright and inverted faces, and compared the ability to generalize across new illumination conditions and novel viewing directions. To test the generalization capacity, subjects were first trained to recognize individual images of unfamiliar faces, in either upright or inverted position.

In each experimental session, three images were used at the training stage, each depicting a different person. The face images were all of males, with the hair line covered, and without distinctive features such as glasses, beard, and the like. After a short training period, the subject learned to identify the three images without errors. He, or she, was then tested on new images of the same three individuals. These new images were taken under different illumination conditions and viewing directions. Altogether,

five different viewing directions were used, separated by 17 degrees
of rotation about the vertical axis, and at each viewing direction
four different illumination conditions were employed.

The first interesting finding was the degree of successful generalization to new viewing conditions. Correct identification was
obtained for over 97% of the new images. In terms of viewing
directions, the maximal separation between the training view and
the test views was 54 degrees, and even for this large angular separation generalization was as good as for the other new views.
As discussed in chapter 1, this generalization capacity cannot be
captured by simple methods of image comparison. The changes
induced in the test images by the variations in viewing direction
and illumination conditions were large, typically larger than the
differences between images of different individuals.

It is particularly remarkable that such good generalization was
possible on the basis of a single image for each face. In previous chapters we have discussed methods that can generalize well
across large variations in viewing direction. The image combination method can obtain good generalization, but not on the basis
of a single image. The 3-D alignment method can similarly obtain
good generalization, provided that an accurate 3-D model is available to the system. It is unlikely that an accurate 3-D model could
be obtained, however, based on a single face image. In principle,
a 3-D model for each given face could be recovered using shape-
from-shading methods (Horn & Brooks 1989), but such methods
are unlikely to be accurate enough to capture the required individual differences between similar faces.

How, then, can good generalization be obtained without the
benefit of multiple images, or an accurate individual 3-D model?
As suggested above, the answer lies in the appropriate use of class-
based processing. It is possible to use some properties that are
common to faces in general in order to help the identification of a
specific face under novel viewing position and illumination. This
raises the following problem: given a new object that belongs to
a familiar object class, how do we use class properties to com-

pensate for variations in novel views of the object? I think that this problem is fundamental to object recognition in general, and should be studied further. The possibilities are rich, and I will mention here only a number of general possibilities. One can use, for example, the 3-D shape of a typical face and its typical transformations, combined with the image of an individual face, to generalize to novel views of the specific individual. One can use a general face model to distinguish in the image between meaningful contours and accidental contours that arise from cast and attached shadows (Cavanagh 1991). It may also be possible to use a specialized shape-from-shading computation that incorporates knowledge about the reflectance properties as well as general shape of typical faces to recover 3-D shape form a single face image.

The study by Moses *et al.* also compared generalization capacity for upright and inverted faces. It is well known that inverted faces are more difficult to recognize than upright ones. This relative difficulty was not, however, of direct concern in this study. The focus was on generalization capacity from familiar to novel views. Subjects were trained to recognize the inverted faces of three different individuals. Because the task was more difficult, the training took somewhat longer, but the final recognition performance on the training set was similar to that of the upright faces. New images were then introduced, showing the same faces but from different viewing directions and under different illumination. The illumination was kept in the horizontal plane, to avoid possible effects of illumination from above *vs.* illumination from below. When tested with the new images, depicting the same faces under different illumination conditions and from novel viewing directions, performance deteriorated, and was significantly worse than the performance for upright faces. For example, the average recognition score for novel viewing conditions was 86.5% compared with 97% for upright faces. For the inverted faces, recognition scores dropped monotonically with changes in orientation or illumination from the original training view. In contrast, for the upright faces there was no significant effect of illumination or viewing position differences over the ranges tested.

These differences in generalization capacity for upright and inverted faces again support the involvement of class-based processes in face identification. Since the images used in the upright and inverted conditions were physically identical, differences in generalization capacity must reflect some differences in the processing applied to these two families of images. Consider, for example, the effect of illumination changes. Theories of recognition often assume that illumination effects can be compensated for by pre-processing the image, in particular by detecting intensity edges and using the resulting edge contours instead of the original grey level image in later recognition stages. This edge-detection process tends to filter out the effects of slow illumination gradients and emphasizes sharp, stable, transitions. But an operation of this type is universal in nature: it does not depend on the particular image used, and it should apply equally well for upright and inverted images. The use of universal shape-from-shading methods suffers from the same limitation. If some general shape-from-shading were used to extract 3-D shape that is independent of illumination effects, then again the same compensation should have applied to both types of images.

The compensation for illumination cannot be, therefore, entirely universal in nature. Instead, it is reasonable to conclude that some class-based processing is involved. According to this view, our visual system has some compensation methods that are particularly effective in compensating for illumination effects for familiar classes of objects, such as upright faces, and are less effective for inverted faces, and for other unfamiliar classes.

In conclusion, class-based processes can play a useful role in identification. According to this view, classification can often precede more specific identification in the chain of processing, although it is likely that a well-known view of a familiar object will still be identified immediately, without the intermediacy of the classification process. If some general level of classification comes first, it will reduce the demands for detailed individual models, and will allow the application of class-specific processing.

The use of class-based processes in recognition can be contrasted with more general, or universal processing on the one hand, and with more specific, or object-based processing on the other (Moses 1993, Moses & Ullman 1991). At the universal level, the processing applies equally well to all objects, it is not restricted to a particular object or a restricted class of objects. The process of edge detection is an example of the universal mode of processing. It can be applied to all input images, and can, under some conditions, produce a representation that is more invariant to the effects of illumination changes. It can also be augmented with additional features of the image intensity distribution, such as intensity ridges and valleys, which are sometimes more stable than intensity edges (Moses 1993). Such processes can be useful; however, they are insufficient for the purpose of recognition.

At the other extreme lies the object-based level. Here, generalization depends on the specific model of an individual object. The linear combination method, for instance, uses a specific object model, in the form of several corresponding images (or pictorial representations), to recognize novel views of this particular object. In between the universal and object-specific level lie generalization methods at the class level. As discussed above, these methods use properties common to a class of objects, such as the typical 3-D shape or reflectance properties of human faces, in the recognition process of a particular individual in this class. These methods are not restricted to an individual object, nor are they applicable to all objects, but they can use some general properties of a class of objects to help the recognition of a specific object in the class.

The class-based level of processing raises many interesting new questions. For example, we can ask how to represent information that pertains to a class of objects, such as faces in general; how to use, for instance, the shape of a typical face in the identification of a specific individual; or how a shape-from-shading method can be combined with face-specific information to recover face shapes

from shaded images. Another question has to do with the classification itself. Before using face-specific information, we must be
able to classify the viewed object as a face image, using a more
general set of processes. We will return to this question later in
this chapter.

6.4   Using Class Prototypes

We mentioned above that classification can aid identification by
reducing the amount of processing that needs to be performed
when comparing an object with multiple internal models. By performing some of the processing stages, such as correspondence
and alignment, at the class level, one can avoid duplicating the
effort for each individual object-model within the class. An example of this use is provided by a method developed by R. Basri,
(1992) within the framework of the image combination approach
to recognition. In this method, objects are matched first with
class-prototypes, and this matching can drastically reduce the
computation required to match the image with all the individual
members of the relevant class.

In this prototype-based method, objects are grouped into classes,
such as a class of faces, cars, chairs, and the like. Each group of
similar objects is represented by a single class prototype. Recall
that in the image combination scheme, an individual object is
represented by a set of corresponding images. Mathematically, we
can think of each object-image as a set of n feature points. An
object model contains several images with known correspondence
between them. A prototype is represented in a similar way: it is
a typical, or average, member of a class of similar objects, also
represented by a small number of corresponding images. Basri's
formulation gives a method for generating an optimal prototype
for a given collection of models, but we will not consider this construction here. We will simply take the prototype to be some
average member of the class in question. It is assumed in this
method that the objects that constitute a class are sufficiently

similar, so that a natural correspondence can be established between different objects in the class. For example, for different faces a correspondence can be established between similar feature points, such as the inner and outer corners of the eyes, the mouth, and the like. This requirement places a limit on the objects that can be grouped together within a single class. If the objects are too different, so that it becomes difficult to establish correspondence between them, then they cannot belong to a single class, and a new class must be formed. The correspondence between the prototype and individual members of the class, and the division into distinct classes, is of course a part of the learning stage, rather than of the actual recognition process.

The first stage in recognizing a new input image consists of comparing it against the class prototypes, rather than against the individual objects. This is done according to the usual image combination method: an image-to-model correspondence of a small number of point or line features is established, the alignment transformation is recovered, and applied to the model. (The transformation is defined in this method by the coefficients of the image combination that brings the model into the closest agreement with the image.) The only difference with respect to the usual image combination method is that here we should not expect the match to be close to perfect: since a prototype is used instead of the precise object model, the method should be more tolerant to mismatches at this stage. The best matching prototype is identified, and further processing is then limited to the class represented by this prototype. On some occasions the classification may happen to be ambiguous, that is, a number of prototypes may compete for the best match. In this case, subsequent processing will be directed to a number of classes rather than a single one.

We have now restricted our attention to the objects within a single class. It may appear at first sight that we now have to repeat the process and test each of the objects in the class. For each candidate object, this test requires establishing a correspondence, and then recovering and applying the best alignment transformation. The main advantage of the scheme is that both the individual correspondence and the recovery of the appropriate alignment transformations are in fact superfluous. With respect to correspondence, the prototype and individual models are already in correspondence, and a single correspondence, between the image and the prototype, has been established in the classification stage. Correspondence with all other members of the same class is immediately established by the composition of these two mappings. With regards to the alignment transformation, Basri has shown that it is possible to pre-align the models in the class with respect to their prototype in such a manner that exactly the same transformation that was used to align the prototype with the image also applies to each of the individual models in the class. In other words, the same set of coefficients that was used to best align the prototype with the new image, can be applied without modifications to each of the individual models in the class.

Intuitively, the pre-alignment of an individual model with respect to its class representative means that both are represented by a similar set of views, taken from similar viewing directions with respect to the objects. Mathematically, this pre-alignment is obtained in the following manner. Suppose that the $i'th$ model of a given class is represented by the matrix M_i. This M_i has k columns, representing k views of the object, and each column contains $2n$ numbers, the x and y coordinates of n points in the object. In a similar manner, P is a $n \times k$ matrix representing the class prototype. Pre-alignment is then obtained by replacing each original model M_i by a new version $\hat{M}_i$, defined by the formula:

$$\hat{M}_i = M_i(P^+M_i)^+$$

where A^+ stands for the pseudo-inverse of the matrix A. If the models are pre-aligned in this manner, then the optimal set of coefficients needed to align the prototype with any given image, also applies, without modifications, to all the individual models in the class.

This method demonstrates in an elegant manner some of the benefits of the classification stage. It should be regarded as an illustrative example, using the specific formulation of the image combination method. However, alternative methods can also benefit from an analogous use of the classification stage. The method focuses on overcoming some bottleneck stages in the computation, and it can substantially reduce the amount of processing required to deal with large collections of objects. As discussed above, there are also additional uses of classification that are important in recognition but were not considered in this example of using class prototypes, such as the use of special transformations that are specific to a certain class of objects (such as facial expressions in the case of face recognition).

6.5   Pictorial Classification

In the case of object identification, an accurate match can be obtained between the model and the viewed object, or their corresponding pictorial descriptions. The reason is that we can have in this case an accurate object-model, and a restricted set of transformations. Therefore, after compensating for the transformations, we can expect the match between the object and the model to be accurate. Additional variations are handled by the use of abstractions that allow the match to take place at a more abstract level than the precise image features.

Can a similar approach apply also to the classification stage? The general goal will be to use a similar set of processes and to match the input image against a prototypical representative, or a number of representatives, of the class in question. The answer is not immediately evident, because in classification we do not have an accurate model, but only a general rough model that represents different individual objects. We cannot expect, therefore, an accurate match between the viewed object and the class prototype, and it is unclear whether the quality of match will be sufficient for classification. One might suspect that in order to capture the essence of a class, the common aspects of the set of faces, airplanes, cats, and so on, one should employ instead of the pictorial approach a more complex, symbolic, and reasoning-like process, perhaps using functional considerations, that is, reasoning about the likely function of the viewed object (Stark & Bowyer 1991).

As mentioned above, it seems that, at least for biological systems, classification is in fact a simpler, more immediate and primitive process than precise identification. It also seems significant in this regard that classification can be obtained from highly reduced images. One can often recognize that a small, low-resolution image contains an object such as a person, a bird, some sort of a car, and so on, even when details and 3-D information are severely reduced. This suggests that a rough pictorial comparison, without detailed 3-D information, is often sufficient for useful classification. Finally, it is also appealing to consider classification and identification as similar processes, with no sharp boundary separating them. If identification is essentially refined classification, rather than a different process, then similar approaches should be applicable to both processes. Since the alignment of pictorial descriptions was suggested as an important component of visual identification, it is of interest to explore the applicability of a simple, fast pictorial approach to object classification.

Some initial computational experiments carried out by Y. Yolles (1996) support the feasibility of such a pictorial approach to classification. Figures 6.1 and 6.2, 6.3 show examples of classifications produced by this experimental scheme.

Figure 6.1 shows examples of objects that were stored in the system's database. About 2000 images of different object classes were stored, and each class contained several different examples (such as several cows, helicopters, cars, etc.) The figure also shows some examples of new input images that the system was required to classify, such as a cow, turtle, lion, toad, etc. that were different from images in the same class already stored in the system's database.

Figure 6.1
Pictorial classification: examples of class-representative stored in the database,
and of new images to be classified.

Figure 6.2
Pictorial classification: examples of classification outputs produced by the classification system. The first image in each row is the input pattern to be classified. The other images are the first four images retrieved by the system in order of increased distance from the input image.

Figure 6.3
Pictorial classification: additional examples. The first image in each row is
the input pattern to be classified. The other images are the first four images
retrieved by the system in order of increased distance from the input image.

Classification of a new input image proceeded along the following lines. The input image was matched against all the images stored in the database. Prior to the match, the image was normalized to bring it into alignment with the stored patterns. The alignment was obtained by extracting the pattern's main orientation, drawing a bounding box around the pattern, and then transforming the box to align with a canonical rectangle (that is, a rectangle of some fixed dimensions). In addition, the input pattern was also mirror-reflected about the vertical axis, so that both the original image and its mirror reflection were matched against the stored patterns. This reflection allows the system to generalize and classify a pattern after being exposed only to a mirror-reflected version of a similar pattern.

It is interesting to note that this capacity to generalize across mirror reflections seems to be an innate capacity of even relatively simple visual systems. Experiments on pattern recognition in animals revealed that they tend to generalize spontaneously to mirror-reflected versions of familiar patterns, and often have difficulties distinguishing a learned pattern from its mirror-reflection, even if the mirror reflected version had never been seen by the animal. This generalization holds for reflection about the vertical, but not the horizontal axis (Sutherland 1960). Human observers also have a similar tendency to generalize from familiar views to mirror-reflected ones (Rock, Wheeler, & Tudor 1989). In physiological studies (Logothetis, Pauls & Poggio 1995), cells were found in the inferior temporal area of the monkey that also exhibit generalization to mirror reflected patterns. After training the animal to recognize a particular view of a 3-D object, some cells responded specifically to the trained view, but also to the same view reflected about the vertical axis.

In Yolles' system, the matching of an input and stored patterns used a comparison measure that was designed to be insensitive to small image distortions, by combining 2-D distances and orientation differences, as described below. This measure was applied to edge representations of the two images. In the stored models, only a subset of the pattern edges, usually the external bounding contours, were used for the comparison; less stable internal contours were not used in the comparison. For the purpose of the comparison, each contour was considered to be composed of many small contour elements, each having a position and orientation. The distance between two such elements was taken to be a combination of the distance between their midpoints and their orientation difference. (The sign of the contrast across the edge was also taken into account; matching was not allowed between edge elements with opposing contrasts.) This is a simple example of a more general "feature distance," where the distance between the elements combines their differences along several dimensions, including orientation, contrast, perhaps color, and the like. Each element in the model was then matched with its nearest neighbor in the input pattern where "nearest" was determined by the feature distance, rather than the 2-D distance alone. Finally, the overall distance between the two patterns was given simply by the total distance between their corresponding elements. The main advantage of this comparison measure is its tolerance to small displacement, rotation, scaling, and other distortions of patterns, and it proved better than, for example, just summing the point-to-point distances across the contours.

The scheme is a simplified one—it combines in a crude manner elements of alignment with simple pictorial comparison, and it also used object parts and abstract labels in a rudimentary manner. More refined versions of the alignment and matching stages, together with other extensions discussed later in this chapter, are clearly needed for the system to be applied under more complex conditions. It is instructive to see, however, that even in this simplified form the scheme produces interesting, sometimes surprising, classifications.

Figures 6.2 and 6.3 show examples of images classified by this scheme. In each panel, the left column (with the number "0" underneath) shows the input pattern to be classified. The other images in each row show the first four patterns retrieved by the system, in order of increasing distance measure from the input pattern. In other words, if the patterns stored in the database are considered as simplified class representatives, then the figure shows for each case the first four representatives retrieved from the entire store of patterns. The scheme makes some interesting mistakes, but on the whole, the patterns of the appropriate class are retrieved in almost all instances.

Alternative Schemes   One can also consider an alternative, and quite natural, method of using an alignment-like method for performing classification. In recognizing rigid 3-D objects, the class of allowable transformations is limited to simple rigid transformations in space. One way of dealing with classes rather than individual objects could be through the use of a more extended set of transformations. For example, some non-rigid distortions could be included to allow the transformation of one car-shape into another, or to distort an individual face into another one (Shapira 1990, Shapira & Ullman 1991). A drawback of such an approach is that classification becomes more complex than identification, rather than a simpler, more primitive task. The alignment problem will now have additional degrees of freedom, and the differences between the viewed object and the stored model will become more complicated to compensate for. In the simple pictorial comparison described above, complex transformations are not compensated for. As a result, the match obtained between the image and model representations will be less accurate. The residual inaccuracy is treated by using a similarity measure that is tolerant to local distortions, and by the use of abstractions that do not rely on a precise pictorial match. Giving up accurate matching reduces the sensitivity of the process to small differences between objects; this is a serious shortcoming for individual identification, but not necessarily for classification. It also increases the risk of matching the viewed object with an incorrect class representative, or, instead of obtaining a single match, a number of possible matches will be obtained, as happened in some of the examples in figure

6.2, 6.3. Provided that the number of possibilities is not too large, this is not a serious drawback, since more specific processing could now be applied to distinguish between the remaining alternatives.

Another possible approach is not to use an alignment scheme at all, but to use instead structural descriptions, such as the RBC description scheme developed by Biederman (1985). This approach has some appeal, since at the class level objects often share some general structural similarity, and in some cases a simple type of structural description may be used. One drawback for the general use of such a method is, again, the problem of relative complexity: initial classification is required to be fast and simple, but recovering a structural description in terms of 3-D primitives can be a demanding task. Classification from reduced images also appears to be more compatible with simple pictorial comparison than with 3-D structural descriptions. It is entirely possible that classification can be obtained by more than a single route. It seems, however, that at the heart of the matter there should be a relatively simple, direct scheme, and this is the main reason for focusing on pictorial matches of the type discussed above.

The results of Yolles' study suggest that relatively simple pictorial comparisons can in fact begin to achieve useful classification. However, the scheme as described above is certainly too simplified. A number of possible extensions are therefore discussed in the next section.

6.5.1   Pictorial Classification: Extensions

Abstractions   An important aspect of recognition, not used in the scheme as outlined above, is the use of abstractions. As discussed in the context of recognition by alignment, it is not enough to limit the comparison of the image and the stored models to the concrete level of matching individual edges, contours, and other image features. The use of abstractions is even more important in classification, compared with identification, due to the differences between individuals in the same class. For example, a deer has antlers, but their precise shape changes among individual mem-

bers of the class. In pictorial classification, the deer class will be
represented by one or more prototypical members, rather than,
for example, a list of distinguishing characteristics of the class. In
matching an individual deer with the class representative, it will
be desirable to use abstract descriptors that will allow the matching of different antlers that do not have exactly the same shape,
but still share a common general shape and branching pattern.

What type of abstract descriptors should be used? This appears to be an important open question in recognition. One common approach that can be regarded as a form of abstraction is
to use multiple-resolution representations. In this approach, a
given object is represented simultaneously at several resolution
levels. Lower resolution representations are typically produced by
progressively blurring the original, high resolution, representation
using gaussians, gabor filters, or the wavelet transform. (Burt &
Adelson 1983, Mallat 1989, Marr & Hildreth 1980, Rosenfeld &
Kak 1982, Witkin 1985). Alternatively, smoothing can be applied
to the contour representation itself (Brady 1984). The low resolution version ignores some of the fine details, and therefore patterns
can match at this level without a tight agreement in the detailed
high-resolution structure. Reduced resolution is, however, only
one possible form of abstraction, and not always the most appropriate one. One could use other types of "abstract labels" along
the lines discussed in chapter 3. In addition to shape abstraction,
other properties, such as color or texture, could also be used to
form abstractions. It will be of interest to study this problem further, and to produce eventually a better theory of abstraction and
its use in classification.

Alignment   The alignment used in the simplified scheme above
is too simplified. It compensated primarily for position, orientation, and scale (separately in two orthogonal directions). In
extending the use of alignment, one can consider, in particular,
the use of model-specific alignment. In a manner similar to the
alignment schemes already discussed, the class prototype can con-

tain information about 3-D structure, as well as possible distortions. For example, a face prototype, and not just the model of an individual face, can contain information about the 3-D shape of a typical face, as well as information about distortions that can occur with facial expressions.

Another problem with the simplified alignment is that it will be sensitive to occlusion, since it relies on the overall dimensions of the object. The use of parts, discussed below, can help in this regard, but it does not by itself provide a full solution to this problem.

The Use of Parts   A third important extension has to do with the use of parts. Again, this is useful for both identification and classification, but becomes more important at the classification level. Because of the intrinsic shape variability, the match between a specific object and a class prototype may be confined initially to only a part of the object. It is therefore desirable for the recognition scheme to be sensitive to a partial match, and also to be able to use the partial match as a starting point and then extend it to additional parts. For example, in matching an animal model, initially only the head may match well, and this should be used to extend the match to the body as well.

Class Boundaries   Finally, a more comprehensive classification scheme is likely to include some specialized means for handling objects that are close to the boundary between two classes. For example, the distinction between two similar animals, or two similar hand-written numerals, such as a "4" and a "9" that can be quite close in shape, may not be obtainable by using the more general classification process. The problem can be overcome in part by storing in the system additional models, for instance, some distorted 4's and 9's, rather than a single class prototype, and in part it may require the triggering of specialized routines (discussed in chapter 9) that can perform disambiguating tasks, such as testing for continuity, closure, and the like, of different parts of the figure.

6.6   Evidence from Psychology and Biology

The discussion above made a number of general points about classification. First, compared with identification, it is a simpler, more immediate task. Second, in terms of the underlying process, it is closely related to identification, and uses some form of aligning pictorial descriptions, Third, classification aids identification by restricting the domain of relevant models, and by the use of class-level processing.

Immediateness of Classification   From a theoretical standpoint, classification could either precede identification, or follow it at a subsequent stage. I have described above the usefulness of classification as a step on the way to more precise identification. One can also consider, however, the opposite point of view, namely, that classification follows identification rather than precedes it. It is possible to classify an object as a "car" for instance, by first matching it against a specific individual model. Having identified it as an instance of a "Chevrolet," say, one can then use more general stored knowledge, namely, that a Chevrolet is a type of car, to then reach the classification stage, and infer that the object is in fact a member of the more general "car" class.

Current recognition schemes that are designed to obtain individual identification could in principle perform classification in this manner. Physiological and biological evidence suggest, however, that as far as the human visual system is concerned, classification is the simpler and more immediate stage in the recognition process.

On the psychological side, problems related to visual classification were studied by E. Rosch and her co-workers (Rosch 1975, Rosch et al. 1976). They found, for example, that recognition is fastest at the level of what they term "basic level classification." This is an intermediate level of classification, such as a car, a guitar, an apple, and so on. It is more general than individual identification, such as a particular make of car, a classical guitar, etc., but more specific than so-called "super-ordinate" classes, such as vehicles, fruits, or musical instruments. The basic level classes are also the categories that people tend to use spontaneously, when they have to name a viewed object. They are also the first to appear during development—children tend to use these categories before they master more specific distinctions, or more general categorizations. The use of super-ordinate categories, for example, that both cars and airplanes belong to the more general class of vehicles, is more cognitive than perceptual in nature. Such categorization is probably an example where classification in fact follows rather than precedes the basic recognition process.

On the biological side, there is an extensive literature on the effects of different types of brain lesions on recognition and classification (Damasio & Damasio 1993, Farah 1990, 1991, Humphreys & Riddoch 1987, Luria 1980, Warrington & Taylor 1978). The details of these interesting studies lie beyond the current discussion. Regarding the immediateness of classification, however, a finding that seems to be quite general in nature is that specific identification is more susceptible to different types of lesions to the visual system, compared with more general classification. Lesions to the temporal cortex, as a result of accidents, viral infections, and other causes, can lead to difficulty in the visual recognition of objects. These problems can take many forms, but in general, the ability to identify individual objects is lost more easily than more general classification. In recognizing faces, for instance, the ability to recognize an image as a face, distinguish between males and females, or major age groups, is often retained even when the ability to identify individuals is severely impaired.

The patient Boswell is a well-known example of the effects of a relatively large lesion to the temporal cortex regions, including medial, polar, and inferotemporal regions (Damasio & Damasio 1993). This patient is unable to recognize faces of family and friends, unique places, or objects. He can, however, recognize them at the more general class level, such as faces, houses, cars, and the like. He can usually assign objects to general, super-ordinate categories, such as a "tool" for different types of tools.

He often uses basic level classes, but in some cases he uses only very general categories, such as "animal" for pictures of a zebra or a camel. It is interesting that Boswell can also recognize correctly facial expressions of both familiar and unfamiliar faces, supporting the notion that facial expressions are handled by class-based processes.

The specific effects of a particular lesion to the visual system can be quite complex. In many cases, however, the deficit associated with unique identification is considerably more pronounced than with basic level classification. This pattern is consistent with the general notion that classification is more basic and immediate than identification.

Pictorial Classification   Regarding the pictorial nature of the classification stage, the evidence is not clear-cut. Rosch, for example, concluded from several experiments that the basic-level classes are represented in a pictorial manner, and more general conceptual categories (such as "vehicles") are no longer pictorial in nature. The experiments showed, for instance, that at the basic level it is possible to recognize a picture generated by averaging members of the class. In fact, the average image is often a good exemplar of the class in question. This kind of pictorial averaging is also possible at the subordinate level (that is, more specific classification), but not at the super-ordinate level. Related results were obtained in studies of classification by young infants (Bomba & Siqueland 1983, Eimas & Miller 1990, Strauss 1979). For example, in a study by Strauss (1979), ten-month old infants were shown a collection of faces that differed along several dimensions, such as the width of the face, separation of the eyes, or nose length. In a subsequent recognition test, the infants treated the average face as the most familiar stimulus seen, although the average face was not presented during the training phase.

In another experiment by Rosch, the task was to detect an object in noisy images. It was found that when the name of the object in the image was given in advance, the task became easier.

This facilitation occurred when the class name was at the basic level classification, such as a "guitar," but not at the more general level, such as a "musical instrument." This is consistent with the notion that basic classes are associated with a typical pictorial representation that can be used when the class name is given. The conclusion from these and related experiments was that basic level classes are represented by some type of pictorial representation. More conceptual classes, such as "furnitures" or "musical instruments" are treated in a different, non-pictorial manner.

Other psychological experiments were taken to support the use of structural descriptions in recognition. For example, Warrington and her collaborators (Warrington & Taylor 1978, Warrington & James 1986) found that people with right posterior lesions tend to have difficulties with non-conventional views of objects, such as objects where the main axis of elongation has been severely foreshortened. This was taken (Marr & Nishihara 1978, Marr 1982) as evidence in support of axis-based structural descriptions. However, other schemes, including alignment, may equally suffer when the object's main axis of elongation is no longer apparent in the image, since this axis is a useful cue for alignment. Furthermore, it appears that the problem of unusual views is more general than the foreshortening of the major axis. The lesion causes, in general, a "narrower span" of perceptual classification. That is, the patients generalize less from a known, or a typical, member of the class. This happens also with meaningless 2-D shapes, suggesting that the problem may lie in the use of some alignment and compensation processes, rather than in the use of 3-D axis-based descriptions. Along the same line, changes in illumination (in recognizing faces) is as effective as changing viewing direction in eliciting recognition deficits in these patients. Again, the problem apparently lies with the ability to compensate for transformations in general, and not necessarily with the ability to create axis-based structural descriptions.

The Use of Classification for Identification It was suggested above that classification can aid more specific identification by reducing the domain of individual models to be considered, and by allowing the use of class-based processing. I have mentioned above an example of a psychophysical study supporting the role of class-level processing in compensating for viewing position and illumination. There are also psychological findings supporting in a more general way the role of classification in subsequent recognition.

An example is the study of M. Potter (1975) using the technique called RSVP—Rapid Sequential Visual Presentation. Usually, when images are shown at a rapid rate of three views per second, half of them do not even look familiar a few minutes later. Potter presented images sequentially at a much faster rate—up to eight per second. Subjects were given a target to look for, and were asked to press a lever when the target appeared. It was found that just giving the class name of the target was as useful in performing the task as showing the precise target in advance. Recognition rates became very high, about 80% at eight images per second, and reaching almost perfect performance at six images a second. It seems, therefore, that knowledge about the general class can facilitate subsequent recognition.

6.7 Are Classes in the World or in Our Head?

When it comes to classification, one general issue that is of interest to consider is how classes are determined.

One view is that classes are "out there," independent of our own perception: "dogs" and "trees" exist in the world as two distinct classes of objects, whether we observe them or not. A certain order exists in the set of objects, and our perceptual system evolved to capture and use it. Some objects, such as the set of all dogs, are relatively similar to one another, and quite different from members of the class of all trees. The clustering of objects into distinct classes is, in this view, objectively defined in the world, independent of the perceiver. The task of a visual recognition system is to detect and faithfully represent these classes, based on their visual images. The main problem with this view is that it appears difficult to define and justify an absolute, objective measure of similarity between objects in the world.

The opposing view is that the division of objects into classes and sub-classes is an order that the perceiver is imposing upon the environment; it is invented rather than discovered. In this view, the classification is determined by the perceptual apparatus rather than the objects themselves. For a given visual system (and other modalities as well; see, for example, classification in the olfactory domain, Ambros-Ingerson, Granger, & Lynch, 1990) the sensory data produced by objects are not just an unstructured collection. Object-images will tend to form clusters that can be taken as the basis for forming classes. Clusters are not objective, but induced by the perceptual machinery. A problem with this view is that it ignores the utility of classes and their relations to objects and their properties. Classes are not just haphazard collections of objects with similar images, but they tend to be composed of objects with some shared properties.

It seems to me that, for the purpose of visual recognition, the natural place to start are classes of objects in the world that exist as "relative classes" rather than "absolute classes." This means that rather than some absolute, objective classes, the formation of object classes depends on a selected set of attributes of interest. For a biological system, attributes of interest may depend on distinctions such as whether the objects are edible or not, whether or not they can move on their own, and how fast, whether they are graspable, and so on. Given a set of attributes, a measure of similarity between objects can be defined, and this can lead to the formation of natural clusters of objects that share similar attributes (Shepard 1987). This clustering is defined in the world, not in the image, since the attributes of interest are not necessarily directly measurable in the image. The clustering depends, however, on the choice of relevant attributes; different attributes will give rise to different clustering. A visual system can then attempt to capture this classification, on the basis of the objects' images. From an evolutionary point of view, different classification systems may evolve, and the one that induces a more useful classification of objects in the world will become advantageous.

To make classification possible in the first place, there must exist some correlation between visual and non-visual attributes. If the objects in some hypothetical environment were all spheres of identical shape, only their properties were different (for instance, some were edible and others not), visual classification would not be possible. In this sense, classification is a world-property, that is, there are some general properties of the world that make visual classification possible. The world does not impose, however, a unique, correct classification. The classification depends on some desired criterion and the attributes of interest, and consequently the giraffe's scheme of classifying plants, for instance, may be different from ours, and more appropriate for its different requirements. At the same time, this does not imply that all classification systems are equally good: given a particular classification criterion some classification schemes can be judged as better than others.

In this view, then, classes are external, but in a relative rather than in an absolute sense. Perceptual systems evolve to reflect and capture useful class structures. Classification schemes can therefore be evaluated and compared, but not in an absolute sense, only relative to given classification criteria.

Conclusions Classification is an important process in its own right, since it allows us to deal effectively with novel objects and apply general class-related knowledge to these objects. Classification is also a useful stage on the way to more specific identification. It can be used to restrict the space of relevant models, it affords considerable saving in terms of the correspondence and alignment processes required, it allows the use of class-specific information, and it makes it possible to generalize from restricted object-specific information.

We have seen some possible methods for performing initial classification. However, we are still a long way from having effective classification methods that can deal with a wide range of natural objects. The development of classification methods, and the use of classification for more specific identification, appear to me as some of the most exciting directions for further studies in visual recognition.

6.8 The Organization of Recognition Memory

The use of classes imposes a certain structure on the organization of the memory used for recognition: related objects form object classes, and these classes are used to facilitate the recognition process. The relation between class and individual is not the only useful relation between object representations stored in recognition memory. In this section, I will briefly comment on additional relations between object representations and how they may be used in the recognition process. From a computational standpoint, problems related to the internal structure of the recognition memory have not yet been examined in detail. Because object recognition schemes were developed so far primarily to deal with small collections of objects, problems related to the structuring of a large number of object models have not been of major concern. We have seen already how class structures can play a useful role in dealing with large collections of objects. As we shall see below, the appropriate structuring of recognition memory could also be useful for dealing with natural scenes, occlusion, and flexible objects.

6.8.1 Part-Whole Relationships

Certain objects that can be recognized on their own can also form parts of larger, more complex objects. For example, an eye is an object that can be recognized in isolation, but it also constitutes a part of a face. It is reasonable to assume that both an eye and a face are somehow represented within our recognition memory. The two are intimately related, and therefore some form of association between the two representations could serve a useful role in their recognition. The two objects usually appear together in the image, and therefore the recognition of one can serve to suggest the presence of the other, together with its expected location, scale, and orientation.

Such part-whole relationships, as well as the relation between different parts, can be useful for dealing with occlusion. For example, an object may be heavily occluded, but the recognition of an unoccluded part could be used to identify the visible parts of the object. Similarly, this relationship can help in dealing with flexible or distorted objects. Due to the distortion, a match may be obtained initially only with a part of the object. The partial match can then be used to select likely object models, and to guide the subsequent matching of the model and the image.

6.8.2   Different Levels of Abstraction

We already mentioned the possibility that a given object may be represented at different levels of abstraction. For example, a coarse representation may be used to obtain a rough initial match, that can then guide the match of a more refined representation. In this case, we clearly want the different representations of the same object to be interrelated in recognition memory. The coarse-fine and part-whole relationships can also be used in combination. For example, an image may be classified first as a standing quadruped. At a subsequent stage, the animal's head can be matched against a number of different animal heads. This second stage combines a transition from a larger object to one of its parts, with a transition from a coarse to a more refined object model.

6.8.3   Object Configurations

Natural object recognition typically involves not the recognition of isolated objects, but recognizing objects in the context of complete scenes. There are strong correlations between objects found in typical scenes such as a living room, a street, or a beach. The presence of an object in a scene can therefore be used to make some object models more likely to appear in the same scene than others. When dealing with a large number of object models stored in recognition memory, examining with higher priority the more likely models will increase the overall efficiency of the recognition process.

The recognition of an object in a scene can not only suggest other probable objects, but also their expected location, size and orientation. The image of a head, for example, can suggest the presence of a hat primarily above the head, rather than at other locations in the scene, and this can be used in the recognition of the hat. Figure 6.4 from Green & Courtis (1966) provides some examples of the powerful effect of object configurations of this kind. As can be seen, many objects in these configurations—hands, a shirt, a glass, a purse, and others—are schematic and ambiguous. They are easily recognized, however, within the appropriate configurations.

This use of object configurations in the recognition process appears to be an important part of our ability to deal effectively with natural scenes. Clearly, a system that can make use of object configurations would be better off than a system that tries to deal with each object in the scene independently. Compared with the use of object parts, such as the eyes, nose, and mouth forming the parts of a face, object configurations within a scene are much more flexible and varied. It is therefore desirable to have a scheme that allows the recognition of one object in the scene to affect the recognition of another without relying on rigid predetermined configurations of specific objects.

A number of psychological studies (Biederman 1972, 1981, Biederman *et al.* 1982, Cave & Kosslyn 1993, Hock *et al.* 1978, Palmer 1975) have shown that the recognition of an object in a scene depends on the presence of other objects in the same scene. For example, Biederman found that recognizing an object in an unusual context, such as a fire hydrant in a bar scene, takes longer and is more prone to errors compared with the same object in a familiar context.

Figure 6.4
Object configurations. Many of the objects in the figures are schematic and ambiguous. They are still easily recognized, however, within the context of the appropriate configurations. From (Green & Curtis, 1966).

The effect of one object on the recognition of another was studied by M. Bar (Bar & Ullman 1993) using object-pairs rather than complete scenes. The experiment used pairs of objects taken from figure 6.4, such as a hat and a shoe, or a hat and a pair of glasses. Each pair contained one object that was relatively easy to recognize, and an object that was more difficult to recognize in isolation (as judged by response time and error rates). Observers were then asked to recognize the two objects presented simultaneously. Two interesting results emerged from this test. First, the recognition of the two objects presented together was faster and more accurate than the recognition of the more difficult object presented on its own (but slower than the easier object presented alone). Second, this beneficial effect depended upon the proper spatial relations between the objects: the hat facilitated the recognition of a pair of glasses below it, but had almost no effect when both objects were presented side by side. The results clearly indicate that the recognition of the first object helped to recognize the second one. The observed effect cannot be obtained by simply associating in memory objects that tend to appear together, since such an association will be independent of the scene's spatial structure. A more sophisticated mechanism that takes into account both the identity of the objects and their spatial relation is required.

In conclusion, the structure of recognition memory makes it possible to use the recognition of one object in the scene to help the recognition of related objects. This process probably plays an important role in the efficient recognition of objects in natural scenes. In the future, it will be of interest to study these aspects of the recognition process further, from both the computational and the psychological perspectives.

7 Image and Model Correspondence

Image-to-model correspondence is a fundamental aspect of recognition by alignment. In the alignment approach, the representations of the viewed object and the stored models maintain their pictorial nature. After compensating for the transformations separating the image and the appropriate internal model, corresponding parts of the two representations will be in close register. In addition to selecting the appropriate stored model, the recognition process in this approach is therefore also accompanied by the establishment of a match, or a mapping, between the image and model pictorial representations.

There are, however, essential differences in the manner correspondence is used in different alignment schemes. The most important difference is between the use of correspondence as a separate stage that drives the alignment process, and correspondence as a final outcome of the alignment process, a distinction that can be summarized as "correspondence first" versus "alignment first." In the former case, a correspondence is first established between selected features in the image and model representations. Based on this match, the alignment transformation is derived and applied to bring the two representations into register. We have seen examples of this approach, in both the 3-D alignment and the image combination methods. In the 3-D alignment method, a small number of corresponding features can be used to determine the transformation in space separating the image and model. Similarly, in the image combination method, corresponding features can be used to derive the parameters of the combination.

In the "alignment first" approach, transformations are applied without the prior establishment of image-to-model correspondence. For example, in the view combination approach, we can search through the space of image combination coefficients. When we hit upon the correct set of coefficients, we will also obtain a close match between the transformed internal model and the viewed image. This will be used to select the model in question, but will also generate, by bringing the two representations into register, a natural mapping between them. In this manner correspondence is eventually established, but it does not constitute a preliminary stage that drives the application of the aligning transformation. This mode of establishing image-to-model correspondence is also used in the deformable templates method (Yuille, Cohen, & Hallinan, 1989), discussed further below. Instead of using correspondence first, the method proceeds by modifying the transformation parameters of the deformable model until a close match is obtained with the input image.

In contrast with alignment, not all approaches to recognition include an image-to-model correspondence as an essential aspect of the recognition process. For example, various feed-forward neural network models of recognition (Fukushima 1986, 1988, Matan *et al.* 1992) proceed without establishing such correspondence. These networks typically represent the possible outcomes of the recognition process by a set of units in the output layer of the network. In recognizing hand-written characters, for example, different output units are used to represent the different characters (Matan *et al.* 1992). During the processing, activation proceeds in the network from layer to layer, leading to the activation of the output units. The result is then determined by the most active output units, but without establishing an explicit correspondence between the image and the model. When the computation is completed, we may know that the input was recognized by the network as an instance of the numeral "4," say, usually with some measure of confidence in the result, but without an explicit correspondence between the parts of the "4" in the image and in the model. Similarly, recognition by invariant properties also performs recognition without establishing image-to-model correspondence. The process proceeds by extracting a number of properties, followed by a classification of the resulting property vector, but without employing image-to-model correspondence.

Is image-to-model correspondence, then, really required for the purpose of recognition? It seems to me that correspondence is, in most cases, an integral aspect of the recognition process. When we recognize an object, we end up knowing not only the identity of the object, but we also know in detail which parts of the image correspond to different parts of the model. This can happen even when the image is a highly distorted version of the model: once we compensate for the distorting transformation, we end up with explicit knowledge about the relative location of the image part with respect to the model. This is illustrated in figure 7.1: the object in the figure is highly distorted, but we can recognize it and we clearly know how parts of the distorted object correspond to a typical example of the same object.

Image-to-model correspondence is also indicated by the fact that when different parts of the image are ambiguous on their own, once the entire object is recognized, the parts often become recognizable as well, based on their agreement with corresponding parts in the model. This is shown in figure 7.2. The top part of figure shows isolated parts of the face figure below. The parts on their own are difficult to recognize (they are, in fact, the eye and ear in the face), but they become recognizable when the entire figure is recognized as a face. Presumably, the recognition of the ambiguous parts relies on the correspondence with the appropriate parts in a stored face-model.

The ability to perform image-to-model correspondence is a useful one: it helps us to identify ambiguous subparts, and allows us to direct our attention to particular parts of the model. If there is a mismatch between a localized part of the image and the corresponding part in the model, the result is not merely an overall decrease in the quality of match between the two, but we can also localize the source of the mismatch and further inspect the corresponding region in the image.

Image-to-model correspondence is, therefore, an integral part of the recognition process. However, establishing the desired correspondence between the image and model is not an easy task. There are two major difficulties associated with this problem. The first has to do with establishing the correct correspondence between an image and a single internal model. Problems here include which features are selected for correspondence, and how

Figure 7.1
An image of a distorted object. Recognition of the object includes image-to-model correspondence as a part of the recognition process.

Figure 7.2
The parts in the top image are difficult to recognize in isolation. In the bottom image, the recognition of the same parts is based on their correspondence with the appropriate parts in a stored face-model.

to determine the match between image and model features. The second difficulty comes from the need to establish correspondence with not just one, but multiple internal models. To select the correct model, correspondence must be established between the viewed object and all the different candidate models that need be considered.

The issue of dealing with multiple internal models was considered briefly in the last chapter, in the context of classification. The use of classification may offer a good way to avoid unnecessary repetitions of the correspondence process. Correspondence between the viewed object and a class prototype can reduce the need for establishing multiple correspondence processes with individual members of the class in question. In this chapter we will concentrate therefore on the problem of establishing an image-to-model correspondence between a single model (that may represent a class prototype), and a viewed object. We will consider first methods for explicitly establishing correspondence between image and model features, and then consider the alternative of establishing a correspondence not as a separate stage, but as a search that forms a part of the alignment process.

Minimal and Full Alignment

In establishing image-to-model correspondence, a distinction can be made between two alternative methods: minimal correspondence, and full correspondence. The first uses a minimal number of corresponding features in the image and model. The second establishes a complete match between the two representations, and transforms one into the other.

In the minimal correspondence approach, the alignment transformation is determined by a small number of corresponding features in the model and the image. The features include pointwise features that are well localized in two dimensions, linear features, such as extended line segments or distinct orientations, and also 2-D regions in the model and the image (Basri & Jacobs 1995). Methods using this approach assume that the set of possible transformations is restricted, usually to rigid 3-D transformations with possible scaling, so that the correct transformation can be recovered using a small number of constraints. (Other families of transformations, such as 2-D Lie transformation groups were also considered, (Brockett 1989).) The selected transformation is then applied to the model or the image, and the resulting degree of match is evaluated. This approach has been used for 3-D alignment by Faugeras & Hebert (1986), Fischler & Bolles (1981), Huttenlocher & Ullman (1987), Shoham & Ullman (1988), Thompson & Mundy (1987), Ullman (1989). Minimal alignment can also be used in the context of the linear combination scheme: a small number of corresponding features is first used to determine the coefficients of the linear combination, the linear combination is then computed, and the result compared with the viewed image.

In the full correspondence approach, a complete match is established between the model and the image. This full match defines a distortion transformation that takes one representation into the other. The linear mapping scheme in section 5.3.3 is an example of a full alignment scheme. In full correspondence schemes, the set of transformations is usually not restricted to rigid transformations alone, complex non-rigid distortions are often included as well.

Full alignment is also needed in the context of the image combination method for another purpose—the construction of internal models. An internal model in the image combination scheme contains a small number of 2-D images, with a known correspondence between them. There is, however, a crucial difference between full alignment used in the recognition process itself and that used for model construction. Model construction can be a considerably slower and more elaborate process, that builds up gradually over time and practice. In contrast, the processes required during recognition must be fast and applicable to many models simultaneously. At the end of this chapter we will consider the problem of establishing correspondence for the purpose of model construction.

7.1   Feature Correspondence

The transformation separating the viewed object and stored model can often be recovered on the basis of a small number of matched image and model features. We have seen in previous chapters that in the case of rigid transformation and scaling, for instance, three features, defined by points and lines, are sufficient to determine the unknown transformation. Given a new image, we first extract from it a set of distinctive features such as corners, inflection points, blob centers, and the like. A similar set of features is also assumed to be associated with the stored model images. The recognition process then proceeds by matching image features with their counterparts in the model. This raises a correspondence problem, namely, how to identify the matching pairs of image and model features.

7.1.1   Successive Search

One possibility is to search through the possible pairings of image and model features, by trying and testing different sets of feature. In the case of a rigid transformation, for example, three feature points already determine the alignment transformation. Given a set P of feature points extracted from the image, and a set M of feature points in the model, a simple way to proceed is to test different triplets of matched features. We try, for example, to match image points p_1, p_2, p_3 with model points m_1, m_2, m_3. This putative pairing defines a transformation that is applied to the entire model. We then test the resulting match between the image and the transformed model. If the match is sufficiently close, the viewed object is considered a possible instance of the model. Otherwise, we proceed to select and test a different triplet of features.

If we know in advance that the projection of model points m_1, m_2, m_3, is guaranteed to appear somewhere in the image, we can keep the model points fixed, and search through different image points until the corresponding feature points are found. In general, however, some of the feature points we search for may be missing from the image, due to occlusion, shadows, noise, or some other failure to extract the features. In the general case, we must therefore search through a large space of possible pairings. If the model we test is in fact an incorrect one, we will have to search through a large number of possibilities before we can reject the model with certainty. Grimson and his colleagues have developed several recognition systems using variations of the search approach outlined above. A detailed description of these systems, together with an analysis of their complexity and performance is described in Grimson (1990a). A number of schemes have extended this approach to deal with possible errors in the measured location of the feature points (Baird 1985, Breuel 1992, Cass 1992). In this case, a model point m_i is not required to match image point p_i exactly. Due to the measurement errors, it is allowed to lie after the alignment transformation in a region surrounding p_i, usually assumed to take the form of a circle or a polygon. For a given pairing between model and image features, the problem is now to find a transformation that will take the model points into the appropriate regions. These methods usually solve this problem by exploring the "transformation space"—an abstract space of all possible 2-D or 3-D transformations that the object may undergo. They proceed by using the bounded error regions to intersect volumes in transformation space. These volumes separate regions of the space that cannot have a possible solution from regions where a solution may still be present. For the correct correspondence, this intersection method eventually results in a small volume, containing the set of all feasible transformations.

The intersection method above applies when the pairing between image and model features is already known. When the correspondence is unknown, one can use again the successive search approach. The difference between the bounded error and the error-free situation is that for each possible pairing we now have to determine a possible transformation based on the bounded error computation, rather than the simpler computation of the exact case. The required computations are quite elaborate, but methods were developed to make them more efficient by storing partial results and thus avoiding unnecessary repetitions in the computations of different possible pairings (Baird 1985, Breuel 1992, Cass 1992). The methods using the successive search approach can match a known model successfully to a sparse and noisy set of data. They do require, however, an extensive search of many different possible matches to obtain a correct solution, and an even more extensive search to reject a potential model. The requirement for an extensive search can be reduced by using some of the methods discussed below.

7.1.2   Pre-alignment

To cut down the search for corresponding image and model features, one possible approach is to use the method of model pre-alignment. This means that multiple copies of the same model are stored, for different alignment keys. An example of employing the pre-alignment method is a scheme by Lamdan, Schwartz, & Wolfson (1987) used for the recognition of planar objects. The treatment of flat objects is considerably easier than more general 3-D objects since the compensating transformations are simpler: the different views of a given object can all be obtained by applying affine transformations to the image (see appendix E). Unlike more general 3-D objects, one can therefore align an image by simply applying an affine 2-D transformation to either the image or the stored model.

The general idea of the method is to prepare and store a separate copy of the model for each possible choice of an alignment key (three feature points) in the image. Given a particular choice of an alignment key in the image, it is possible to bring the viewed object into a normalized form in terms of size, position, orientation and the like. Different choices of features will result, however, in different normalized forms of the object. We therefore consider, prior to recognition, all possible alignment keys in the model, and for each one store a separate copy of the model in a normalized form with respect to the alignment key in question. Given a new image, we extract a set of three feature points, use them to normalize the image, and compare the normalized image with all the model versions stored in memory.

More specifically, the pre-alignment method proceeds in the following manner. Given an alignment key of three (non-colinear) points, p_1, p_2, p_3, it is always possible to apply an affine transformation A that will map these points onto a fixed, "canonical" triplet of points, for example, the three points: $(0, 0), (1, 0), (0, 1)$. When A is applied to a model M, the result (in which p_1 is mapped to $(0, 0)$, p_2 to $(1, 0)$, p_3 to $(0, 1)$) is said to be in a canonical form. During the model construction phase, a copy of the model is stored in a canonical form for each triplet of possible alignment points. During recognition, a triplet of alignment features is identified in the image and used to bring the viewed object to a canonical form. The transformed image is then compared in parallel with all the copies of all the models stored in memory. A search over different possible pairings of feature points will no longer be necessary since a canonical form of the model, corresponding to the particular choice of image feature points, has already been computed and stored in recognition memory.

This approach can be practical for flat objects, or for 3-D objects containing a significant flat face, but not for general 3-D objects. It is also desirable in this method that the number of possible alignment features will not be large, otherwise the number of stored copies of the same object may become unmanageable. These limitations restrict the applicability of the pre-alignment method, making it unsuitable for the general case of three-dimensional objects.

7.1.3   Labeled features and parts

The search for corresponding image and model features can be reduced significantly, and even eliminated, if the alignment features being used are not indistinguishable: if each feature somehow carries a unique label, then the correspondence process can use these identifying labels to constrain the match. Image features can indeed be labeled in several ways. For example, feature points can be classified into different types, such as corners, tips, endpoints, blob centers, and inflection points (Huttenlocher & Ullman 1987). The matching process can then match, for instance, corner points in the image with corners, but not with inflection points, in the model. Relations between features can also be used for labeling. For example, the alignment method developed by Huttenlocher (Huttenlocher & Ullman 1987) identified pairs of feature points connected by an image contour. The matching of a given point then places strong constraints on the possible matching of other points. Feature labeling is also possible using not the shape of the feature point but its rough location. Such labeling becomes possible if the aligning transformations are known to be limited. For example, a feature near the top of the object will not be paired with feature points near the bottom of the object. A rough description of the object in terms of overall shape, major parts, or large structures, could also be used. Correspondence can then start by matching corresponding parts, and the matching of specific features can follow. For example, a feature may be labeled as lying inside an elongated part, or near the bottom flat part of the object, and then be matched with a similar feature in the model.

7.1.4 Rough Alignment

A related possible method for reducing the correspondence search is by using a stage of rough alignment. This means that before establishing a precise point-to-point correspondence, large discrepancies between the image and the model in terms of overall location, scale, and orientation, are removed in a preliminary stage. For example, to compensate for overall change in location, it is possible to compute a "center of mass" for both the model and the viewed object, and then translate one of the two representations so that the two centers of mass coincide. Technically, the center of mass is simply the average $x-$ and $y-$coordinates of a shape's points. Scale can be normalized, for example, by drawing the smallest rectangle (or some other shape) containing the figure, and then scaling the rectangle to a pre-determined fixed size.

Since the rough alignment already removes much of the difference between the image and model representations, corresponding features will now be closer to each other. Consequently, the search for matching features can be limited to small regions. The size of the search region will depend, of course, on the quality of the rough alignment process. If the remaining distortions are small, then the search can be eliminated altogether, and features will simply be matched with their nearest corresponding counterparts.

Labeling and rough alignment as described in these sections have not yet been studied extensively. If they can be performed with sufficient reliability, then the search for corresponding features may be reduced. One limitation of current methods for performing rough alignment is their reliance on global properties of the viewed object, such as its center of mass, overall size, or object moments used to compensate for changes in orientation. Such global methods require good segmentation, and they run into problems in the case of partial occlusion. It seems, therefore, that rough alignment can be a very useful stage, but that it will be desirable to find methods that are less global, and less sensitive to the problems of partial occlusion or incomplete segmentation.

7.2   Contour Matching

The process of image-to-model correspondence can also be based on the matching of extended smooth contours, rather than isolated feature points. If the image contains extended smooth contours, it will become difficult to identify and match localized feature points. It is relatively easy under such conditions to know with some certainty that a given point along an image contour should match some point along a neighboring contour in the model, but it will be difficult to determine the precise matching location along the contour.

A similar problem arises in the context of motion correspondence (Hildreth 1984, Marr & Ullman 1981). The problem in motion computation is to match images at successive time frames, rather than an image with a stored model. Here, again, it is possible to perform either isolated feature matching (Ullman 1979) or extended contour matching. A contour matching method for motion correspondence was developed by Hildreth (1984). The method assumes that the match is roughly known, and then proceeds to determine it more precisely. This assumption is illustrated in figure 7.3. Point $\mathbf{p}$ on contour c is known to match a point $\mathbf{p}'$ on contour c', but the exact location of $\mathbf{p}'$ is unknown, as in 7.3a. This problem is inherently ambiguous, since there are not enough constraints to impose a unique solution for $\mathbf{p}'$. In solving the matching problem, it is often assumed that the displacement from $\mathbf{p}$ to $\mathbf{p}'$ can be described as the sum of two components: a normal component, which is normal to c at $\mathbf{p}$, and a tangential component, along the tangent to c' (at the intersection point $\mathbf{q}$ on c'), as in 7.3b. This assumption is approximately true as long as the displacement is small, and the contours are not too curved. Some variations of this decomposition have also been used; for example, the component N can be replaced by the nearest neighbor on c' to p.

The problem then reduces to determining, at each point, the unknown tangential component. The problem is still under constraint, and in Hildreth's method the match is determined by establishing the smoothest possible solution that is compatible with the data. A motion field along the contour c is compatible with the data if, at any point along the contour, the normal component of the displacement vector coincides with the measured normal component. Of all these compatible motion fields, the preferred solution is the one that varies the least. (The variation is defined mathematically as: $\int_c \|\frac{dv}{ds}\|^2$, where s is a length parameter of the curve.)

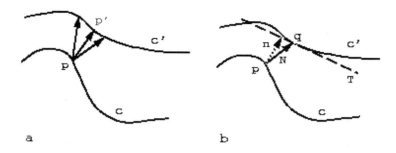

Figure 7.3
Establishing a match between two contours. *a.* Point **p** on contour c is known
to match a points **p**′ on contour c', but the exact location of **p**′ is unknown. *b.*
The displacement of point **p** can be described as the sum of two components:
a normal component N, that is normal to c at **p**, and a tangential component
T, along the tangent to c' (at the intersection point **q** on c'). The segment n,
used in the appendix, is perpendicular to T.

7.2.1   Locally Affine Match

One technical difficulty with the minimal variation method is its
computational complexity: methods for deriving the minimum
variation velocity field require iterative computations that take
time to converge (Hildreth 1984, Horn & Schunk 1981). The
intuitive reason for the multi-iteration computation is that the
best displacement vector at each point depends on its compati-
bility with the output at neighboring positions and therefore the
displacement vectors interact and modify one another until they
reach an optimal equilibrium. This behavior is problematic in motion analysis, where it is required to cope with rapidly changing
stimuli, and also in the context of recognition, where it may be
required to perform the correspondence computation between the
image and multiple models. A more efficient contour correspondence method uses the constraint of locally affine match instead
of minimum variation (Bachelder & Ullman 1992). This method
assumes that the matching between contours can be approximated
locally by an affine transformation. This is equivalent to assuming local planarity, since the image transformation induced by a

planar patch moving in 3-D is a 2-D affine transformation. In assuming local planarity we constrain the transformation between the image and model to be locally affine and therefore the problem becomes more restricted: locally, the match is determined by the six unknown parameters of the affine transformation. These parameters can be recovered by a simple and efficient computation. The method then proceeds by matching locally planar segments of the object contours.

We will next see how to recover this transformation using the local match between contours. The assumption on the form of the transformation entails that each contour point $\mathbf{p} = (x, y)$ in the first image maps to a contour point $\mathbf{p}' = (x', y')$ in the second image by the following simple equation

$$\mathbf{p}' = A\mathbf{p} + \mathbf{t} \qquad\qquad (7.2.1)$$

where the 2×2 matrix A accounts for the two-dimensional linear transformation, including shearing, scaling, and rotation, and the vector $\mathbf{t}$ accounts for two-dimensional translation in the image plane. We now have to use image measurements to determine the four elements of A and the two components of the displacement $\mathbf{t}$.

It is not difficult to see that from each contour point we can derive a single equation constraining the unknown transformation. The transformation is required to map the point $\mathbf{p}$ to a new point $\mathbf{p}'$ somewhere along the appropriate constraint line. A known point-to-point match is sufficient to provide two independent equations, and a match restricted to a line supplies a single equation regarding the unknown transformation. Given six or more measurements of this type, the local transformation can be recovered by solving a system of linear equations.

The unknowns in this system can be written as a vector $\mathbf{a}$, of six components:

$$\mathbf{a} = \begin{bmatrix} A_{00} & A_{10} & A_{01} & A_{11} & t_x & t_y \end{bmatrix}^T \qquad\qquad (7.2.2)$$

where $A_{00}, A_{10}, A_{01}, A_{11}$, are the components of A, and t_x, t_y are the two components of the translation. These unknowns are determined by a system of linear equations of the form:

$$\mathbf{Ca} = \mathbf{d} \tag{7.2.3}$$

The matrix $\mathbf{C}$ and the vector $\mathbf{d}$ are determined from measurements in the image, and they are then used to recover the unknown vector $\mathbf{a}$. The equations themselves together with some more details are described in appendix D. It is worth noting that the same computation can naturally combine feature and contour matching. At a number of well-localized feature points, such as points of high curvature, sharp inflections, or the centers of small blobs, the exact point-to-point correspondence may be known. In this case, each pointwise match supplies not only one, but two independent equations. The affine transformation can then be recovered from a system of equations that mixes both contour and point constraints.

Figures 7.4 and 7.5 produced by I. Bachelder show several examples of matching contour images using the locally affine match.

The figures show four examples: a rotating wireframe, a rotating curved space-curve, a car and a head model. Each example contains four panels. The first shows the two contour images to be matched: one can be considered as the internal model, the other as the viewed object. The second panel shows the initial perpendicular components used for the matching (these are the vectors $\mathbf{n_i}$ above). The third panel shows the computed locally-affine match, and the fourth shows the correct match, that can be compared with the computed one.

Two main points about the locally affine match are noteworthy. First, the efficiency of the method, compared with multi-iteration methods: the computation within each neighborhood does not require a lengthy iterative process, but consists primarily of solving a small system of linear equations. The computations at different parts of the contour are independent and can proceed in parallel.

The second point concerns the quality of the results. The method is based on assumptions that are difficult to assess in

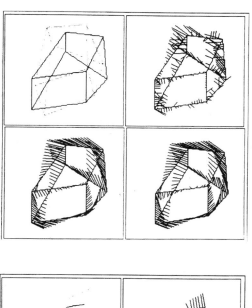

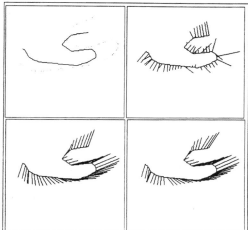

Figure 7.4
Matching contour images using the method of local affinity. Each example shows (1) the two contour images to be matched, one shown in solid and the second in dotted line, (2) the initial perpendicular components, (3) the locally-affine match, (4) the correct match between the images. First example: rotating wireframe object. Second example: a rotating smooth space curve. The initial perpendicular displacement are quite different from the true displacement, but the final affine match is in good agreement with the actual correspondence.

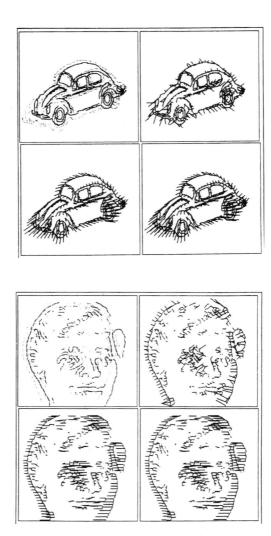

Figure 7.5
Third example: a car model. Fourth example: a face model. Figure produced
by I. Bachelder.

a quantitative manner. For example, it is difficult to assess the accuracy of the normal component decomposition, namely, that the displacement at a point can be described as the sum of a normal and tangential components as described above (figure 7.3). Similarly, local affinity is violated in regions that are not entirely planar. The results of the simulations, as in 7.4 and 7.5, show that the matching is quite satisfactory, even for rather complex objects.

A limitation of this method that should be stressed is that it requires a stage of rough alignment that will bring corresponding contours into reasonable match. This is also true for the next method that relies on model-based constraints rather than local affinity.

7.2.2   Model-Guided Contour Match

The main idea behind the model-guided match is that we can use known properties of the model itself, rather than general properties such as smoothness or local planarity, to constrain the image-to-model correspondence. An example is the contour matching scheme developed by Lipson and Ullman (Lipson 1993). The starting point for this method is similar to the locally affine scheme summarized in figure 7.3: along the contours, only the normal components of the match are known, the tangential components are the unknowns to be recovered. In addition, the exact point-to-point match may be known at special feature points. In the locally affine method, the unknowns are recovered based on an affinity constraint. Here, we bring to bear the three-dimensional structure of the model, using the linear combination approach. Technically, each point supplies again a single equation, and the constraints at a number of points can be combined to form a system of linear equations that can be used to derive the correspondence as well as the coefficients of the image combination. The basic idea is outlined briefly below, the method is described in more detail in (Lipson, 1993).

In the image combination method, the object model is represented by a small number (say, three) of corresponding images. Let us assume in figure 7.3 that contour c belongs to one of the model images and contour c' belongs to the viewed object. Point $\mathbf{p}$ in the model corresponds to some point $\mathbf{p'}$ on the object contour. We do not know the location of $\mathbf{p'}$ exactly, but we know that it lies along the constraint line passing through $\mathbf{q}$. The general idea is now simple: we seek to determine the three coefficients of the image combination that will make $\mathbf{p'}$ lie on the required constraint line. The details of this computation are as follows. The fact that the unknown point $\mathbf{p'}$ lies on the constraint line through $\mathbf{q}$ can be expressed as:

$$p'_x = q_x + \alpha v_x \qquad\qquad\qquad (7.2.4)$$
$$p'_y = q_y + \alpha v_y$$

where v_x, v_y are known (they give the direction of the constraint line), but α is not.

We now use the model as an additional source of constraints. We know that the viewed object can be expressed as the linear combination of the three model images. In particular, the still unknown point $\mathbf{p'}$ will be given by the combination of the point $\mathbf{p}$ and its counterparts in the two other model images. The basic idea is simple: we want to discover coefficients for the linear combination that will map each image point to a new point along its constraint line. This can be expressed as:

$$p'_x = a_1 m_{1x} + a_2 m_{2x} + a_3 m_{3x} \qquad\qquad (7.2.5)$$
$$p'_y = b_1 m_{1y} + b_2 m_{2y} + b_3 m_{3y}.$$

Here a_1, a_2, a_3 and b_1, b_2, b_3 are the unknown coefficients of the linear combination. The last two equations can be combined to yield a single equation, in which the only unknowns are the parameters of the image combination:

$$v_y(a_1 m_{1x} + a_2 m_{2x} + a_3 m_{3x}) - v_x(b_1 m_{1y} + b_2 m_{2y} + b_3 m_{3y}) \quad (7.2.6)$$
$$= v_y q_x - v_x q_y.$$

We need at least six equations of this type, supplied by six different points. Instead, many more points can be used, to deal with noise and inaccuracies, and the system is then solved in the least squares sense. Following the recovery of the unknown coefficients, the model-to-image correspondence also follows immediately.

Figures 7.6, 7.7, 7.8, produced by P. Lipson at MIT, show examples of using model-guided correspondence. In the first example, the computation is applied to the car images. The figure shows the three model images (top row), which are three partial edge images of a VW car. A new view of the same object (middle row, left), is compared with one of the model images (middle row, right). Finally, the new view is compared with the image combination obtained by the model-guided correspondence.

Figure 7.7 shows the method applied to a face image. The five images, $m_1 - m_5$ constitute the internal model. Image a is a novel view of the same face, which is superimposed in b on the fourth model image. 7.7c shows the result of the method following a single iteration, and d the match following 10 iterations. In figure 7.8, a match is attempted between the same model and a different face, shown in 7.8a. This face is superimposed on the fourth model image in b. Results of the matching process after a single iteration and after 10 iterations are shown in 7.8c and d. It can be seen that the match with the incorrect model is not as accurate as the match with the correct model, in figure 7.7, especially at the internal contours. Faces are generally similar, and therefore even the wrong model approximates the novel image, however many of the internal contours are missing or displaced. The final image, 7.8e, shows the transformed model alone. This is a combination of the original model images, selected by the method to approximate the novel input image as closely as possible.

7.3 Correspondence-less Methods

In contrast with the previous approaches, the "correspondence-less" methods do not use feature correspondence to recover the

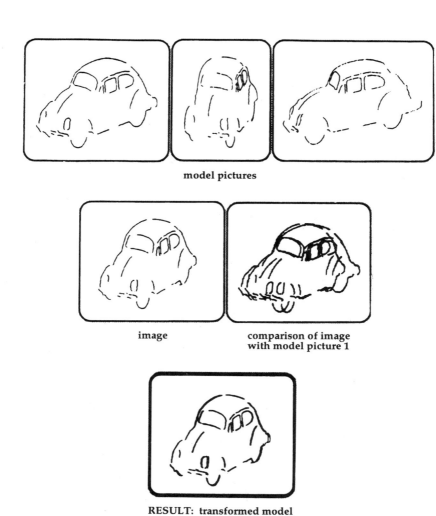

model pictures

image   **comparison of image
                              with model picture 1**

**RESULT: transformed model
superimposed on the image**

Figure 7.6

Model-guided match. The three model images are shown on the top row, they
are partial edge maps of a car. The new view of the same object (middle row,
left), is compared with one of the model images (middle row, right). On the
bottom row, the new view is compared with the image combination obtained
by the model-guided correspondence. The initial discrepancy between the
image and model is large, but following the model-guided matching process a
good agreement is obtained.

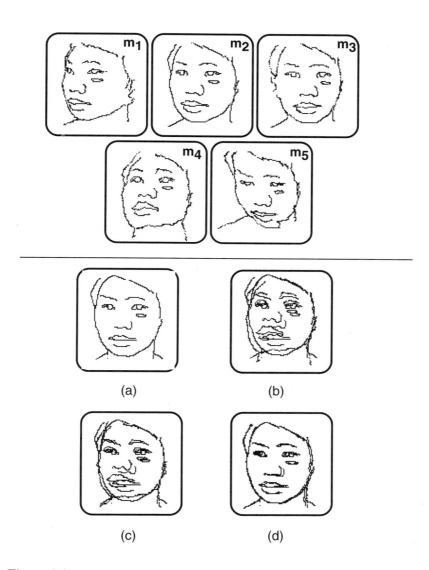

(a)   (b)

(c)   (d)

Figure 7.7
Model-guided match applied to a face image. Images m_1 through m_5 constitute the face model. *a.* A novel face image. *b.* The novel image superimposed on m_4. *c.* The resulting match after one iteration. *d.* The resulting match after 10 iteration.

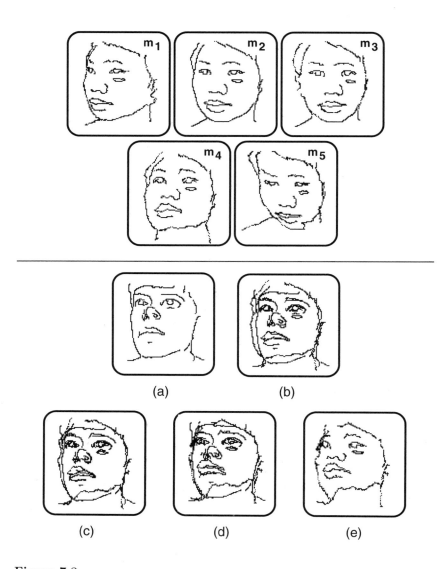

(a)   (b)

(c)   (d)   (e)

Figure 7.8
Matching a face image with the incorrect face model. Images m_1 through m_5 are the same face model as before. *a*. A novel face image. *b*. The novel image superimposed on m_4. *c*. The resulting match after one iteration. *d*. The resulting match after 10 iteration. *e*. The transformed model alone, at the end of 10 iterations. Figure produced by P. Lipson.

transformation. Instead, a search is conducted in the space of possible transformations. Mathematically, the set of possible transformations $\{T_\alpha\}$ is parametrized by a parameter vector α, and a search is performed in the parameter space to determine the best value of α.

The deformable templates method (Yuille, Cohen & Hallinan 1988, Yuille & Hallinan 1992) is an example of this approach. In this method an object-model contains a number of adjustable parameters for varying its shape. For example, a face recognition module may contain a deformable template for the shape of the mouth. This mouth template will contain a typical mouth shape, together with a set of parameters that control various aspects of the shape, such as the mouth's width, height, curvature, and the like. During recognition, these parameters are adjusted by a search process (such as gradient descent) to minimize the difference between the model and the viewed object.

At the beginning of this chapter we mentioned a similar possibility of performing such a search in the context of the view combination approach, to determine the value of the required coefficients. A particular image combination is defined by a small number of coefficients, for example, three for the $x-$ and three for the $y-$direction. One can start from some initial value of the six parameters and then improve the match by using, for instance, gradient descent in the space of parameters.

One potential problem with such a search is that it may require many iterations to converge to a good match. A second problem is that the search may by stuck in a local minimum and then fail to find the correct match. There are search methods that can get around these problems, at the price of exploring in parallel multiple potential solutions. For a biological system that is slow but inherently parallel, this is an attractive tradeoff. In chapter 10, that deals with biological aspects of recognition and information processing by the visual cortex, this possibility is considered in more detail.

7.4   Correspondence Processes in Human Vision

One question that naturally arises regarding image-to-model correspondence is whether our own visual system operates in this manner. That is, whether it establishes a correspondence between the viewed image and a stored model as an intermediate stage in the recognition process.

The answer is not known, but it is interesting to note in this regard the capacity of the visual system to perform efficient correspondence in another domain—that of motion perception. When two similar images are presented in rapid alternation, we often see not a disappearance of one image and the appearance of another, but a smooth motion distorting one image into the other. This is known as the phenomenon of apparent motion. In perceiving apparent motion, the visual system effectively establishes a correspondence between the two images. This process has been investigated extensively from the psychophysical standpoint, and a number of computational schemes were proposed for establishing motion correspondence (Ullman 1979, Scott & Longuet-Higgins 1991).

An example of motion correspondence is shown in figure 7.9, produced by Y. Shapira (1990). The figure shows two different car images. The one on top is a sketch of a prototypical car. The one at the bottom was obtained by an edge detection process from the image of a toy car. Due to shadows and noise there are missing and spurious edges in this image. When these two images were presented in rapid alternation, observers saw them in apparent motion. The two images were shown not one above the other, as in the figure, but superimposed, at the same location: one disappeared, the other appeared at the same location, was then replaced again by the first image, and so on. Using a computer display, observers then indicated, using screen cursors, pairs of points that appeared in perceptual correspondence. The numbers in the figure indicate corresponding features as perceived by the observers. That is, the point labeled, for instance, by "1" in the first figure was seen to move and match point "1" in the second image. It can be seen that the perceived motion tended to match corresponding features. For example, the four corners of the window (marked "21") in one image matched the window corners in the second image.

The example above is from the domain of motion rather than recognition, but it is interesting to note that the correspondence established during apparent motion appears to provide sufficient information for the purpose of recognition. This was illustrated in an experiment by R. Basri that combined motion correspondence established perceptually with the linear combination scheme for recognition (Ullman & Basri 1991). As we have seen, the image combination scheme requires some form of image-to-model correspondence. Instead of using a computer algorithm, the correspondence was established perceptually by using the procedure outlined above, and then used by the recognition algorithm. The results were as accurate as those obtained by our computer-based correspondence algorithms, and were sufficient to discriminate reliably between the two similar car models (the VW and the SAAB) used in the experiment.

If reliable correspondence can be established by the motion system, could a similar process be used for the purpose of recognition? The answer is not known, but two differences between recognition and motion should be pointed out. First, in motion correspondence the discrepancy between successive images is usually not too large, in terms of scale difference, orientation change and so on. In recognition the differences might be larger, but they can be reduced by using a stage of rough alignment. Second, in recognition correspondence is established not only once, but several times, with all the candidate models that must be considered. However, by the appropriate use of classification, the number of distinct image-to-model correspondences that need to be established may be quite restricted. In the future, computational experiments, combining classification with the recognition of a large number of objects may shed some light on these issues.

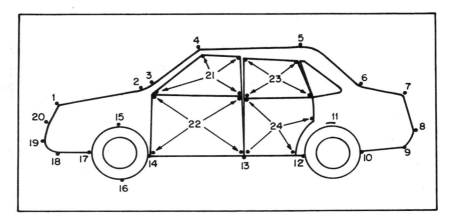

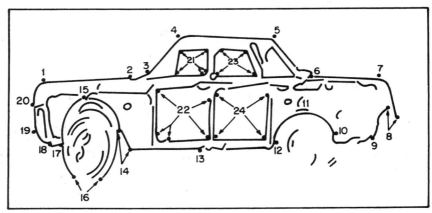

Figure 7.9
Correspondence established perceptually, in apparent motion presentation.
The two images were presented in alternation, shown at the same location in
rapid succession. The numbers indicate the features that were perceived as
corresponding (moving from one location to the other). Figure produced by
Y. Shapira

7.5   Model Construction

In the image combination approach, a model is constructed from a number of pictures with known correspondence between them. The required correspondence for this purpose is a full one, in contrast with the recognition stage that can use sparse matching features. For 3-D alignment, having several pictures with known correspondence is also useful, since a full 3-D model can be constructed from such data (Ullman 1979).

The problem of establishing correspondence for the purpose of model construction is different from that of performing image-to-model correspondence during recognition. During model construction one can often actively explore the object, and track selected features as the viewing point is changed in a controlled manner. Methods for actively exploring objects to derive information about them in an optimal manner have been the object of considerable research in the field of so-called "active vision" (see, e.g., Blake & Yuille, 1992). In addition, model construction is an "off line" process, it is not subject to the same time constraints as the recognition process itself. Model construction can therefore use more elaborate and time-consuming processes.

The techniques discussed above for image-to-model correspondence can also be employed for the purpose of model construction. In addition, two techniques have been used to aid the establishment of full correspondence of the type needed for model construction. The first is the use of so-called epipolar lines. The basic idea is that, following the establishment of a small number of corresponding features, the matching of any additional feature is constrained to lie along a known line (Ullman 1979, Koenderink & Van Doorn 1991). To use this fact, we first establish a number of pointwise matches between features in two views of the same object (four corresponding points are sufficient in the case of orthographic projection). For any other point in one of the views, the search for its counterpart in the other view can now be limited to a single line, and this facilitates considerably the search for the appropriate match. The line itself (called the "epipolar" line) is derived in a straightforward manner from the four corresponding features (Koenderink & Van Doorn 1991, Shashua 1992). When we already have two model views in full correspondence and we wish to add a third one, the correspondence task gets simpler, because now we already have constraints from two different images.

A second method that can help in establishing full correspondence relies on the use of the actual grey level in the image, rather than contours and feature points. The idea is to use the fact that as the viewing point moves around the object, and assuming that this motion is not too large, the grey level value of a given point will remain approximately constant. This is true in particular for so-called lambertian reflection (Horn & Brooks 1989, Woodham 1984). For objects with lambertian reflection properties, the grey level at a given point depends only on the angle formed between the surface normal at the point in question and the direction of the light source. These factors do not change when only the observation point is modified. It is preferable in this respect to leave the object stationary and move the observation point rather than keep the observation point fixed and rotate the object to obtain a new view. For the purpose of recognition, this can be obtained by actively moving the observation point around the object during the model construction stage (Aloimonos, Weiss & Bandyopadhyay 1988, Blake & Yuille 1992). Under such conditions, grey level based correspondence techniques (Horn & Schunk 1981) can be used to help the model acquisition. Shashua (1992) combined the use of epipolar lines and grey level correspondence to construct internal models for 3-D object recognition. By using a small number of corresponding features the epipolar lines are derived, and the match along these lines is determined by using the correlation of small grey level patches. The method can give good results when applied in an incremental fashion. That is, to obtain correspondence over large changes in viewing angle it is necessary to use intermediate views, so that the differences between neighboring views will not be too large.

The issue of full correspondence, and the use of image grey level values in corresponding images, is also related to the problem of dealing with illumination changes, examined in the next section. The issue is considered here rather than earlier because the discussion used material from chapters 5, 6, and the current chapter.

7.6   Compensating for Illumination Changes

In considering the possible variations in the image of a given object, we have focused so far primarily on shape changes, induced by either changes in viewing position, or, to some extent, distortions of the object itself. Another important source of variability comes from changes in the illumination conditions. The image itself, which is a two-dimensional distribution of light intensity values, changes significantly with changes in illumination. How can a recognition system deal with, and compensate for, such changes?

The answer is not entirely known, but there has been primarily one dominant approach to the problem, based on the notion of edge detection (Canny 1986, Davis 1975, Haralick 1980, Marr & Hildreth 1980). The idea is to find in the light intensity distribution that forms the image features that are affected as little as possible by changes in the illumination conditions. The best known example of such features are intensity edges, which are contours where the light intensity changes relatively abruptly from one level to another. Such edges are often associated with object boundaries, and with material changes on an object's surface. When the illumination changes, the absolute light intensities change as well, but the locations of edges caused by physical surface discontinuities remain on the whole stable. The edge image is often somewhat less informative to the human eye compared with the original grey level image. Theoretically, however, the information is usually preserved in the edge image (Curtis & Oppenheim 1990). The main advantage of the edge image, compared with the original image, is that the edge map is less affected by changes in the illumination conditions. This invariance is not complete, however:

many edges do not maintain their exact locations, some object edges might appear or disappear, some spurious edges will result from shadows and specularities, and so on. It appears, therefore, that although the use of relatively stable features such as edges, and possibly intensity ridges and valleys (Pearson, Hanna, & Martinez, 1990, Moses 1993) can play a useful role, it is unlikely to provide a full solution to the problem. The result is not always sufficiently stable, and it ignores grey level variations that can be useful in the recognition process. We have also seen in chapter 6, in discussing illumination effects in the recognition of normal and inverted faces, that compensation for illumination is unlikely to come from universal processing such as edge detection alone.

7.6.1   Illumination and Image Combination

In chapter 5 we have seen how image combination and interpolation can be used to deal with shape changes caused by changes in viewing position and object distortions. A similar approach was used by Shashua (1992) and Moses (1993) to deal with illumination changes. The general idea is the following. The image intensity at a point depends on the relative orientation between the surface at this point and the direction of illumination. But because space is three-dimensional, if we know the effect of illumination for a small number of directions, we can then generalize to other directions as well.

To see in more detail how combinations of grey level images can be used, we have to know something about the relationship between image intensity and surface properties. Let us consider first the simple case of a lambertian, or matte surface. This is a surface that contains no specular component. The image intensity at a given point is determined by the angle between the surface (represented by the surface normal) and the direction from the surface to the light source. This can be expressed simply as the product:

$$I = \hat{\mathbf{n}} \cdot \mathbf{E}$$

where $\hat{\mathbf{n}}$ is the surface normal, and $\mathbf{E}$ a vector pointing in the direction of the light source, with magnitude corresponding to the intensity of the light source (we are assuming for now a single distant light source). Suppose that we have seen three different images, with three different orientations of the light source. These three images can now be used to deal with new illuminations by noting that any new direction can be expressed as a combination of the old ones.

The light intensity from a given point in the three images is given by

$$I_1 = \hat{\mathbf{n}} \cdot \mathbf{E_1}$$
$$I_2 = \hat{\mathbf{n}} \cdot \mathbf{E_2}$$
$$I_3 = \hat{\mathbf{n}} \cdot \mathbf{E_3}.$$

(7.6.7)

The object itself is assumed to remain stationary, and therefore the surface normal $\hat{\mathbf{n}}$ at the point in question remains fixed, but the object is illuminated from three different directions. We also ignore for now the fact that some of the points may in fact be in shadow for a given illumination, and examine only the points that are illuminated by the three different light sources.

Given a new illumination, represented by the vector $\bar{\mathbf{E}}$, the intensity changes to $\bar{I} = \hat{\mathbf{n}} \cdot \bar{\mathbf{E}}$. But $\bar{\mathbf{E}}$ can be expressed using $\mathbf{E_1}, \mathbf{E_2}, \mathbf{E_3}$ as basis vectors (except for degenerate cases, where they are coplanar), that is,

$$\bar{\mathbf{E}} = a_1 \mathbf{E_1} + a_2 \mathbf{E_2} + a_3 \mathbf{E_3}$$

for some constants a_1, a_2, a_3. Consequently,

$$\bar{I} = a_1 I_1 + a_2 I_2 + a_3 I_3.$$

The constants a_1, a_2, a_3 come from the relationship between the illumination directions; they do not depend on the particular point we examined. Therefore, the relation above holds for all illuminated points. In other words, the new grey level image is a simple combination of the old ones. The combination of face images in chapter 5, figure 5.2, used such a linear combination of grey values at corresponding points.

The discussion above made a number of simplifying assumptions. Some points may be in shadow, not directly illuminated in one of the illumination conditions. The illumination itself may be complex, including extended light sources and multiple reflections, and not simply a single distant light source. The surface is not likely to be entirely lambertian, most surfaces include also a specular reflectance component.

With respect to shadow effects, it is useful to distinguish between two kinds of shadows, called "attached" and "cast" (Cavanagh 1991). An attached shadow occurs when the surface points away from the light source ($\mathbf{n} \cdot \mathbf{E} < 0$). A cast shadow is the result of one object "standing in the way" and obscuring the light source from another object. Cast shadows are difficult to treat because the effect is non-local, being dependent on other objects in the scene. Attached shadows can be treated to some extent by the image combination method (Shashua 1992). The predicted grey level at a cast shadow may become negative, and can then be ignored or set to the value 0, or a small background value.

The effects of extended illumination and non-lambertian reflection functions can be treated to some extent analytically (Shashua 1992). In practice, the main effect is an increase in the number of grey level images required for a faithful reconstruction. Hallinan (1994) examined face images under varying illumination conditions. By performing principal component analysis he found that a small number of grey-level images (about five to seven) were sufficient to approximate, by simple linear combinations as above, new images of the same face, under a wide range of illumination conditions. He also found that the first few basis images ("eigenfaces," Turk & Pentland 1991) tended to be quite similar across a range of faces, suggesting the possibility of modeling in a similar manner not only illumination effects for a specific face, but also effects that are common to faces in general and can be applicable to novel face images.

7.6.2   Combining Geometric and Illumination Changes

The method of image combination was applied so far independently to changes in viewing direction and changes in illumination conditions. In realistic cases, changes occur, of course, simultaneously in both viewing and illumination conditions. Shashua (1992) applied an image combination method to such images.

The combined method used a minimum of three images, using two viewing directions and three different illumination directions. These can be denoted as:

$$(V_1, E_1), (V_2, E_2), (V_1, E_3).$$

The two viewing directions are denoted here by V_1, V_2, and the three illumination directions by E_1, E_2, E_3. The first view, V_1 is used here with two different illumination conditions, E_1 and E_3, and the second view, V_2, is used with its own illumination condition. During the model construction phase, an auxiliary image was used, the image (V_2, E_1). This is the second viewing direction but with the first illumination direction, and it is obtained by simply moving the observation point with respect to the first image.

The model construction phase requires a correspondence between the model images. The first and last images are taken from the same viewing direction and therefore their correspondence is immediate. The auxiliary image is used to facilitate the correspondence between the first and second images. Between the first and the auxiliary image, the viewing direction changes, but the illumination direction is fixed. Consequently, the full correspondence method described earlier can be applied. Between the auxiliary image and the second model-image the viewing direction does not change, and therefore correspondence is immediate.

Following the model construction, both geometric and illumination changes are compensated for by using a method that is quite similar to the view combination method discussed in previous chapters. First, correspondence is established between the

novel image and the first model image. A minimal correspondence
of a small number of features is sufficient at this stage. The corresponding points, with their grey levels, can be used to recover
the coefficients of the image coordinates (as in the usual linear
combination method), as well as the coefficients of the grey level
combination (a_1, a_2, a_3 in the discussion above). We can now generate a predicted grey level image, P, using the model images.
Essentially, the transformed coordinates are determined using the
linear combination scheme of the previous chapters, and the grey
level at each point is determined using the combination of grey
level images described above. To see how this is applied, consider
the first model image, I_1. For each point x, y in I_1, its corresponding coordinates x', y' in the predicted image P are given as
an image combination of I_1 and I_2. This stage is identical to the
linear combination scheme described in chapter 5. The grey level
at x', y' is then determined by the combination of the grey levels in
the three images I_1, I_2, I_3. The internally generated image is then
compared with the input image. Since both the effects of viewing
direction and illumination have been compensated for, with the
exception of residual errors, the two should agree well as grey level
images. The same method can be extended in a straightforward
manner to include additional stored views, thereby increasing the
accuracy of the predicted image, or to deal directly with perspective rather than orthographic projection.

7.6.3 Compensating for Illumination at the Object and Class Levels

The method above for dealing with grey level images illustrates the
general point that illumination effects can be treated by object-
specific processes. The common approach to the problem of illumination in recognition is to utilize illumination-invariant features,
in particular, edge-maps produced by edge detection techniques.
The method described in the last section uses a very different approach: it uses a specific object model to predict and compensate
for variations in grey level resulting from illumination changes.

The psychophysical experiment using upright and inverted faces, described in chapter 6, suggests the possiblity of dealing with illumination effects at an intermediate level, by using general class information, or information associated with a prototypical representative, rather than a specific object. As already mentioned, human observers had difficulties in compensating for illumination effects when the objects in question were inverted faces. This suggests that compensating for illumination involves more that producing illumination-invariant edge maps. At the same time, the observers generalized well across illumination changes from a single image of an unknown face. Since it is difficult to generate an accurate 3-D model from a single face image, it is reasonable to assume that the compensation process can use information about faces in general to deal with variations in illumination applied to a specific face.

It will be interesting to study, from a computational standpoint, methods for dealing with illumination effects at the class, rather than the specific object level. This problem is related to the issue of classification discussed in the previous chapter—how to perform initial classification, and how to then use class-level information in subsequent identification stages.

8 Segmentation and Saliency

Objects are usually not seen in isolation, but embedded in larger scenes, next to, and sometimes partially occluded by, other objects. The recognition task examined so far focused on the recognition of a single, isolated object. The task becomes much more complicated when the object is not isolated, but "buried" within the context of a larger scene.

To recognize an individual object in the scene, it would be useful to somehow separate as much as possible the image of the object in question from the remainder of the scene. A common approach has therefore been to precede the recognition process by a stage called "segmentation." The goal of the segmentation stage is to isolate from the image a sub-structure that corresponds to the image of a single object. If such a goal can be realized, then the task of the subsequent recognition process will be simplified—it will be reduced to the recognition of single isolated objects.

The notion of "segmentation" is similar to related notions that are used in perception and image processing, including grouping, partitioning, perceptual organization, and figure-ground separation. All these notions have to do with the identification of meaningful structures in the image. Sometimes the emphasis is on the subsequent goal of recognition (Biederman 1985, Lowe 1985, Pentland 1986, Walters 1986), in other cases more emphasis is put on detecting structures that appear as perceptually coherent units (Hochberg & Silverstein 1956, Leeuwenberg 1971, Olson & Attneave 1970). In our case, the focus will be on the goal of recognition.

The definition of the segmentation stage also depends on whether we approach the problem as starting from the image—it is then natural to consider the partitioning of the image into smaller structures—or as starting from a collection of small image units such as edge fragments, in which case it becomes more natural to consider the problem of grouping the elements into larger structures. Many of the classical studies of the Gestalt school of perception (Kanizsa 1979, Koffka 1935) were concerned with the rules of grouping elementary image elements into larger structures, based on properties such as proximity, colinearity, similarity in color and contrast, common direction of motion, and the like.

Given what we know about the early processing stages in the visual cortex, it will be reasonable to treat the segmentation problem as involving grouping processes. In the primary visual cortex, for example, the image is represented by the activity of units tuned to local features, such as small oriented line and edge fragments. Similarly, in most image processing and computer vision schemes, the image is first analyzed locally, to produce, for example, an edge map, composed of a large collection of local edge elements. The term "segmentation" will therefore include grouping processes that start from the image described mainly in terms of local elements, and proceed to identify larger structures.

8.1   Is Segmentation Feasible?

What exactly is the goal of the segmentation process? A naive answer might be something like: "find the different objects in the image." That is, divide the image into distinct structures, corresponding to the different objects in the scene.

This answer is unsatisfactory for several reasons. First, there is a problem with the definition of an "object" in this regard. What is the image of a "single object?" D. Marr raises this problem by asking: "Is a nose an object? is a head one? ...What about a man on horseback?" (Marr 1982, p. 270).

A related issue is that the task of segmenting an object out of the image in a bottom-up manner prior to recognition is probably too demanding. It proved very difficult to separate complete objects, such as a car, a house, or a person, from complex natural scenes. But is it really necessary, for the purpose of recognition, to separate the entire object from its background, or perhaps some partial results would be sufficient? Is segmentation performed in a bottom-up manner, or does it require "top-down" processes? Is segmentation really a separate stage that precedes recognition, or is it intertwined with the recognition process?

These questions are important for the understanding of the segmentation process, and in fact it seems that the lack of a clear conception of the task and its requirements is responsible in part for the lack of satisfactory progress in this area. It will be better, however, to consider some of these problems only after discussing in more detail specific aspects of the segmentation problem. We will therefore resume the discussion of these general issues in the last section of this chapter.

The focus of this chapter is primarily on bottom-up processes in image segmentation. To this end, I will first discuss some evidence supporting the existence of "autonomous" segmentation processes in human vision. I will then briefly describe a procedure that can extract fairly complex image structures, often disconnected, based on local geometric properties of image contours.

8.2   Bottom-up and Top-down Segmentation

We have already introduced some of the distinctions between low-level and high-level processes in vision. In the context of segmentation, low-level aspects will mean processes that perform grouping and segmentation operations on the basis of image properties, such as proximity, colinearity, similarity of contrast, color, motion, texture, and the like. High-level processes in segmentation are those that use known object shapes to perform segmentation and grouping, for example, by looking for a particular object in the image, and using the identified object in the segmentation process.

In some cases, the segmentation process in human vision appears to rely heavily on high-level processes that employ knowledge about objects to to be able to identify certain image structures as corresponding to a particular object. In R.C. James's well-known image of the Dalmatian dog, for instance, (Gregory 1970, Marr 1982), it appears unlikely that the portion of the image containing the dog can be identified in a purely bottom-up manner, based on image properties alone. Segmentation and recognition in this case are strongly coupled, and both are aided by the knowledge that one is looking for a dog. Figure 8.1 reproduced from Kundel & Nodine (1983) is a similar example of top-down effects on segmentation. The image depicts the head of a cow that is difficult to identify because the face image cannot be easily segmented from the background. When the face is perceived, its segmentation from the background is clearly aided by high-level effects that rely on our knowledge concerning the shape of a cow's face. This is reflected in figure 8.1b that illustrates two line-drawings, produced by two observers, based on the images in 8.1a. One of them clearly perceived the cow's face, the other did not. The line sketch of the face can be used to distinguish the cow's face in the original image, 8.1a, demonstrating the effect of high-level processes on the segmentation and interpretation of the image.

There is considerable evidence, however, that human vision also contains processes that perform grouping and segmentation prior to, and independent of, subsequent recognition processes. One type of evidence comes from brain lesions leading to recognition problems. For example, Luria (1980) has described cases where the recognition of isolated objects remained relatively intact, but became severely impaired for non-isolated objects, when recognition also required the separation of an object from partially overlapping or touching distractors.

An illustration of the power of low-level segmentation processes is shown in figure 8.2, originally produced by Bregman (1984). The figure depicts several two-dimensional objects partially occluded by an ink blot. With the occluder present, the image organizes itself effortlessly into distinct objects. When the occluder is removed, the scattered fragments of the letters fail to organize. Knowledge concerning the content of the scene is of limited help: it is as if the visual system makes a decision at a low level as to which parts of the scene belong together, and there is only a limited cognitive high-level control over this decision.

a

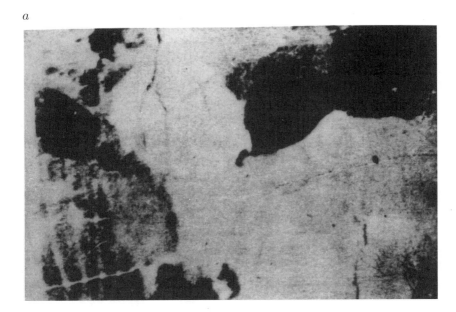

b

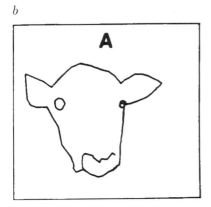
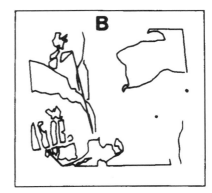

Figure 8.1
The cow-head in *a* is difficult to discern because segmentation from the background is difficult. *b*. A and B are two line drawings produced by two observers looking at the image in *a*. The sketch of the cow-head in *b* can be used to facilitate the interpretation of the image in *a*. Reproduced from Kundel & Nodine (1983).

Figure 8.2
A number of partially occluded objects. When the occluder (an ink blot) is explicitly shown, segmentation becomes easier. The objects here are recognizable: several instances of the letter "B". (After Bregman (1984).

Figure 8.3
Similar to the previous figure, but using nonsense shapes. Segmentation is
again considerably easier when the occluder is explicitly shown.

A related illustration is Nakayama's "face behind the fence" demonstration (Nakayama, Shimojo & Silverman 1989). In this example, a face partially occluded by horizontal bars is easily recognizable when the unoccluded parts lie behind, but not in front of, the occluding bars. Again, it appears that the visual system makes a decision regarding the parts that belong together, to form a single object. Under the occlusion condition, the face-parts are treated as a single object. When the face-parts are in front, they are treated independently and do not form a single recognizable face. Knowledge about the face has again limited influence on the segmentation process. Additional support for segmentation processes operating in early vision comes from demonstrations of motion and stereo capture (Ramachandran 1986), where segmentation processes appear to precede and influence the organization of motion and binocular stereo matching in the image. For example, the motion of the boundary of a square can influence the perceived motion inside, but not outside, the square. This points to an early separation between the inside of an object and the surrounding background. Similarly, in demonstrations produced by Adelson (1993), the perceived brightness of surfaces can be affected by the segmentation of the images into different surfaces.

These and many other studies indicate that the visual system attempts, at the early processing stages, to organize the image into coherent units, and to decide what parts of the image belong together. This organization process involves a remarkably sophisticated integration of a variety of both static and dynamic cues.

From a physiological standpoint there is some evidence that segmentation processes may start as early as in visual area V2, an area that receives its input directly from the primary visual area V1, and is placed low in the stream of visual processing.In V2, some of the units are sensitive to subjective contours (von der Heydt, Peterhans, & Baumgartner, 1984), as well as to the coherent motion of a colinear row of dots relative to the background (Peterhans & von der Heydt 1991). It is likely that the analysis of these cues is related to the perception of occlusion and to image

segmentation, and therefore V2 is likely to play a role in image segmentation processes. There is also some evidence for the possible
implication of area V1 in segmentation processes. Grosof, Shapley
and Hawken (1993) reported evidence for the detection of some
types of subjective contours already in V1. Lamme, Van Dijk and
Spekreijse (1992), using recordings of visually evoked potentials,
obtained some evidence implicating areas V1 in texture segregation tasks. A similar view was supported by physiological findings
of Zipser *et al.* (1994). They found that the responses of V1 cells
are often enhanced when the receptive field of the recorded unit
falls within a region that becomes figure-like in appearance, by
making it distinct from the background in terms of depth, orientation, luminance, or color. Another visual area, termed area MT,
appears to participate in processes involved in the segmentation
of moving stimuli. Psychophysical studies have shown that two
overlapping gratings that move together are sometimes perceived
as a single rigidly-moving plaid pattern, and sometimes they separate into two independently moving surfaces, defined by the two
component gratings. The dominant perception can be affected
by subtle cues: for example, under luminance conditions that support the perception of one of the gratings as a transparent surface,
the motion usually breaks down into its two independent components. In studies by Stoner and Albright (1992), it was shown that
single units in visual area MT in the monkey exhibit a similar behavior. Under luminance conditions that promote the perception
of transparency, many cells tend to signal the motion direction
of the component gratings. The same cells responded better to
the direction of the entire plaid under conditions that promoted
the perception of the plaid as a single surface. These neurons are
therefore not just simple "motion filters," but are somehow involved in processing that is affected by segmentation cues. Area
MT therefore appears to be involved in segmentation processes
that involve the use of motion as well as other, non-motion cues,
such as luminance, and possibly binocular disparity.

Segmentation involves a number of different processes, using different sources of information, including contour and region properties, stereoscopic disparity, texture, color, and motion. Zucker (1987) drew a distinction between one-dimensional grouping processes that create extended contours and boundaries, and two-dimensional processes that separate regions in the image. Image segmentation based on two-dimensional texture and color properties of image regions has been the topic of many studies in the field of human perception (e.g., Beck 1982, Julesz 1975, 1981, Treisman 1982). Texture- and color-based segmentation was also studied extensively in computational vision (see summaries in Ballard & Brown 1982, Haralick 1979, Nevatia 1982, Pavlidis 1992, Pratt 1991), together with other region-based segmentation methods (Ballard & Brown 1982, Mitiche & Aggarwal 1985, Nalwa 1993, Pavlidis 1977, Pong *et al.* 1984, Rosenfeld & Kak 1982), and will not be reviewed here. Models were also proposed for integrating together one-dimensional grouping processes along edges and contours with two-dimensional, region-based processes (Grossberg 1993, 1994, Sejnowski & Hinton 1985). The focus of this chapter will be limited, however, to some aspects of one-dimensional grouping of contours and boundaries. These contours can originate from lines and edges in the image, and also from lines of discontinuities in image properties such as texture, motion, or depth, as will be discussed further below. Such contour-based processes are important in segmentation on their own right, and can also be integrated with complementary region-based processes (Geman & Geman 1984, Mumford & Shah 1989).

8.3   Extracting Globally Salient Structures

When we look at an image such as figure 8.4a, it appears that our attention is somehow immediately drawn to the main object which we then recognize as a car. For most observers, the car is found immediately, without the need to scan the image systematically, and without first attempting to recognize some structures in other parts of the image.

Structures that attract our attention need not be recognizable objects. In figure 8.4 b-d, for example, the round blobs are relatively easy to detect as the most salient, figure-like structures in these images. These are examples of segmentation and selection processes that appear to operate early and define certain parts of the image as figure-like based on geometric properties of the contours. In this section, a method is developed for extracting salient structures of this type.

In examining the processes that make such structures salient in our perception, it is useful to draw a distinction between local and global saliency. Our attention is sometimes drawn to an item in the image because this item differs in some local property from neighboring elements; for example, a green dot in an image of red dots, or a vertical line segment surrounded by horizontal ones. This phenomenon of local saliency has been investigated in a number of psychological studies (e.g., Treisman & Gelade 1980, Julesz 1981). In other cases (such as figure 8.4c,d) the salient structure has no conspicuous local part, with a distinguishing local property such as color, orientation, contrast, or curvature. Although the elements comprising the structure are not individually salient, their arrangement makes the figure as a whole somehow globally figure-like and conspicuous. In the more general case, the saliency of an image structure may be determined by the combination of both local and global aspects. For example, the saliency of the blobs in figure 8.4 can be further enhanced by increasing their contrast with respect to the background.

The next section describes a model that has been developed to extract certain classes of globally salient structures from images (Shashua & Ullman 1988). This process is not intended to offer a complete solution to the segmentation of such images, but, as we will see in more detail later, to provide a useful stage in solving the problem.

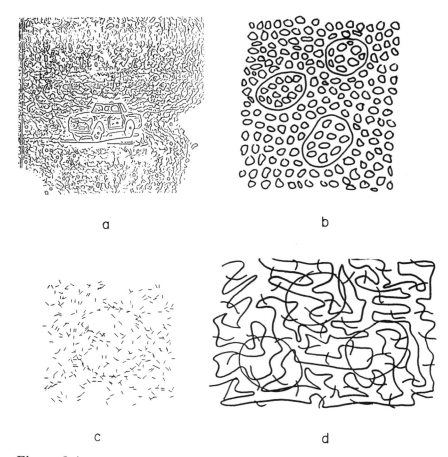

a   b

c   d

Figure 8.4
In each of these contour images certain structures are more salient and figure-
like than the background contours. The salient structure can be of a recognizable object, as in *a*, or just blob-like shapes. Global properties of the contour
affect the perceived saliency.

8.3.1   Defining a Saliency Measure

The model for extracting salient image structures proceeds by computing a measure of saliency at each point in the image. A successful model of this type will assign high saliency measure to image structures that are also salient in human perception, and should provide an efficient method for extracting from the image the conspicuous structures such as the car or the blobs in figure 8.4.

For simplicity, the input image is assumed to be composed of contours. Such contours may be, for example, the lines and edges extracted from the image by line and edge detection processes. They may also come from other sources, for example, from processes that detect boundaries of discontinuity in depth, surface orientation, or motion. The saliency measure in the model increases with the contour's length, and decreases with its curvature or curvature variation; that is, the measure is designed to favor image contours that are long and smooth. In this section I will concentrate on a version that does not take curvature variation into account: the saliency measure simply increases with overall length, and decreases with total curvature. The use of length and curvature parameters was motivated by psychophysical observations regarding the effect of these parameters, and the exact form of the saliency measure was determined by computational considerations that are discussed in more detail below. The grouping of boundary fragments into extended smooth curves is similar to the general notion of "good continuation" used by the Gestalt school of perceptual psychology (Koffka 1935) and, more specifically, to methods of contour grouping based on curvilinearity (Marr 1982, Mohan & Nevatia 1989, Zucker 1987).

The following section is more technical in nature, but its essence can be summarized in simple terms. We first define a saliency measure that increases with the contour's length and smoothness. We then describe a scheme that organizes edge fragments in the image into extended contours, fills in the gaps, and computes the saliency along all the image contours. We show that the scheme, described as a simple parallel network of interconnected line elements, in fact computes the saliency measure defined in this section.

In defining the mathematical form of the saliency measure, it is convenient to consider first a single contour Γ in the image, and ignore all others. The contour is composed of a sequence of small line elements, that may be detected by local line (or edge) detecting units. Let p be a point on Γ, and $S_\Gamma(p)$ be the saliency measure at point p assuming that Γ is the only relevant curve (see figure 8.5). The saliency at p is then given by:

$$S_\Gamma(p) = \sum_i w_i \sigma_i \qquad (8.3.1)$$

In this expression σ_i is the local saliency of the i'th edge element along the curve. For now, σ_i can be thought of simply as having the value "1" for every edge element i, and "0" if the edge element is missing (that is, there is a gap in the curve). More generally, the values of σ_i provide the link between local and global saliency. The idea is that the σ_i's are determined by a local saliency measure; they increase, for example, for higher contrast, or when the i'th edge element differs significantly from its neighbors in color, or orientation. In this manner the scheme can provide a measure of the global saliency based on length and curvature, while at the same time taking into account the local saliency of the individual components.

In the expression above the overall saliency is obtained by a weighted sum of the local contributions σ_i along Γ. The weight w_i of the i'th element is taken to be:

$$e^{-c_i} \qquad (8.3.2)$$

where c_i is the total curvature of the contour from p up to the i'th element. (Mathematically, the total curvature is defined as $\int \kappa^2$, where κ is the curvature at a point.) This is a reasonable choice: the weight achieves the maximal value of 1 for a straight line, and decreases monotonically as the curvature increases.

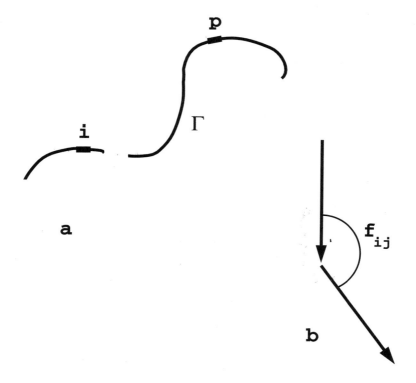

Figure 8.5
Computing the saliency measure. *a.* The saliency of p on the curve Γ is a weighted contribution from all the points on the curve. The contribution falls off with distance and overall curvature. *b.* A part of the network computing the saliency. The network is constructed from interconnected line-detecting elements. The connection strength f_{ij} between neighboring elements is maximal when they are colinear, and falls off with the angle between them.

The saliency measure defined so far depends on a particular curve Γ. The final saliency at p is given by:

$$S(p) = max_\Gamma S_\Gamma(p). \tag{8.3.3}$$

The maximum is taken over all possible curves terminating at p. (This computes the contribution to p from one side of the curve, the contribution from the other side is determined in a similar manner.) In practice, it is also convenient to use a similar definition, but limited to curves of length N:

$$S_N(p) = max_{\Gamma_N} S_{\Gamma_N}(p) \tag{8.3.4}$$

where Γ_N stands for Γ restricted to length N. It is important to note that the optimum is sought over all possible curves, including fragmented ones. In the case of the fragmented circle in figure 8.4, for example, the scheme will in effect consider all the possible curves running through any number of the individual line segments in the figure. This task may appear prohibitive: to determine the salient figure, one must consider all possible curves through all the elements in the image, and along each one integrate the curvature-based saliency measure defined above. As it turns out, the saliency measure described above can in fact be computed by a surprisingly simple, locally connected, network described below.

8.3.2   Computing the Saliency Measure by a Simple Local Network

To detect the globally salient structures in the image, the saliency measure $S(p)$ is computed at each image point p by a locally connected network of processing units. The processing elements can be thought of as local "line detectors" that respond to the presence of lines or edges in the image. The entire image is covered by a grid of $n \times n$ points, where each point corresponds to a specific x, y location in the image. At each point p there are k "orientation elements" coming into p from neighboring points, and the same number of orientation elements leaving p to nearby points. Each orientation element p_i (the i'th orientation element at point p) responds to an input image by signaling the presence of the corresponding line segment in the image. A lack of activity at p_i means that the corresponding line segment is not present in the image. The activity level of the element p_i, denoted by E_{p_i}, will eventually correspond to the saliency of this line element.

The computation by the network proceeds in two stages. The first consists of the initial measurements of local saliency by the individual units. The second consists of interactions between the unit that update the initial measurements in a process that embodies the preference for smooth long contours.

The initial activity is determined by the local saliency of the element, denoted by σ_i. This local saliency is determined by comparing the element in question with surrounding elements along a number of dimensions. For example, if the i'th element has high contrast, or if it is very different from the surrounding elements in color, orientation or direction of motion, then its local saliency will be high. To account for global rather than local saliency, the activity $E(p_i)$ is then modified by interactions with the neighboring elements, so that eventually it also measures the length and the curvature of the contour passing through p_i.

The activity $E(p_i)$ is updated by the following simple local computation:

$$
\begin{aligned}
E_{p_i}^{(0)} &= \sigma_i \\
E_{p_i}^{(n+1)} &= \sigma_i + \rho \max_{p_j} E_{p_j}^{(n)} f_{i,j}
\end{aligned}
\tag{8.3.5}
$$

where p_j is one of the k possible neighbors of p_i. In this formula, $f_{i,j}$ are "coupling constants" between neighboring line elements. The main property of these coupling constants is that they decrease with the angle between successive elements (see figure 8.5). A particular choice of the coupling constants above can ensure that the computed saliency will depend directly on the total curvature along the contour (although curvature is not measured directly, as in the scheme developed by Zucker, Dobbins & Iverson 1989). The factor ρ is of secondary importance; it makes the contributions of distant locations smaller than that of nearby elements along the curve (for more detail, see Shashua & Ullman 1988).

The saliency computation as defined above is simple and local: at each step in the iteration at a given element, the element simply adds the maximal contribution of its k neighbors to its original local saliency σ_i.

The interesting point about this computation is that by using the simple updating formula for the quantity E_{p_i}, the network computes the desired measure $S(p)$, defined above (in 8.3.3), at every point p. For a limited number of iterations, the network will compute the saliency measure $S_N(p)$, and will converge to $S(p)$ as the number of iterations increases. It may appear surprising that such a simple local computation is sufficient for this task, since the saliency measure S at a point p in the image is in fact a rather elaborate measure. For each possible curve Γ passing through p, it must compute a measure S_Γ, and select the best one (with highest S_Γ). The computation achieves all of this without explicitly tracing and then examining different curves. Although the number of possible curves of length N increases exponentially as the number N grows, the computation is only linear in the length N. The mathematical analysis and more details of this process can be found in Shashua & Ullman (1988).

Figure 8.6 shows examples of the computation applied to several figures. The first is the car image in figure 8.4a (only a portion of the image is shown). The figure on the left is a "saliency map" after 30 iterations of the computation. In this representation, the wider, lighter contours are those with higher saliency $E(p)$. It can be seen that the activity in the background is reduced compared with the activity in the figure. The figure on the right shows the five most salient contours by the end of the 30 iterations.

Although the process successfully selects the main object in this image, it should be noted that, in general, the saliency computation described above is not intended to model the entire process of selecting out a candidate object from the image. A more plausible view is that such a selection process is obtained in two stages. The

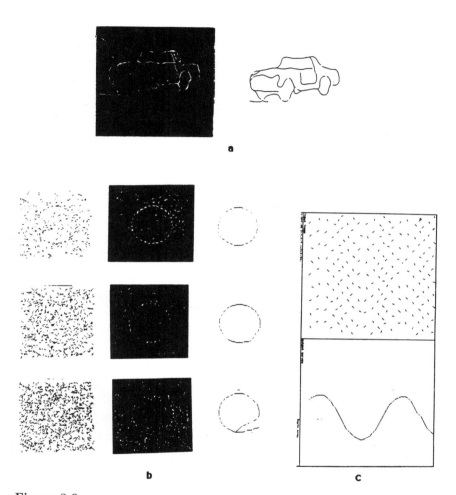

Figure 8.6

Examples of the saliency computation. The figure shows the input image,
the saliency map after several iterations, and the final output of the most
salient contours. (*a*). The car image in 8.3a. Left: the saliency map after 30
iterations. Right: the five most salient contours. (*b*). Left: the input images,
blobs buried in noise. Center: the saliency map after 10 iterations. Right:
the most salient contours in the respective maps. (*c*). Top: a sine curve in
a noisy background. Bottom: the output produced by the saliency network.
After Shashua & Ullman (1988).

first stage, which is applied uniformly and in parallel across the entire image, selects and "highlights" a small number of contours. A candidate object can then be selected by processing these preferred contours further. This second stage can be more serial, and applied preferentially to the contours selected in the first stage, rather than to all the contours in the image. This "completion" stage is discussed in more detail in a subsequent section.

Figure 8.6b shows a fragmented circle embedded in increasing amounts of noise. The left column illustrates the input figures. It can be noted that in the first two images the circle is immediately discernible by our perceptual system despite the gaps and the high noise level. The second column shows the saliency map after 10 iterations, and the right column shows the most salient contour by the end of the 10 iterations (see Shashua & Ullman 1988 for details regarding the selection and tracing of the salient contours in the saliency map). The performance of the scheme appears to be comparable to human perception. It is also worth noting that the gaps in the original figure are filled-in in the course of the computation.

Figure 8.6c was devised by J. Beck from the University of Oregon. Beck has noted that the figure is a challenging one, but still perceivable by human observers. It is also interesting because it is not a simple closed compact figure. Schemes that are sensitive specifically to blob-like structures will not be able to extract such long curved structures. The scheme described above has some preference for closed figures, but, like human vision, can detect any smooth extended structure.

The scheme above prefers smooth, extended boundaries. But clearly a wiggly, jagged contour will also stand out as the main figure against a background of smooth contours. What causes the increased saliency in this case? The answer is that this can be based simply on local saliency. In particular, the jagged contour has loci of high curvature that make it stand out against the smooth background. This is therefore a relatively simple case, and straightforward extensions of the scheme described above should be able to deal with such a case as well.

8.3.3 Contours of Discontinuity

The examples above all used explicit image contours, that is, contours that originate from intensity edges and lines in the image. A similar computation can be applied also to contours that originate from discontinuity not in image intensity, but in other image properties, such as texture, motion, or depth. For example, when separate objects move independently in the field of view, the motion pattern they induce in the image will usually have contours of discontinuity around the objects' boundaries. Similarly, object boundaries will often be associated with discontinuities in texture and depth. Such contours of discontinuity can therefore serve as useful cues for segmentation.

The detection of contours of discontinuity can use a similar computation to the detection of salient curves described above. For instance, consider the detection of object boundaries based on contours of discontinuity in image motion. Motion discontinuities can be detected in the image by locating places of relatively sharp transitions in either velocity or direction of motion. However, such local measurements of motion discontinuity often result in a set of fragmented and inaccurate indications of the loci of discontinuities (Spoerri & Ullman 1987). A natural second stage is therefore to "glue" together the results of the first stage, looking again for contour fragments that form together smooth, long boundaries, as in the saliency computation described above (Spoerri 1991). As a result, local measurements of possible discontinuities that are fragmented and somewhat fuzzy are grouped together to form sharper and more complete contours that often correspond to object boundaries.

8.4   Saliency, Selection, and Completion

The saliency computation outlined above achieves two related goals. First, it starts from local contour elements and links them together to create larger image structures. Such processes of grouping, or "chunking" (Mahoney & Ullman 1988) serve a useful role not only in recognition, but also for visual routines, discussed in the next chapter. Second, the computation produces a "saliency map" of the image. In this map image structures are assigned a measure of saliency that depends on both local properties, such as contrast, color, motion, or disparity, and more global properties, such as length and overall curvature.

However, the saliency map by itself falls short of the goal of the segmentation stage. The main reason is that, because it uses simple and limited criteria for creating larger structures, the process does only a partial job. It can group and highlight useful image structures, but it often still leaves them partial and disconnected. When applied to a structure such as the car image in figure 8.4, it will highlight a number of disconnected pieces, and will leave out parts of the structure that could be joined naturally with the selected structures, provided that one uses grouping criteria that are more sophisticated than merely relying on length and curvature. This suggests that for the purpose of recognition, it would be useful to select first one of the structures in the saliency map, and then analyze it further, with the goal of completing it, or appending to it additional contours (or other image structures) associated with it. This will divide the computation into two different stages. The first is the saliency computation: it is applied to the entire image, and, on the basis of simple criteria, produces larger image structures together with their measure of saliency. The second is the completion stage: it focuses on one of the structures and completes it on the basis of more elaborate criteria. In between the two comes a stage of selection, that is, selecting one of the structures produced in the first stage for further analysis by the completion stage (see Koch & Ullman 1985). Because the second stage is spatially focused and not applied to the entire image, it can employ more serial operations and specialized routines, such as boundary tracing and area filling, discussed in chapter 9, and also processes that are top-down in nature, discussed in chapters 9 and 10. According to this proposal, segmentation will include the following stages:

• Salient segments are detected (in parallel) across the image. This includes both the creation of larger image structures and the creation of a saliency map.

• A salient segment or a set of segments is selected.

• A completion operation is then performed, that completes the selected set by adding associated contours to it.

8.4.1 Completion

The criteria for completion, namely, for deciding which contours should "go together" with the initially selected set, is an interesting open question. One obvious criterion is the use of line continuity. Smooth continuation is already included to some degree in the saliency computation described above. However, if a part of a contour has been selected, and this part has a smooth continuation that is still disconnected from the first part, the two can be grouped together in the completion stage.

In addition to smooth continuation, one can envision a number of additional completion operations, that append to an initial set of contours additional segments that are likely to belong to the same set. Examples are shown in figure 8.7.

The use of vertices: If an already selected line segment terminates in a vertex, other edges of the vertex may be added by the completion process, see 8.7a. The use of co-termination as well as other properties sometimes called "non-accidental" properties for the purpose of segmentation has been suggested and studied by Binford (1981), Palmer (1982), Witkin and Tenenbaum (1983), Lowe (1985), Biederman (1985), and Fischler and Bolles (1986). The general idea is to make use of configurational properties in

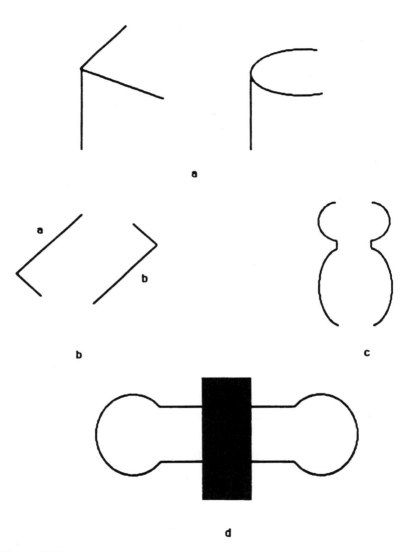

Figure 8.7
Contours that will be grouped together by the completion stage. *a.* Segments
co-terminating in a vertex. *b.* Complementing structures, forming a local
convex figure. *c.* Symmetric contours. *d.* Occlusion.

the image that are unlikely to arise purely by accident. For example, lines in the image that co-terminate in a vertex may in fact be separated in 3-D space, and just happen to project as a 2-D vertex from a particular viewing direction. This possibility is, however, unlikely, and it is more likely that the lines meet physically in space, to create a 3-D vertex. It is therefore reasonable to group them together in the image and assume that they belong to a single 3-D object. The use of such non-accidental properties is important: it increases the likelihood that the segmentation process will group successfully image structures that belong to the same 3-D object. The grouping together of extended smooth curves discussed above can also be seen as an instance of using a non-accidental property for the purpose of grouping.

Complementing structures: Complementing structures that form together, for example, a local convex figure as in 8.7b, could be used for completion. If one was selected, the completion stage will add the second. Grouping criteria of this type were used by Jacobs (1988) is his *Groper* contour-grouping algorithm.

Symmetric contours: If a selected contour has a symmetric counterpart (including the case of parallel segments), the symmetric parts will be selected together, as in 8.7c. The human perceptual system is efficient at detecting symmetry (Barlow & Reeves 1979, Bruce & Morgan 1975, Julesz 1971), and a number of methods have been developed in computer vision for detecting mirror and rotational symmetry, and using symmetry in segmentation (Brady 1982, Fleck 1986, Mohan & Nevatia 1989, Rosenfeld 1986, Subirana-Vilanova 1990).

Occlusion: If a part of an occluded shape has been selected, other parts may be added during the completion stage, as in 8.7d. Grossberg (1993) suggested that contours may also be filled in behind the occluder and may be used for recognition even when they are not perceptually visible in the image.

8.5   What Can Bottom-up Segmentation Achieve?

At the beginning of this chapter we raised a number of questions regarding the goal of the segmentation process. What can be reasonably expected from a bottom-up segmentation process? Can one expect to delineate complete objects in the image prior to recognition? And what should be considered as an object—an eye, a face, the entire person?

From the point of view of recognition, one can circumvent philosophical aspects of the question of what an object "really" is. For the purpose of recognition, we can assume that certain 3-D objects are represented somehow in recognition memory, for example, by collections of their images, as in the view combination approach. The representation of objects in memory is expected to reflect some relevant aspects of the environment: there are reasons for treating a cup, say, as one object, and a plate as another, rather than forming an object from parts of the cup together with parts of the plate. However, the question of what exactly is an object need not concern us here.

The representation of objects in memory includes parts-whole relationships. That is, both an eye and a face can be stored as objects for the purpose of recognition, together with the fact that an eye forms a part of a face. It will be useful in this regard to distinguish the notion of a "part" from that of a "portion." An eye is a part of a face, and it is also a separate object in its own right. However, if only 75% of the eye are visible in the image, the visible piece will be called a portion of the eye, but it will not constitute a separate part. In these terms, segmentation can be viewed as a process that attempts to extract from the image structures that correspond to significant portions of stored object representations.

Such a goal would be both useful and attainable. It may be difficult to delineate in a bottom-up manner complete objects, but, by using processes of the type discussed above, it should be possible in many cases to pull out from the image a set of contours and regions that correspond to a significant portion of an object representation stored in memory. This limited goal should be sufficient for the purpose of recognition. The recognition schemes examined earlier, such as 3-D alignment and image combination do not require a complete and perfect segmentation. We can consider, for example, recognition by 3-D alignment, using for alignment a small set of corresponding image and model features. The main requirement from the segmentation process in this case is to "pull out" a set of features that belong to a single object stored in memory. This will be enough for successful alignment, which will then help to delineate the full object in the image. As we can see from this example, the goal of segmentation is determined by the subsequent recognition processes. Segmentation is not required to be perfect or complete, and in fact, the identification of the full object in the image is obtained not only by the initial segmentation stage, but also by the subsequent alignment and recognition processes.

And what about objects and parts—should we expect the segmentation stage to pull out from the image the eye, or the complete face? If one object also forms a part of another object, the segmentation process should be capable of pulling out significant portions of either one. The question then arises as to which one should be processed first. A similar problem arises in fact simply from the presence of multiple objects in the scene: that they are not recognized simultaneously, we have to somehow determine the order of processing. I will not examine this problem of sequential ordering further, except to comment that it appears possible to limit the number of natural candidates produced by the segmentation stage at a given location.assuming

To illustrate this, Y. Yolles (1989) has implemented a segmentation scheme that produces, at a given location in the image, not a single candidate structure, but a number of structures at increasing scales. The system is given an image and a selected location. It then performs a number of bottom-up grouping operations, based on properties of the image, but without any knowledge concerning the shapes of specific objects. It finally produces a number of image structures around the selected location at a number of different scales. The number of structures produced at a selected location is usually small, and they usually correspond to portions of objects, such as an eye and a face, a wheel and a car, and so on. Subsequent processes will then select one of these structures for further processing. In summary, as far as recognition is concerned, the goal of the segmentation stage is to extract image structures that correspond to significant portions of stored object representations. This goal is more limited than the description of the image as the union of all the objects comprising the scene. For recognition purposes, a structure extracted during the segmentation stage need not correspond to a complete object. The segmentation can be partial, but it is desired to be "conservative," that is, not to mix together pieces of different objects.

The fact that parts of objects can be objects in their own right is not a major complication for recognition. An eye can be represented as an object and recognized on its own, and at the same time be a part of a face, and either object could be selected first for recognition. In the course of performing recognition, it is also desirable that the recognition of a part will facilitate the recognition of the larger object, and, conversely, if the larger object is recognized first, it should facilitate the recognition of the parts. As discussed at the end of chapter 6, this requirement has implications for the organization of recognition memory. Rather than storing object representations in memory as independent entities, they should be stored in a structured manner that includes the part-whole relationships.

The discussion of the segmentation process suggested the use of several sub-stages, including grouping and the creation of larger image structures, the assignment of saliency, the selection of a structure for further processing, and the completion of the selected structure. The computation described in this chapter focused on the first two stages—it can group together small contour or edge fragments and produce a saliency map, based on the criteria of smoothness and length. The process demonstrates how useful image structures can be extracted by a simple bottom-up process. This is, however, only a limited part of the overall process. For example, segmentation is determined not only by contour properties, but also by the properties of the enclosed regions. The issues of selection and completion, including the treatment of occlusion, also need further elaboration from both the computational and psychological perspectives.

The psychophysical evidence also supports the existence of quite elaborate processes of perceptual organization that operate already at the early stages of visual processing, and that depend on both local (such as contrast, depth, color, and motion) and more global (such as length and overall curvature) properties. From a biological standpoint, low-level visual areas, such as V2 and MT (and possibly V1) may be involved in this type of processing.

To implement the interactions between local elements used in the saliency computation, the processing in these areas may use the lateral connections within a given cortical area, or perhaps interconnections between neighboring cortical areas. It will be of interest to examine further in physiological studies segmentation mechanisms of the type discussed in this chapter. For example, one could examine the response of orientation-selective units in different visual areas to stimuli of the kind shown in 8.4. In particular, one could test whether the response of a unit increases when it is embedded in a salient configuration outside the unit's own receptive field. Another interesting possibility is to test whether the grouping of the elements into a larger unit can be signaled by increased firing synchrony among the appropriate units, rather than by increased activation (Gray *et al.* 1989).

9 Visual Cognition and Visual Routines

The use of shape and spatial information is not limited to the tasks of object recognition and classification. We also use visual analysis of shape and spatial relations for other tasks, such as manipulating objects, planning and executing movements in the environment, selecting and following a path, and the like. In assembling objects and parts, for instance, we can use our visual perception to decide how different parts may fit together, and then plan and guide our movements accordingly. Problems of this type can be solved without implicating object recognition. They do require, however, the visual analysis of shape and spatial relations among parts. This visual analysis of shape properties and spatial relations is called here "visual cognition."

The visual extraction of spatial information is remarkably flexible and efficient. We can look for instance at an image such as figure 9.1 and obtain, almost at a glance, answers to a variety of possible questions regarding shape properties and spatial relations. For example, in figure 9.1a, the task is to determine visually whether the X lies inside or outside the closed curve. Observers can establish this relation effortlessly, unless the boundary becomes highly convoluted. The answer appears to simply "pop out," and we cannot give a full account of how the decision was reached. It is interesting to note that this capacity appears to be associated with relatively advanced visual systems. The pigeon, for example, that shows an impressive capacity for figure classification and recognition (Herrnstein 1984), is essentially unable to perform this task in a general manner. It can respond correctly only for simple figures, and appears to base its decision on simple local cues such as the convexity or concavity of the contour nearby (Herrnstein et al., 1989).

Figure 9.1b is an example of establishing a shape property, in this case, judging the elongation of ellipse-like figures. (The terms "shape property" refer to a single item, while spatial relations, such as "above," "inside," "longer-than," and the like, involve two or more items.) The visual system is quite precise at detecting such elongations: reliable judgements of elongation can

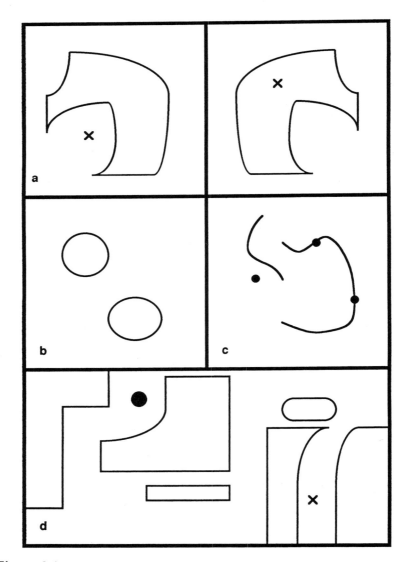

Figure 9.1
Examples of several "visual cognition" tasks involving the analysis of shape
properties and spatial relations. (*a*) Inside/outside relation: it is easy to determine whether the "X" lies inside or outside the closed figures. (*b*) Elongation
judgements. (*c*) The task is to determine whether two black dots lie on a
common contour. (*d*) The task is to determine whether the black disk can be
moved to the location of the "X" without colliding with nearby shapes.

be obtained when the major axis of the ellipse is $4 - 5\%$ longer than the minor axes (Cave 1983). Interestingly, the judgements become more difficult when the axes themselves, without the ellipses, are present. This suggests that the judgement is not based on the extraction and comparison of the main axes, and it remains unclear what mechanisms in fact subserve this and related shape judgements. In figure 9.1c the task is to determine whether two black dots lie on a common contour. Again, a solution is obtained by "merely looking" at the figure. In figure 9.1d the task is more complex—to determine whether the black disk can be moved to the location of the X without colliding with any of the other shapes. We can use our visual capacities to somehow "simulate" the motion and obtain the correct answer.

These figures and tasks are artificial, but similar visual cognition problems also occur in natural settings, in the course of object manipulation, planning actions, reasoning about objects in the scene, navigation, and the like, and are solved routinely by the visual system. We also make use of visual aids such as diagrams, charts, sketches and maps, because they draw on the system's natural capacity to manipulate and analyze spatial information, and this ability can be used to help our reasoning and decision processes.

Spatial analysis of this kind does not require object recognition, that is, it does not depend on object naming or on whether we have seen the objects in the past. It does require, however, the analysis of shape and spatial relations among shapes. The visual system can perform a wide variety of visual cognition tasks with remarkable proficiency, that cannot be mimicked at present by artificial computer vision systems.

In view of the fundamental importance of the task, it is not surprising that our visual system is indeed remarkably adept at establishing a variety of spatial relations among items in the visual input. This proficiency is evidenced by the fact that the perception of spatial properties and relations that are complex from a computational standpoint nevertheless often appears immediate and effortless. The apparent immediateness and ease of perceiving spatial relations is, however, deceiving: it conceals in fact a complex array of processes that have evolved to establish certain spatial relations with considerable efficiency. This makes the problems of visual cognition intriguing and challenging: What mechanisms and processes in human vision are responsible for these computations? How can machines achieve similar capacities?

The mechanisms underlying such visual cognition are still ill-understood. It is still unclear what internal shape processes are used, even in simple configurations, such as comparing the length of two line segments. How is such a comparison actually accomplished? Can the system somehow apply an "internal yardstick" to the segments, shift them internally to test their overlap, or use some other method? The answer to such questions remains at present unknown. I will discuss here a possible approach, based on the notion of visual routines (Ullman 1984). Let me summarize first the basic idea, and then discuss the approach in more detail.

The approach assumes that the perception of shape properties and spatial relations is achieved by the application of so-called "visual routines" to the early visual representations. These visual routines are efficient sequences of basic operations that are "wired into" the visual system. Routines for different properties and relations are then composed from the same set of basic operations, using different sequences. Using a fixed set of basic operations, the visual system can assemble different routines and in this manner extract an essentially unbounded variety of shape properties and spatial relations. Within this framework, to understand visual cognition in general, it will be required to identify the set of basic operations used by the visual system. An explanation of how we determine a particular relation such as "above," "inside," "longer-than" or "touching," would require a specification of the visual routine used to extract the shape or property in question.

9.1 Perceiving "Inside" and "Outside"

An Example: Perceiving "Inside" and "Outside" It will be useful to examine in more detail a specific example of our perception of spatial relations in a scene: the example will make clear that our effortless perception of shape properties and spatial relations is in fact a complex process, whose exact nature remains at present quite mysterious. The example will also serve to introduce the notion of visual routines, and how they may be applied to the extraction of abstract shape properties and spatial relations.

To consider a concrete example, let us assume that the visual input consists of a single closed curve, and a small "X" figure (as in figure 9.1a), and one is required to determine visually whether the X lies inside or outside the closed curve. The correct answer appears to be immediate and effortless, and the response is usually fast and accurate (Varanese 1983). One possible reason for our proficiency in establishing inside/outside relations is their potential value in figure-ground segmentation: if the bounding contour of an object has been identified, features inside the contour belong to the objects, and features outside it to the surround (see also Sutherland (1968) and Kovás & Julesz (1994) on inside/outside relations in perception).

The immediate perception of the inside/outside relation is subject to some limitations: when the bounding contour becomes highly convoluted, the distinction between inside and outside becomes more difficult. These limitations are not very restrictive, however, and the computations performed by the visual system in distinguishing "inside" from "outside" exhibit considerable flexibility: the curve can have a variety of shapes, and the positions of the X and the curve do not have to be known in advance. In mathematics, the "Jordan curve theorem" states that a simple closed plane curve separates the plane into two disjoint regions, its inside and outside. It may appear surprising that this is a theorem that requires an elaborate proof, since the concepts of inside and outside are intuitively clear to us, and we "see" that the theorem must be true. This is probably based on our visual cognition capacity to deal effectively with spatial analysis.

The processes underlying the perception of inside/outside relations are as yet unknown. In the following section I will examine two methods for computing "insideness" and compare them with human perception. The comparison will then serve to introduce the general discussion concerning the notion of visual routines and their role in visual perception.

9.1.1   The Ray-Intersection Method

Shape perception and recognition is often described in terms of a hierarchy of "feature detectors" (Barlow 1972, Milner 1974). According to these hierarchical models, simple features such as short edge and line segments are detected early in the chain of visual processing by specially constructed feature-detecting units. These feature detectors are then combined to produce higher order units such as, say, corner and triangle detectors, leading eventually to the detection and recognition of complete objects. It does not seem possible, however, to construct in such a manner an "inside/outside detector" from a combination of elementary feature detectors. Approaches that are more procedural in nature have therefore been suggested instead.

A simple procedure that can establish whether a given point lies inside or outside a closed curve is the method of ray-intersections. To use this method, a ray is drawn, emanating from the point in question, and extending to "infinity." For practical purposes, "infinity" is a region that is guaranteed somehow to lie outside the curve. The number of intersections made by the ray with the curve is recorded. (The ray may also happen to be tangent to the curve without crossing it at one or more points. In this case, each tangent point is counted as two intersection points.) If the resulting intersection number is odd, the origin point of the ray lies inside the closed curve. If it is even (including zero), then it must be outside (see figure 9.2a, b).

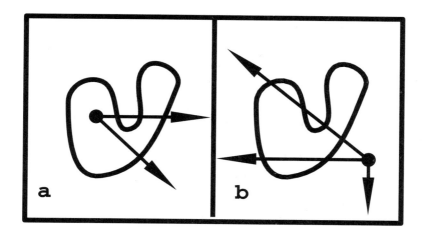

Figure 9.2
The ray-intersection method for establishing inside/outside relations. When
the point lies inside the closed curve, the number of intersections is odd (*a*);
when it lies outside, the number of intersections is even (*b*).

This procedure has been implemented in computer programs
(Evans 1968, Winston 1977, chapter 2), and it may appear rather
simple and straightforward. The success of the ray-intersection
method is guaranteed, however, only if rather restrictive constraints are met. First, it must be assumed that the curve is
closed, otherwise an odd number of intersections would not be in-
dicative of an "inside" relation (see figure 9.3*a*). Second, it must
be assumed that the curve is isolated: in figure 9.3*b* and *c*, point
p lies within the region bounded by the closed curve *c*, but the
number of intersections is even.

These limitations of the ray-intersection method are not shared
by the human visual system: in all of the above examples the correct relation is easily established. In addition, some variations of
the inside/outside problem pose almost insurmountable difficulties
to the ray-intersection procedure, but not to human vision. Suppose that in figure 9.3*d* the problem is to determine whether any
of the points lies inside the curve *C*. Using the ray-intersection

procedure, rays must be constructed from all the points, adding significantly to the complexity of the solution. In figure 9.3e and f the problem is to determine whether the two points marked by dots lie inside the same curve. The number of intersections of the connecting line is not helpful in this case in establishing the desired relation. In figure 9.3g the task is to find an innermost point—a point that lies inside all of the three curves. The task is again straightforward, but it poses serious difficulties to the ray-intersection method. It can be concluded from such considerations that the computations employed by our perceptual system are different from, and often superior to, the ray-intersection method.

9.1.2 The "Coloring" Method

An alternative procedure that avoids some of the limitations inherent in the ray-intersection method uses the operation of activating, or "coloring" an area. Starting from a given point, the area around it in the internal representation is somehow activated. This activation spreads outward until a boundary is reached, but it is not allowed to cross the boundary. Depending on the starting point, either the inside or the outside of the curve, but not both, will be activated. This can provide a basis for separating inside from outside. An additional stage is still required, however, to complete the procedure, and this additional stage will depend on the specific problem at hand. One can test, for example, whether the region surrounding a "point at infinity" has been activated. Since this point lies outside the curve in question, it will thereby be established whether the activated area constitutes the curve's inside or the outside. In this manner a point can sometimes be determined to lie outside the curve without requiring a detailed analysis of the curve itself.

Alternatively, one may start at an infinity point, using for instance the following procedure: (1) move towards the curve until a boundary is met, (2) mark this meeting point, (3) start to track the boundary, in a clockwise direction, activating the area on the right, (4) stop when the marked position is reached. If a termi-

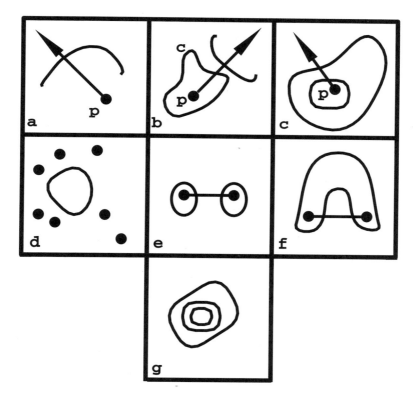

Figure 9.3
Limitations of the ray-intersection method. *a.* An open curve: the number of intersections is odd, but *p* does not lie inside *C*. *b, c.* Additional curves may change the number of intersections, leading to errors. *d − g.* Variations of the inside/outside problem that render the ray-intersection method ineffective. In *d* the task is to determine visually whether any of the dots lie inside *C*; in *e, f*, whether the two dots lie inside the same curve; in *g* to find a point that lies inside all three curves.

nation of the curve is encountered before the marked position is reached, the curve is open and has no inside or outside. Otherwise, when the marked position is reached again and the activation spread stops, the inside of the curve will be activated. Both routines are possible, but, depending on the shape of the curve and the location of the X, one or the other may become more efficient. A similar procedure can be used to solve some of the other problems. For example, to test whether two locations lie inside the same enclosing curve, as in 9.3e, f, the activation will start at one location, and its spread to the second location will be tested.

The coloring method avoids some of the main difficulties with the ray-intersection method, but it also falls short of accounting for the performance of human perception in similar tasks. It seems, for example, that for human perception the computation time is to a large extent scale-independent. That is, the size of the figures can be increased considerably with only a small effect on the computation time (Varanese 1983). In contrast, in the activation scheme outlined above, computation time will increase with the size of the figures. The basic coloring scheme can be modified to increase its efficiency and endow it with scale independence, for example by performing the computation simultaneously at a number of resolution scales (Jolicoeur, Ullman & MacKay 1991). Even the modified scheme will have difficulties, however, competing with the performance of the human perceptual system. Evidently, elaborate computations will be required to match the efficiency and flexibility exhibited by the human perceptual system in establishing inside/outside relationships.

It is interesting to note, with respect to coloring, that a fast coloring operation for the purpose of visual processing was implemented in an analog VLSI device developed by Luo, Koch, and Mathur (1992). This "figure-ground" chip labels all the points inside a contour with one voltage value and all the points outside the contour with a different voltage. The basic idea is to simply let the voltage spread in a resistive network, and separate electrically the inside of a region from its outside. The structure that carries out this operation is constructed from a regular grid of points connected by resistors and switches. The presence of an edge between two grid points causes the switch at the corresponding location to open, and in this manner the inside and the outside of the contour become disconnected. (A mechanism is also incorporated to complete small breaks in the contour.) When the voltage at a selected point is set to a relatively high "figure" value, the voltage at all connected points will rise to this value, while the background points will remain at the lower "background" value.

The goal of the above discussion was not to examine the perception of inside/outside relations in particular, but to introduce the problems associated with the seemingly effortless and immediate perception of spatial relations. The main conclusions from the discussion are, first, that the efficient and flexible computation of spatial relations is a complex task, and, second, that a natural approach to the problem involves the internal application of a sequential process, somewhat similar to a computer program, to the image representation.

The discussion so far used a specific example—perceiving "inside" and "outside" to raise some of the main issues and possible directions. I next turn to a more general discussion of the difficulties associated with the perception of spatial relations and shape properties, and the implications of these difficulties to the processing of visual information.

9.2   Spatial Analysis by Visual Routines

In this section we will examine the general requirements imposed by the visual analysis of shape properties and spatial relations. The difficulties involved in the analysis of spatial properties and relations are summarized below in terms of three requirements that must be met by the "visual processor" that performs such an analysis. The three requirements are (i) the capacity to establish abstract properties and relations (abstractness), (ii) the capacity to establish a large variety of relations and properties, including newly defined ones (open-endedness), and (iii) the requirement to cope efficiently with the complexity involved in the computation of spatial relations (complexity).

9.2.1   Abstractness

The perception of inside/outside relations provides an example of the visual system's capacity to analyze abstract spatial relations. In this section the notion of "abstract" properties and relations and the difficulties raised by their perception will be briefly discussed.

Intuitively, the concept of being "inside" is abstract, because it does not refer to any particular shape, but can appear in many different forms. More formally, a shape property P defines a set S of shapes that share this property. The property of closure, for example, divides the set of all curves into the set of closed curves that share this property, and the complementary set of open curves. Similarly, a relation such as "inside" defines a set of configurations that satisfy this relation. Clearly, in many cases the set of shapes S that satisfy a property P can be large and unwieldy. It therefore becomes impossible to test a shape for property P by simply comparing it against all the members of S stored in memory. To be more accurate, the problem lies in fact not simply in the size of the set S, but in what may be called the size of the *support* of S.

An observation by Sutherland (1960, 1968) on pattern recognition in simple animals can help to illustrate this distinction. In perceptual experiments, octopuses were trained to successfully distinguish squares from diamonds of different sizes and locations. As it turned out, however, the animals then responded to triangles as equivalent to diamonds. Apparently, what they actually used to make the distinction was the property of having a pointy top, while ignoring the rest of the shape. This property of having a pointy top depends on a small local region (at least for convex shapes), and it can be tested without analyzing the entire shape.

Without getting into detailed definitions, it is clear that because of the restricted support such properties are easier to compute.

When the set of supports is small, the recognition of even a large set of objects can still be accomplished by simple means such as direct template matching. This means that a small number of patterns is stored, and matched against the figure in question. When the set of supports is prohibitively large, a template matching decision scheme will become impossible: we cannot store, for example, all instances of closed curves in the image. The classification task may nevertheless be feasible if the set of shapes sharing the property in question contains certain regularities. This roughly means that the recognition of a property P can be broken down into a set of operations in such a manner that the overall computation required for establishing P is substantially less demanding than the storing of all the shapes in S. The set of all closed curves, for example, is not just a random collection of shapes, and closure can obviously be established without storing all possible instances of closed plane curves. For a completely random set of shapes containing no regularities, simplified recognition procedures will not be possible. The minimal program required for the recognition of the set would in this case be essentially as large as the set itself (c.f. Kolmogorov 1968).

The above discussion can serve to define what is meant here by "abstract" shape properties and spatial relations. This notion refers to properties and relations with a prohibitively large set of supports that can nevertheless be established efficiently by a computation that captures the regularities in the set. For example, closure is an abstract property because it must be established by some process that makes use of general characteristics of closed curves. Our visual system can clearly establish abstract properties and relations of this type. The implication is that it should employ sets of processes for establishing shape properties and spatial relations. The perception of abstract properties such as insideness or closure would then be explained in terms of the computations employed by the visual system to capture the regularities underlying different properties and relations. These computations would be described in terms of their constituent operations and how they are combined to establish different properties and relations.

We have seen already examples of possible computations for the analysis of inside/outside relations. It is suggested that processes of this general type are performed by the human visual system in perceiving inside/outside relations. The operations employed by the visual system may prove, however, to be different from those considered above. To explain the perception of inside/outside relations it would be necessary, therefore, to unravel the constituent operations that are actually employed by the visual system, and how they are used in different situations.

9.2.2   Open-Endedness

As we have seen, the perception of an abstract relation is quite a remarkable feat even for a single relation, such as insideness. Additional complications arise from the requirement to establish not only one, but a large number of different properties and relations. A reasonable approach to the problem would be to assume that the computations that establish different properties and relations share their underlying elemental operations. In this manner a large variety of abstract shape properties and spatial relations can be established by different processes assembled from a fixed set of elemental operations. The term "visual routines," already mentioned above, will be used to refer to the processes composed out of the set of elemental operations to establish shape properties and spatial relations.

A further implication of the open-endedness requirement is that a mechanism is required by which new combinations of basic operations can be assembled to meet new computational goals. One can impose goals for visual analysis, such as "determine whether the green and red elements lie on the same side of the vertical line." That the visual system can cope effectively with such goals suggests that it has the capacity to create new processes out of the basic set of elemental operations.

9.2.3   Complexity

The open-endedness requirement implied that different processes should share elemental operations. The same conclusion is also suggested by complexity considerations. The complexity of basic operations such as the bounded activation (discussed in more detail below) implies that different routines that establish different properties and relations and use the bounded activation operation would have to share the same mechanism rather than have their own separate mechanisms.

A special case of the complexity consideration arises from the need to apply the same computation at different spatial locations. The ability to perform a given computation at different spatial positions can be obtained by having an independent processing module at each location. For example, the orientation of a line segment at a given location is determined in the primary visual cortex in our brain largely independent of other locations: the machinery for detecting a line segment of a particular orientation is duplicated many times within this visual area. In contrast, the computations of more complex relations such as inside/outside independent of location cannot be explained by assuming a large number of independent "inside/outside modules," one for each location. Routines that establish a given property or relation at different positions are likely to share some of their machinery, similar to the sharing of elemental operations by different routines.

Certain constraints will be imposed upon the computation of spatial relations by the sharing of elemental operations. For example, the sharing of operations by different routines will restrict the simultaneous perception of different spatial relations. The application of a given routine to different spatial locations will be similarly restricted. In applying visual routines the need will consequently arise for the sequencing of elemental operations, and for selecting the location at which a given operation is applied.

In summary, the requirements discussed above of abstractness, open-endedness, and complexity, suggest the following conclusions:

1. Spatial properties and relations are established by the application of visual routines to a set of early visual representations.

2. Visual routines are assembled from a fixed set of elemental operations.

3. New routines can be assembled to meet newly specified processing goals.

4. Different routines share elemental operations.

5. A routine can be applied to different spatial locations.

The processes that perform the same routine at different locations are not independent.

6. In applying visual routines mechanisms are required for sequencing elemental operations and for selecting the locations at which they are applied.

9.3   Conclusions and Open Problems

The discussion so far suggests that the immediate perception of seemingly simple spatial relations often requires in fact complex computations that are difficult to unravel. The general proposal is that using a fixed set of basic operations, the visual system can assemble visual routines that are applied to the visual representations to extract abstract shape properties and spatial relations.

The use of visual routines to establish shape properties and spatial relations raise fundamental problems at the levels of computational theory, algorithms, and the underlying mechanisms. A general problem on the computational level is to establish which spatial properties and relations are important for different visual tasks. On the algorithmic level, the problems are how these relations are computed, and what would be a useful complete set of basic operations. These are challenging problems, since the processing of spatial relations and properties by the visual system is remarkably flexible and efficient. When these algorithmic issues become better understood, it will also become possible to consider the construction of a "routine processor" with similar capabilities for practical use in machine vision applications. On the mechanism level, the problem is to find out how visual routines are implemented in neural networks within the visual system. To conclude this section, the main problems raised by the notion of visual routines are listed below, divided into four main categories.

- *The elemental operations.* In the examples discussed above the computation of inside/outside relations employed operations such as drawing a ray, counting intersections, boundary tracing, and area activation. The same basic operations can also be used in establishing other properties and relations. In this manner a variety of spatial relations can be computed using a fixed and powerful set of basic operations, together with means for combining them into different routines.

The first problem that arises therefore is the identification of the elemental operations that constitute the basic "instruction set" in the composition of visual routines.

- *Integration.* The second problem is how the elemental operations are integrated into meaningful routines. This problem has two aspects. First, the general principles of the integration process; for example, whether different elemental operations can be applied simultaneously. Second, there is the question of how specific routines are composed in terms of the elemental operations. An account of our perception of a given shape property or relation such as elongation, above, next-to, inside/outside, taller-than, and the like, should include a description of the routines that are employed in the task in question, and the composition of each of these routines in terms of the elemental operations.

- *Controlling the routines.* The questions in this category are how visual routines are selected and controlled; what triggers the execution of different routines during the performance of visual tasks, and how the order of their execution is determined.

• *Compilation of new routines.* We have seen already that visual routines can be applied in a flexible manner that depends on the task, as well as the properties of the scene being analyzed. Problems that naturally arise, therefore, are how new routines are generated to meet specific needs, and how they are stored and modified with practice. These are interesting problems, but they will not be discussed in detail in this chapter.

In the next section, I will turn to the first of these issues, that is, the elemental operations used by visual routines.

9.4   The Elemental Operations

In this section, we examine the set of basic operations that may be used in the construction of visual routines. In trying to explore this set of internal operations, at least two approaches can be followed. The first is the use of empirical psychological and physiological evidence. The second is computational: one can examine the kind of basic operations that would be useful in principle for establishing a large variety of relevant properties and relations. In particular, it would be useful to examine complex tasks in which we exhibit a high degree of proficiency. For such tasks, processes that match the human system in performance are difficult to devise. Consequently, their examination is likely to provide useful constraints on the nature of the underlying computations.

In exploring such tasks, the examples I will use below employ mainly schematic drawings rather than natural scenes. The reason is that simplified artificial figures allow more flexibility in adapting the pattern to the operation under investigation. As long as we examine visual tasks for which our proficiency is difficult to account for, we are likely to be exploring useful basic operations even if we use simplified drawings rather than natural scenes. In fact, our ability to cope efficiently with artificially imposed visual tasks underscores two essential capacities in the computation of spatial relations. First, that the computation of spatial relations is flexible and open-ended: new relations can be defined and computed efficiently. Second, it demonstrates our capacity to accept non-visual specification of a task and immediately produce a visual routine to meet these specifications.

The empirical and computational studies can then be combined, for example, by comparing the complexity of various visual tasks in the model and in human vision. That is, the theoretical studies can be used to predict how different tasks should vary in complexity, and the predicted complexity measure can be gauged against human performance. We have seen above an example along this line, in the discussion of the inside/outside computation.   Predictions regarding relative complexity, success, and failure, based upon the ray-intersection method prove largely incompatible with human performance, and consequently the employment of this particular method by the human perceptual system can be ruled out.   In this case, the argument is also supported by theoretical considerations showing the inherent limitations of the ray-intersection method.

In this section, only some initial steps towards examining the basic operations problem will be taken. I will examine a number of plausible candidates for basic operations, discuss some available evidence, and raise problems for further study. Only a few operations will be examined; they are not intended to form a comprehensive list. Since the available empirical evidence is scant, the emphasis will be on computational considerations of usefulness. Finally, some of the problems associated with the assembly of basic operations into visual routines will be briefly discussed.

9.4.1   Shifting the Processing Focus

A fundamental requirement for the execution of visual routines is the capacity to control the location at which certain operations take place. For example, the operation of area activation will be of little use if the activation starts simultaneously everywhere. To be of use, it must start at a selected location, or along a selected contour. More generally, in applying visual routines it would be useful to have a "directing mechanism" that will allow the application of the same operation at different spatial locations. It is natural, therefore, to start the discussion of the elemental operations by examining the processes that control the locations at which these operations are applied.

Directing the processing focus (that is, the location to which an operation is applied) may be achieved in part by moving the eyes (Norton & Stark 1971). But this is clearly insufficient: many shape properties and relations can be established without eye movements. A capacity to shift the processing focus internally is therefore required.

Problems related to the possible shift of internal operations have been studied empirically, both psychophysically and physiologically. These diverse studies still do not provide a complete picture of the shift operations and their use in the analysis of visual information. They do provide, however, strong support for the notion that shifts of the processing focus play an important role in visual information processing, starting from early processing stages. The main directions of studies that have been pursued are reviewed briefly in the next two sections.

Psychological Evidence A number of psychological studies have suggested that the focus of visual processing can be directed, either voluntarily or by manipulating the visual stimulus, to different spatial locations in the visual input. They are listed below under three main classes.

The first line of evidence comes from reaction time studies suggesting that it takes some measurable time to shift the processing focus from one location to another. In a study by Eriksen & Schultz (1977), for instance, it was found that the time required to identify a letter increased linearly with the eccentricity of the target letter, the difference being on the order of 100 milliseconds at three degrees from the fovea center. Such a result may reflect the effect of shift time, but, as pointed out by Eriksen & Schultz, alternative explanations are also possible, in particular, that the processing time in general increases with increased distance from the center of the visual field. More direct evidence comes from a study by Posner, Nissen & Ogden (1978). In this study a target was presented seven degrees to the left or right of fixation. It was shown that if the subjects correctly anticipated the location at which the target will appear using prior cuing (an arrow at fixation), then their reaction time to the target in both detection and identification tasks was consistently lower (without eye movements). For simple detection tasks, the gain in detection time for a target at seven degrees eccentricity was on the order of 30 milliseconds.

A related study by Tsal (1983) employed peripheral rather than central cuing. In his study a target letter could appear at different eccentricities, preceded by a brief presentation of a dot at the same location. The results were consistent with the assumption that the dot initiated a shift towards the cued location. If a shift to the location of the letter is required for its identification, the cue should reduce the time between the letter presentation and its identification. If the cue precedes the target letter by k milliseconds, then by the time the letter appears the shift operation is already k milliseconds under way, and the response time should decrease by this amount. The facilitation should therefore increase linearly with the temporal delay between the cue and target until the delay equals the total shift time. Further increase of the delay should have no additional effect. This is precisely what the experimental results indicated. It was further found that the delay at which facilitation levels off (presumably the total shift time) increases with eccentricity, by about eight milliseconds on average per one degree of visual angle.

A second line of evidence comes from experiments suggesting that visual sensitivity at different locations can be somewhat modified with a fixed eye position. Experiments by Shulman, Remington & Mclean (1979) can be interpreted as indicating that a region of somewhat increased sensitivity can be shifted across the visual field. A related experiment by Remington (1978, described in Posner 1980), showed an increase in sensitivity at a distance of eight degrees from the fixation point 50–100 milliseconds after the location had been cued.

A third line of evidence that may bear on the internal shift operations comes from experiments exploring the selective read-out from some form of short-term visual memory (Sperling 1960, Shiffrin, McKay & Shaffer 1976). In such an experiment, an observer is briefly presented with a complex visual stimulus, for example, a collection of numbers arranged in a square matrix. Under such conditions, the observer can recall information from the display only in a very partial manner. If, following the visual presentation, the observers are directed to a particular location in the display, for instance, the third number in the second row, the recollection is usually close to perfect. These experiments suggest that some internal scanning can be directed to different locations a short time after the presentation of a visual stimulus.

The Shift Operation and Selective Visual Attention Many of the experiments mentioned above were aimed at exploring the concept of "selective attention." This concept has a variety of meanings and connotations (Estes 1972), many of which are not related directly to the proposed shift of processing focus in visual routines. The notion of selective visual attention often implies that the processing of visual information is restricted to a small region of space, to avoid "overloading" the system with excessive information. Certain processing stages have, according to this description, a limited total "capacity" to invest in the processing, and this capacity can be concentrated in a spatially restricted region. Attempts to process additional information would detract from this capacity, causing interference effects and deterioration of performance. Processes that do not draw upon this general capacity are, by definition, pre-attentive. In contrast, the notion of processing shift discussed above stems from the need for spatially-structured processes, and it does not necessarily imply such notions as general capacity or protection from overload. For example, the "coloring" operation used above for separating inside from outside started from a selected point or contour. Even with no capacity limitations such coloring would not start simultaneously everywhere, since a simultaneous activation will defy the purpose of the coloring operation. The main problem in this case is in coordinating the process, rather than excessive capacity demands. As a result, the process is spatially structured, but not in a simple manner as in the "spotlight model" of selective attention. In the course of applying a visual routine, both the locations and the operations performed at the selected locations are controlled and coordinated according to the requirements of the routine in question. Therefore, as far as the shift operation is concerned, it is of interest to demonstrate phenomena of attention shift under conditions that do not overwhelm the capacity of the visual system.

Many of the results mentioned above are nevertheless in agreement with the possible existence of a directable processing focus. They suggest that the redirection of the processing focus to a new location may be achieved in two ways. The experiments by Posner (1980) and by Shulman, Remington & Mclean (1979) suggest that it can be "programmed" to move along a straight path using central cuing. In other experiments, such as Remington's and Tsal's, the processing focus is shifted by being attracted to a peripheral cue.

Physiological Evidence Shift-related mechanisms have been explored in the monkey physiologically in the superior colliculus, and in a number of cortical areas: the posterior parietal lobe (area 7) the frontal eye fields, visual areas V1, V2, V4, MT, MST, and the inferior temporal lobe. The general idea of these experiments has been to study whether the response of units in the visual system can be modified by somehow manipulating the experimental animal's attention to different locations in the visual field. It is of interest to examine these studies in connection with the shift operation for two reasons: first, to examine whether there is physiological evidence in support of the proposed shift operation, and second, to try to find out which brain area may be the "controller" that directs the location of processing.

In the superficial layers of the superior colliculus of the monkey, a sub-cortical structure associated with the control of eye movements, many cells have been found to have an enhanced response to a stimulus when the monkey uses the stimulus as a target for a subsequent saccadic eye movement (Goldberg & Wurtz 1972). This enhancement is not strictly sensory in the sense that it is not produced if the stimulus is not followed by a saccade. It also does not seem strictly associated with a motor response, since the temporal delay between the enhanced response and the saccade can vary considerably (Wurtz & Mohler 1976s). The enhancement phenomenon was suggested as a neural correlate of "directing visual attention," since it modifies the visual input and enhances it at selective locations when the sensory input remains constant (Goldberg & Wurtz 1972). The intimate relation of the enhancement to eye movements, and its absence when the saccade is replaced by other responses (Wurtz & Mohler 1976a, Wurtz, Goldberg & Robinson 1982) suggest, however, that this mechanism is specifically related to saccadic eye movements rather than to operations associated with the shifting of an internal processing focus. Similar enhancement that depends on saccade initiation to a visual target has also been described in the frontal eye fields (Wurtz & Mohler 1976) and in prestriate cortex, probably area V4 (Fischer & Boch 1981).

Another area that exhibits a similar phenomenon of a facilitated region that can be shifted around, but not exclusively in relation to saccades, is area 7 of the posterior parietal lobe of the monkey. Using recordings from behaving monkeys, Mountcastle and his collaborators (Mountcastle 1976, Mountcastle *et al.* 1975,) found three populations of cells in area 7 that respond selectively (i) when the monkey fixates an object of interest within its immediate surrounding (fixation neurons), (ii) when it tracks an object of interest (tracking neurons), and (iii) when it saccades to an object of interest (saccade neurons). (Tracking neurons were also described in area MST, Newsome & Wurtz 1982.) Studies by Robinson, Goldberg & Stanton (1978) indicated that all of these neurons can also be driven by passive sensory stimulation, but their response is considerably enhanced when the stimulation is "selected" by the monkey to initiate a response. On the basis of such findings it was suggested by Mountcastle (as well as by Robinson *et al.* 1978, Posner 1980, Wurtz, Goldberg & Robinson 1982) that mechanisms in area 7 are responsible for "directing visual attention" to selected stimuli. These mechanisms may be primarily related, however, to tasks requiring hand-eye coordination for manipulation in reachable space (Mountcastle 1976), and there is at present no direct evidence to link them with visual routines and the shift of processing focus discussed above.

In area TE of the inferotemporal cortex units were found whose responses depend strongly upon the visual task performed by the animal. Fuster & Jervey (1981) described units that responded strongly to the stimulus' color, but only when color was the relevant parameter in a matching task. Richmond & Sato (1982) found units whose responses to a given stimulus were enhanced when the stimulus was used in a pattern discrimination task, but not in other tasks (for instance, when the stimulus was monitored to detect its dimming). Again, it has been suggested that such responses may be linked in general to some form of selective visual attention, but they are not directly implicated in an internal shifting operation.

An elegant experiment concerning physiological mechanisms of selective visual attention is the study of Moran & Desimone (1985) in visual areas V4 and IT of the monkey. In this experiment, two different stimuli were presented simultaneously within the receptive field of a neuron. One was an effective stimulus, the other ineffective. For example, if the unit responded selectively to a red vertical bar, such a bar was used as the effective stimulus, and a horizontal green bar could be used as the ineffective stimulus. By using a shape matching task, the animal's attention was drawn to the effective stimulus on some trials, and to the ineffective stimulus on others. The main finding was that although the physical stimulation was identical in the two conditions, the response was considerably reduced when attention was drawn to the ineffective stimulus. In the initial studies, these attentional effects were found only when the two stimuli were both within the receptive field of the recorded unit, but further studies found similar effects for stimuli with larger separations as well (Luck *et al.* 1992). These results are consistent with the possibility that the recorded units are related to the direction of visual processing to different locations. Van Essen and his collaborators (Connor, Gallant & Van Essen 1993) have tested this possibility further by directing the monkey's attention to different locations, and at the same time plotting the sensitivity profile of the receptive field to a small bar stimulus. They found that in many cases the center of gravity of the receptive field in fact shifted, in the direction of the attentional cue. They have also developed a biological model by which shifts of the center of processing can be obtained (Anderson & Van Essen 1987).

Finally, responses in the pulvinar (Gattas *et al.* 1979, Desimone *et al.* 1990) were shown to be strongly modulated by attentional and situational variables. Combined with the extensive connectivity of the pulvinar to multiple visual areas in the cortex, this led to the suggestion that the pulvinar may be (either by itself or in combination with other structures) the "controller" of location in directing visual attention.

Physiological evidence of a different kind comes from visual evoked potential (VEP) studies. With fixed visual input and in the absence of eye movements, changes in VEP can be induced by instructing the subject to "attend" to different spatial locations (e.g., van Voorhis & Hillyard 1977). This evidence may not be of direct relevance to visual routines, since it is not clear whether there is a relation between the voluntary "direction of visual attention" used in these experiments and the shift of processing focus in visual routines. VEP studies may nonetheless provide at least some evidence regarding the possibility of internal shift operations.

In assessing the relevance of these physiological findings to the shifting of the processing focus it would be useful to distinguish three types of interactions between the physiological responses and the visual task performed by the experimental animal. The three types are task-dependent, task-location dependent, and location-dependent responses.

A response is task-dependent if, for a given visual stimulus, it depends upon the visual task being performed. Some of the units described in area TE, for instance, are clearly task-dependent in this sense: their response depends on whether the task requires shape or color discrimination. In contrast, units in area V1 for example, appear in several studies to be task-independent. Task-dependent responses suggest that the units do not belong to the purely bottom-up generation of the early visual representations, and that they may participate in the application of visual routines. Task-dependence by itself does not necessarily imply, however, the existence of shift operations. Of more direct relevance to shift operations are responses that are both task- and location-dependent. A task-location dependent unit would respond preferentially to a stimulus when a given task is performed at a given location. Unlike task-dependent units, it would show a different response to the same stimulus when an identical task is applied to a different location. At the same time, unlike the spotlight metaphor of visual attention, it would show different responses when different tasks are performed at the same locations.

There is at least some evidence for the existence of such task-location dependent responses. The response of a saccade neuron in the superior colliculus, for example, is enhanced only when a saccade is initiated in the general direction of the unit's receptive field. A saccade towards a different location would not produce the same enhancement. The response is thus enhanced only when a specific location is selected for a specific task.

Unfortunately, many of the other task-dependent responses have not been tested for location specificity. It would be of interest to examine similar task-location dependence in tasks other than eye movement, and in the visual cortex rather than the superior colliculus. For example, the units described by Fuster & Jervey (1981) showed task-dependent response (they responded strongly during a color matching task, but not during a form matching task). It would be interesting to know whether the enhanced response is also location-specific; for example, whether during a color matching task, when several stimuli are presented simultaneously, the response would be enhanced only at the location used for the matching task.

Finally, of particular interest would be units referred to above as location-dependent (but task-independent). Such a unit would respond preferentially to a stimulus when it is used not in a single task but in a variety of different visual tasks. Such units may be part of a general "shift controller" that selects a location for processing independent of the specific operation to be applied. Of the areas discussed above, the responses in area 7, the superior colliculus, and TE, do not seem appropriate for such a "shift controller." The pulvinar remains a possibility worthy of further exploration in view of its rich pattern of reciprocal and orderly connections with a variety of visual areas (Beneveneto & Davis 1977, Rezak & Beneveneto 1979, Robinson & Petersen 1992).

Selecting a Location   Computational considerations strongly suggest the use of internal shifts of the processing focus, and this notion is supported by psychological evidence, and to some degree by physiological data. A related issue to consider is how specific locations are selected for further processing. There are various manners in which such a selection process could be realized. On a digital computer, for instance, the selection can take place by providing the coordinates of the next location to be processed: "move to location x = 5cm, y = 8 cm from the bottom-left corner of the screen." This is probably not how locations are being selected for processing in the human visual system. What determines, then, the next location to be processed, and how is the processing focus moved from one location to the next?

In this section we shall consider one mode of operation which seems to be used by the visual system in shifting the processing focus. This is based on the extraction of certain salient locations in the image, and then shifting the processing focus to one of these distinguished locations. The salient locations are detected in parallel across the base representations, and can then serve as "anchor points" for the application of visual routines. As an example, suppose that a page of printed text is to be inspected for the occurrence of the letter "A." In a background of similar letters, the "A" will not stand out, and considerable scanning will be required for its detection (Nickerson 1966). If, however, all the letters remain stationary with the exception of one which is jiggled, or if all the letters are red with the exception of one green letter, the odd-man-out will be immediately identified. The identification of the odd-man-out letter proceeds in several stages. First the odd-man-out location is detected on the basis of its unique motion or color properties. Next, the processing focus is shifted to this odd-man-out location. As a result of this stage, visual routines can be applied to the figure. By applying the appropriate routines, the figure is identified. A similar process also played a role in the inside/outside example above. It was noted that one plausible strategy is to start the processing at the location marked by the X figure. This raises a problem, since the location of the X and of the closed curve were not known in advance. If the X is somehow sufficiently salient, it can serve to attract the processing focus, and then the execution of the appropriate routine can start immediately at that location.

To conclude, one way in which the focus of processing can be manipulated is by moving it to a salient location in the scene. A question that naturally arises at this point, is: what defines a distinguished location, that can be used for the purpose of shifting the processing focus and applying further operations?

From psychophysical studies it appears that certain odd-man-out locations that are sufficiently different from their surroundings can attract the processing focus directly, and eliminate the need for lengthy scanning. For example, differences in orientation and direction of motion can be used for this purpose, while more complex distinctions, such as the occurrence of the letter "A" among similar letters, cannot define a distinguished location.

By using visual search and other techniques, Treisman and her collaborators (Treisman 1977, Treisman & Gelade 1980, see also Beck & Ambler 1972, 1973, Pomerantz *et al.* 1977) have shown that color and simple shape parameters can define distinguished locations. For example, the time to detect a target blue X in a field of brown T's and green X's does not change significantly as the number of distractors is increased (up to 30 in these experiments). The target is immediately distinguished by its unique color. Similarly, a target green S letter is detectable in a field of brown T's and green X's in constant time. In this case it is probably distinguished by certain shape parameters, such as orientation and curvature.

The notion of a limited set of properties that can be processed "pre-attentively" agrees well with Julesz' studies of texture perception (see Julesz 1981 for a review). In detailed studies, Julesz and his collaborators have found that only a limited set of features, which he termed "textons," can support immediate texture discrimination. These textons include color, elongated blobs of specific sizes, orientations, and aspect ratios, and the terminations of these elongated blobs.

These psychological studies are also in general agreement with physiological evidence. Properties such as motion, orientation, color, and binocular disparity, were found to be extracted in parallel by units that cover the visual field. These units appear to be driven in a bottom-up manner, and their responses are almost unchanging when the animal is awake, anesthetized, or naturally sleeping (Livingston & Hubel, 1981). On physiological grounds these properties are suitable, therefore, for defining distinguished locations prior to the application of visual routines.

It is interesting to note that apparently only simple differences in these early-computed properties can be used to define distinguished locations, prior to the application of visual routines. For example, several studies by Treisman and her collaborators examined the problem of whether different properties measured at a given location can be combined to define a distinguished odd-man-out location. They have tested, for instance, whether a green T could be detected in a field of brown T's and green X's. The target in this case matches half the distractors in color, and the other half in shape. It is the combination of shape and color that makes it distinct. Earlier experiments have established that such a target is distinguished if it has a unique color or shape. The question now was whether the conjunction of two such properties is also immediately distinguished. The empirical evidence indicates that items cannot be immediately distinguished by a conjunction of properties: the time to detect the target increases linearly in the conjunction task with the number of distractors. The results obtained in such studies (Treisman & Gelade 1980) were consistent with a serial self-terminating search in which the items are examined sequentially until the target is reached.

In summary, one way of shifting the processing focus around in the course of applying visual routines is by first extracting a set of distinguished locations in the scene, and then shifting the processing focus towards one of these locations. In defining the distinguished locations, a small number of elementary properties such as orientation, contrast, color, motion, binocular disparity, and perhaps a few others, are computed in parallel across the early visual representations, prior to the application of visual routines. Simple differences in these properties can then be used to define distinguished locations. These locations can then be used in visual routines by moving the processing focus directly to one of the distinguished locations, without the need for extensive search or systematic scan.

9.4.2 Bounded Activation (Coloring) and the Incremental Representations

The bounded activation, or "coloring" operation, was suggested above in examining the inside-outside relation. It consisted of the spread of activation over a surface in the visual representation emanating from a given location or contour, and stopping at discontinuity boundaries. I will discuss below the coloring operation together with some general notion of creating "incremental representations" for subsequent processing.

The results of the coloring operation may be retained for further use by additional routines. Coloring provides in this manner one method for defining larger units in the initial visual representations: the "colored" region becomes a unit to which routines can be applied selectively. An example along this line is illustrated in figure 9.4a. The visual task here is to identify the subfigure marked by the black dot. One may have the subjective feeling of being able to concentrate on this subfigure, and "pull it out" from its complicated background. It is easily seen in the figure that the marked subfigure has the shape of the letter G. The area surrounding the subfigure in close proximity contains a myriad of irrelevant features, and therefore identification would be difficult, unless processing can be directed to this subfigure. The suggestion is, then, that the figure is first separated from its surroundings by using the area activation operation. Recognition routines could then concentrate on the activated region, ignoring the irrelevant contours. This example uses an artificial stimulus, but the ability to identify a region and process it selectively is equally useful for the recognition of objects in natural scenes.

The use of coloring to define a region of interest to which subsequent processing can be applied provides an example of the distinction between the early visual representations (also called "base representations"), and the subsequent, or "incremental" represen-

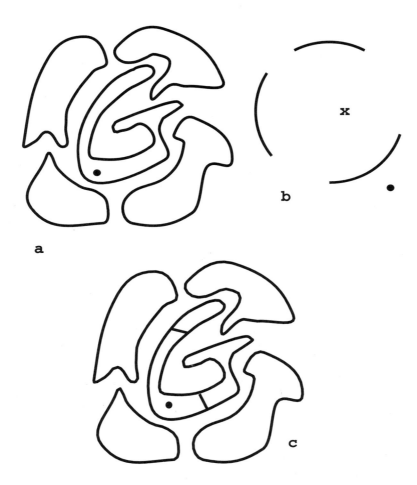

Figure 9.4
Examples of the "coloring" operation. In *a*, the visual task is to identify
the subfigure containing the black dot. This figure (the letter "G") can be
recognized despite the presence of confounding features in close proximity
to its contours. The capacity to "pull out" the figure from the irrelevant
background may involve the bounded activation operation. In *b* the boundaries
are fragmented: the curve is defined by a dashed line, but inside/outside
judgements are still immediate. In *c*, additional internal lines are introduced
into the G-shaped subfigure. If bounded activation is used to "color" this
figure, it must spread across the internal contours.

tations (Ullman 1984). The earlier representations are produced prior to the application of visual routines. They are produced in an unguided bottom-up manner, determined by the visual input and not by the goal of the processing. They are also spatially uniform, in the sense that, with the exception of a scaling factor, similar processes are applied across the visual field, or large parts of it. Examples of early visual representations include the extraction of edges and lines from the image, the computation of motion, disparity, and color.

In contrast with these early processes, the application of visual routines, and the properties and relations they extract, are not determined by the input alone. For the same visual input different aspects will be made explicit at different times, depending on the goals of the computation. Unlike the base representations, the computations by visual routines are not applied uniformly over the visual field (for example, not all of the possible inside/outside relations in the scene are computed), but only to selected objects. Another distinction between the two stages is that the construction of the early representations is essentially fixed and unchanging, while visual routines are open-ended and permit the extraction of newly defined properties and relations.

For various visual tasks, the analysis of visual information therefore divides naturally into two distinct successive stages: the creation of the base representations, followed by the application of visual routines to these representations. The application of visual routines can define objects within the base representations and establish properties and spatial relations that cannot be established within the base representations. It should be noted that many of the relations that are established at this stage are defined not only in the image but also in three-dimensional space. Many spatial judgements we make naturally depend in fact primarily on three-dimensional relations rather than on projected, two-dimensional ones (see, for example, Joynson & Kirk 1960, Lappin & Fuqua 1983). The implication is that various visual routines such as those used in comparing distances operate upon a three-dimensional representation, rather than a representation that resembles the two-dimensional image. Since the base representations already contain three-dimensional information, the visual routines applied to them can also establish such properties and relations in three-dimensional space.

Discontinuity Boundaries for Coloring   The activation operation is supposed to spread until a discontinuity boundary is reached. This raises the question of what constitutes a discontinuity boundary for the activation operation. In figure 9.4a, lines in the two-dimensional drawing served for this purpose. In more natural scenes, it is expected that discontinuities in depth, surface orientation, and texture, will all serve a similar role. The use of boundaries to check the activation spread is not straightforward: it appears that in certain situations the boundaries do not have to be entirely continuous in order to block the coloring spread. In figure 9.4b, a curve is defined by a fragmented line, but it is still immediately clear that the X lies inside and the black dot outside this curve. If activation is to be used in this situation as well, then incomplete boundaries should have the capacity to block the activation spread. It is interesting to note that inside/outside judgements using dashed boundaries appear to require somewhat longer times compared with continuous curves, suggesting that fragmented boundaries may indeed require additional processing (Varanese 1983).

Finally, the activation is sometimes required to spread across certain boundaries. For example, in figure 9.4c, which is similar to figure 9.4a, the letter G is still recognizable, in spite of the internal bounding contours. To allow the coloring of the entire subfigure in this case, the activation must spread across internal boundaries.

In conclusion, the bounded activation, and in particular, its interactions with different contours, is not a simple process. It is possible that as far as the activation operation is concerned,

boundaries are not defined universally, but may be defined somewhat differently in different routines.

A Possible Mechanism for Bounded Activation   The "coloring" spread can be realized by using only simple, local operations. The activation can spread in a network in which each
element excites all of its neighbors. A second network containing a map of the discontinuity boundaries can be used to check
the activation spread. An element in the activation network will
be activated if any of its neighbors is "turned on," provided that
the corresponding location in the second, control network, does
not contain a boundary. The turning on of a single element in
the activation network will thus initiate an activation spread from
the selected point outwards, that will fill the area bounded by
the surrounding contours. Each element may also have neighbor-
hoods of different sizes, to allow a more efficient, multi-resolution
implementation. In such a multi-scale scheme, the time to color
a shape becomes almost independent of the shape's size. Such
schemes were developed and implemented by Shafrir (1985) and
by Mahoney and Ullman (1988).

In this scheme, an "activity layer" serves for the execution of
the basic operation, subject to the constraints in a second "control
layer." The control layer may receive its content (the discontinuity boundaries) from a variety of sources, which thereby affect the
execution of the operation. An interesting question to consider is
whether the visual system incorporates mechanisms of this general sort. If this were the case, the interconnected network of
cells in cortical visual areas may contain distinct subnetworks for
carrying out the different elementary operations. Some layers of
cells within the retinotopically organized visual areas would then
be best understood as serving the execution of basic operations.
Other layers receiving their inputs from different visual areas may
serve in this scheme for the control of these operations.

We still know very little about the kind of computations that
are taking place in the visual system in the course of performing

visual cognition tasks, but an interesting point to consider is that if such networks for executing and controlling basic operations are in fact incorporated in the visual system, they will have important implications for the interpretation of physiological data. In exploring such networks, physiological studies that attempt to characterize units in terms of their optimal stimuli would run into difficulties. The activity of units in such networks would be better understood not in terms of high-order features extracted by the units, but in terms of the basic operations performed by the networks. The testing and interpretation of units in these networks would depend not on finding the optimal stimulus conditions for the unit, but rather on the visual tasks that cause the unit to be active. Elucidating the basic operations would be helpful in providing clues for understanding the activity in such networks and their patterns of interconnections.

9.4.3   Boundary Tracing

Since contours and boundaries of different types are fundamental entities in visual perception, a basic operation that could serve a useful role in visual routines is the tracking of contours in an internal visual representation. A simple example that will benefit from the operation of contour tracing is the problem of determining whether a contour is open or closed. If the contour is isolated in the visual field, an answer can be obtained by detecting the presence or absence of contour terminators. This strategy would not apply, however, in the presence of additional contours. This is an example of the "figure in a context" problem (Minsky & Papert 1969): figural properties are often substantially more difficult to establish in the presence of additional context. In the case of open and closed curves, it becomes necessary to relate the terminations to the contour in question. The problem can be solved by tracing the contour and testing for the presence of termination points on the traced contour.

Another simple example which illustrates the role of boundary tracing is shown in figure 9.5a. The question here is whether

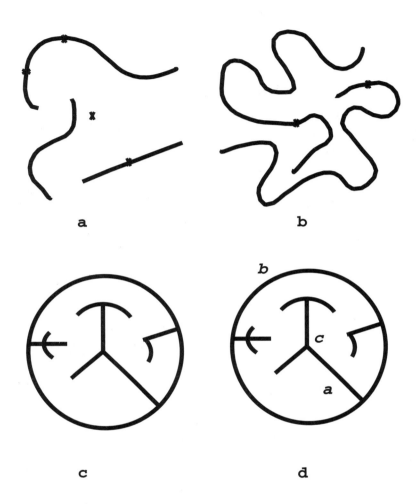

Figure 9.5
Examples of the boundary tracing operation. In *a*, the task is to determine visually whether two small X's lie on the same curve. This simple task requires in fact the application of a visual routine that is likely to include the use of a tracing operation. In *b* the task is similar, but the figure, after the study of Jolicoeur, Ullman & Mackay (1986), was designed to change the separation of the two X's when they appeared on the same curve, while keeping their direct distance fixed. In *c*, the task is to determine visually whether there is a part connecting the center of the figure to the surrounding circle. In *d* the solution is labeled. The interpretation of such labels also relies upon the use of common natural visual routines.

there are two small X's lying on a common curve. The answer seems immediate and effortless, but how is it achieved? Clearly, it cannot be mediated by a fixed array of two-X's-on-a-curve detectors. This simple perception conceals in fact a more elaborate chain of events that involves the application of a visual routine. In response to the question, a routine has been compiled and executed. An appropriate routine for this task can be constructed if the repertoire of basic operations included a shift to the X's and the tracking of curves. The tracking provides in this task a useful role of integrating information from different parts of the same contour, in the presence of other contours nearby.

Another example of the possible use of boundary tracing goes back to the inside/outside example discussed above. Tracking can be used in conjunction with the area activation operation to establish inside/outside relations, by moving along a boundary, coloring only one side. If the curve is closed, its inside and outside will be separated. Otherwise, the fact that the curve is open will be established by the coloring spread, and by reaching a termination point while tracking the boundary.

The possible use of an internal tracing process has been investigated in a number of studies (Jolicoeur & Ingleton 1991, Jolicoeur, Ullman & Mackay 1986, 1991, McCormick & Jolicoeur 1991, 1992, Pringle & Egeth 1988), and the results clearly support the use of a contour tracing operation. For example, in a study by Jolicoeur, Ullman & Mackay (1986), subjects were presented with stimuli composed of two separate curves. In all trials there was a small X at the fixation point, intersecting one of the curves. A second X could lie either on the same or on the second curve, and the observer's task was to decide as quickly as possible whether the two X's lay on the same or different curves. The physical distance separating the two X's was always the same, (1.8 degree of visual angle). When the two X's lay on the same curve, their distance along the curve could be changed, however, in increments of 2.2 degrees of visual angle, measured along the curve.

The main result from a number of related experiments was that the time to detect that the two X's lay on the same curve increased monotonically, and roughly linearly, with their separation along the curve. This result suggests the use of a tracing operation, proceeding along the curve from the location of the first X to the second. The short presentation time (250 milliseconds) precluded the tracing of the curve using eye movements, hence the tracing operation must have been performed internally. Similar results were obtained for a range of different stimuli, including simple configurations such as isolated arcs (Pringle & Egeth 1988) and straight lines (Jolicoeur, Ullman & Mackay 1991).

Although the task in this experiment apparently employed a rather elaborate visual routine, it nevertheless appeared immediate and effortless. Response times were relatively short, about 750 milliseconds for the fastest condition. When subjects were asked to describe how they performed the task, the main response was that the two X's were "simply seen" to lie on either the same curve or on different curves. No subject reported any scanning along a curve before making a decision.

Other studies have revealed additional interesting properties of the tracing operation. In a study by Jolicoeur, Ullman & Mackay (1991), it was found that the speed of tracing depended on properties of the curve, in particular its curvature and the proximity to other contours in the scene. The average speed of tracing in these experiments was about 40 degrees of visual angle, measured along the curve, per second, but it could be higher or lower, depending upon the conditions in the scene (Pringle & Egeth 1988). Tracing speed was highest for straight contours, and decreased systematically with the contour's curvature. The tracing speed was also higher when the curve was isolated in the visual field, free of nearby clutter, and slowed down in the presence of nearby contours. Finally, it turns out that within a broad range the tracing time is invariant to the absolute size of the pattern (Jolicoeur & Ingleton 1991, Pringle & Egeth 1988). If the entire display is simply scaled by a factor of, say, two, the tracing time does not double, but remains essentially unchanged. As mentioned above, the tracing time does depend on the curvature and proximity to other curves, but the relevant factors are the relative rather than the absolute distances. If the curve length is doubled, but at the same time all the other parameters, such as the distances to nearby curves, are also doubled, then the tracing time will not be affected.

It seems from these studies that internal boundary tracing is a fairly sophisticated operation, that attempts to perform the tracing as efficiently as possible. Perhaps the simplest implementation of a boundary tracing operation would be to march in a fixed step-size from one point to the next along the curve. Such a process will be insensitive, however, to parameters such as curvature and proximity to other curves. A more efficient process would adjust itself to the properties of the scene. One could use a coarser tracing mechanism for relatively straight, isolated contours, and a finer mechanism for a highly curved contour or a cluttered environment. This could be likened to the use of an adjustable beam moving along the curve. When the traced curve is relatively straight and isolated, one could use a larger beam, moving in larger steps along the curve. In the presence of nearby clutter, for instance, a smaller beam, moving in smaller steps, will be used (see Jolicoeur, Ullman & Mackay, 1991, McCormick & Jolicoeur 1991, for further discussion). Mahoney and Ullman (1988) proposed a similar mechanism, in which the curve is first divided into "chunks" of optimal size, and curve tracing subsequently proceeds along a succession of such chunks. If internal tracing is indeed one of a small set of basic operations, it is perhaps not surprising to find out that a fairly efficient and sophisticated mechanism is used for the task.

It is also interesting to note that when the same task employed colored curves, such as a green and a red one, the distance effect, and the effects of curvature and proximity, all but disappeared. The task could now be solved by using a simplified strategy, of checking whether the two X's lie locally on a curve of the same color. It appears that the visual system makes use of this shortcut, and adjusts the strategy used, even without deliberate or conscious planning, to the available information.

The example above employed the tracking of a single contour. In other cases, it would be advantageous to activate a number of contours simultaneously. In figure 9.5c, for instance, the task is to establish visually whether there is a path connecting the center of the figure to the surrounding contour. The solution can be easily obtained by looking at the figure, but again, it must involve in fact a complicated chain of processing. To cope with this seemingly simple problem, visual routines must (i) identify the location referred to as "the center of the figure," (ii) identify the outside contour, and (iii) determine whether there is a path connecting the two. (It is also possible to proceed from the outside inwards.) In analogy with the area activation, the solution can be found by activating contours at the center point and examining the activation spread to the periphery. In figure 9.5d, the solution is labeled: the center is marked by the letter c, the surrounding boundary by b, and the connecting path by a. Labeling of this kind is common in describing graphical material. To be unambiguous, such notations must rely upon the use of common, natural visual routines. The label b, for example, is detached from the figure and does not identify explicitly a complete contour. The labeling notation implicitly assumes that there is a common procedure for identifying a distinct contour associated with the label.

Finally, it should be noted that the examples illustrated above used contours in schematic line drawings. However, if boundary tracking is indeed a basic operation in establishing properties and spatial relations, it is expected to be applicable not only to such contours, but also to the different types of contours and discontinuity boundaries in the early representations, such as boundaries defined by discontinuity in depth, motion, and texture. It should also be able to deal with incomplete boundaries, and to cope with the presence of intersections and branching points along the contour.

In summary, the tracing and activation of boundaries are useful operations in the analysis of shape and the establishment of spatial relations. Psychophysical studies provide strong support for the employment of such internal tracing by the visual system. This is a complicated operation since flexible, reliable tracing should be able to cope with breaks, crossings, and branching, and with different resolution requirements.

9.4.4 Marking

In the course of applying a visual routine, the processing shifts across the base representations from one location to another. To control and coordinate the routine, it would be useful to have the capability to keep at least a partial track of the locations already visited.

A simple operation of this type is the marking of a single location for future reference. This operation can be used, for instance, in establishing the closure of a contour. As noted in the preceding section, closure cannot be tested in general by the presence or absence of terminators, but can be established using a combination of tracing and marking. The starting point of the tracing operation is marked, and if the marked location is reached again the tracing is completed, and the contour is known to be closed.

Figure 9.6a shows a similar problem, which is a version of a problem examined in the previous section. The task here is to determine visually whether there are two X's on the same curve. Once again, the correct answer is perceived immediately. To establish that only a single X lies on the closed curve, one can use the above strategy of marking the X and tracking the curve. When the tracing is completed, we know that we have reached the same X, as opposed to a second one. Again, the problem cannot be solved by pre-existing detectors specialized for the task. Instead it is suggested that this simple perception of the X on the curve involved the application of visual routines that employ operations such as marking and tracing.

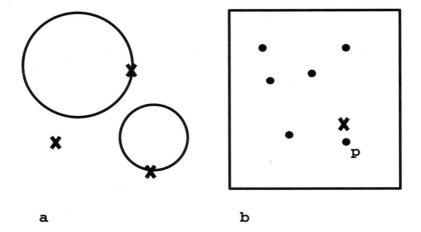

a   b

Figure 9.6
The use of marking. The task in *a* is to determine visually whether there are
two X's on a common curve. The task could be accomplished by employing
marking and tracing operations. *b*. The use of an external reference: the
position of point *p* can be defined and retained relative to the predominant X
nearby.

Many other tasks may benefit from the marking of more than a single location (Pylyshyn 1988). A simple example is visual counting, that is, determining as fast as possible the number of distinct items in view (Atkinson, Campbell & Francis 1969, Kowler & Steinman 1979). For a small number of items visual counting is fast and reliable. When the number of items is four or less, the perception of their number is so immediate, that it gave rise to conjectures regarding special "Gestalt" mechanisms that can somehow respond directly to the number of items in view, provided that this number does not exceed four (Atkinson, Campbell & Francis 1969).

It is in fact possible, in principle, to construct special counting mechanisms of this type. For example, in their book "Perceptrons," Minsky and Papert (1969, chapter 1) describe parallel networks that can count the number of elements in their input (see also Milner 1974). Counting is based on computing the predicates "the input has exactly M points" and "the input has between M and N points" for different values of M and N. For any given value of M, it is possible to construct a special network that will respond only when the number of items in view is exactly M. Unlike visual routines which are composed of elementary operations, such a network can adequately be described as an elementary mechanism by itself, responding directly to the presence of M items in view (Ullman 1980). Unlike the shifting and marking operations, the computation is performed by these networks uniformly and in parallel over the entire field.

Counting can also be performed, however, not by elaborate networks, constructed specifically for this task, but by simple visual routines that employ elementary operations such as shifting and marking. It could be achieved by shifting the processing focus among the items of interest without scanning the entire image systematically. In more complicated displays, shifting and marking can also be used for visual counting by scanning the entire scene in a fixed predetermined pattern.

There are two main differences between counting by visual routines of one type or another on the one hand, and by specialized counting networks on the other. First, unlike the perceptron-like networks, the process of determining the number of items by visual routines can be decomposed into a sequence of elementary operations. The problem of decomposing perceptual processes into simpler components is an interesting issue that lies at the heart of the controversy concerning Gibson's notion of "direct perception" (Ullman 1980). Second, in contrast with a counting network that is specially constructed for the task of detecting a prescribed number of items, the same elementary operations employed in the counting routine also participate in other visual routines. Although we do not know how counting of this type is in fact achieved by the visual system, counting by visual routines appears more attractive than the counting networks. It does not seem plausible to assume that visual counting is essential enough to justify specialized networks dedicated to this task alone. In other words, visual counting is simply unlikely to be by itself an elementary operation. It is more plausible that visual counting can be performed efficiently as a result of our general capacity to generate and execute visual routines, and the availability of the appropriate elementary operations that can be harnessed for the task.

Marking and the Integration of Information in a Scene
The marking of a location for later reference requires a coordinate system, or a frame of reference, with respect to which the location is defined. One general question regarding marking is, therefore, what is the referencing scheme in which locations are defined and remembered for subsequent use by visual routines. One possibility is to maintain an internal "egocentric" spatial map that can then be used in directing the processing focus. The use of marking would then be analogous to reaching in the dark: the location of one or more objects can be remembered, so that they can be reached (approximately) in the dark without external reference

cues. It is also possible to use an internal map in combination with external referencing. For example, the position of point q in figure 9.6b can be defined and remembered using the prominent X figure nearby. In such a scheme it becomes possible to maintain a crude map with which prominent features can be located, and a more detailed local map in which the position of the marked item is defined with respect to the prominent feature.

To be useful in the natural analysis of visual scenes, the marking map should also be preserved across eye motions. This means that if a certain location in space is marked prior to an eye movement, the marking should point to the same spatial location following the eye movement. Such a marking operation, combined with the incremental representation, can play a valuable role in integrating the information across eye movements and from different regions in the course of viewing a complete scene. Suppose, for example, that a scene contains several objects, such as a man at one location, and a dog at another, and that following the visual analysis of the man-figure we shift our gaze and processing focus to the dog. The visual analysis of the man figure has been summarized in the incremental representation, and this information is still available at least in part as the gaze is shifted to the dog. In addition to this information we keep a spatial map, a set of spatial pointers, which tell us that the dog is at one direction, and the man at another. Although we no longer see the man clearly, we have a clear notion of what exists where. Roughly speaking, the "what" is supplied by the incremental representations, and the "where" by the marking map.

In such a scheme, we do not maintain a full panoramic representation of the scene (Rayner 1978). After looking at various parts of the scene, our representation of it will have the following structure. There would be a retinotopic representation of the scene in the current viewing direction. To this representation we can apply visual routines to analyze the properties of, and relations among, the items in view. In addition, we would have markers to the spatial locations of items in the scene already analyzed. These markers can point to peripheral objects, and perhaps even to locations outside the field of view (Attneave & Pierce 1978). If we are currently looking at the dog, we would see it in fine detail, and will be able to apply visual routines and extract information regarding the dog's shape. At the same time we know the locations of the other objects in the scene (from the marking map) and what they are (from the incremental representation). We know, for example, the location of the man in the scene. We also know various aspects of his shape, although it may now appear only as a blurred blob, since they are summarized in the incremental representation. To obtain new information, however, we would have to shift our gaze back to the man-figure, and apply additional visual routines.

We have examined above a number of plausible elemental operations including shift, bounded activation, boundary tracing, and marking. These operations would be valuable in establishing abstract shape properties and spatial relations, and some of them are partially supported by empirical data. They certainly do not constitute a comprehensive set, but it appears that a small set of operations will still be sufficient to perform rather elaborate visual computations.

Visual routines that are much more complex than the simple tasks used in the discussion above have been used in computational studies by Chapman (1991, 1992) in the context of a sophisticated computer system that interprets its environment visually in the course of playing an interactive video game. The computer program developed by Chapman simulates the activities of a human player of the game. The program is presented with a screen of the kind used in many computer games. The screen is in fact not presented visually, but its content is made available to the computer program. The task of the program is to produce commands for moving the game's characters on the screen and for producing various actions, such as picking up objects or shooting at an opponent. Producing the appropriate commands at any given instant in the game requires the analysis of the visual display to determine, for instance, a path to a desired target, obstacles to avoid, directions of potential threats, possible hiding places, and the like. This is performed by the program by applying appropriate visual routines, determined by the various tasks, to an internal image of the changing game display. Although the tasks were varied and sometimes quite complex, different combinations of a small and fixed set of basic operation proved sufficient to perform all the visual analysis regarding shapes and their relations required for playing the game successfully. Another example is a system developed by Romanycia. Using a somewhat augmented set of basic operations, the system can respond to queries about the image, and extract a variety of shape properties and spatial relations, for example, finding line crossings, concave and convex regions, closed curves, isolated triangles, vertical rectangles, triangles inside squares, vertical bars that are parts of triangles, convex shapes inside closed curves, and so on.

The discussion in the last few sections of the basic operations and their use in establishing spatial relations illustrates that in perceiving spatial relations the visual system accomplishes with intriguing efficiency highly complicated tasks. There are two main sources for the complexity of these computations. First, as was illustrated above, from a computational standpoint, the efficient and reliable implementation of each of the elemental operations poses challenging problems. It is evident, for instance, that a sophisticated specialized processor would be required for an efficient and flexible bounded activation operation, or for the tracing of contours and boundaries. In addition to the complications involved in the realization of the individual elemental operations, new complications are introduced when the elemental operations are assembled into meaningful visual routines. As illustrated by the inside/outside example, in perceiving a given spatial relation different strategies may be employed, depending on various parameters of the stimuli such as the complexity of the boundary, or the distance of the X from the bounding contour. The immediate perception of spatial relations often requires, therefore, selection among possible routines, followed by the coordinated application

of the elemental operations comprising the visual routines. Some
of the problems involved in the assembly of the elemental operations into visual routines are discussed briefly in the next section.

9.5   The Assembly and Storage of Routines

The use of visual routines allows a variety of properties and relations to be established using a fixed set of basic operations. We
have discussed above a number of plausible basic operations. In
this final section I will raise some of the general problems associated with the construction of useful routines from combinations
of basic operations.

The appropriate routine to be applied in a given situation depends on the goal of the computation, and on various parameters
of the configuration to be analyzed. We have seen, for example,
that the routine for establishing inside/outside relations may depend on various properties of the configuration: in some cases it
would be efficient to start at the location of the X figure, in other
situations it will be more efficient to start at some other locations,
or from the bounding contour. As another example, suppose that
we are trying to locate an item defined by the combination of two
properties, such as a vertical red item in a field of vertical green
and horizontal red distractors, as in (Treisman 1977, Treisman &
Gelade 1980). There are at least two alternative strategies for
detecting the target: one may either scan the red items, testing
for orientation, or scan the vertical items, testing for color. The
distribution of distractors in the field determines the relative efficiency of these alternative strategies. In such cases it will useful,
therefore, to precede the application of a particular routine with
a stage where certain relevant properties of the configuration to
be analyzed are sampled and inspected.

We have also seen in discussing the tracing operation that when
additional information was available, such as differently colored
curves, the strategy for solving the two-x's-on-a-curve changed.
This appears to be a general situation—the same goal can often

be reached by different routines, and various parameters of the scene, such as the density and distribution of objects and their properties, will determine which routine is more appropriate.

This introduces the "assembly problem" of visual routines, that is, the problem of how routines are constructed in response to specific goals, and how this generation is controlled by aspects of the scene to be analyzed. In the above examples, a goal for the computation was set up externally, and an appropriate routine was applied in response. In the course of performing visual cognition tasks, routines are usually invoked in response to internally generated goals. Some of these routines may be stored in memory rather than assembled anew each time they are needed. These stored visual routines constitute "perceptual programs" somewhat analogous to stored "motor programs" for executing movements. The repeated execution of a familiar visual task may then use pre-assembled routines for inspecting relevant features and relations among them. Since routines can also be generated efficiently by the assembly mechanism in response to specific goals, it would probably be sufficient to store routines in memory in a skeletonized form only. The assembly mechanism will fill in details and generate intermediate routines when necessary. The perceptual activity will be guided by setting pre-stored goals that the assembly process will then expand into detailed visual routines.

The application of pre-stored routines rather then assembling them again each time they are required can lead to improvements in performance and the speed-up of performing familiar perceptual tasks. These improvements can come in fact from two different sources. First, assembly time will be saved if the routine is already "compiled" in memory. Second, stored routines may be improved with practice, as a result of either external instruction, or by modifying routines when they fail to accomplish their tasks efficiently. In the final chapter of the book we will discuss cortical mechanisms that could be used in the assembly, storage, and application of visual routines.

9.6 Routines and Recognition

Visual routines are useful for a variety of visual tasks that arise in
the course of reasoning about objects in the scene, visual search,
the manipulation of objects and planning of actions, navigation
in the environment, the use of visual aids such as diagrams and
maps, and the like. What about visual recognition—are visual
routines also used in the course of visual object recognition?

Recognition and visual routines are both important parts of
high level vision, but they are generally separate processes. As
we have seen in discussing object recognition, the general capacity to establish abstract shape properties and spatial relations is
usually not required in the recognition of specific 3-D objects.
To recognize a familiar 3-D object, we typically use specialized
recognition processes that compare the current view with stored
models, as discussed in previous chapters, rather than the processes of visual routines discussed in this chapter. The specialized
recognition mechanisms are useful for the specific task of object
recognition, but are not suitable for general visual cognition tasks.
To inspect a map, for instance, and locate the largest city between
the lake and the highway, the mechanisms of object recognition
are no longer sufficient (although they may be employed as a part
of performing the task), and we will use other processes of visual
routines. Biologically, the processes related to visual routines may
be associated primarily with the so-called dorsal system of visual
processing, and the recognition process with the ventral processing stream (Ungerleider & Mishkin 1982, Ungerleider & Haxby
1994).

Under some cases, however, visual routines could also serve a
useful role for the purpose of object recognition. This is not surprising since, as discussed in the introduction, recognition is a general term, and more than a single process can be used for the task
of identifying or classifying an object. Routines can be employed,
for example, to scan a large object that cannot be perceived effectively in a single glance, or we may use boundary tracing to

trace the stream of connected characters in recognizing cursive handwriting. As was mentioned in the previous chapter, some of the processes of image segmentation, in particular selection and completion, also involve the use of visual routines. As another example, visual routines can be used to distinguish between two closely similar objects. To distinguish between two similar cars, for instance, or between highly similar faces, we may first perform a more general recognition, and then execute a "disambiguating routine" that inspects special distinguished locations, looking for the shape of a specific part, or a special marking and the like. In such cases final recognition is obtained by the combination of general recognition mechanisms, of the type discussed in previous chapters followed by the application of appropriate disambiguating routines.

10 Sequence Seeking and Counter Streams: A Model for Information Flow in the Visual Cortex

In this chapter computational considerations discussed throughout this book, combined with psychophysical and biological data, are used to propose a model for the general flow of information in the visual cortex. The model uses a process called "sequence-seeking" which is a search for a sequence of transformations and mappings that link an input image with a stored object representation. This process has two main characteristics: it is bi-directional, bottom-up as well as top-down, and it explores in parallel a large number of alternative sequences.

From a biological standpoint, this computation is performed by a structure called "counter-streams." This structure is composed of two complementary pathways, an ascending one from low to high visual areas, and a descending one going in the opposite direction, from high to low visual areas. Roughly, the suggestion is that the ascending pathway performs bottom-up processing, starting from the image and proceeding to high-level visual areas. The descending pathway is performing top-down visual processing, starting with stored models in higher level visual areas and proceeding to lower regions. Within each pathway, multiple processing sequences are explored. The integration of bottom-up with top-down processing is achieved by the interactions between the two complementary processing streams. A biological embodiment of this model in cortical circuitry is proposed. The model serves to account for known aspects of cortical interconnections and to derive new predictions.

The focus of the model is on the task of visual recognition and the structure of the visual cortex. The proposed computation has, however, useful generic aspects, and the possible applicability of the scheme to other domains will also be briefly considered. The first part of this chapter will focus on the computations being performed, and the second on details of the biological model. The second part assumes some familiarity with the principle features of cortical anatomy and physiology. Good summaries of the biological background can be found in (Crick & Asanuma 1986, Hubel 1988, Zeki 1993).

10.1 The Sequence-seeking Scheme

As we have seen throughout this book, object recognition is complicated by the large variations that exist between different images of the same object. To obtain effective recognition, it is therefore insufficient to perform a direct matching between the input and the stored patterns. Considerable processing is required to compensate for the effects of viewing direction, illumination, occlusion, and deformations in the object itself. The discussion in previous chapters led to several conclusions regarding the general nature of the processes involved in object recognition, including the use of pictorial representations, the combination of universal bottom-up with top-down, object and class-specific processes, the establishment of a correspondence between the image and the stored model, and the role of classification on the way to individual identification. These conclusions will be used below to motivate key aspects of the proposed model.

10.1.1 Bi-directional Processing

The approach to recognition developed in the previous chapters includes as a major component the manipulation and matching of pictorial representations. This matching is complicated by the fact that the image and model representations can be initially quite dissimilar. The recognition process therefore includes processes that compensate for the initial discrepancy between the two representations. These compensation processes make use of stored information based on accumulated past experience, at both the object and class levels.

In most of the alternative approaches to recognition, including the invariant properties scheme as well as the structural description method, compensation is obtained without consulting the stored internal models: recognition proceeds by processing the incoming image to obtain a new representation that is invariant to the effects of viewing conditions, such as illumination and viewing direction. These representations are matched at a final stage with object models stored in memory. In contrast, in the schemes discussed earlier (including 3-D alignment and the view-combination methods) the stored models play a much more active role. For example, the compensation for the 3-D viewing direction does not require the extraction from the image of a 3-D invariant description. Instead, the compensation is based primarily on the use of 3-D information stored with the object model, either at the level of the object's general class, or at the level of the specific object model. Similarly, effects of object deformations, such as facial expressions, are compensated for by applying class-specific processes, as opposed to some universal bottom-up processes. In the case of illumination effects, which are often assumed to be handled by purely bottom-up processes, evidence was also cited supporting the view that they are compensated in part by class-specific processes adapted, for example, to the class of upright faces.

The use of stored information in the recognition process can take various forms. For example, to compensate for the effect of viewing direction, the method of 3-D alignment uses the explicit manipulation of an internal 3-D model, while the image combination method uses for the same purpose combinations of stored views. The crucial point for the current discussion is not the particular method used, but the basic strategy of using stored object- and class-specific information. We have seen that the compensation for viewing conditions on the basis of the image alone is difficult, and may require the extraction of precise 3-D shape as well as the illumination conditions. Instead of relying exclusively on bottom-up processing of the input image, the recognition process can be aided by using the results of accumulated past experience with the same or similar objects. For example, the human visual system is repeatedly exposed to face images, seen from different directions and under a variety of illumination conditions. It would be clearly advantageous to use some general learned properties of faces in the recognition of a novel face image. These properties include the 3-D shape of a typical face, the effects of illumination, shadows, and specularities, as well as common facial expressions.

Bottom-up and Top-down Processing   We have already used above and in previous chapters the notions of "bottom-up" and "top-down" processing, which are frequently used terms in the psychology of perception as well as in computer vision. The distinction is that bottom-up processes are involved in the analysis of the incoming image, and top-down processes originate with stored models and information associated with them. The term "top-down" is sometimes used in a more restricted sense, to refer to the influence on perception of expectations and high-level contextual information; for example, the kind of knowledge one can bring to bear when one is entering a familiar office. Here, the term is used in a broader sense, to refer to processing applied to the stored models rather than the incoming image. Such processes can use knowledge about individual objects and object classes in the recognition process, including information concerning 3-D shape, the effect of illuminations, and deformations that an object may undergo.

In computer vision, the integration of bottom-up with top-down processing has been a major concern. During the 70's, the emphasis was placed heavily on top-down processes. Fundamental difficulties with building computer vision systems led to the view that the processing must be guided primarily by knowledge associated with stored models of objects and scenes, and systems in the 70's were constructed using this approach (Freuder 1974, Tenenbaum & Barrow 1976). Following in part the work of Marr (1982), the emphasis shifted towards bottom-up processing, but it became also evident that a key issue is the integration of bottom-up with top-down processing (Grimson 1990a, Marr 1982, Tsotsos 1990), and both processes are used in current recognition systems (e.g., Grimson 1990a, Lowe 1985, Ullman 1989, Yuille & Hallinan 1992).

In many neural network models the emphasis has been placed on bottom-up processing. Networks of the back-propagation type, for example (Rumelhart, Hinton & Williams 1986, Matan *et al.* 1992) are essentially feed-forward networks, where the computation proceeds in one direction from the input layer through successive intermediate stages to the output layer. The flow of information in the opposite direction is used for a different purpose—modifying the network when the errors in its output become too large. The general view expressed by Hubel and Wiesel in describing their findings regarding the visual cortex (Hubel & Wiesel 1962, 1968) also emphasizes the bottom-up direction. This informal model regards visual information processing as the successive extraction of increasingly elaborate image features. Different cell types in the visual cortex, in particular simple, complex, and hyper-complex V1 units, were originally thought to form the first stages of this hierarchy. Some neural network models, such as the Neocognitron (Fukushima 1988), attempted to simulate this mode of processing and apply it to pattern recognition problems.

In contrast with this approach, the computational studies examined in previous chapters argue in favor of a more balanced combination of bottom-up and top-down processing. As we have seen, the processes of object recognition, including the difficult tasks of compensating for the effects of viewing direction, illumination, occlusion and object deformation, can benefit from the use of information associated with objects and object classes, acquired through past experience. A major requirement for a model of information processing in the visual cortex is therefore the capacity to combine efficiently bottom-up processing starting at the image and proceeding to high-level cortical areas, with top-down processing, starting at stored object representations, and proceeding from high to low visual areas. As will be discussed in more detail later, the structure of the cortex clearly supports this possibility. A major characteristic of cortical interconnections is the reciprocity of the connections between visual areas. If a visual area in the cortex sends ascending connections to another visual area higher up in the hierarchy of visual processing, then, as a general rule, the second area sends reciprocal connections to the first. (This connectivity, including the so-called lateral interconnections, will be examined in more detail in the second part of this chapter.) A key ingredient of the proposed model is the suggestion that, roughly speaking, the ascending pathways in the visual cortex subserve mainly bottom-up processing, and the descending pathways mainly top-down processing. Certain interactions between the streams provide a mechanism for integrating the two types of processing.

It is worth noting that in the matching of pictorial descriptions discussed in previous chapters, the use of bi-directional processing, top-down as well as bottom-up, is considerably more natural than in alternative approaches to recognition, because similar processes can be applied to the incoming image and to stored object models. This can be contrasted, for example, with schemes based on the use of invariant properties, discussed in chapter 2. Bottom-up processes are used in these schemes to extract from the image a vector of property values, but it is not apparent how to proceed in the opposite direction, that is, how processing could be applied to the property vector in a top-down fashion to help the recognition process.

10.1.2   Exploring Multiple Alternatives

A second general strategy proposed by the current model is based on a combination of computational considerations and biological constraints. Computational experience with object recognition schemes, including 3-D alignment and the view-combination method, have shown that the recovery of the appropriate compensation transformations often require considerable search. For example, some of the best-performing recognition systems using 3-D alignment (Fischler & Bolles 1986, Grimson 1990a, Huttenlocher & Ullman 1990, Lowe 1985, Thompson & Mundy 1987), search for the best match between an input shape and a candidate internal model by exploring and comparing multiple (e.g., in the hundreds) possible 3-D poses of the internal model. As a simple illustration of the problems involved, suppose that to compensate for possible size variations, we wish to normalize the input image in size, that is, scale it either up or down, to bring it into agreement with a predetermined canonical size. One problem that arises is how do define and measure the size of the input image. Typical measures used in practice include the apparent area of the object in the image, or the size of the smallest shape (such as a square or ellipse) containing the viewed object. Such measures can give an estimate of the object's size, but a precise value is difficult to obtain. For example, when applied to a face image, the measured size will change with changes in viewing direction, will be affected by shadows and occlusion, will change with the hairdo, and so on. This is a simple example of an ubiquitous problem: the alignment process cannot be performed instantly and uniquely, since a search for the appropriate parameters in usually unavoidable. This may seem a somewhat practical consideration, but it has significant implications due to the inherent slowness of neuronal systems.

In current computer systems the multiple comparisons are performed sequentially, at a rapid succession. In much slower neuronal networks, timing considerations (Maunsell & Gibson 1992, Rolls, Tovee & Lee 1991, Thorpe et al. 1991) place rather stringent restrictions on the use in recognition of long chains of calculations, or the use of iterative relaxation processes (Geman & Geman 1984, Poggio, Torre & Koch 1985, Mumford 1992). A visual cortical area may introduce an average delay of about 10-15 milliseconds, and there are several (about six) stations spanning the hierarchy from V1 to anterior IT. This suggests that visual processing should usually require a limited number of sweeps through the system.

Neuronal systems are slow, but inherently parallel, and therefore a useful strategy is to explore multiple alternatives simultaneously, rather than explore and refine them in sequence. In some widely used neural network models, such as back-propagation (Rumelhart, Hinton & Williams 1986) or the Hopfield model (Hopfield 1982), the simultaneous computation of competing alternatives is usually not used explicitly. It is interesting to note, however, that in several neural network models in areas such as arm control (Jordan & Jacobs 1993), or handwriting recognition (Matan et al. 1992), the explicit exploration of multiple alterna-

tives proved useful in dealing with complex problems that were
not handled effectively by more standard models. For example, in
a network developed at AT&T for reading hand-written numerals
(Matan *at al.* 1992), the letter identification stage is preceded by a
process that segments the string into individual characters. This
turned out to be a difficult task, and the segmentation was often unreliable. The approach adopted was to perform explicitly a
number of different candidate segmentations, and later select the
best solution among the different alternatives. The network also
uses multiple-scale analysis: it processes the same input through
separate mechanisms tuned to different scales of the letters, and
again selects at the end the best alternative. This design proved
to perform better than a single network trained to become scale-
invariant. Another example is a network developed for controlling
the 3-D movements of a simplified arm (Jordan & Jacobs 1993).
The training of standard neural networks indexNeural network
models failed to converge to a satisfactory solution to this control problem. An approach that proved successful was to train a
number of different sub-networks, each one capable of providing
a good solution under restricted conditions. The combined problem is then treated by letting the different networks work on the
problem individually, followed by a gating and selection stage.

10.1.3   The Counter-streams Structure

The main conclusions reached so far are illustrated pictorially in
figures 10.1 and 10.2 in the domain of face recognition. Figure
10.1a illustrates the problem: the discrepancy between the stored
model and the novel image is initially large, and the two cannot
be matched directly. Figure 10.1b illustrates the combination of
bottom-up and top-down processing. The processes compensating
for the image-to-model differences are applied in part to the stored
model and in part to the incoming image. Top-down processing
is involved in dealing with the effects of viewing direction, facial
expression, and illumination. Bottom-up processing is used in
the figure to handle variations due to position and scale. The

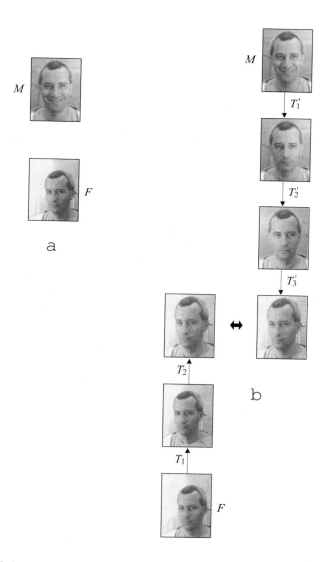

Figure 10.1
a. The stored model and the input image are initially different, and cannot be matched directly. M represents the stored model, F is the novel image. *b.* During the recognition process, bottom-up processes are applied to the incoming image, and top-down processes are applied to the stored model.

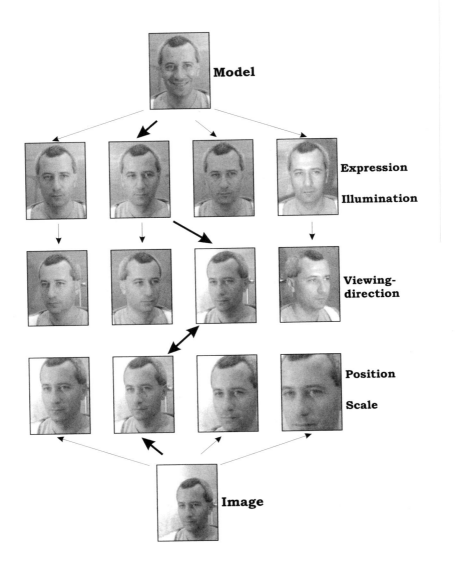

Figure 10.2
Illustration of two main properties of the sequence-seeking process: it uses
bi-directional processing, and the simultaneous exploration of multiple alternatives. The top image represents a stored face model, and the bottom image
is the novel view to be matched with the model. In this example, scale and position are processed by bottom-up processing; facial expression, illumination,
and viewing position, by top-down processing.

model is depicted as a picture to represent the use of pictorial descriptions in the recognition process. However, the stored model is actually not just a grey level image, but a more abstract pictorial representation that also contains more than a single view.

In this figure, a single stream of processing is applied from both directions. How are the appropriate transformations selected at each stage by the system? As discussed above, this is obtained by evaluating in parallel multiple competing alternatives. Figure 10.2 illustrates the exploration of multiple alternatives in the two processing streams. The image at the top represents again a stored internal model of a face, and the image at the bottom is the novel input to be matched with the model.

The novel view differs from the stored model in viewing direction, illumination, and facial expression, demonstrating the limitation of direct image matching. The figure illustrates schematically the two properties of the compensation process discussed so far: the bi-directional processing and the exploration of multiple alternatives. Processes applied to the image are involved, for example, in compensating for differences in position and scale. This is represented in the figure by multiple internal images, at different positions and scales, generated in a bottom-up manner on the ascending stream of processing. Processes applied to the stored model are used in handling the effects of facial expression, illumination, and viewing position. This is represented by multiple internal images, at different illumination and viewing directions, generated from the stored model on the descending stream. The figure does not propose specific methods for performing the compensation processes, but stresses the bi-directional processing, the parallel exploration of multiple alternatives, and the use of pictorial representation in the recognition process.

The flow of the computation is diagrammed more schematically in figure 10.3. The basic operation in this scheme is to seek a sequence of processing steps linking a pattern of activity (S in 10.3) in one cortical area with stored representations (such as M_1, M_2) in another. The pattern S may arise from the image of

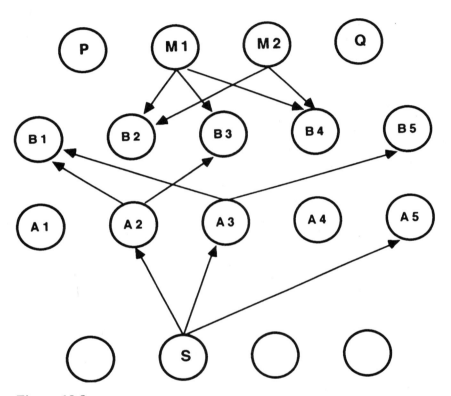

Figure 10.3
The sequence-seeking computation seeks a sequence of pattern-activations
linking a source pattern (S) in one area with stored representations (M_1, M_2)
in another. Nodes represent patterns of activity (co-active populations of
neurons), arrows indicate how patterns activate subsequent patterns. In expanding sequences only a subset of patterns will be activated initially, and
will later decay and be replaced by others. The processing is bi-directional,
and a linking sequence is successfully established when the two searches meet
somewhere in a large network of interconnected patterns.

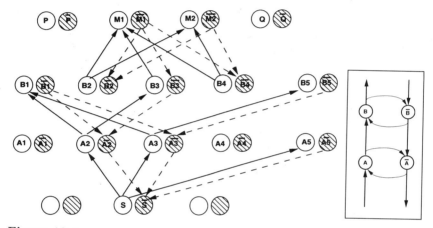

Figure 10.4
Similar to the previous figure, except that each node is split into two complementary ones. The ascending and descending streams proceed along complementary pathways. When a track is being traversed in one stream, it leaves
behind a primed trace in the complementary stream. Inset shows the basic unit of the counter-streams structure. Patterns A, B on the ascending,
$\bar{A}, \bar{B}$ on the descending path. Thin arrows denote connections of the priming
type. This repeating unit is embedded in a network of richly interconnected
patterns.

an object, for example, a familiar face, and the patterns M_i represent stored object models, perhaps in visual area IT. As discussed above, the recognition of the viewed object involves multiple processing stages, applied in part to the incoming pattern and in part to the stored models, in an attempt to establish a match between the incoming pattern and a stored model. Intermediate patterns in the diagram correspond to different representations of the object, for example, at different 3-D orientations and scales. The figure shows a part of a network that in reality will be much larger.

Biologically, the nodes in this schematic figure represent patterns of activity of sub-populations of neurons acting together, possibly with some degree of synchrony (Abeles 1991, Engel *et al.* 1992). That is, each of the patterns, such as A_1, A_2, A_3, is a population of perhaps a few hundred co-active neurons. As in many neural models (Hopfield 1982, Marr 1970, Willshaw, Buneman & Longuet-Higgins 1969), the populations are overlapping, that is, a given neuron can be used in more than a single pattern. The arrows in the diagram indicate how patterns activate subsequent patterns, for instance, S can activate A_2, A_3, and A_5. Since different patterns may share neurons, implementation constraints will place some limitations on the co-activation of patterns; for example, patterns (B_2, B_3, B_4) may be prohibited from being all active together. In expanding the sequences down from M_1, only a subset of these patterns will therefore be activated initially, and will later decay and be replaced by other patterns.

The search is bi-directional, and a linking sequence is successfully established when the two streams of activation meet somewhere in this large network of interconnected patterns. For example, the recognition of a face image can be obtained in this scheme if processing the input image and processing the stored model can both lead to the same, or a sufficiently similar, intermediate face representation.

How can a successful link of patterns between the input and a stored model be found by the system? The proposed scheme (figure 10.4) has two main components. First, the ascending and descending streams proceed along separate, complementary pathways. Second, when a track is being traversed in one stream, it is assumed to leave behind a primed trace in the complementary stream, making it more readily excitable, as explained further below. The scheme shown schematically in 10.4 is similar to 10.3, except that each node is now split into two complementary nodes (populations of neurons), for instance, B_2 in 10.3 is now split into B_2 on the ascending pathway and its complementary pattern $\bar{B}_2$ on the descending one.

The full bi-directional search now proceeds as follows. A number of sequences originating at S begin to be activated along the ascending pathway. At the same time, sequences originating at M_1 and M_2 begin to expand downwards along the descending pathway. (We will see below how some models, such as M_1, M_2, can be selected from a larger population of stored patterns.) Whenever a track (sub-sequence) is being traversed on either stream, the complementary track remains in a primed state, ready to be activated. Not all of the possible sequences are expanded simultaneously, and already-primed patterns are activated with priority. The result will be a mechanism that searches for linking sequences in the network. Suppose that by the time S has activated A_2 along the ascending stream, the track $\bar{M}_1 \rightarrow \bar{B}_3 \rightarrow \bar{A}_2$ had already been traversed in the descending stream. This is an example of a linking taking place between the two streams: that is, a node, or group of neurons, on the ascending streams (A_2 in the example) and its counterpart ($\bar{A}_2$) on the descending stream, have both been activated within a limited time interval (up to a few hundred milliseconds in the case of typical recognition).

The activity will then proceed along the primed traces, since, for example, A_2 will next activate B_3 (which is primed) rather than alternative, non-primed nodes. This will result, therefore, in the immediate activation of the complete sequences $S \rightarrow M_1$ and $\bar{M}_1 \rightarrow \bar{S}$, establishing a complete link between the source and target patterns. This will also select M_1 as the stored pattern corresponding to the input image S, thereby serving to recognize S as an instance of M_1. In this manner, as a result of the priming, the top-down processing guides and paves the way for the bottom-up processing. The task of relating the sensory input to the appropriate stored representation is achieved by the cooperation of bottom-up and top-down processing, and by exploring, in each direction, multiple alternatives.

This scheme of processing is motivated directly by the proposed roles of the two processing streams, namely, that the ascending stream supports top-down, and the descending stream bottom-up processing. This proposal implies a certain degree of separation between the pathways. The separation between the streams is necessary to avoid possible intermixing between data supported by the input and states explored internally by the system. This distinction is crucial in a system that uses both top-down and bottom-up processes. For example, top-down processing can initiate the activation of an internal model (such as $\bar{M}_1$ in 10.4), but this event must be distinguished in the system from the activation of an internal model (M_1 in 10.4) on the ascending stream by a sequence originating at the sensory input. In other words, the bottom-up activation actually indicates the presence of the corresponding pattern in the image, whereas the top-down activation is akin to a hypothesis explored internally by the system. The separation between the processing streams is not entirely symmetric, in the sense that the descending pathway must be prevented from directly activating the ascending one, but in the opposite direction, activation of descending sequences by ascending patterns is not precluded.

The priming interaction is motivated by the assumption that recognition requires the activation of an object model stored in a high-level visual area. The matching itself can take place at any intermediate level in the network, and this match is therefore required to guide the activation towards the appropriate stored model. This is obtained in the model by the priming interaction.

The linking process described above has two additional benefits. First, a link between the ascending and descending streams can take place at any intermediate level. This has the advantage that the overall task can be split in a flexible manner between bottom-up and top-down processing. In some cases, such as the recognition of a highly familiar object, the process will be primarily bottom-up, since compensation for viewing direction, illumination, and the like, will not be required. Less familiar views will require a more substantial contribution of the top-down processes, and the relative contribution of the two processes can change in the system from one situation to another. Second, to establish a link, the ascending and descending patterns need not arrive at a given node simultaneously; a meeting is also possible between an active pattern and a pattern that had been active some time before and decayed, but left a primed trace in the complementary stream. This is convenient because strict coincidence of activated patterns is not required.

In terms of connectivity, the excitatory connections between patterns are predominantly reciprocal, obeying the following general rule (figure 10.4b): whenever A is connected to B, there is a back-connection from $\bar{B}$ to $\bar{A}$, with cross-connections between A and $\bar{A}$ and B and $\bar{B}$. (Inhibitory connections also play a role, but will not be discussed.) The cross-connections are assumed to have a priming effect: when B, for instance, is activated, it also provides input to $\bar{B}$, making it more readily excitable by a subsequent input along the descending stream. The reciprocity of the connections is an inherent aspect of the model, and it is also a distinguishing feature of cortical connectivity (although some exceptions have been noted, Distler et $al.$ 1991, Rockland, Saleem & Tanaka, 1992). It should also be noted that although the counter-streams structure uses "forward" and "backward" connections, it does not necessarily imply a simple hierarchical structure; it can incorporate a more general structure as long as the above connectivity rule is obeyed.

In summary, the model proposes a general form of computation, called sequence-seeking, and a particular structure, called counter-streams, that supports the required flow of information. The sequence-seeking process has two main characteristics: it is bi-directional, and it explores multiple alternatives simultaneously. The basic structure of the counter-streams model is relatively straightforward, comprising two complementary networks going in opposite directions, with interaction between them primarily (but not exclusively) in the form of enhancing patterns across the two streams. In later sections of this chapter we will examine in more detail the proposed relation of this structure to cortical circuitry.

10.1.4 The Role of the Anatomical Back Projections

A point worth stressing is the role assigned by the model to the descending, or feedback, projections in the visual cortex. These connections have attracted considerable attention since it was found that they tend to be as massive as the forward pathways, and they tend as a rule to reciprocate the forward connections (that is, when a forward connection exists between two cortical regions, the reciprocal back projection almost always exists as well). This pattern of connections is surprising if one considers visual processing as an essentially bottom-up process.

The current model makes a simple proposal: the top-down pathways are used as the anatomical substrate for top-down processing. This role can be contrasted with other models, where the descending projections are used for different purposes: controlling selective attention (Fukushima 1986, Koch 1987), grouping and figure-ground segregation (Okajima 1991, Sporns, Tononi & Edelman 1991), learning processes (Zipser & Rumelhart 1990), modulating cortical output to other visual centers (Sandell & Schiller 1982), or to correlate and synchronize the activity of interrelated neuronal groups (Tononi, Sporns & Edelman 1992).

In proposing this role for the descending pathways it is worth noting that the use of top-down processing in the proposed model is more extensive than in alternative models of visual processing. As already mentioned, top-down processing is sometimes taken to refer to the use of high-level contextual knowledge in perceptual processing. For example, in an office scene one expects to find certain objects such as a desk, a chair, and a telephone, and top-down processing refers to the use of such expectations in the perceptual process. In this view top-down processing is more cognitive than visual in nature. The visual processing is performed mainly by bottom-up processing applied to the incoming image, and top-down processing becomes effective primarily when the visual input becomes ambiguous, as a result of poor lighting conditions, severe occlusion, and the like. In contrast with this limited role, computational studies of visual recognition have shown the need and the feasibility of using top-down processing as an integral part of the recognition process. The use of top-down processing in this view includes the use of stored information required to deal with the effects of viewing direction, illumination, occlusion, and object deformation. Consequently, the top-down processing is expected to be as extensive as, and roughly symmetric to, the bottom-up part.

10.1.5   Model Selection

The bi-directionalprocess raises an important question regarding the activation of stored models for top-down processing. To initiate appropriate top-down processing, some initial selection and subsequent refinement of a relevant subset of stored models is required. The next two sections discuss two mechanisms for this task, both supported by evidence regarding human perception.

Initial Classification   One mechanism of model selection is provided by the mechanism of initial classification. It has been suggested in chapter 6 that as an intermediate stage on the way to individual identification an object is often classified first more broadly as a face, a car, a bird, and the like. The classification may even be non-unique, that is, a number of competing interpre-

tations may still exist at this stage. Following the initial classification some stored models will become more likely then others,
and will be activated and processed with higher priority. For example, an object may be classified as a face prior to its individual
identification, and following classification, face-related sequences
will be expanded preferentially. Biologically, fast classification will
involve the activation (or inhibition) of high-level patterns on the
descending stream by low-level ascending patterns, resulting in
the preferred activation of the selected patterns. This interaction
is similar to the priming interaction between the pathways, with
the exception that in this case the ascending pathway can activate,
rather than facilitate, the descending one. The fast initial selection of subsets of models will not be limited to the activation of
object models at a single "topmost" level; intermediate models at
different levels along the descending stream can also be activated
and serve as the starting points for descending sub-sequences. For
example, in addition to the selection of a complete face model, intermediate models of face-parts can also be activated, and perhaps
also stored models of some basic image configurations of the type
described by Fujita *et al.* (1992) in the study of visual area IT. To
achieve fast initial selection, this process may use some of the direct connections that are known anatomically to take a relatively
short route on the way from low to high visual areas (such as the
connections from area V4 to AIT, or from V3 and VP to area TF;
Felleman & Van Essen 1991).

The Use of Context   A second mechanism for model selection
is provided by the effects of expectation and context. The essential idea is that temporal and spatial correlations can influence the
likelihood of different models. Knowledge about the current situation can thereby be used to influence the activation or priming
of a subset of models that will then become preferential sources
for descending sequences.

As discussed at the end of chapter 6, context can have a powerful influence on the processing of visual information (as well

as in other perceptual and cognitive domains). A pair of similar elongated blobs in the image may be ambiguous, but in the appropriate context, for instance, under the bed, they may be immediately recognized as a pair of slippers.

Familiar objects can often be recognized in the absence of context, but in dealing with less familiar objects, or with complex scenes, or when the viewing conditions are degraded, the role of context increases in importance and can become indispensable. Even when context is not strictly required, the appropriate visual context still facilitates the recognition process, and makes it faster and more reliable (Biederman *et al.* 1982, Palmer 1975, Potter 1975). Context information that helps the observer expect a certain class of objects facilitates recognition significantly, and when objects are placed in an unusual context, recognition is hampered. Under natural conditions, useful context information is almost always present, and this accounts in part for our capacity to deal effectively with complex scenes.

Context effects can operate in the framework of the sequence-seeking scheme by the prior priming of some of the patterns (populations of neurons). The effect will be similar to the mutual priming of the ascending and descending streams, but over longer time-scales. (Priming between the streams may last for tens to hundreds of milliseconds, context effects should last for considerably longer, up to minutes or hours.) Sequences passing through the primed patterns will then become facilitated. In the above example, the location of the blobs, under the bed, will prime patterns representing objects that are commonly found in that location, making slippers a likely interpretation.

The general notion of priming internal representations is a common one (Kosslyn 1994), but its effects in the framework of the sequence-seeking scheme are particularly broad. When certain patterns are activated, for instance, by noticing and identifying the bed in the image, they will initiate sequences of their own, and an entire set of patterns will end up in a primed state. Later on, other sequences passing through a primed trace will be facilitated, compared with the non-primed sequences. The resulting effect is that a context pattern A may help to bring about the activation of B not as a result of direct pre-wired association, but because an intermediate sub-sequence leading from A to B had been previously facilitated. Context effects will therefore have indirect and wide-spread influence.

The spread of context effects may capture some of the fundamental aspects of context effects in humans. Human perception and cognition appear to have an almost uncanny capacity (which is remarkably difficult to reproduce in artificial systems) for bringing in relevant context information in a broad and flexible manner. It seems that broad and indirect context effects of this kind can be reproduced by the sequence-seeking computation.

10.1.6   Learning Sequences

Recognition in the sequence-seeking scheme can become faster and more efficient by the learning of past successful sequences. A successful sequence is a sequence of pattern activations linking an input pattern with a stored model. When faced again with a similar input, the computation will follow the sequence that proved successful in the past rather than search anew for a possible link between the input and a stored representation.

The counter-streams structure makes it possible to use a simple and local learning rule to reinforce selectively complete, successful sequences. The reason is that every pattern along a successful sequence will receive both a direct activation and a priming signal from the complementary track. In contrast, patterns on dead-end tracks will receive one or the other, but not both. The approximate temporal coincidence of the two signals can therefore be used to preferentially strengthen the successful sequence. This rule is local, since it depends on the activation of a single pattern. Yet it is sufficient to reinforce preferentially successful sequences forming an uninterrupted link between source and target patterns. Following practice, out of the huge number of possible sequences, those that proved useful in the past will be explored with higher priority in future uses of the network.

From a biological standpoint, this is a favorable and perhaps surprising property of the counter-streams structure. As in other models of learning in neuronal networks, learning is accomplished by the modification of synaptic efficacy, and the change is determined locally by the activity of the pre- and post-synaptic units. One might expect difficulties in using such a local rule to distinguish complete from dead-end sequences, since this involves a global distinction that depends on the entire sequence of activation. Yet, because the counter-streams structure combines patterns of activation flowing in both directions, the local rule is sufficient for learning globally successful sequences. The synaptic mechanism responsible for the learning of sequences is also expected to have some special properties not found in more standard Hebbian models. In particular, the synaptic modification is expected to be more effective in neurons in the primed compared with the non-primed state.

In the process of reinforcing successful sequences, changes due to learning are distributed throughout the system, and are not confined to high-level centers specializing in learning (Sejnowski 1986). Recent studies of learning certain perceptual skills suggest that low-level visual areas are indeed involved in the modifications that take place during the learning process (Karni & Sagi 1991).

In addition to the learning of complete sequences, as above, the system may also be engaged in the learning of the individual stages, that is, the different steps comprising the processing sequences. This aspect of the learning is treated, for example, by Poggio (1990). However it remains outside the scope of the current discussion, since the focus here is not on the specifics of individual processes, but on their overall common structure.

10.1.7 Searching for the Best Sequence

Due to the parallel exploration of multiple alternatives, and to the tuning of the system by past experience, straightforward recognition tasks will require little or no search. More complex tasks will require a search through the space of possible sequences for the appropriate transformations that will bring the viewed object and the stored model into close alignment.

In previous chapters we have discussed possible methods for determining the required transformations between the stored model and a novel view. For example, one possible method for dealing with the effect of viewing direction is to determine the required transformation uniquely on the basis of a small number of corresponding features. Another possibility is simply to try out a number of alternatives and then select the most appropriate one. Consider for example the problem of compensating for a possible scale difference between a novel view and a stored object model. This can be accomplished by first recovering the required transformation uniquely based, for example, on the matching of corresponding features, and then applying the normalizing transformation to the viewed object or the stored model. An alternative approach, mentioned earlier in this chapter, is to perform a multiscale analysis by generating internally a number of copies at a number of different scales, and then selecting the best-matching one. To avoid excessive search, it will be useful to first perform a rough alignment, as discussed in chapter 7, that will narrow down the range of scale corrections that must be applied. Similarly, in compensating for 3-D viewing direction, illumination, and object deformation, instead of recovering uniquely the required transformations, the alternative approach is to generate and test in parallel a number of competing alternatives. As discussed in previous chapters, this will be based on the use of stored information regarding possible object changes, associated with both specific objects and object classes. This simple search approach replaces a sequential and relatively sophisticated computation by a simpler, parallel, but more extensive process. For standard computers, the sequential sophisticated computation is usually the method of choice. For a biological system, however, the simpler parallel approach is probably more suitable.

We have tested in simulations some aspects of a process that searches in parallel for the appropriate alignment transformations. The overall structure of the search is simple. It tries out in parallel a set of N competing possibilities. The size of this set will be determined in practice by hardware limitations. If none of the alternatives produce a sufficiently close match, the process selects a subset of k patterns, and explores a new set of N patterns around the selected subset. The process uses the fact that the matching between patterns is not an all-or-nothing event, but a graded one. Some sequences will lead to better matches than others, and will then serve as starting points for exploring additional sequences, leading in turn to an improved match. This process is related to the method of Bayesian optimization (Mockus 1989), and also has some features in common with a family of optimization and search procedures known as "genetic algorithms" (Holland 1975, Goldberg 1989). Recent evaluations have shown such methods to behave quite efficiently (Brady 1985, Peterson 1990). Our own simulations in the context of pattern matching have also shown that computations based on sequence-seeking compare favorably with alternative methods, such as gradient descent and simulated annealing.

Some of the simulations were applied to a database of Japanese characters shown in figure 10.5. The search in this case was in a six-dimensional transformation space, because the input characters could be scaled, rotated, shifted, stretched, and sheared with respect to the stored patterns.

Figure 10.6 shows a simulation of a simplified sequence-seeking process applied to such 2-D patterns. This simulation, as well as the other examples in this section, were performed by A. Zeira at the Weizmann Institute. The example is intended not as a realistic model, but to illustrate the process in a simple example. The task is to recognize an input shape (example in 10.6a) by comparing it with stored shapes. To make the task more difficult, noise was added to the input images. The search in this example was two-dimensional—the input shape was displaced in the x,

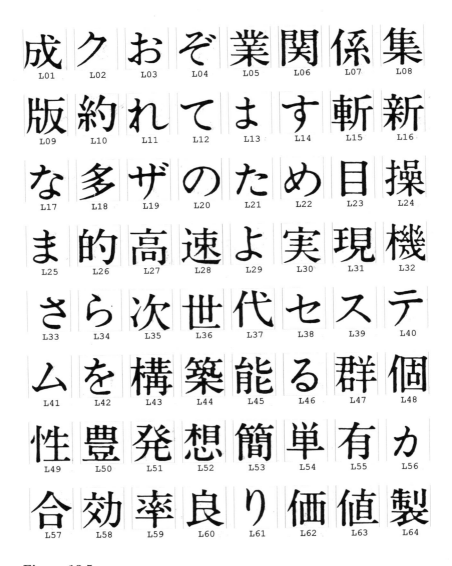

Figure 10.5
A database of characters used in the simulations of the sequence-seeking process.

y directions with respect to the stored pattern. The objective function to be minimized by the search, which is the degree of match as a function of displacement, is a complex function that contains multiple minima. Level-contours of this function (that is, contours of constant function values, similar to elevation contours) are shown in 10.6b. The correct solution is represented by the deep valley in the middle, but there are many additional local minima.

To determine the optimal match between the input shape and the stored pattern, one possibility is to displace the input shape by different amounts in x and y, and compare each displaced version with the model until the best match is obtained. Instead, the simulation used a different strategy to test aspects of the bidirectional search employed by the sequence-seeking computation. The search in the x and y directions was divided into two parts. The model M was shifted in x, to generate a number of copies M_i at different horizontal locations. The input image was shifted in y, generating displaced copies I_k. This is a simplified example of splitting the computation between the two directions. In more realistic cases of 3-D recognition the internal transformations applied to the model will be more complex, and will depend, for example, on its 3-D structure. The search proceeds by comparing the displaced versions of the input and stored patterns. A good match between a pair M_i, I_k, then leads to the generation of new copies around the corresponding displacement x_i, y_k. The results were compared with the one-directional version, where M remained fixed, and copies of the image $I_{j,k}$ were generated by shifting I in both the x and y directions.

The procedure used to generate the new "offsprings" around the existing patterns was a simple genetic-like algorithm: the likelihood of generating a new sample increases near good past samples (as determined by the function f_1 in 10.6c), and decreases with the density of past samples. (The shape of f_1 was guided by theoretical considerations that will not be detailed here.) This function is computed in the vicinity of past samples. For example, if a good match was obtained between the input displaced horizon-

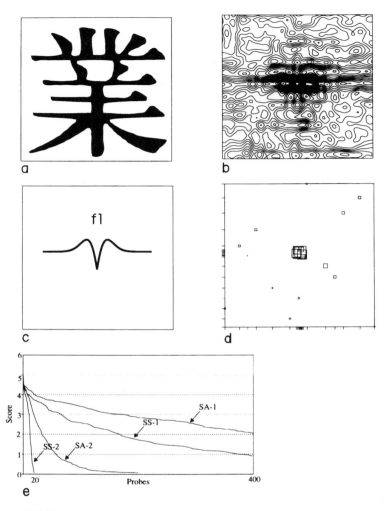

Figure 10.6
Simulation of a simplified bi-directional process, used to match a noisy input shape by comparing it with stored shapes (example in *a*). The input shape is displaced in the *x*, *y* directions with respect to the stored pattern. The objective function to be minimized is complex and contains multiple minima (level contours in *b*). The likelihood of generating a new sample increases near good past samples, and decreases with the density of past samples. Bias towards good sample points was determined by f_1 in *c*. (*d*) A representation of the search following 20 displacements in *x* and *y*. The marks show the selected displacements, the squares show the degree of match obtained at some *x, y* displacements, coded by size. (For each x_i, the best matching y_k is shown, similarly for the y_j's). The search combines exploration of the domain with concentration around good matches. (*e*) Match-quality as a function of number of patterns explored for one (SS-1), and two-directional (SS-2) versions of the sequence-seeking search, compared with one- (SA-1) and two-directional (SA-2) versions of simulated annealing. Reproduced from Ullman (1995).

tally by $\bar{x}$ units and the stored pattern displaced vertically by $\bar{y}$ units, new displacements will be generated around the successful values $(\bar{x}, \bar{y})$. However, if the match was poor, or if many patterns with a similar displacement were already compared, then the likelihood of attempting further solutions in the vicinity of $(\bar{x}, \bar{y})$ will decrease. In this manner the past samples induce over the search-space a likelihood function, and the next samples occur at maxima of this function. The process is simple: it proceeds by trying a number of alternatives, and then selecting and refining successful solutions.

The simulations of the simplified bi-directional search show that the process has a number of favorable general properties. First, the search locates the optimal match efficiently, as shown in 10.6e. (The score is in units of σ, the standard deviation of the terrain in b.) It proved more efficient in the pattern matching task than commonly used minimization methods such as simulated annealing (SA in 10.6e) or gradient descent using multiple starting points. Second, the bi-directional scheme in these examples is considerably more efficient in terms of the number of patterns explored than a one-directional process (SS-1 vs. SS-2 in 10.6e). This advantage will hold as long as the number of stored patterns to be explored is not too large. Third, the use of past results in guiding the search biases the process to concentrate in more promising regions, compared with SA and gradient descent. Finally, this process exhibits good capacity to escape local minima in reaching for the global solution.

The examples used a simplified task, but the search-space was of significant size (up to a million locations) and contained multiple local minima. Further experiments were also applied to face images, as shown in figure 10.7. In this case the stored model consisted of two face images, shown at the top of the figure, with correspondence established between them. The transformations explored by the process included rotation in depth around the vertical y-axis, scaling, translation, and rotation in the image plane.

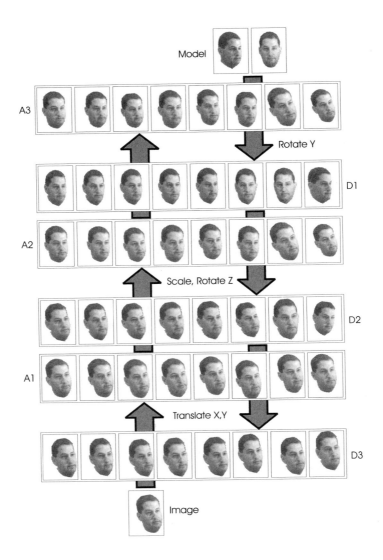

Figure 10.7
The sequence-seeking process applied to face images. The stored model consists of the two top images, with known correspondence. The transformations performed during recognition included rotation in depth around the vertical y-axis, scaling, translation, and rotation in the image plane. A1, A2, A3 are patterns on the ascending stream, D1, D2, D3 on the descending one.

The rotation in depth was obtained from the model images using the view-combination method. In the ascending direction, rotation in depth was not applied. The use of such transformations, that are applied in one direction only, requires some additions to the scheme that will not be detailed here. As before, the scheme performs the recognition task without establishing feature correspondence, and without explicitly recovering the transformation parameters. The scheme simply tries multiple alternatives, and selects the best ones.

The computational experiments suggest that a search of this type, combining bi-directional search with the exploration of multiple alternatives can be quite efficient. At the same time, it is worth stressing that in many recognition tasks the search is not expected to be extensive, for several reasons. First, the use of rough alignment will limit, as mentioned above, the range of the required compensating transformation. Second, the use of past experience can lead to a direct and immediate match. Suppose that V is a view of a familiar, frequently seen object. The view V itself may then become a part of the stored object representation, eliminating the need for compensating transformations. Alternatively, the sequence required to match V with the appropriate stored model can be learned and reinforced with time. This sequence will be consequently explored with high priority, eliminating again the need for search. In the model discussed above, the acquired increased efficiency with practice will not be limited to the view V itself, but will generalize to similar views: if the input view is similar to V, the search will still be efficient because it will use the learned sequence as a starting point and explore additional sequences in its vicinity. In conclusion, the compensating transformations required to match the input with a stored model will usually require little or no search. When a search becomes necessary, it will be performed efficiently by the sequence-seeking process.

10.1.8   Generic Aspects of Sequence-Seeking

The discussion of the sequence-seeking process focused on the domain of visual recognition. However, the process of establishing a sequence of transformations, mappings, or states, linking source and target representations, provides a useful general mechanism for various aspects of perception as well as for non-perceptual functions. For example, the planning of a motor action can be cast at some level in terms of seeking a sequence of possible moves linking an initial configuration with a desired final state. Movement trajectories could be based in a sequence-seeking scheme on a repertoire of elementary movements, and these basic movements will then be transformed (scaled, stretched, rotated, etc.) and concatenated together to generate more complex movements. In analogy with sequence-seeking in vision, movement planning could also utilize a bi-directional search that explores in parallel multiple alternatives. Similarly, more general planning and problem solving can also be formulated in terms of establishing a sequence of transformations, mappings, or intermediate states, linking some source and target representations (as proposed, for example, by Newell & Simon's (1972) GPS model, Quillian's (1968) semantic net theory, see also Winston 1992), and they may therefore benefit from computations similar to the sequence-seeking scheme. I will not discuss these general problems further, beyond raising the possibility that general aspects of the sequence-seeking process provide a useful computational scheme that could be applied, with appropriate modifications, to different cognitive tasks. This possibility is consonant with the widespread hypothesis (e.g., Barlow 1985, Creutzfeldt 1978, Crick & Asanuma 1986, Edelman 1978, Martin 1988a, White 1989) regarding the possible existence of some general cortical mechanisms that are applicable, with suitable local modifications, to a broad range of different tasks.

10.2   Biological Embodiment

In this section, biological aspects of the model will be discussed. It is suggested that the general connectivity structure of the cortex is highly suitable for supporting the bi-directional, multi-path computation of the sequence-seeking model. The model is used to interpret key aspects of cortical connectivity, to derive new predictions, and to raise problems for further study. The discussion will focus primarily on general features of the model, such as the ascending and descending streams, and the laminar distribution and general pattern of connections between and within cortical areas. Several aspects of a more specific nature will also be considered, to illustrate possible predictions and questions for further study.

The sequence-seeking model requires two pathways going in opposite directions with the appropriate cross-connections. A schematic diagram proposing how the counter-streams structure may be embedded in cortical connections is shown in figure 10.8a. The proposed embodiment is presented in schematic outline only, focusing on a number of central aspects, but without discussing details or possible variations of the model.

The ascending stream goes through layer 4, which is the main input layer in the cortex, to a sub-population of the superficial layers above it, denoted in the figure as AS (for Ascending Superficial), and then projects to layer 4 of the next cortical area (II in the figure). The descending stream goes through a different sub-population of the superficial layers (DS, for Descending Superficial) to DI (for Descending Infra), a subpopulation of the infragranular layers (often in layer 6), and from there to DS of a preceding area. The connections can also skip one step (or occasionally more) in the stream, such as AS directly to AS on the ascending stream, and DS $\rightarrow$ DS or DI $\rightarrow$ DI on the descending stream (thin lines in figure 10.8a.)

Layer 5 is left out of the diagram because, according to the model, this layer (or a part of it) is involved primarily not in the

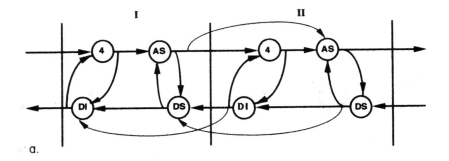

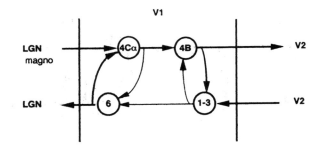

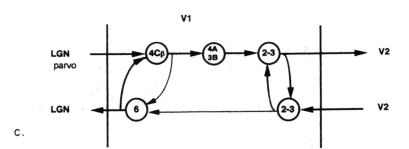

Figure 10.8

a. How the basic counter-stream structure may be embodied in cortical connectivity. The structure contains two interconnected streams, an ascending and a descending one. The ascending path goes through layer 4 and the ascending superficial population (AS) to the next area. The descending path goes from the descending superficial (DS) population to DI (descending infra) and back to the first area. Thin arrows show pathways that "leap over" a step in the stream. Inhibitory and long-range intra-areal connections are not shown. See text for more details. *b.* A schematic representation of the main connections according to the model along the magnocellular stream from the LGN via V1 to V2. (V1 is also connected to other visual areas, not shown in the diagram). The connections are drawn in a manner suggested by the model and *a* above. Thick arrows: established connections; thin arrows: connections predicted by the model. *c.* The main connections according to the model along the parvocellular stream from the LGN via V1 to V2. Thick arrows: established connections; thin arrows: connections predicted by the model.

main streams, but with their control, in cooperation with subcortical structures. There are at least two reasons for assuming that layer 5 (or parts of it, such as 5b of the macaque's V1) may be involved in control functions. First, its orderly connections to subcortical structures (such as from visual cortex to the pulvinar and the superior colliculus, structures implicated in controlling attentionand eye movements, Desimone *et al.* 1990) that are reciprocally connected in turn in a topographic manner to multiple visual areas. Second, the firing pattern of a population of pyramidal cells in this layer that "...can initiate synchronized rhythms and project them on neurons in all layers" (Silva, Amitai & Connors, p. 434).

Note that the counter-streams structure suggests a natural organization in about five to six main layers: one or two performing control functions, two (an input and an output layer) for the ascending and two for the descending streams. Furthermore, the main layers are assigned in the model a characteristic functional role, and this appears to be compatible with the relatively uniform pattern of the laminar distribution of inter-area connections. The division between the roles of the different layers is likely to be in reality less clear-cut, and there are known variations and specialized sub-laminations. However, the goal of the diagram is to emphasize the possible common underlying structure according to the model, rather than to account for possible variations.

It is interesting to note that from a developmental standpoint the layered cortical structure appears to develop in two stages, possibly from distinct origins (Marin-Padilla 1978, Deacon 1990). The most superficial and deepest layers develop first, and all other layers develop subsequently in between them. These two structures may be the precursors of the descending and ascending streams, respectively (Deacon 1990, Mumford 1993). This developmental view is compatible with the notion of the two distinct and interconnected streams constituting the two main building blocks of the counter-streams structure.

10.2.1   Connections of V1: Data and Predictions

To give a more specific example, figure 10.8*b, c* shows an expanded
version of the connectivity diagram, applied to cortical area V1
(which is somewhat special, but for which the data are more comprehensive than for other visual areas), and its connections to the
LGN below it and cortical area V2 above. V1 is also connected
to other visual areas that are not shown in the diagram. The input to area V1 is comprised of two sub-populations of cells in the
LGN, the magno- and parvocellular inputs.

Figure 10.8*b* shows the connections in the macaque of the magnocellular stream, 10.8*c* of the parvocellular stream, (Rockland
and Lund 1983, Lund 1988a, 1988b, Martin 1988a). The diagram
shows the main connections; some additional secondary ones exist
but will not be considered. The connections are drawn in a manner
suggested by the model, and they include both known connections
(thick arrows) and connections predicted by the proposed scheme
but for which empirical evidence is partial or lacking (thin arrows).
As can be seen, the pattern of connections in the two streams is in
general agreement with the counter-streams structure and figure
10.8*a*.

If the general hypothesis regarding the counter-streams structure is broadly correct, then a number of predictions can be made
regarding the main connectivity patterns within and between areas. One general prediction is the possible distinction between
the AS and DS sub-populations. This separation reflects the most
straightforward implementation of the scheme; however, some alternatives can exist without violating the constraints of the model.

A separation between the ascending and descending populations
is evident in the connections involving layer 4: the ascending projections terminate in layer 4, the descending projections always
avoid it. In the superficial layers the situation is more difficult
to assess, and the available evidence is at present restricted. In
the magnocellular projection from V1 to V2 this separation is re-
spected: the forward projection originates mainly in 4B, while the

back projection is mainly to other layers (figure 10.8*b*). It is further expected that even when the superficial layers provide both the source and the target of connections to another area, there will in fact often be a separation to the AS/DS sub-populations. If these populations exist, they should be connected in a reciprocal manner. A related expectation derived from the model is the existence of priming-typesynaptic interactions. That is, excitatory synaptic input that by itself may not be very effective in driving the target cells, but that facilitates the effects of subsequent inputs to these cells.

An example at the other end of the spectrum, that is, a highly specific expectation, is that in the magnocellular stream the model suggests reciprocal interconnections between layer 4B (playing the part of AS in the model), and layers 1-3, the recipients of descending projections from V2 (DS in the model). Moreover, the same superficial cells connected to 4B will also be the recipients of descending projections from V2. The projection from 4B to the superficial layers is well established. It is also known (Lund 1988a) that 4B pyramidal cells send apical dendrites to the superficial layers where the connection may take place.

The model also includes a reciprocal connection between layer 4 and the LGN-projecting cells in layer 6. The projection from 6 to 4 is well-established in both the cat (McGuire *et al.* 1984) and monkey (Lund 1988a), and there is support for the opposite connection as well (Lund & Boothe 1975). It is also interesting to note in this regard that the population of layer 6 cells projecting back to the LGN were found (in the cat) to be the same cells that are also connected to layer 4C, by axonal collaterals and dendritic arbors (Katz, Burkhalter & Dreyer 1984), in accordance with the connectivity in 10.8*b, c*.

The connections between layers 4 and 6 are expected to have a priming effect in the model (not necessarily the only effect, see Bolz & Gilbert 1986, Martin 1988b), and this notion has some physiological support. It was found (Ferster and Lindström 1985) that using electrical activation of layer 6 cells by antidromic activation increased the probability of layer 4 firing, and most cells fired multiple spikes in response to each ascending stimulation. Under the opposite conditions, when layer 6 was inactivated, the main observed effect was the reduction in excitability of layer 4 cells (Grieve, Murphy & Sillito, 1991). This priming of layer 4, which is the main input layer to the visual cortex, can be viewed as reflecting the expectations of the visual cortex, attempting to detect expected patterns in the image.

From an anatomical standpoint, EM reconstructions (McGuire *et al.* 1984) have shown terminations of layer 6 axons on smooth and sparsely spiny cells. In the cortex, smooth cells are usually inhibitory and spiny cells are usually excitatory. These findings were therefore interpreted as connections to inhibitory interneurons in layer 4, unlike the prediction of the model that suggests a projection onto layer 4 spiny cells. Detailed recent data by Ahmed *et al.* (1994) support, however, the model's prediction, and indicate that the major target of layer 6 pyramidal output to layer 4 are in fact the spiny stellate cells rather than inhibitory interneurons.

Layer 6 is also involved in the model in the descending pathway (although, as mentioned above, layers 5 and 6 are often further divided into distinct sublayers, and the identification of layer 6 with the Descending Infra population in the model is not always straightforward.) The involvement of layer 6 in the descending pathway, as either the origin or the target of the descending projection, has been demonstrated in many visual areas, including V1, V2, V3, V4, TEO, MT, MST, VIP, PO, LIP (Andersen *et al.* 1990, Felleman & Van Essen 1984, Maunsell & Van Essen 1983, Lund *et al.* 1981, Rockland, Saleem & Tanaka 1992, Rockland & Virga 1989).

10.2.2 Lateral Connections between Areas

Connections between cortical areas (not only visual, but also somatosensory and motor) can be classified into "forward," "backward," and "lateral" connections, on the basis of the laminar distribution of their source and destination (Rockland & Pandya

1979, Maunsell & Van Essen 1983, Friedman 1983, Van Essen 1985, Zeki & Shipp 1988, Andersen *et al.* 1990, Boussaud *et al.* 1990, Felleman & Van Essen 1991). Lateral connections terminate in all layers, and their origin is bi-laminar, from the supra as well as infra layers. (These lateral connections between areas should not be confused with the horizontal connections within a region.) The lateral pattern is relatively complex; it is therefore interesting that a number of its main features can be derived almost directly from the model. The counter-streams structure does not require a distinct, third type of connections. It allows, however, forward and backward connections simultaneously in both directions, and it can include lateral connections by simply assuming that they are the union of ascending and descending connections. If this view is correct, then the main connections participating in the lateral connection can be inferred from the basic scheme (figure 10.8a). According to the model, they include the direct connections: AS → 4, and DI → DS, as well as the connections that leap over one stage in the diagram, namely, AS → AS, DS → DS,DI, and DI → DI.

The origin of the projections according to the model would be bi-laminar, and the terminations would span all layers, in agreement with the observed pattern. This can also provide an explanation for the problem of irregular terminations (Felleman & Van Essen 1991), that occurs when the pattern of terminations is at odds with the usual distinctions between forward, backward, and lateral connections. This can happen, for example, when some of the terminations are restricted to layer 4 of the target area while others show columnar terminations. This pattern was termed F/C (for a mixture of "four" and "columnar") paradoxical termination, since termination in layer 4 is a signature for ascending connections, while a columnar termination signifies lateral connections. In the counter-streams structure, the point to note is that the lateral connections from the superficial layers of area A to target area B are composed of two sub-projections: ascending (AS → 4) and descending (DS → DS, DI). Anterograde labeling of the upper layers of area A can therefore show mixed patterns of terminations, such as 4 alone, or a columnar termination, in agreement with the F/C paradoxical termination. It can also (by labeling the DS alone) show a bi-laminar pattern of connections, and this can account for the other types of irregular terminations.conclusive

The detailed nature of these connections is still not entirely clear. However, the proposed account serves to illustrate two points. First, that some of the apparent complexities may have a natural explanation within the counter-stream structure. Second, if the account is generally correct, it provides support for the existence of the AS and DS subpopulations in the model.

10.2.3   Priming Mechanisms

A central prediction of the model concerns the existence of synaptic interactions of the priming type. These are synaptic inputs that by themselves will not be sufficient under normal conditions to drive the target cells, but will increase the efficacy of subsequent inputs to these cells. A more conventional view is that if the synaptic input fails to reach threshold it will decay and die out, and will have little effect on subsequent processing. Here the expectation is that some sub-threshold interactions will have long-lasting effects on subsequent processing.

Although priming interactions have not been studied directly, some known or physiologically plausible mechanisms could play a role in such priming interactions. Priming can be obtained for example by long-lasting depolarization, combined with subsequent input, added either linearly or nonlinearly. A long-lasting depolarization can be caused by a number of possible mechanisms, including the activation or inactivation of ionic channels with a slow time course (Amitai *et al.* 1993, Hirsch & Gilbert 1991, Markram & Sackman 1994, McCormick 1990, Wilson 1995), NMDA receptors (Miller, Chapman, & Stryker 1989), or the activation of distal parts of the dendritic tree (Stratford *et al.* 1989). This depolarization will facilitate subsequent inputs by summation (Miller, Chapman, & Stryker 1989), or by a nonlinear interaction (Esguerra

Kwon, & Sur 1989, Koch 1987, Sherman *et al.* 1990). From the sequence-seeking model one might expect in fact to find not a single mechanism, but a number of different ones, operating at a range of different time-scales. Related to the priming effect, one might also expect a "reset" mechanism, that resets primed neurons to a non-primed state following activation. Although the details are not known, it appears that synaptic mechanisms for priming connections are physiologically plausible, and it will be of interest to try to test them empirically.

10.2.4   Effects of the Feedback Projection

According to the sequence-seeking scheme, the physiological effects of the descending projections can assume two different forms: either the priming and modulation of the ascending stream, or the direct activation of a lower area. Both effects have been observed in physiological studies, modulatory (Nault *et al.* 1990, Sandell & Schiller 1982), as well as direct excitatory effects (Mignard and Malpeli 1991, Cauller & Kullics 1991). They are also supported by functional imaging studies showing that low-level visual areas can be activated by tasks such as visual imagery (Kosslyn *et al.* 1993). Further predictions of the model regarding the modulatory effects include: (i) similar modulatory effects are also likely to be exerted by ascending signals on descending ones, (ii) the two effects of the back-projections may be segregated into two distinct sub-populations: in figure 10.4*b*, $\bar{B}$ can be directly driven along the descending stream, but patterns such as B on the ascending stream are expected to show modulatory effects.

10.3   Summary

In summary, the computation proposed by the sequence-seeking model is a bi-directional process performed by the combination of top-down and bottom-up streams of processing. Bottom-up processing is supported by the ascending pathways, top-down processing by the descending ones. In each direction, different alternatives are explored in parallel. The scheme incorporates a number of basic lessons from computational vision and perceptual psychology. Essential properties of the scheme include the simultaneous exploration of multiple alternatives, the relatively simple, uniform, and extensible structure, the flexible use of 'bottom-up' and 'top-down' sequences that can meet at any level, the roles of context and of fast classification, and the learning of complete sequences by a simple local reinforcement rule.

The model combines the proposed computation with a number of known as well as predicted aspects of cortical circuitry. Given the still limited knowledge regarding cortical structures and the computations they perform, the model addresses mainly general aspects of the computation. The combination of the proposed computation and structure serves to suggest a framework that offers a computational account for several basic features of cortical circuitry, such as the predominantly reciprocal connectivity between cortical areas, the forward, backward and lateral connection types, the regularities in the distribution patterns of inter-area connections, the organization in 5-6 layers, and the effects of back projections, as well as a number of more specific details. It also poses problems for further study at the structural as well as computational levels.

A Alignment by Features

A.1 Three-Point Alignment: Existence and Uniqueness

In this appendix we show that the alignment of a 3-D object with an image can be performed uniquely (up to sign) on the basis of three corresponding model and image points. This result concerning three-point alignment will follow from the proposition below that relates affine transformations of the plane and similarity transformations in space. Roughly, it says that each affine transformation in the plane is the projection of a unique similarity transformation in space.

Proposition 1: Any affine transformation of the image plane can be produced by the orthographic projection of a 3-D similarity transformation of the plane. The 3-D transformation is unique, up to a reflection about the image plane, and translation in depth.

Comments: The image plane P is the plane $z = 0$. An affine transformation A of P is $L(P) + d$, where $L(P)$ is linear and d a translation. A similarity transformation T of P is composed of a translation in space D, rotation in space R, and scaling by a factor s ($s > 0$). The orthographic projection π of a point (x, y, z) in space is (x, y) in the image plane. Given A, we are looking for T such that $\pi T = A$. Without loss of generality we can assume that $d = 0$ (no translation in the image plane). The reason is that under orthographic projection $\pi D = d$ (translation in space and the image plane coincide, translation in depth remains undetermined), and therefore the translation component is immediately recoverable. The problem is therefore to determine, given $L(P)$, s, R such that $\pi(sR) = L(P)$. (That is, expressing a linear transformation of the plane as the orthographic projection of a rotation in space accompanied by scaling). We will show that s, R always exist and are unique, up to reflection of the transformed plane about the image plane (which is an inherent ambiguity of orthographic projection).

Proof: Given a linear transformation L of the plane we can determine its effect on a pair of perpendicular unit vectors ϵ_1, ϵ_2. That is, $\|\epsilon_1\| = \|\epsilon_2\| = 1$, $\epsilon_1 \cdot \epsilon_2 = 0$, $L(\epsilon_1) = \epsilon_1'$, $L(\epsilon_2) = \epsilon_2'$. We seek a rotation in space R, and scaling s, such that $\pi s R(\epsilon_1) = \epsilon_1'$, $\pi s R(\epsilon_2) = \epsilon_2'$. Let $sR(\epsilon_1)$ be v_1, $sR(\epsilon_2)$ be v_2. $v_1 = \epsilon_1' + c_1\hat{z}$, $v_2 = \epsilon_2' + c_2\hat{z}$ where c_1, c_2 are the unknown depth coordinates of v_1 and v_2 respectively. Since rotation and scaling preserve orthogonality:

$$v_1 \cdot v_2 = 0 \tag{A.1.1}$$

therefore:

$$(\epsilon_1' + c_1\hat{z}) \cdot (\epsilon_2' + c_2\hat{z}) = 0$$
$$c_1 c_2 = -\epsilon_1' \cdot \epsilon_2'. \tag{A.1.2}$$

Let us denote $-\epsilon_1' \cdot \epsilon_2' = c_{12}$, which is measurable in the image. Following uniform scaling $\|v_1\| = \|v_2\|$, therefore

$$c_1^2 - c_2^2 = \|\epsilon_2'\|^2 - \|\epsilon_1'\|^2 \tag{A.1.3}$$

or $c_1^2 - c_2^2 = k_{12}$, where k_{12} is measurable in the image. The two equations:

$$c_1 c_2 = c_{12}$$
$$c_1^2 - c_2^2 = k_{12} \tag{A.1.4}$$

always have exactly two real solutions for c_1, c_2, that differ only in sign.

One way of verifying this is to define a complex number $z = c_1 + ic_2$. Then $z^2 = k_{12} + ic_{12}$. Therefore z^2 is known, and c_1, c_2 are simply determined by the square roots of z. There are exactly two solutions, for z, of the form $c_1 + ic_2$ and $-c_1 - ic_2$.

This shows that the transformation sR of the plane always exists and is unique, up to a reflection about the image plane. That is, one transformation takes $\epsilon_1 \rightarrow \epsilon_1' + c_1\hat{z}$, $\epsilon_2 \rightarrow \epsilon_2' + c_2\hat{z}$, the other takes $\epsilon_1 \rightarrow \epsilon_1' - c_1\hat{z}$, $\epsilon_2 \rightarrow \epsilon_2' - c_2\hat{z}$.

The fact that sR transforms ϵ_1 to v_1 and ϵ_2 to v_2 determines sR completely. It is also clear that a solution always exists for any choice of ϵ'_1 and ϵ'_2. (See appendix 2 for an explicit calculation of s, R.)

Comment: We have seen that for a space with dimension $n = 2$, an affine transformation can be produced as the orthographic projection of a similarity transformation in a space with dimension $n + 1$. Is this true for higher dimensions as well (e.g., for $n = 3$)? The answer is negative, as can be verified by considering the number of independent parameters required to specify the transformations.

A linear transformation is specified by n^2 independent parameters. Rotation and scaling in a space of $n + 1$ dimensions requires $n + 2$ parameters. For $n > 2$, $n + 2 < n^2$.

Proposition 1 above has been formulated in terms of an affine transformation of the plane. Since an affine transformation is uniquely determined by three non-colinear points, we immediately obtain:

Proposition 2:   Let (P_1, P_2, P_3) and (P'_1, P'_2, P'_3) be two sets of three non-colinear points in the plane. Then there exists a transformation T in space, composed of rotation, translation, and scaling, such that $\pi T P_i = P'_i$, $i = 1, 2, 3$. The transformation is unique, up to reflection of the points $T P_i$ about the image plane and translation in depth.

Comment: A proposition similar to the above has been proposed, without a complete proof, by Kanade & Kender (1983). For the perspective rather than orthographic case, Fischler & Bolles (1981) suggested, without a complete proof, that six corresponding points may be required for alignment. Finding six corresponding points in the image and model may be difficult. In addition, perspective effects are often small, leading to instability in the computation. It appears, therefore, that the use of orthographic projection accompanied by scale change provide a useful approximation for performing alignment.

A.2   Three-Point Alignment: Computation

In this section we show briefly how the proof above can be used for actually performing the alignment based on three corresponding points in the model and in the image.

The problem is the following. We are given the 3-D coordinates of three non-colinear points. Without loss of generality we can assume that the points lie initially in the image plane $z = 0$. We are next given the image of the same points (with known correspondence) following a transformation T. The image is an orthographic projection on the image plane, and T is composed of rotation R and scaling s. The objective is to determine R and s. As discussed above, the translation component can be ignored, and we assume that the object is fixed at one point. With this point as the origin, T transforms the other two points: $\pi T(P_1) = P_1'$, $\pi T(P_2) = P_2'$. In the image plane, an affine transformation A that maps $P_1 \to P_1'$, $P_2 \to P_2'$ is easy to determine. A is a 2×2 matrix, $AP_1 = P_1'$. $AP_2 = P_2'$. This gives four equations for the components of A. (In fact two sets of equations with two unknowns in each. The equations are independent for non-colinear points.) Having determined A, we can compute its effect on two perpendicular unit vectors $A\hat{x} = (x_1, y_1)$ $A\hat{y} = (x_2, y_2)$.

We now compute c_1, c_2 using the equations:

$$
\begin{aligned}
c_1 c_2 &= c_{12} \\
c_1^2 - c_2^2 &= k_{12}
\end{aligned}
\tag{A.2.5}
$$

where

$$
\begin{aligned}
c_{12} &= -(x_1 x_2 + y_1 y_2) \\
k_{12} &= (x_2^2 + y_2^2) - (x_1^2 + y_1^2).
\end{aligned}
\tag{A.2.6}
$$

From A.2.5 c_1 and c_2 can be recovered:

$$
c_1^4 - k_{12} c_1^2 - c_{12}^2 = 0.
\tag{A.2.7}
$$

This is a quadratic equation in c_1^2. There will be one real solution $c_1^2 > 0$, and another $c_1^2 < 0$. (This can be shown directly, or based on the uniqueness result above). c_2 is also determined up to a common sign. That is, the solutions to A2.1 are (c_1, c_2) and $(-c_1, -c_2)$.

To obtain T explicitly, we compute its effect on the vector $\hat{z}$. Let $T(\hat{z}) = (x_3, y_3, c_3)$. The direction of $T\hat{z}$ is along $(x_1, y_1, c_1) \times (x_2, y_2, c_2)$, and because of the scaling its length is given by $x_3^2 + y_3^2 + c_3^2 = x_1^2 + y_1^2 + c_1^2$, hence $T\hat{z}$ is determined uniquely. T is then given explicitly by the matrix

$$T = \begin{matrix} x_1 & x_2 & x_3 \\ y_1 & y_2 & y_3 \\ c_1 & c_2 & c_3 \end{matrix} \quad \text{or by:} \quad T' = \begin{matrix} x_1 & x_2 & -x_3 \\ y_1 & y_2 & -y_3 \\ -c_1 & -c_2 & c_3 \end{matrix}$$

As discussed above, the difference between T and T' is a reflection of the points about the image plane. From this it is also easy to factor out s and R $(s^2 = x_1^2 + x_2^2 + x_3^2)$.

B The Curvature Method

In this appendix we examine the relationships between the radii of curvature of a fixed point of the boundary, but at different orientations. Consider a surface defined by the implicit function $F(x, y, z) = 0$, F twice differentiable. Assuming an orthographic projection, where Z is the visual axis, the rim is defined by the set of points on the surface where $F_z(x, y, z) = 0$. Let $p_0 = (x_0, y_0, z_0)$ be a rim point, that is $F(p_0) = F_z(p_0) = 0$. We assume that either $F_x(p_0) \neq 0$ or $F_y(p_0) \neq 0$ and that $F_{zz}(p_0) \neq 0$. By this we ignore points with infinite radius of curvature and inflection points. These points may change their place unexpectedly during rotation. We next want to derive expressions for the radii of curvature r_x, r_y, and then for intermediate orientations r_α in terms of r_x, r_y.

Lemma 1: Let $F(x, y, z) = 0$ be a surface description, and let $p_0 = (x_0, y_0, z_0)$ be a rim point, i.e. $F(p_0) = F_z(p_0) = 0$. The curvature radii of p_0 with respect to the Y and X axes are given by

$$
\begin{aligned}
r_x &= -\frac{F_x}{F_{zz}} \\
r_y &= -\frac{F_y}{F_{zz}}.
\end{aligned}
\tag{B.0.1}
$$

Proof: Consider the space curve defined by the implicit function $F(x, y_0, z) = 0$. According to the implicit function theorem, since $F_x(p_0) \neq 0$ and $F_{zz}(p_0) \neq 0$, $x(z)$ is a well defined function in a neighborhood of p_0, and

$$
\begin{aligned}
\frac{d}{dz} F_z &= F_{zz} + F_{zx}\left(\frac{dx}{dz}\right) = \frac{1}{F_x}(F_{zz}F_x - F_{zx}F_z) \\
\frac{d}{dz} F_x &= F_{xz} + F_{xx}\left(\frac{dx}{dz}\right) = \frac{1}{F_x}(F_{xz}F_x - F_{xx}F_z).
\end{aligned}
$$

And since

$$
\frac{d^2 x}{dz^2} = \frac{d}{dz}\left(\frac{dx}{dz}\right) = \frac{d}{dz}\left(-\frac{F_z}{F_x}\right) = \frac{-(\frac{d}{dz}F_z)F_x + (\frac{d}{dz}F_x)F_z}{F_x^2}.
\tag{B.0.2}
$$

We obtain

$$\frac{d^2x}{dz^2} = \frac{-F_{zz}F_x^2 + F_{zx}F_xF_z + F_{xz}F_xF_z - F_{xx}F_z^2}{F_x^3}. \tag{B.0.3}$$

$F_z(p_0) = 0$, therefore

$$\frac{dx}{dz}(z_0) = 0$$

$$\frac{d^2x}{dz^2}(z_0) = -\frac{F_{zz}}{F_x}. \tag{B.0.4}$$

For a curve $x(z)$, the radius of curvature at z_0 is given by

$$r(t) = \frac{1}{k(t)} = \frac{\left(1 + \frac{dx}{dz}(z_0)\right)^{3/2}}{\frac{d^2x}{dz^2}(z_0)}. \tag{B.0.5}$$

Substituting the appropriate terms we obtain:
$r_x = -\frac{F_x}{F_{zz}}$, and similarly $r_y = -\frac{F_y}{F_{zz}}$.

Proposition 1: Let $F(x, y, z) = 0$ be a surface description, and let p_0 be a rim point, i.e. $F(p_0) = F_z(p_0) = 0$. Let V_α be an axis lying in the image plane and forming an angle α with the positive X-axis. The radius of curvature at p_0 with respect to V_α is given by

$$r_\alpha = r_y \cos\alpha - r_x \sin\alpha. \tag{B.0.6}$$

Proof: Let $G(x', y', z) = 0$ be the surface $F(x, y, z) = 0$ rotated about the Z-axis by the angle $-\alpha$, that is,

$$G(x', y', z) = F(x'\cos\alpha - y'\sin\alpha, x'\sin\alpha + y'\cos\alpha, z). \tag{B.0.7}$$

After such a rotation V_α coincides with the X-axis, therefore

$$r_\alpha^F = r_{y'}^G. \tag{B.0.8}$$

Where r^F, r^G are radii of curvature for the surfaces F, G respectively. According to lemma 1

$$r_{y'}^G = -\frac{G_{y'}}{G_{zz}}. \tag{B.0.9}$$

Since

$$
\begin{aligned}
G_{y'} &= -F_x \sin\alpha + F_y \cos\alpha \\
G_z &= F_z = 0 \\
G_{zz} &= F_{zz}
\end{aligned}
$$

we obtain

$$
r_\alpha = \frac{-F_y \cos\alpha + F_x \sin\alpha}{F_{zz}} = r_y \cos\alpha - r_x \sin\alpha. \tag{B.0.10}
$$

Proposition 2: Let $F(x,y,z) = 0$ be a surface description, and let p_0 be a rim point, i.e., $F(p_0) = F_z(p_0) = 0$. Let $\mathbf{r} = (r_x, r_y)$ be the curvature vector at p_0, and let $\mathbf{t}$ be the tangent vector to the silhouette at p_0. Then $\mathbf{r} \cdot \mathbf{t} = 0$, that is, $\mathbf{r} \perp \mathbf{t}$.

Proof: The point p_0 satisfies the two constraints $F(p_0) = 0$ and $F_z(p_0) = 0$. According to the implicit function theorem, since $F_y(p_0) \neq 0$, $F_{zz}(p_0) \neq 0$, $y(x)$, $z(x)$ are well defined functions in a neighborhood of p_0. The tangent vector $\mathbf{t}$ to $y(x)$ is in the direction $(1, \frac{dy}{dx})$ in the XY plane, and since $\frac{dy}{dx} = -\frac{F_x}{F_y}$, $\mathbf{t}$ is the direction $(-F_y, F_x)$. According to Lemma 1, the vector of curvature radii is given by

$$
\mathbf{r} = (r_x, r_y) = (-\frac{F_x}{F_{zz}}, -\frac{F_y}{F_{zz}}). \tag{B.0.11}
$$

Therefore

$$
\mathbf{r} \cdot \mathbf{t} = \frac{F_x F_y}{F_{zz}} - \frac{F_x F_y}{F_{zz}} = 0. \tag{B.0.12}
$$

C Errors of the Curvature Method

In this appendix we derive an expression of the error obtained when the curvature method is applied to a canonical ellipsoid rotating about the vertical axis. We then show that a similar error is obtained when the ellipsoid is rotating about any axis in space. Finally, we compute the error resulting from applying the curvature method to a non-canonical ellipsoid.

C.1 Rotation About the Vertical Axis

The surface of a canonical ellipsoid can be expressed as:

$$\frac{x^2}{a^2} + \frac{y^2}{b^2} + \frac{z^2}{c^2} = 1. \tag{C.1.1}$$

Let $p_1 = (x_1, y_1)$ be a point on its silhouette. Assume the ellipsoid is rotating about the vertical (Y) axis by an angle θ. Let $p_2 = (x_2, y_2)$ be the appeared position of p_1 following the rotation, and let $\hat{p}_2 = (\hat{x}_2, \hat{y}_2)$ be the approximated position of p_2 according to the curvature method. The relative error for the case of an ellipsoid that is rotating about the Y-axis is given by

$$E = \frac{\hat{x}_2 - x_2}{x_1}.$$

Proposition: The error is given by

$$E(\frac{c^2}{a^2}, \theta) = \cos\theta + \frac{c^2}{a^2}(1 - \cos\theta) - \sqrt{\cos^2\theta + \frac{c^2}{a^2}\sin^2\theta}. \tag{C.1.2}$$

Proof: The rim of a canonical ellipsoid contains the surface points for which $z = 0$. Therefore, the silhouette is defined by

$$\frac{x^2}{a^2} + \frac{y^2}{b^2} = 1. \tag{C.1.3}$$

After the ellipsoid is rotated by an angle θ about the Y-axis, it is described by

$$\frac{(x\cos\theta - z\sin\theta)^2}{a^2} + \frac{y^2}{b^2} + \frac{(x\sin\theta + z\cos\theta)^2}{c^2} = 1. \tag{C.1.4}$$

And its silhouette is given by

$$\frac{x^2}{a^2 \cos^2 \theta + c^2 \sin^2 \theta} + \frac{y^2}{b^2} = 1. \tag{C.1.5}$$

The position of $p_2 = (x_2, y_2)$ is therefore

$$x_2 = \frac{x_1}{a}\sqrt{a^2 \cos^2 \theta + c^2 \sin^2 \theta}$$

$$y_2 = y_1. \tag{C.1.6}$$

Next we calculate $\hat{p}_2$. Denote the surface of the canonical ellipsoid by the form $F(x, y, z) = 1$. According to Lemma 1 (appendix A) the curvature radius with respect to the Y-axis is given by

$$r_x = -\frac{F_x}{F_{zz}} = -\frac{c^2 x}{a^2}. \tag{C.1.7}$$

When the ellipsoid rotates about the Y-axis by an angle θ, the position of p_2 is estimated by the curvature method to be

$$\hat{x}_2 = x_1 \cos \theta - \frac{c^2 x_1}{a^2}(1 - \cos \theta)$$

$$\hat{y}_2 = y_1. \tag{C.1.8}$$

Consequently, the relative error is given by

$$E(\frac{c^2}{a^2}, \theta) = \frac{\hat{x}_2 - x_2}{x_1} = \cos \theta + \frac{c^2}{a^2}(1 - \cos \theta) - \sqrt{\cos^2 \theta + \frac{c^2}{a^2} \sin^2 \theta}.$$

The error is therefore a function of θ and $\frac{c^2}{a^2}$.

C.2   Rotation in 3-D Space

In this section we consider the case of a canonical ellipsoid rotating arbitrarily in 3-D space. A rotation in 3-D space can be decomposed into three successive rotations, about the Z-, Y- and Z-axes. The last rotation can be ignored since it does not deform the image and therefore does not change the errors. (The first rotation cannot be ignored since it determines the actual axis of the second rotation.) Let

$$\frac{(x \cos \alpha + y \sin \alpha)^2}{a^2} + \frac{(-x \sin \alpha + y \cos \alpha)^2}{b^2} + \frac{z^2}{c^2} = 1 \tag{C.2.9}$$

be the surface of a canonical ellipsoid rotated about the Z-axis by an angle α. We now examine this ellipsoid as it rotates about the Y-axis by an angle θ.

Proposition: The error is given by

$$E(\frac{C^2}{A^2}, \theta) \tag{C.2.10}$$

where $\frac{C^2}{A^2} = \frac{c^2}{a^2}\cos^2\alpha + \frac{c^2}{b^2}\sin^2\alpha$.

Proof: In order to prove this proposition we have to show that every horizontal section of the ellipsoid defined above is an ellipse with an aspect ratio $\frac{C^2}{A^2}$ as given in the proposition.

Any nonempty intersection of an ellipsoid and a plane is either a point or an ellipse. The section is nonempty when $y^2 \leq a^2\sin^2\alpha + b^2\cos^2\alpha$, and is a point when a strict equality holds. Given the canonical ellipsoid following its rotation about the Z-axis by an angle α, we show that the boundaries of its horizontal section can be represented as

$$\frac{(x - x_0)^2}{A^2} + \frac{z^2}{C^2} = 1 \tag{C.2.11}$$

which describes a canonical ellipse displaced along the X-axis. To establish the above relation, we show that for a constant value of y the surface equation of the rotated ellipsoid reduces to equation of the displaced ellipse. The two equations are identical if there exists a constant $k \neq 0$ such that the following equation system holds

$$kC^2 = \frac{\cos^2\alpha}{a^2} + \frac{\sin^2\alpha}{b^2}$$

$$kC^2 x_0 = y\sin\alpha\cos\alpha(\frac{1}{b^2} - \frac{1}{a^2})$$

$$kA^2 = \frac{1}{c^2}$$

$$kC^2(A^2 - x_0^2) = 1 - y^2(\frac{\sin^2\alpha}{a^2} + \frac{\cos^2\alpha}{b^2}). \tag{C.2.12}$$

We obtain a system of four equations in four unknowns, A^2, C^2, x_0 and k. We now show that when $y^2 < a^2\sin^2\alpha + b^2\cos^2\alpha$ this system has a unique solution with positive values for A^2 and C^2.

Denote the right side of the four equations by

$$p = \frac{\cos^2 \alpha}{a^2} + \frac{\sin^2 \alpha}{b^2}$$

$$q = y \sin \alpha \cos \alpha (\frac{1}{b^2} - \frac{1}{a^2})$$

$$r = \frac{1}{c^2}$$

$$s = 1 - y^2 (\frac{\sin^2 \alpha}{a^2} + \frac{\cos^2 \alpha}{b^2}).$$

The solution to the system above is given by

$$x_0 = \frac{kC^2 x_0}{kC^2} = \frac{q}{s}$$

$$A^2 = \frac{kC^2(A^2 - x_0^2) + kC^2 x_0^2}{kC^2} = \frac{ps + q^2}{p^2}$$

$$C^2 = \frac{kC^2(A^2 - x_0^2) + kC^2 x_0^2}{kA^2} = \frac{ps + q^2}{pr}$$

$$k = \frac{kA^2}{A^2} = \frac{p^2 r}{ps + q^2}. \qquad \text{(C.2.13)}$$

Notice that $p, r > 0$. This system therefore has a unique solution with positive values for A^2 and C^2 when $ps + q^2 > 0$. This inequality is satisfied when $y^2 < a^2 \sin^2 \alpha + b^2 \cos^2 \alpha$.

Now, we can compute the value of the ratio $\frac{C^2}{A^2}$ from this equation system by dividing the first equation by the third one

$$\frac{C^2}{A^2} = \frac{c^2}{a^2} \cos^2 \alpha + \frac{c^2}{b^2} \sin^2 \alpha. \qquad \text{(C.2.14)}$$

Therefore, any horizontal section of this ellipsoid is an ellipse with an aspect ratio of $\frac{C^2}{A^2}$, and since translation does not affect the results of the curvature method, the error is given by

$$E(\frac{C^2}{A^2}, \theta)$$

Where A^2 and C^2 are the parameters of the ellipse, and θ is the rotation angle about the Y-axis.

C.3 Intermediate Models

In this section we derive an expression of the error obtained when the curvature method is applied to an ellipsoid that is rotated about the Y-axis (rather than a canonical ellipsoid), as discussed in chapter 4. Let

$$\frac{(x \cos \alpha - z \sin \alpha)^2}{a^2} + \frac{y^2}{b^2} + \frac{(x \sin \alpha + z \cos \alpha)^2}{c^2} = 1 \qquad (C.3.15)$$

be the surface of a canonical ellipsoid rotated about the Y-axis by an angle α. Assume this ellipsoid is modeled by the curvature method. We consider now the error produced by using this model as the ellipsoid rotates about the Y-axis by an angle θ.

Proposition: The relative error is given by

$$E_\alpha(\frac{c^2}{a^2}, \theta) = \cos \theta + z' \sin \theta + r'(1 - \cos \theta)x'' \qquad (C.3.16)$$

where

$$z' = -\frac{\sin \alpha \cos \alpha (1 - \frac{c^2}{a^2})}{\cos^2 \alpha + \frac{c^2}{a^2} \sin^2 \alpha}$$

$$r' = \frac{\frac{c^2}{a^2}}{(\cos^2 \alpha + \frac{c^2}{a^2} \sin^2 \alpha)^2}$$

$$x'' = \sqrt{\frac{\cos^2(\alpha + \theta) + \frac{c^2}{a^2} \sin^2(\alpha + \theta)}{\cos^2 \alpha + \frac{c^2}{a^2} \sin^2 \alpha}}.$$

Proof: Let $p_1 = (x_1, y_1)$ be a point on the silhouette of the ellipsoid. Let z_1 be its depth value, and let r_1 be its curvature value with respect to the Y-axis. Then

$$x_1 = \frac{x}{a}\sqrt{a^2 \cos^2 \alpha + c^2 \sin^2 \alpha}$$

$$y_1 = y$$

$$z_1 = \frac{-x \sin \alpha \cos \alpha (a^2 - c^2)}{a\sqrt{a^2 \cos^2 \alpha + c^2 \sin^2 \alpha}}$$

$$r_1 = \frac{xac^2}{(a^2 \cos^2 \alpha + c^2 \sin^2 \alpha)^{\frac{3}{2}}} \qquad (C.3.17)$$

where $p = (x, y)$ is the corresponding point on the silhouette of the ellipsoid in its canonical position.

Let $p_2 = (x_2, y_2)$ be the appeared position of p_1 after a rotation about the Y-axis by an angle θ, p_2 is given by

$$x_2 = \frac{x}{a}\sqrt{a^2 \cos^2(\alpha + \theta) + c^2 \sin^2(\alpha + \theta)}$$

$$y_2 = y. \tag{C.3.18}$$

Let $\hat{p}_2 = (\hat{x}_2, \hat{y}_2)$ be the position of p_2 approximated by the curvature method

$$\hat{x}_2 = x_1 \cos\theta + z_1 \sin\theta + r_1(1 - \cos\theta)$$

$$\hat{y}_2 = y. \tag{C.3.19}$$

Since $y_1 = y_2 = \hat{y}_2$, the error is defined by

$$E_\alpha = \frac{\hat{x}_2 - x_2}{x_1}$$

Let

$$z' = \frac{z_1}{x_1}$$

$$r' = \frac{r_1}{x_1}$$

$$x'' = \frac{x_2}{x_1} \tag{C.3.20}$$

and we obtain the expressions given in the proposition.

D Locally Affine Matching

In this appendix we discuss the matching of two contour images, using the assumption of local planarity, or that the transformation can be described locally as an affine transformation. Additional discussion of this method can be found in (Bachelder & Ullman 1992). The description refers to figure 7.3 in chapter 7.

Assuming a locally affine mapping between the two contour images, each contour point $\mathbf{p}_i = (x_i, y_i)$ in the first image maps to a contour point $\mathbf{p}'_i = (x'_i, y'_i)$ in the second image, given be the equation:

$$\mathbf{p}'_i = A\mathbf{p}_i + \mathbf{t}. \tag{D.0.1}$$

The 2×2 matrix A expresses the two-dimensional linear transformation, and the vector $\mathbf{t}$ denotes the translation in the image plane.

We know that $\mathbf{p}'_i$ is constrained to lie on a line, called the "constraint line". Let $\mathbf{n}$ be the perpendicular from $\mathbf{p}'_i$ to the constraint line, and $\hat{\mathbf{n}}$ be the unit vector in this direction.

The vector $(\mathbf{p}_i + \mathbf{n} - \mathbf{p}'_i)$ is oriented along the constraint line and $\mathbf{n}$ is perpendicular to it, therefore:

$$\hat{\mathbf{n}}^T (\mathbf{p}_i + \mathbf{n} - \mathbf{p}'_i) = 0. \tag{D.0.2}$$

Substituting (D.0.1) into (D.0.2) yields

$$(A\mathbf{p}_i)^T \hat{\mathbf{n}} + \mathbf{t}^T \hat{\mathbf{n}} = \mathbf{p}_i^T \hat{\mathbf{n}} + |\mathbf{n}|. \tag{D.0.3}$$

Therefore, we obtain from each point a single linear equation constraining the six parameters of the affine transformation.

The six unknown parameters of the affine transformation can be represented by the vector $\mathbf{a}$:

$$\mathbf{a} = \begin{bmatrix} A_{00} & A_{10} & A_{01} & A_{11} & t_x & t_y \end{bmatrix}^T. \tag{D.0.4}$$

Then for a given point $\mathbf{p}_i$ with normal $\mathbf{n}_i$ equation (D.0.3) can be rewritten as

$$\mathbf{c}_i \mathbf{a} = d_i. \tag{D.0.5}$$

Both $\mathbf{c}_i$ and $\mathbf{d}_i$ are given in terms of quantities that are measured in the image:

$$\mathbf{c}_i = \left[\; \hat{n}_{i_x} x_i \quad \hat{n}_{i_x} y_i \quad \hat{n}_{i_y} x_i \quad \hat{n}_{i_y} y_i \quad \hat{n}_{i_x} \quad \hat{n}_{i_y} \;\right] \tag{D.0.6}$$

$$d_i = \mathbf{p}_i^T \hat{\mathbf{n}}_i + |\mathbf{n}_i|. \tag{D.0.7}$$

To solve for the affine transformation we need at least six points, providing six constraints. For k points we obtain a system of equations that can be summarized as:

$$C\mathbf{a} = \mathbf{d} \tag{D.0.8}$$

where C is a $k \times 6$ matrix whose rows are $\mathbf{c}_1 \ldots \mathbf{c}_k$, and $\mathbf{d}$ is a vector with elements $d_1 \ldots d_k$. It is possible to use more than the minimum of six constraints, and then (D.0.8) above will be solved in the least-squares sense. This can be obtained by solving the system:

$$C^T C \mathbf{a} = C^T \mathbf{d}. \tag{D.0.9}$$

In some matching problems, the exact point-to-point correspondence may be known for some special contour points, such as corners, terminators, points of high curvature, inflection points, or small blobs. Such point-to-point matches can be naturally incorporated into the computation of the affine transformation. In this case, each pointwise match supplies not only one, but two independent equations. The affine transformation can be then recovered from a system of equation that mixes both contour and point constraints.

In some degenerate cases, the affine transformation will not be determined uniquely by the data. Consider, for example, the case of a circle in one image that maps onto another circle in the second image, of a different scale and at a new location. Since a circle is unaffected by a pure rotation, it is clear that if a transformation A is a possible mapping between the two shapes, any other transformation A' that differs from A by adding some arbitrary rotation is a different possible solution. In this case it will make sense to prefer the transformation that involves the least rotation. Under some conditions the uniqueness of the solution may depend on the size of the neighborhood used to derive the affine transformation. For example, if the neighborhood is too small, it may contain a single line segment which is insufficient for determining the transformation uniquely. A solution can then be obtained by using the smallest neighborhood size that still gives a unique solution. For a more detailed discussion of these issues, including the mixing of line and point constraints, the non-unique solutions and the selection of an appropriate neighborhood size see (Bachelder & Ullman 1992).

E Definitions

E.1 Projections

An image is a two-dimensional projection of a three-dimensional object. A number of different schemes are used to model this projection process. The simplest model is the so-called *orthographic* projection, shown in figure E.1a. In this model all the rays projecting object points to their corresponding image points are parallel, and perpendicular to the image plane. If we choose a coordinate system such that the image plane becomes the $X - Y$ plane, and the projection is along the Z axis, then in the projection a point simply "loses" its Z coordinate. That is, a 3-D object point X, Y, Z, becomes an image point x, y, with $x = X$, $y = Y$. In addition, the orthographic model can allow overall scale changes of the image. When scaling is included, the projection model is also called *weak perspective*. The model is convenient, but inaccurate. It provides a reasonable approximation when the object is in the center of the field of view, and when the distance between the object and the imaging device is large compared with the dimensions of the object itself.

A more accurate description of the correct projection is provided by the *perspective* projection, shown in figure E.1b. Here, all the projection rays meet at a common point, the center of the perspective (also called "central") projection. As in the orthographic projection, the image surface is usually assumed to be a plane. In reality it may have other shapes, for example, in the human eye the retina forms a nearly spherical shape. The origin of the 3-D coordinate system is the center of projection. It is again convenient to consider the image as parallel to the $X - Y$ plane of the coordinate system, with Z constituting the depth dimension. The image origin is the intersection of the Z axis with the image plane. The projection then takes the form:

$$x = \frac{f}{Z}X, \quad y = \frac{f}{Z}Y \tag{E.1.1}$$

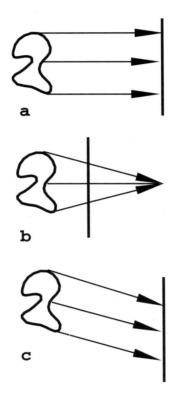

Figure E.1
Commonly used models of the projection from a 3-D object to the 2-D image.
(a). Orthographic projection: the projection rays are parallel, and perpendicular to the image plane. (b). Perspective projections: the projection rays all
meet at a common point. (c). Paraperspective projection: the projection rays
are parallel, but not perpendicular to the image plane, and the projection also
includes a scale factor.

where f is the distance of the image plane from the origin.

The third projection model, in figure E.1c, is called *paraperspective*. In this case the projection rays are parallel, but not necessarily perpendicular to the image plane. As in the weak perspective model, over scale changes are also allowed. This model was analyzed by Aloimonos (1990), Sugimoto & Murota (1993), and was shown to provide a good approximation to the perspective projection.

E.2 Affine Transformation

In a number of places we have used the notion of an affine transformation applied either to a 3-D object or to a 2-D image. An affine transformation combines a linear transformation with a uniform displacement. That is, given a point p in R^n, the transformation has the form:

$$p' = \mathbf{L}p + \mathbf{d} \qquad (\text{E.2.2})$$

where $\mathbf{d}$ is a displacement and $\mathbf{L}$ is a linear transformation, that is:

$$\mathbf{L}(ap + bq) = a\mathbf{L}p + b\mathbf{L}q \qquad (\text{E.2.3})$$

The relevant cases for us are in two and three dimensions. In two dimensions, $\mathbf{L}$ can be represented by a 2×2 matrix and $\mathbf{d}$ is a 2-D vector. Similarly, in 3-D $\mathbf{L}$ is represented by a 3×3 matrix, and $\mathbf{d}$ is a 3-D vector.

All the orthographic images of a planar patch are related by affine transformations. This makes planar objects much easier to recognize compared with the recognition of 3-D objects. Given a single (orthographic) image of a planar object, we can generate additional views by simply applying affine transformations to this image.

Bibliography

Abeles, M. 1991. *Corticonics*. Cambridge: Cambridge University Press.

Abu-Mostafa, Y.S. & Pslatis, D. 1987. Optical neural computing. *Scientific American, 256*, 66-73.

Adelson, E.H. 1993. Perceptual organization and the judgement of brightness. *Science*, 262, 2042-2044.

Ahmed, B., Andersen, J.C., Douglas, R.J., Martin, K.A.C. & Nelson, J.C. 1994. Polyneural innervation of spiny stellate neurons in cat visual cortex. *Journal of Comparative Neurology*, 339, 1-11.

Albright, T.D. 1992. Form-cue invariant motion processing in primate visual cortex. *Science*, 255, 1141-1143.

Aloimonos, J. 1990. Perspective approximations. *Image and Vision Computing*, 8(3), 177-192.

Aloimonos, J., Weiss, I. & Bandyopadhyay, A. 1988. Active vision. *International Journal of Computer Vision*, 1, 333-356.

Ambros-Ingerson, Granger, R. & Lynch, G. 1990. Simulation of Paleocortex performs hierarchical clustering. *Science* , 247, 1344-1348.

Amitai, Y., Friedman, A., Connors, B.W. & Gutnick, M.J. 1993. Regenerative activity in apical dendrites of pyramidal cells in neocortex. *Cerebral Cortex*, 3, 26-38.

Andersen, R.A., Asanuma, C., Essick, G. & Siegel, R.M. 1990. Cortico-cortical connections of anatomically and physiologically defined subdivisions within the inferior parietal lobule. *Journal of Comparative Neurology*, 296, 65-113.

Anderson, C.H. & Van Essen, D.C. 1987. Shift circuits: A computational strategy for dynamic aspects of visual processing. *Proceedings of the National Academy of Science, USA*, 84, 6297-63301.

Atkinson, J., Campbell, F.W. & Francis, M.R. 1969. The magic number 4 ± 0: A new look at visual numerosity judgments. *Perception*, 5, 327-334.

Attneave, F. & Pierce, C.R. 1978. The accuracy of extrapolating a pointer into perceived and imagined space. *American Journal of Psychology*, 91(3), 371-387.

Bachelder, I.A. & Ullman, S. 1992. Contour matching using local affine transformation. *Proceeding of IEEE Conference on Pattern Recognition and Image Processing*, 798-801.

Baird, H.S. 1985. *Model-Based Image Matching Using Location*. Cambridge, MA: MIT Press.

Bajcsy, R. & Solina, F. 1987. Three dimensional object representation revisited. *Proceedings of the International Conference on Computer Vision*, 231-240.

Baker, H. 1977. Three-dimensional modeling. *Proceedings of the 5th International Joint Conference on Artificial Intelligence*, 649-655.

Ballrad, D.H. & Brown, C.M. 1982. *Computer Vision*. Englewood Cliffs, NJ: Prentice-Hall.

Ballrad, D.H. & Brown, C.M. 1982. *Computer Vision*. Englewood Cliffs, NJ: Prentice-Hall.

Bar, M. & Ullman, S. 1993. Spatial context in recognition. *The Weizmann Institute of Science, Technical Report CS93-22*.

Barlow, H.B. 1972. Single units and sensation: A neuron doctrine for perceptual psychology? *Perception*, 1, 371-394.

Barlow, H.B. 1985. Cerebral cortex as model builder. In: D. Rose & V.G. Dobson (eds)., *Models of the Visual Cortex*, New York: John Wiley and Sons, Ltd.

Barlow, H. & Reeves, B. 1979. The versatility and absolute efficiency of detecting mirror symmetry in random dot displays. *Vision Research*, 19, 783-793.

Basri, R. 1992. Recognition by Prototypes. *A.I. Memo 1391, The Artificial Intelligence Lab., M.I.T.*.

Basri, R. 1994. Paraperspective equals affine. *The Weizmann Institute of Science, Technical Report CS94-19*.

Basri, R. & Jacobs, D.W. 1995. Recognition using region correspondences. *Proceedings of the International Conference on Computer Vision*, 8-15.

Basri, R. & Ullman, S. 1993. The alignment of objects with smooth surfaces. *Computer Vision, Graphics, and Image Processing*, 57(3), 331-345.

Beck, J. 1982. Textural segmentation. In: J. Beck (ed.), *Organization and Representation in Perception*, Hillsdale N.J.: Lawrence Erlbaum Assoc.

Beck, J. & Ambler, B. 1972. Discriminability of differences in line slope and in line arrangement as a function of mask delay. *Perception & Psychophysics*, 12(1), 33-38.

Beck, J. & Ambler, B. 1973. The effects of concentrated and distributed attention on peripheral acuity. *Perception & Psychophysics*, 14(2), 225-230.

Beneveneto, L.A. & Davis, B. 1977. Topographical projections of the prestriate cortex to the pulvinar nuclei in the macaque monkey: an autoradiographic study. *Experimental Brain Research*, 30, 405-424.

Besl, P.J. & Jain, R. C. 1985. Three–dimensional object recognition. *Computing surveys*, 17(1), 75-145.

Biederman, I. 1972. Perceiving real-world scenes. *Science*, 177, 77-80.

Biederman, I. 1981. On the semantic of a glance at a scene. In: M. Kubovy & J.R. Pomerantz (eds.), *Perceptual Organization*, Hillsdale, NJ: Lawrence Erlbaum Assoc.

Biederman, I. 1985. Human image understanding: Recent research and a theory. *Computer Vision, Graphics, and Image Processing*, 32, 29-73.

Biederman, I. & Cooper, E.E. 1992. Size invariance in visual object priming. *Journal of Experimental Psychology: Human Perception and Performance*, 18, 121-133.

Biederman, I. & Gerhardstein, P.C. 1993. Recognition of depth-rotated objects: Evidence and conditions for three-dimensional viewpoint invariance. *Journal of Experimental Psychology: Human Perception and Performance*, 19, 1162-1182.

Biederman, I., Mazzanotte, R.J. & Rabinowitz, J.C. 1982. Scene perception: detecting and judging objects undergoing relational violations. *Cognitive Psychology*, 14, 143-177.

Bienenstock, E. & Doursat, R. 1991. Issues of representation in neural networks. In: A. Gorea (ed.)m *Representations of Vision*, Cambridge: Cambridge Univ. Press,

Binford, T.O. 1981. Inferring surfaces from images. *Artificial Intelligence*, 17, 205-244.

Blake, A. & Yuille, A. (eds.), 1992. *Active Vision*. Cambridge, MA: MIT Press.

Blake, A. & Cipolla, R. 1990. *Proceedings of the first European Conference on Computer Vision*, 465-474.

Bolles, R.C. & Cain, R.A. 1982. Recognizing and locating partially visible objects: The local-feature-focus method. *International Journal of Robotics Research*, 1(3), 57-82.

Bolz, J. & Gilbert, C.D. 1986. Generation of end-inhibition in the visual cortex via interlaminar connections. *Nature*, 320, 362-365.

Bomba, P.C. & Siqueland, E.R. 1983. The nature and structure of infant form categories. *Journal of Experimental Child Psychology*, 35, 294-328.

Boussaud, D., Ungerleider, L.C. & Desimone, R. 1990. Pathways for motion analysis: Cortical connections of the medial superior temporal and fundus of the superior temporal visual areas in the macaque. *Journal of Comparative Neurology*, 296, 462-495.

Brady, M. 1982. Smoothed local symmetries and local frame propagation. *Proceeding of IEEE Conference on Pattern Recognition and Image Processing*, 629-633.

Brady, M. 1984. Representing shape. *IEEE International Conference on Robotics*, 256-264.

Brady, M., Ponce., J., Yuille, A. & Asada, H. 1985. Describing surfaces. *A.I. Memo 882, The Artificial Intelligence, 17*, 285-349.

Brady, R.M. 1985. Optimization processes gleaned from biological evolution. *Nature*, 317, 804-806.

Bregman, A.S. 1984. Auditory scene analysis. *Proceedings of the Seventh International Conference on Pattern Recognition*, 168-175.

Breuel, T.M. 1992. Geometric aspects of visual object recognition. *Ph.D. Thesis, Department of EECS, Massachusetts Institute of Technology*.

Brockett, R.W. 1989. Least squares matching problems. *Linear Algebra and its Applications*, 1-17.

Brooks, R. 1981. Symbolic reasoning among 3-dimensional models and 2-dimensional images. *Artificial Intelligence*, 17, 285-349.

Brown, C.M. 1981. Some mathematical and representational aspects of solid modeling. *IEEE Transactions on Pattern Analysis and Machine Intelligence*, 3(4), 444-543.

Bruce, V. & Morgan, M. 1975. Violations of symmetry and repetition in visual patterns. *Perception*, 4, 239-249.

Bülthoff, H.H. & Edelman, S. 1992. Psychophysical support for a two-dimensioanl view interpolation theory of object recognition. *Proceedings of the National Academy of Science USA*, 89, 60-64.

Bundesen, C. & Larsen, A. 1975. Visual transformation of size. *Journal of Experimental Psychology: Human Perception and Performance*, 1, 214-220.

Burns, J., Weiss, R. & Riseman, E. 1992. The non-existence of general case view invariants. In: J.L. Mundy & A. Zisserman (eds.), *Geometric Invariance in Computer Vision*. Cambridge, MA: MIT Press.

Burt, P.J. & Adelson, E.H. 1983. The laplacian pyramid as a compact image code. *IEEE Transactions of Communication*, COM-31, 532-540.

Cass, T.A. 1992. Polynomial time object recognition in the presence of clutter, occlusion, and uncertainty. *Proceedings of the European Conference on Computer Vision*, 834-842.

Canny, J. 1986. A computational approach to edge detection. *IEEE Transactions on Pattern Analysis and Machine Intelligence*, 8(6), 34-43.

Cauller, L.J. & Kullics, A.T. 1991. The neural basis of the behaviorally relevant N1 component of the somatosensory-evoked potential in SI cortex of the awake monkey: evidence that backward cortical projections signal conscious touch sensation. *Experimental Brain Research*, 84, 607-619.

Cavanagh, P. 1991. What's up in top-down processing? In: A. Gorea (ed.), *Representations of Vision*, Cambridge: Cambridge University Press.

Cave, C.B. & Kosslyn, S.M. 1993. The role of parts and spatial relations in object identification. *Perception*, 22, 229-248.

Cave, K.R. 1983. The importance of axes and curvature in simple shape recognition. *Undergraduate Thesis, Harvard University*.

Cave, K.R. & Kosslyn, S.M. 1989. Varieties of size-specific visual selection. *Journal of Experimental Psychology: General*, 118, 148-164.

Cerella, J. 1986. Pigeons and perceptrons. *Pattern Recognition*, 19(6), 431-438.

Chapman, D. 1991. *Vision, Instruction, and Action*. Cambridge, MA: MIT Press.

Chapman, D. 1992. Intermediate vision: architecture, implementation, and use. *Cognitive Science*, 16(4), 491-537.

Chien, C.H. & Aggarwal, J.K. 1987. Shape recognition from single silhouette. *Proceedings of the International Conference on Computer Vision*, 481-490.

Chien, C.H. & Aggarwal, J.K. 1989. Model construction and shape recognition from occluding contours. *IEEE Transactions on Pattern Analysis and Machine Intelligence*, 11(4), 372-389.

Clemens, D.J. & Jacobs, D.W. 1990. Space and time bounds on indexing 3-D models from 2-D images. *IEEE Transactions on Pattern Analysis and Machine Intelligence*, 13(10), 1007-1017.

Clowes, M.B. 1967. Perception, picture processing, and computers. In: N.L. Collins & D. Michie (eds.), *Machine Intelligence*, 1, 181-197, Edinburgh, Oliver & Boyd.

Connell, J.H. 1985. Learning shape descriptions: Generating and generalizing models of visual objects. *MIT Artificial Intelligence Technical Report 853*.

Connor, C.E., Gallant, J.L. & Van Essen, D.C. 1993. Effects of focal attention on receptive field profiles in area V4. *Society of Neuroscience Abstract*, 19, 974.

Corballis, M.C. 1988. Recognition of disoriented shapes. *Psychological Review*, 95, 115-123.

Creutzfeldt, O.D. 1978. The neocortical link: Thoughts on the generality of structure and function of the neocortex. In: M.A.B. Brazier & H. Petsche (eds.), *Architectonics of the Cerebral Cortex*, New York: Raven Press.

Crick, F. & Asanuma, C. 1986. Certain aspect of the anatomy and physiology of the cerebral cortex. In: J.L. McClelland & D.E. Rumelhart (eds.), *Parallel Distributed Processing*, (Vol. 2), Cambridge, MA: MIT Press.

Curtis, S.R. & Oppenheim, A.V. 1990. Reconstruction of multidimensional signals from zero crossings. In: S. Ullman & W. Richards, (eds.), *Image Understanding 1989*, Norwood, NJ: Ablex Publishing Crop.

Cutting, J.E. & Kozlowski, L.T. 1977. Recognizing Friends by Their Walk: Gait Perception Without Familiarity Cues, *Bulletin of the Psychonometric Society*, 5, 353-356.

Damasio, A.R. & Damasio, H. 1993. Cortical systems underlying knowledge retrieval: evidence from human lesion studies. In: T.A. Poggio & D.A. Glaser (eds.), *Exploring Brain Functions: Models in Neuroscience.* New York: John Wiley and Sons.

Damasio, A.R., Damasio, H. & Tranel, D. 1990. Impairment of visual recognition as clues to the processing of memory. In: G.M. Edelman, W.E. Gall & W.M. Cowan (eds.), *Signal and Sense: Local and Global Order in Perceptual Maps*, New York: John Wiley and Sons.

Dane, C. & Bajcsy, R. 1982. An object-centered three-dimensional model builder. *Proceedings of the 6th International Conference on Pattern Recognition*, 348-350.

Daugman, J.G. 1989. Complete discrete 2-d Gabor transforms by neural networks for image analysis and compression. *IEEE Transactions on Biomedical Engineering*, 36(1), 107-114.

Davis, L.S. 1975. A survey of edge detection techniques. *Computer Graphics and Image Processing*, 4, 248-270.

Deacon, T.W. 1990. Rethinking mammalian brain evolution. *American Zoologist*, 30, 629-706.

Desimone, R., Wessinger, M., Thomas, L. & Schneider, W. 1990. Attentional control of visual processing: cortical and subcortical mechanisms. *The Brain: Cold Spring Harbor Symposia on Quantitative Biology*. Cold Spring Harbor Laboratory Press, 963-971.

Dill, M., Wolf, R. & Heisenberg, M. 1993. Visual pattern recognition in *Drosophila* involves retinotopic matching. *Science*, 365, 751-753.

Distler, C., Ungherleider, L.G., Boussaud, D. & Desimone, R. 1991. Cortical connections of temporal-lobe area TEO in macaque. *Supplement No. 4 to the European Journal of Neuroscience*, 56.

Edelman, G.M. 1978. Group selection and phasic re-entrant signalling: A theory of higher brain functions. In: G.M. Edelman & V.B. Mountcastle (eds.), *The Mindful Brain*, Cambridge, MA: MIT Press.

Edelman, S. & Bülthoff, H.H. 1992. Orientation dependence in the recognition of familiar and novel views of three-dimensional objects. *Vision Research*, 32, 2385-2400.

Eimas, P.D. & Miller, J. L. 1990. Infant categories and categorization. In: G.M. Edelman, W.E. Gall & W.M. Cowan (eds), *Signal and Sense: Local and Global Order in Perceptual Maps*, New York: John Wiley and Sons.

Eley, M.G. 1982. Identifying rotated letter-like symbols. *Memory and cognition*, 10, 25-32.

Engel, A.K., König, P., Kreiter, A.K., Schillen, T.B. & Singer, W. 1992. Temporal coding in the visual cortex: new vistas on integration in the nervous system. *Trends in Neuroscience*, 15, 218-226.

Engel, F.L. 1974. Visual conspicuity and selective background interference in eccentric vision. *Vision Research*, 14, 459-471.

Eriksen, C.W. & Schultz, D.W. 1977. Retinal locus and acuity in visual information processing. *Bulletin of the Psychonomic Society*, 9(2), 81-84.

Esguerra, M., Kwon, Y.H. & Sur, M. 1989. NMDA and non-NMDA receptors mediate retinogeniculate transmission in cat and ferret LGN *in vitro. Society of Neuroscience Abstracts*, 15, 175.

Estes, W.K. 1972. Interactions of signal and background variables in visual processing. *Perception & Psychophysics* 12(3), 278-286.

Evans, T.G. 1968. A heuristic program to solve geometric analogy problems. In: M. Minsky (ed.), *Semantic Information Processing*, Cambridge, MA: MIT. Press.

Farah, M.J. 1990. *Visual Agnosia: Disorders of object recognition and what they tell us about normal vision*. Cambridge, MA: MIT Press.

Farah, M. J., 1991. Patterns of co-occurrence among associative agnosias: Implications for visual object representation. *Cognitive Neuropsychology*, 8(1), 1-19.

Faugeras, O.D. 1984. New steps towards a flexible 3-D vision system for robotics. *Proceedings of the 7th International Conference on Pattern Recognition*, 796-805.

Faugeras, O.D. 1993. *Three-Dimensional Computer Vision*. Cambridge, MA: MIT Press.

Faugeras, O.D. & Hebert, M. 1986. The representation, recognition and location of 3-D objects. *International Journal of Robotics Research*, 5(3), 27-52.

Felleman, D.J & Van Essen, D.C. 1984. Cortical connections of area V3 in macaque extrastriate cortex. *Society of Neuroscience Abstracts*, 10, 933.

Felleman, D.J. & Van Essen, D.C. 1991. Distributed hierarchical processing in primate visual cortex. *Cerebral Cortex*, 1-47.

Ferster, D. & Lindström, S. 1985. Synaptic excitation of neurons in area 17 of the cat by intracortical axon collaterals of cortico-geniculate cells. *Journal of Physiology*, 367, 233-252.

Fischer, B. & Boch, R. 1981. Enhanced activation of neurons in prelunate cortex before visually guided saccades of trained rhesus monkey. *Experimental Brain Research*, 44, 129-137.

Fischler, M.A. & Bolles, R.C. 1981. Random sample consensus: a paradigm for model fitting with application to image analysis and automated cartography. *Communications of the ACM*, 24(6), 381-395.

Fischler, M.A. & Bolles, R.C. 1986. Perceptual Organization and curve partitioning. *IEEE Transactions on Pattern Analysis and Machine Perception*, 8(1), 100-105.

Fleck, M. 1986. Local rotational symmetries. *Proceedings of IEEE Conference on Computer Vision and Pattern Recognition*, 332-334.

Freeman, H. & Chakravarty, I. 1980. The use of characteristic views in the recognition of three-dimensional objects. In: E. Gelsema & L. Kanal (eds.), *Pattern Recognition in Practice*, Amsterdam: North-Holland.

Freeman, W.J. 1979. EEG analysis gives model of neuronal template matching mechanism for sensory search with olfactory bulb. *Biological Cybernetics*, 35, 221-234.

Freuder, E.C. 1974. A computer vision system for visual recognition using active knowledge. *MIT A.I. Technical Report 345*.

Friedman, D.P. 1983. Laminar patterns of termination of corticocortical afferents in the somatosensory system. *Brain Research*, 273, 147-151.

Fu, K.S. 1974. *Syntactic Methods in Pattern Recognition*. N.Y.: Academic Press.

Fujita, I, Tanaka, K., Ito, M. & Cheng, K. 1992. Columns for visual features of objects in monkey inferotemporal cortex. *Nature*, 360, 343-346.

Fukushima, K. 1986. A neural network model for selective attention in visual pattern recognition. *Biological Cybernetics*, 55(1), 5-15.

Fukushima, K. 1988. Neocognitron: A hierarchical neural network capable of visual pattern recognition. *Neural Networks*, 1, 119-130.

Fuster, J.M. & Jervey, J.P. 1981. Inferotemporal neurons distinguish and retain behaviorally relevant features of visual stimuli. *Science*, 212, 952-955.

Garey, M.R. & Johnson, D.S. 1979. Computers and Intractability. San Francisco: Freeman.

Gattas, R, Oswaldo–Cruz, E. & Sousa, A.P.B. 1979. Visual receptive fields of units in the pulvinar of cebus monkey. *Brain Research*, 160, 413-430.

Geman, S. & Geman, D. 1984. Stochastic relaxation, Gibbs distributions, and the Bayesian restoration of images. *IEEE Transactions on Pattern Analysis and Machine Perception*, 6, 721-741.

Giblin, P. & Weiss, R. 1987. Reconstruction of surfaces from profiles. *Proceedings of the International Conference on Computer Vision*, 136-144.

Gibson, E.J., Owsley, C.J. & Johnston, J. 1978. Perception of invariants by five-month-old infants: differentiation of two types of motion. *Developmental Psychology*, 14(4), 407-415.

Gibson, J.J. 1950. *The perception of the visual world.* Boston: Houghton Mifflin.

Gibson, J.J. 1979. *The ecological approach to visual perception.* Boston: Houghton Mifflin.

Goldberg, D. E. 1989. *Genetic Algorithms in Search, Optimization, and Machine Learning.* Reading, MA: Addison-Wesley.

Goldberg, M.E. & Wurtz, R.H. 1972. A ctivity of superior colliculus in behaving monkey. II. Effect of attention of neural responses. *Journal of Neurophysiology*, 35, 560-574.

Gould, J.L. 1985. How bees remember flower shapes. *Science*, 227, 1492-1494.

Gray, C.M., König, P., Engel, A.K. & Singer, W. 1989. Oscillatory responses in cat visual cortex exhibit inter-columnar synchronization which reflects global stimulus properties. *Nature, 338*, 334-337.

Green, R.T. & Courtis, M. C. 1966. Information theory and figure perception: The metaphor that failed. *Acta Psychologica*, 25, 12-36.

Gregory, R.L. 1970. *The Intelligent Eye.* London: Weidenfield & Nicholson

Grimsdale, R.L., Sumner, F.H., Tunis, C.J. & Kilburn, T. 1959. A system for the automatic recognition of patterns. Proceedings of the Institute of Electrical Engineering, 106(26), 210-221.

Grimson, W.E.L. & Lozano-Perez, T. 1987. Localizing overlapping parts by searching the interpretation tree. *IEEE Transactions on Pattern Analysis and Machine Intelligence*, 9(4), 469-482.

Grimson, W.E.L. 1981. *From Images to Surfaces.* Cambridge, MA: MIT Press.

Grimson, W.E.L. 1990a. *Object Recognition by Computer.* Cambridge, MA: MIT Press. .

Grimson, W.E.L. 1990b. The combinatorics of heuristic search termination for object recognition in cluttered environments. *Proceedings of the European Conference on Computer Vision*, 552-556.

Grieve, K.L., Murphy, P.C. & Sillito, A.M. 1991. Inhibitory and excitatory components to the subcortical and cortical influence of layer VI cells in the cat visual cortex. *Society of Neuroscience Abstracts*, 17, 629.

Gross, C.G. 1992. Representation of visual stimuli in inferior temporal cortex. *Philosophical Transactions of the Royal Society, London, B*, 335, 3-10.

Grossberg, S. 1993. A solution of the figure-ground problem for biological vision. *Neural Networks*, 6, 463-483.

Grossberg, S. 1994. 3-D vision and figure-ground separation by visual cortex. *Perception & Psychophysics*, 55(1), 48-120.

Grosof, D.H., Shapley, R.M. & Hawken, M.J. 1993. Macaque V1 neurons can signal 'illusory' contours. *Nature*, 365, 550-552.

Hallinan, P.W. 1994. A low-dimensional representation of human faces for arbitrary lighting conditions. *Technical Report, Robotics Laboratory, Harvard University*.

Haralick, R.M. 1979. Statistical and structural approaches to texture. *Proceedings of the IEEE*, 67(5), 786-804.

Haralick, R.M. 1980. Edge and region analysis for digital image data. *Computer Graphics and Image Processing*, 12, 60-73.

Herrnstein, R.J. 1984. Objects, categories, and discriminative stimuli. In H.L. Roitblat, T.G. Bever, & H.S. Terrace (eds.), *Animal Cognition*, Hillsdale N.J.: Lawrence Erlbaum Assoc.

Herrnstein, R.J., Vaughan, W., Mumford, D.B. & Kosslyn, S.M. 1989. Teaching pigeons an abstract relational rule. *Perception & Psychophysics*, 46, 56-64.

Hildreth, E.C. 1984. The computation of the velocity field. *Proceedings of the Royal Society, London, B*, 221, 189-120.

Hirsch, J.A. & Gilbert, C.D. 1991. Synaptic physiology of horizontal connections in the cat's visual cortex. *Journal of Neuroscience*, 11(6), 1800-1809.

Hochberg, J. & Silverstein, A. 1956. A quantitative index of similarity: Proximity versus difference in brightness. *American Journal of Psychology*, 69, 456-458.

Hock, H.S., Romanski L., Galie, A. & Williams, C.S. 1978. Real-world schemata and scene recognition in adults and children *Memory and Cognition*, 6, 423-431.

Hoffman, D. 1983. The interpretation of visual illusions. *Scientific American*, 249 (6), 154-162.

Hoffman, D. & Richards, W. 1986. Parts of Recognition. In: A.P. Pentland (ed.), *From Pixels to Predicates*, Norwood N.J.: Ablex Publishing Corp.

Holland, J.H. 1975. *Adaptation in Natural and Artificial Systems*. Ann Arbor: University of Michigan Press.

Hopfield, J.J. 1982. Neural networks and physical systems with emergent collective computational abilities. *Proceedings of the National Academy of Science, USA*, 79, 2554-2558.

Horn, B.K.P. & Brooks, M. 1989. *Seeing Shape from Shading*. Cambridge, MA: MIT Press.

Horn, B.K.P. & Schunk, B.G. 1981. Determining optical flow. *Artificial Intelligence*, 17, 185-203.

Horn, B.K.P. 1986. *Robot Vision*. Cambridge, MA: MIT Press.

Huang, T. S. & Lee, C. H. 1989. Motion and structure from orthographic projections. *IEEE Transactions on Pattern Analysis and Machine Intelligence*, 2(5), 536-540.

Hubel, D. 1988. *Eye, Brain and Vision*. New York: Scientific American Library.

Hubel, D.H. & Wiesel, T.N. 1962. Receptive fields, binocular interaction, and functional architecture in the cat's visual cortex. *Journal of Physiology*, 160, 106-154.

Hubel, D.H. & Wiesel, T.N. 1968. Receptive fields and functional architecture of monkey striate cortex. *Journal of Physiology*, 195, 215-243.

Humphreys, G.W. & Riddoch, M.J. 1987. *To see but not to see: A case study of visual agnosia*. Hillsdale, NJ: Erlbaum.

Huttenlocher, D.P. & Ullman, S. 1987. Object recognition using alignment. *Proceedings of the International Conference on Computer Vision*, 102-111.

Huttenlocher, D.P. & Ullman, S. 1990. Recognizing solid objects by alignment with an image. *International Journal of Computer Vision*, 5(2), 195-212.

Jacobs, D.W. 1988. The use of grouping in visual object recognition. *MIT A.I. Lab. Technical Report TR 1023*.

Johansson, G. 1973. Visual perception of biological motion and a model for its analysis, *Perception & Psychophysics*, 14(2), 201-211.

Jolicoeur, P. 1985. The time to name disoriented natural objects. *Memory & Cognition*, 13, 289-303.

Jolicoeur, P. 1990. Orientation congruency effects on the identification of disoriented shapes. *Journal of Experimental Psychology: Human Perception and Performance*, 16, 351-364.

Jolicoeur, P. & Ingleton, M. 1991. Size invariance in curve tracing. *Memory & Cognition*, 19, 21-36.

Jolicoeur, P., Ullman, S. & MacKay, M. 1986. Curve tracing: a possible elementary operation in the perception of spatial relations. *Memory & Cognition*, 14, 129-140.

Jolicoeur, P., Ullman, S. & MacKay, M. 1991. Visual curve tracing properties. *Journal of Experimental Psychology, Human Perception & Performance*, 17(4), 997-1022.

Jordan, M. & Jacobs, R.A. 1993. Hierarchical mixtures of experts and the EM algorithm. *MIT Computational Cognitive Science Technical Report 9301.*

Joynson, R.B. & Kirk, N.S. 1960. The perception of size: An experimental synthesis of the associationist and gestalt accounts of the perception of size. Part III. *Quarterly Journal of Experimental Psychology,* 12, 221-230.

Julesz, B. 1971. *Foundations of Cyclopean Perception.* Chicago: Chicago University Press.

Julesz, B. 1975. Experiments in the visual perception of texture. *Scientific American,* 232, 34-43.

Julesz, B. 1981. Textons, the elements of texture perception, and their interactions. *Nature,* 290, 91-97.

Kanade, T. & Kender, J.R. 1983. Mapping image properties into shape constraints: skewed symmetry, affine transformable patterns, and the shape from texture pardigm. In: J. Beck, B. Hope & A. Rosenfeld (eds.), *Human and Machine Vision,* 237-257. New York, Academic Press.

Kanizsa, G. 1979. *Organization in Vision: Essays in Gestalt Perception.* New York: Praeger.

Karni, A, & Sagi, D. 1991. Where practice makes perfect in texture discrimination: Evidence for primary visual cortex plasticity. *Proceedings of the National Academy of Science, USA,* 88, 4966-4970.

Katz, L.C., Burkhalter, A. & Dreyer, W.J. 1984. Fluorescent latex microspheres as a retrograde neuronal marker for *in vivo* and *in vitro* studies of visual cortex. *Nature,* 310, 498-500.

Koch, C. 1987. The action of the corticofugal pathway on sensory thalamic nuclei: A hypothesis. *Neuroscience,* 23, 399-406.

Koch, C. & Ullman, S. 1985. Shifts in selective visual attention: towards the underlying neural circuitry. *Human Neurobiology,* 4, 219-227.

Koffka, K. 1935. *Principles of Gestalt Psychology.* New York: Harcourt, Brace & World.

Koenderink, J.J. 1984. What does the occluding contour tell us about solid shapes? *Perception,* 13, 321-330.

Koenderink, J.J. & Van Doorn, A.J. 1979. The internal representation of solid shape with respect to vision. *Biological Cybernetics,* 32, 211-216.

Koenderink, J.J. & Van Doorn, A.J. 1981. The shape of smooth objects and the way contours end. *Perception 11,* 129-137.

Koenderink, J.J. & Van Doorn, A.J. 1991. Affine structure from motion. *Journal of the Optical Society of America,* 8, 377-385.

Kohonen, T. 1978. *Associative Memories: A System Theoretic Approach.* Berlin: Springer-Verlag.

Kolmogorov, A.N. 1968. Logical basis for information theory and probability theory. *IEEE Transactions on Information Theory,* 14(5), 662-664.

Kositsky, M. 1994. Classification by union of ellipsoids. *M.Sc. Thesis, The Weizmann Institute of Science, Rehovot, Israel.*

Kosslyn, S.M. 1994. *Image and Brain.* Cambridge, MA: MIT Press.

Kosslyn, S.M, Alpert, N.M., Thompson, W.L., Maljkovic, V., Weise, S.B., Chabris, C.F., Hamilton, S.E., Rauch, S.L. & Buonanno, F.S. 1993. Visual mental imagery activates topographically organized visual cortex: PET investigations. *Journal of Cognitive Neuroscience,* 5, 263-287.

Kovács, I. & Julesz, B. 1994. Perceptual sensitivity maps within globally defined visual shapes. *Nature,* 370, 644-646.

Kowler, E. & Steinman, R.M. 1979. Miniature saccades: eye movements that do not count. *Vision Research,* 19, 105-108.

Kundel, H.L. & Nodine, C.F. 1983. A visual concept shapes image perception. *Radiology,* 146(2), 363-368.

Lamdan, Y., Schwartz, J.T. & Wolfson, H. 1988. On the recognition of 3-D objects from 2-D images. *IEEE International Conference of Robotics and Automation,* 1407-1413.

Lamme, V.A.F., Van Dijk, B.W. & Spekreijse, H. 1992. Texture segregation is processed by primary visual cortex in man and monkey. Evidence from VEP experiments. *Vision Research,* 32(5), 797-807.

Lappin, J.S. & Fuqua, M.A. 1983. Accurate visual measurement of three-dimensional moving patterns. *Science,* 221, 480-482.

Larsen, A. 1985. Pattern matching: effects of size ration, angular difference in orientation, and familiarity. *Perception & Psychophysics,* 38, 63-68.

Leeuwenberg, E. 1971. A perceptual coding language for visual and auditory patterns. *American Journal of Psychology,* 84(3), 307-349.

Linainmaa, S., Harwood, D. & Davis, L.S. 1985. Pose determination of a three-dimensional object using triangle pairs. *Technical Report CAR-TR-143,* Center for Automation Research, University of Maryland.

Lipson, P.R. 1993. Model guided correspondence. *Ms.C. Thesis, Department of EECS, Massachusetts Institute of Technology.*

Liu, Z., Knill, D.C. & Kersten, D. 1995. Object classification for human and ideal observers. *Vision Research,* 35(4), 549-568.

Livingstone, M.L. & Hubel, D.H. 1981. Effects of sleep and arousal on the processing of visual information in the cat. *Nature,* 291, 554-561.

Logothetis, N.K., Pauls, J., Bülthoff, H.H. & Poggio, T. 1994. View-dependent object recognition in monkeys. *Current Biology,* 4, 401-414.

Logothetis, N.K., Pauls, J., Bülthoff, H.H. & Poggio, T. 1995. Shape representation in the inferior temporal cortex of monkeys. *Current Biology,* 5, 552-563.

Longuet-Higgins, C.H. 1981. A computer algorithm for reconstructing a scene from two projections. *Nature,* 293, 133-135.

Lowe, D.G. 1985. *Perceptual Organization and Visual Recognition.* Boston: Kluwer Academic Publishing.

Lowe, D.G. 1987. Three-dimensional object recognition from single two-dimensional images. *Journal of Artificial Intelligence*, 31, 355-395.

Luck, S.J., Chelazzi, L., Hillyard, S.A. & Desimone, R. 1992. Attentional modulation of responses in area V4 of the macaque. *Society of Neuroscience Abstracts*, 18, 147.

Lund, J.S. 1988a. Excitatory and inhibitory circuitry and laminar mapping strategies in primary visual cortex of the monkey. In: G.M. Edelman, W.E. Gall & W.M. Cowan (eds.), *Signal and Sense: Local and Global Order in Perceptual Maps*, New York: John Wiley and Sons.

Lund, J.S. 1988b. Anatomical organization of macaque monkey striate visual cortex. *Annual Review of Neuroscience*, 11, 253-288.

Lund, J.S. & Boothe, R.G. 1975. Interlaminar connections and pyramidal neuron organization in the visual cortex, area 17, of the macaque monkey *macaca mulatta. Journal of Comparative Neurology*, 159, 305-334.

Lund, J.S., Hendrickson, A.E., Orgen, M.P. & Tobin, E.A. 1981. Anatomical organization of primate visual cortex VII. *Journal of Comparative Neurology*, 202, 19-45.

Luo, J., Koch, C. & Mathur, B. 1992. Figure-ground segregation using an analog VLSI chip. *IEEE Microelectronics*, 46-57.

Luria, A. 1980. *Higher Cortical Functions in Man.* N.Y: Basic Books.

Mahoney, J.V. & Ullman, S. 1988. Image chunking defining spatial building blocks for scene analysis. In: Z. Pylyshyn (ed.), *Computational Processes in Human Vision*, Norwood, N.J., Ablex Publishing Company, 169-209.

Mallat, S.G. 1989. A theory for multiresolution signal decomposition: The wavelet representation. *IEEE Transactions on Pattern Analysis and Machine Intelligence*, 11, 674-693.

Marin-Padilla, M. 1978. Dual origin of the mammalian neocortex and evolution of the cortical plate. *Anatomy and Embryology*, 152, 109-126.

Markram, H. & Sackman, B. 1994. Calcium transients in dendrites of neocortical neurons evoked by single subthreshold excitatory postsynaptic potentials via low-voltage-activated calcium channels. *Proceedings of the National Academy of Science, USA*, 91, 5207-5211.

Marr, D. 1970. A theory for cerebral neocortex. *Proceedings of the Royal Society, London, B*, 176, 161-234.

Marr, D. 1977. Analysis of occluding contour. *Philosophical Transactions of the Royal Society, London, B*, 275, 483-524.

Marr, D. 1982. *Vision.* San Francisco: Freeman.

Marr, D. & Hildreth, E.C. 1980. Theory of edge detection. *Proceedings of the Royal Society, London, B*, 207, 187-217.

Marr, D. & Nishihara, H.K. 1978. Representation and recognition of the spatial organization of three dimensional shapes. *Proceedings of the Royal Society, London, B*, 200, 269-291.

Marr, D. & Ullman, S. 1981. Directional selectivity and its use in early visual processing. *Proceedings of the Royal Society, B*, 211, 151-180.

Martin, K.A.C. 1988a. From singe cells to simple circuits in the cerebral cortex. *Quarterly Journal of Experimental Physiology*, 73, 637-702.

Martin, K.A.C. 1988b. The lateral geniculate nucleus strikes back. *Trends in Neuroscience*, 11(5), 192-194.

Matan, O., Burges, C.J.C., Le Cun, Y. & Denker, J.S. 1992. Multi-digit recognition using a space displacement neural network. In: J. Moody, S. Hanson & R. Lippmann (eds.), *Neural Information Processing Systems, 4*, San Mateo, CA: Morgan Kaufmann, 488-495.

Maunsell, J.H.R. & Gibson, J.R. 1992. Visual response latencies in striate cortex of the macaque monkey. *Journal of Neurophysiology*, 68(4), 1332-1344.

Maunsell, J.H.R. & Van Essen, D.C. 1983. The connections of the middle temporal visual area (MT) and their relationship to a cortical hierarchy in the macaque monkey. *Journal of Neuroscience*, 3, 2563-2586.

McCormick, D.A. 1990. Membrane properties and neurotransmitter actions. In: G.M. Shepard (ed.), *The Synaptic Organization of the Brain*, 3rd edition, New York: Oxford University Press.

McCormick, P.A. & Jolicoeur, P. 1991. Predicting the shape of distance function in curve tracing: Evidence for a zoom lens operator. *Memory & Cognition*, 19(5), 469-486.

McCormick, P.A. & Jolicoeur, P. 1992. Capturing visual attention and the curve tracing operation. *Journal of Experimental Psychology, Human Perception & Performance*, 18(1), 72-89.

McGuire, B.A., Hornung, J.-P. & Gilbert, C.D. 1984. Patterns of synaptic input to layer 4 of cat striate cortex. *Journal of Neuroscience*, 4, 3021-3033.

Mignard, M. & Malpeli, J.G. 1991. Paths of information flow through visual cortex. *Science*, 251, 1249-1251.

Miller, K.D., Chapman, B. & Stryker, M.P. 1989. Visual responses in adult cat visual cortex depend on N-methyl-D-aspartate receptors. *Proceedings of the National Academy of Science, USA*, 86, 5183-5187.

Milner, P.M. 1974. A model for visual shape recognition. *Psychological Review*, 81(6), 521-535.

Minsky, M. & Papert, S. 1969. *Perceptrons*. Cambridge, MA: MIT Press.

Mitiche, A. & Aggarwal, J.K. 1985. Image segmentation by conventional and information integrating techniques: a synopsis. *Image and Vision Computing*, 3(2), 50-62.

Mockus, J. 1989. *Bayesian Approach to Global Optimization*. Boston: Kluwer Academic Publishers.

Mohan, R. & Nevatia, R. 1989. Perceptual organization for computer vision. *IBM Research Report RC 15177.*

Moran, J, & Desimone, R. 1985. Selective attention gates visual processing in the extrastriate cortex. *Science,* 229, 782-784.

Morton, J. 1969. Interaction of information in word recognition. *Psychological Review,* 76, 165-178.

Moses, Y. 1993. Face recognition: generalization to novel images. *Ph.D. Thesis, Applied Math. and Computer Science, The Weizmann Institute of Science, Israel.*

Moses Y. & Ullman S. 1991. Limitations of non model-based recognition schemes, *Proceedings of the European Conference on Computer Vision,* 820-828.

Moses Y. & Ullman S. 1992. Non-negligibile paramaters for face recognition. *Proceedings of the 9th Israeli Conference on A.I. and Computer Vision,* 265-283.

Moses, Y., Edelman S. & Ullman S. 1993a. Generalization to Novel Images in Upright and Inverted Faces, *The Weizmann Institute of Science, Technical Report CS93-14.*

Moses, Y. & Ullman, S. 1993. Generalization across viewing position and illumination conditions in face identification. *Proceeding of "Looking at People" Workshop at the International Joint Conference on Artificial Intelligence,* 1-7.

Moses, Y. Adini, Y. & Ullman, S. 1994. Face recognition: the problem of compensating for illumination changes. *Proceedings of the European Conference on Computer Vision,* 286-296.

Mountcastle, V.B. 1976. The world around us: neural command functions for selective attention. The F.O. Schmitt Lecture in Neuroscience 1975. *Neuroscience Research Program Bulletin,* 14, 1-47.

Mountcastle, V.B., Lynch, J.C., Georgopoulos, A., Sakata, H. & Acuna, A. 1975. Posterior parietal association cortex of the monkey: command functions for operations within extrapersonal space. *Journal of Neurophysiology,* 38, 871-908.

Mundy, J.L. & Zisserman, A. (eds.), 1992. *Geometric Invariance in Computer Vision,* Cambridge, MA: MIT Press.

Mumford, D. 1992. On the computational architecture of the neocortex. II. The role of cortico-cortical loops. *Biological Cybernetics,* 66, 241-251.

Mumford, D. 1993. Neural architectures for pattern-theoretic problems. In: C. Koch & J.L. Davis (eds.), *Large Scale Neuronal Theories of the Brain,* Cambridge MA: MIT Press.

Mumford, D. & Shah, J. 1989. Boundary detection by minimizing functionals. In: S. Ullman & W. Richards, (eds.), *Image Understanding 1989,* Norwood, NJ: Ablex Publishing Crop.

Murray, J.E., Jolicoeur, P., McMullen, P.A. & Ingleton, M. 1993. Orientation-invariant transfer of training in the identification of rotated natural object. *Memory & Cognition*, 21, 604-610.

Nakayama, K., Shimojo, S. & Silverman, G.H. 1989. Stereoscopic depth: its relation to image segmentation, grouping, and the recognition of occluded objects. *Perception*, 18, 55-68.

Nalwa, V.S. 1993. *A Guided Tour of Computer Vision*. Reading, MA: Addison-Wesley.

Nault, B., Michaud, Y., Morin, C., Casanova, C. & Molotchnikoff, S. 1990. Responsiveness of cells in area 17 after local interception of the descending path from area 18. *Society of Neuroscience Abstracts*, 16, 1219.

Neisser, U. 1967. *Cognitive Psychology*. New York: Prentice-Hall.

Nevatia, R. 1982. *Machine Perception*. Englewood Cliffs, NJ: Prentice-Hall.

Newell, A. & Simon, H.A. 1972. *Human Problem Solving*. P Englewood Cliffs, NJ: Prentice-Hall.

Newsome, W.T. & Wurtz, R.H. 1982. Identification of architectonic zones containing visual tracking cells in the superior temporal sulcus of macaque monkeys. *Investigations of Ophthalmology & Visual Science*, supplement 3, 22, 238.

Nickerson, R.S. 1966. Response times with memory-dependent decision task. *Journal of Experimental Psychology*, 72(5), 761-769.

Noton, D. & Stark, L. 1971. Eye movements and visual perception. *Scientific American*, 224(6), 34-43.

Okajima, K. 1991. A recurrent system incorporating characteristics of the visual system: a model for the function of backward neural connections in the visual system. *Biological Cybernetics*, 65, 235-241.

Olson, R.K. & Attneave, F. 1970. What gives rise to similarity grouping? *American Journal of Psychology*, 83, 1-21.

Palmer, S.E. 1975. The effects of contextual scenes on the identification of objects. *Memory & Cognition*, 3(5), 519-526.

Palmer, S.E. 1977. Hierarchical structure in perceptual representation. *Cognitive Psychology*, 9, 441-474.

Palmer, S.E. 1978. Structural aspects in visual similarity. *Memory & Cognition*, 6(2), 91-97.

Palmer, S.E. 1982. The psychology of perceptual organization: A transformational approach. In: J. Beck, B. Hope & A. Rosenfeld (eds.), *Human and Machine Vision*, New York, Academic Press.

Pavlidis, T. 1977. *Structural Pattern Recognition*. New York: Springer-Verlag.

Pavlidis, T. 1982. *Algorithms for Graphics and Image Processing*. Rockville, MD: Computer Science Press.

Pearson, D., Hanna, E. & Martinez, K. 1990. Computer-generated cartoons. In: H. Barlow, C. Blakemore, & Weston-Smith, M (eds.), *Images and Understanding*, NY: Cambridge University Press.

Pentland, A.P. 1986. Perceptual organization and the representation of natural form. *Artificial Intelligence*, 28, 293-331.

Peterhans, E. & von der Heydt, R. 1991. Elements of form perception in monkey prestriate cortex. In: A. Gorea (ed.), *Representations of Vision*, Cambridge: Cambridge University Press.

Peterson, C. 1990. Parallel distributed approaches to combinatorial optimization: Benchmark studies on traveling salesman problem. *Neural Computation*, 2, 261-269.

Perret, D.I., Rolls, E.T. & Caan, W. 1982. Visual neurons responsive to faces in the monkey temporal cortex. *Experimental Brain Research*, 47, 329-342.

Perret, D.I., Smith, P.A.J., Potter, D.D., Mistlin, A.J., Head, A.S., Milner, A.D. & Reeves, M.A. 1985. Visual cells in the temporal cortex sensitive to face view and gaze direction. *Proceedings of the Royal Society, B*, 223, 293-317.

Pitts, W. & McCulloch, W.S. 1947. How we know universals: The perception of auditory and visual forms. *Bulletin of Mathematical Biophysics*, 9, 127-147.

Pomerantz, J.R., Sager, L.C. & Stoever, R.J. 1977. Perception of wholes and of their component parts: some configural superiority effects. *Journal of Experimental Psychology, Human Perception & Performance*, 3(3), 422-435.

Poggio, T. 1990. A theory of how the brain might work . *The Brain: CSH Symposia on Quantitative Biology*, NY: CSH Laboratory Press, 899-910.

Poggio, T. & Edelman, S. 1990. A network that learns to recognize three-dimensional objects. *Nature*, 343, 263-266.

Poggio, T. & Girosi, F. 1990. Regularization algorithms for learning that are equivalent to multilayer networks. *Science*, 247, 978-982.

Poggio, T., Torre, V. & Koch, C. 1985. Computational vision and regularization theory. *Nature*, 317, 314-319.

Pong, T.C., Shapiro, L.G., Watson, L.T. & Haaralick, R.M. 1984. Experiments in segmentation using a facet model region grower. *Computer Vision, Graphics, and Image Processing*, 25, 1-23.

Posner, M.I. 1980. Orienting of attention. *Quarterly Journal of Experimental Psychology*, 32, 3-25.

Posner, M.I., Nissen, M.J. & Ogden, W.C. 1978. Attended and unattended processing modes: the role of set for spatial location. In: H.L. Pick & I.J. Saltzman (eds), *Modes of Perceiving and Processing Information*, Hillsdale, N.J.: Lawrence Erlbaum Assoc.

Potmesil, M. 1983. Generating models of solid objects by matching 3-D surface segments. *Proceedings of the 8th International Joint Conference on Artificial Intelligence*, 1089-1093.

Potter, M.C. 1975. Meaning in visual search. *Science*, 187, 565-566.

Pratt, W.K. 1991. *Digital Image Processing*. New York: John Wiley & Sons.

Preparata, F.P & Shamos, M.I. 1985. *Computational Geometry.* N.Y.: Springer-Verlag.

Pringle, R. & Egeth, H.E. 1988. Mental curve tracing with elementary stimuli. *Journal of Experimental Psychology, Human Perception & Performance,* 14(4), 716-728.

Pylyshyn, Z. 1988. Here and there in the visual field. In: Z. Pylyshyn (ed.), *Computational Processing in Human Vision,* Norwood NJ: Ablex.

Quillian, M.R. 1968. Semantic memory. In: M. Minsky (ed.), *Semantic Information Processing,* Cambridge, MA: MIT Press.

Ramachandran, V.S. 1986. Capture of stereopsis and apparent motion by illusory contours. *Perception & Psychophysics,* 39(5), 361-373.

Rayner, K. Eye movements in reading and information processing. *Psychological Bulletin,* 85(3), 618-660.

Rezak, M. & Beneveneto, A. 1979. A comparison of the organization of the projections of the dorsal lateral geniculate nucleus, the inferior pulvinar and adjacent lateral pulvinar to primary visual area (area 17) in the macaque monkey. *Brain Research,* 167, 19-40.

Richmond, B.J. & Sato, T. 1982. Visual responses of inferior temporal neurons are modified by attention to different stimuli dimensions. *Society of Neuroscience Abstracts,* 8, 812.

Roberts, L.G. 1965. Machine perception of three-dimensional solids. In: J.T. Tippett, D.A. Berkowitz, L.C. Clapp, C.J. Koester, & A. Vanderburgh, Jr., (eds), *Optical and Electro-Optical Information Processing,* Cambridge, MA: MIT Press.

Robinson, D.L., Goldberg, M.G. & Stanton, G.B. 1978. Parietal association cortex in the primate: sensory mechanisms and behavioral modulations. *Journal of Neurophysiology,* 41(4), 910-932.

Robinson, D.L. & Petersen, S.E. 1992. The pulvinar and visual salience. *Trends in Neuroscience,* 15(4), 127-132.

Rock, I. 1973. *Orientation and Form.* N.Y.: Academic Press.

Rock, I. & Di Vita, J. 1987. A case of viewer-centered object perception. *Cognitive Psychology,* 19, 280-293.

Rock, I., Wheeler, D. & Tudor, L. 1989. Can we imagine how objects look from other viewpoints? *Cognitive Psychology,* 21, 185-210.

Rockland, K.S. & Lund, J.S. 1983. Intrinsic laminar lattice connections in primate visual cortex. *Journal of Comparative Neurology,* 216, 303-318.

Rockland, K.S. & Pandya, D.N. 1979. Laminar origins and terminations of cortical connections of the occipital lobe in the rhesus monkey. *Brain Research,* 179, 3-20.

Rockland, K.S. & Virga, A. 1989. Terminal arbors of individual "feedback" axons projecting from area V2 to V1 in the macaque monkey: A study using immunohistochemistry of anterogradely transported *Phaseolus vulgaris*-leucoagglutinin. *Journal of Comparative Neurology,* 285, 54-72.

Rockland, K.S., Saleem, K. & Tanaka, K. 1992. Widespread feedback connections from areas v4 and TEO. *Society of Neuroscience Abstracts*, 22, 390.

Rolls, E.T. 1984. Neurons in the cortex of the temporal lobe and in the amygdala of the monkey with responses selective for faces. *Human Neurobiology*, 3, 209-222.

Rolls, E.T., Tovee, M.J. & Lee, B. 1991. Temporal response properties of neurons in the macaque inferior temporal cortex. *Supplement No. 4 to the European Journal of Neuroscience*, 84.

Romanycia, M.H.R. 1987. The design and control of visual routines for the computation of simple geometric properties and relations. *Technical Report 87-34, Department of Computer Science, The University of British Columbia*.

Rosch, E. 1975. The nature of mental codes for color categories. *Journal of Experimental Psychology: Human Perception and Performance*, 1, 303-322.

Rosch, E., Mervis, C.B., Gray, W.D., Johnson, D.M. and Boyes-Braem, p. 1976. Basic objects in natural categories. *Cognitive Psychology*, 8, 382-439.

Rosenfeld, A. & Kak, A.C. 1982. *Digital Picture Processing*. New York: Academic Press.

Rosenfeld, A. 1986. Axial representation of shape. *Computer Vision, Graphics and Image Processing*, 33, 156-173.

Rumelhart, D.E, Hinton, G.E. & Williams, R.J. 1986. Learning representations by back-propagating errors. *Nature*, 323, 533-536.

Sagi, D. & Julesz, B. 1985. "Where" and "what" in vision. *Science*, 228, 1217-1219.

Sandell, J.H. & Schiller, P.H. 1982. Effect of cooling area 18 on striate cortex cells in the squirrel monkey. *Journal of Neurophysiology*, 48, 38-48.

Schiller, P.H., Finlay, B.L. & Volman, S.F. 1976. Quantitative studies of single-cell in monkey striate cortex. I. Spatiotemporal organization of receptive fields. *Journal of Neurophysiology*, 39(6), 1288-1319.

Schiller, P.H. & Lee, K. 1991. The role of the primate extrastriate area V4 in vision. *Science*, 251, 1251-1253.

Schiller, P.H. 1995. Effect of lesion in visual cortical V4 on the recognition of transformed objects. *Science*, 376, 342-344.

Scott, G.L. & Longuet-Higgins, H.C. 1991. An algorithm for associating the features of two images. *Proceedings of the Royal Society, B*, 223, 293-317.

Sejnowski, T.J. 1986. Open questions about computation in cerebral cortex. In: J.L. McClelland & D.E. Rumelhart (eds.), *Parallel Distributed Processing* (Vol. 2), Cambridge, MA: MIT Press.

Sejnowski, T.J. & Hinton, G.E. 1985. Separating figure from ground with a Boltzmann Machine. In: M.A. Arbib & A.R. Hanson (eds.), *Vision, Brain, and Cooperative Computation*, Cambridge, MA: MIT Press.

Selfridge, O.G. 1959. Pandemonium: A paradigm for learning. In: *The Mechanization of Thought Processes*, London: H.M. Stationary Office.

Shafrir, A. 1985. Fast region coloring and the computation of inside/outside relations. *Ms.C. Thesis, Department of Applied Math. and Computer Science, The Weizmann Institute of Science, Rehovot, Israel.*

Shapira. 1990. A pictorial approach to object classification and recognition across shape changes. *Ph.D. Thesis, Department of Applied Math. and Computer Science, The Weizmann Institute of Science, Rehovot, Israel.*

Shapira, Y. & Ullman, S. 1991. A pictorial approach to object classification. *Proceedings of the 12th International Conference on Artificial Intelligence,* 1257-1263.

Shashua, A. 1994. Trilinearity in visual recognition by alignment. *Proceedings of the European Conference on Computer Vision,* 479-484.

Shashua, A. 1992. Geometry and photometry in 3-D visual recognition. *Ph.D. Thesis, Department of EECS, Massachusetts Institute of Technology.*

Shashua, A. 1995. Algebraic function for recognition. *IEEE Transactions on Pattern Analysis and Machine Perception,* 17(8), 779-789.

Shashua, A. & Ullman, S. 1988. Structural saliency. *Proceedings of the International Conference on Computer Vision,* 482-488.

Shepard, R.N. 1987. Toward a universal law of generalization for psychological science. *Science,* 237, 1317-1323.

Shepard, R.N. and Cooper, L.A. 1982. *Mental Images and Their Transformations.* Cambridge, MA: MIT Press.

Shepard, R.N. and Metzler, J. 1971. Mental rotation of three-dimensional objects. *Science,* 171, 701-703.

Sherman, S.M., Scharfman, H.E., Lu, S.M., Guide, W. & Adams, P.R. 1990. N-methyl-D-aspartate (NMDA) and non-NMDA receptors participate in EPSPs of cat lateral geniculate neurons recorded in thalamic slices. *Society of Neuroscience Abstracts,* 16, 159.

Shiffrin, R.M., McKay, D.P. & Shaffer, W.O. 1976. Attending to forty-nine spatial positions at once. *Journal of Experimental Psychology, Human Perception & Performance,* 2(1), 14-22.

Shoham, D. & Ullman, U. 1988. Aligning a model to an image using minimal information. *Proceedings of the International Conference on Computer Vision,* 259-263.

Shulman, G.L., Remington, R.W. & McLean, I.P. 1979. Moving attention through visual space. *Journal of Experimental Psychology, Human Perception & Performance,* 5, 522-526.

Silva, L.R., Amitai, Y. & Connors, B.W. 1991. Intrinsic oscillations of neocortex generated by layer 5 pyramidal neurons. *Science,* 251, 432-435

Sperling, G. 1960. The information available in brief visual presentations. *Psychological Monographs, 74,* (11, Whole No. 498).

Spoerri, A. 1991. The early detection of motion boundaries. *MIT A.I. Lab. Technical Report TR 1275*.

Spoerri, A. & Ullman, S. 1987. The early detection of motion boundaries. *Proceedings of the International Conference on Computer Vision*, 209-218.

Sporns, O., Tononi, G. & Edelman, G.M. 1991. Modeling perceptual grouping and figure-ground segregation by means of active reentrant connections. *Proceedings of the National Academy of Science, USA*, 88, 129-133.

Stark, L. & Bowyer, K. 1991. Achieving generalized object recognition through reasoning about association of function to structure. *IEEE Transactions on Pattern Analysis and Machine Intelligence*, 13(10), 1097-1104.

Stoner, G.R. & Albright, T.D. 1992. Neural correlates of perceptual motion coherence. *Nature*, 358, 412-414.

Stratford, K., Mason, A., Larkman, A., Major, G. & Jack, J. 1989. The modeling of pyramidal neurons in the visual cortex. In: R. Durbin, C. Miall, & G. Mitchison (eds). *The Computing Neuron*, Reading, MA: Addison-Wesley.

Strauss, M.S. 1979. Abstraction of prototypical information by adults and 10-month-old infants. *Journal of Experimental Psychology: Human Learning and Memory*, 5(6), 618-632.

Sutherland, N.S. 1959. Stimulus analyzing mechanisms. In: *The Mechanization of Thought Processes*, London: H.M. Stationary Office.

Sutherland, N. 1960. Visual discrimination of orientation by *octopus:* mirror images. *British Journal of Psychology*, 51, 9-18.

Sutherland, N.S. 1968. Outline of a theory of visual pattern recognition in animal and man. *Proceedings of the Royal Society, London, B*, 171, 297-317.

Subirana-Vilanova, B. 1990. Curved inertia frames and the skeleton sketch: finding salient frames of reference. *Proceedings International Conference on Computer Vision*, 702-708.

Sugimoto, A. & Murota, K. 1993. Object recognition by combination of perspective images. *Proceedings of SPIE*, 183-195.

Tarr, M.J. & Pinker, S. 1989. Mental rotation and orientation dependence in shape recognition. *Cognitive Psychology*, 21, 233-282.

Tarr, M.J. & Pinker, S. 1991. Orientation-dependent mechanisms in shape recognition: further issues. *Psychological Science*, 2, 207- 209.

Tou, J.T. & Gonzales, R.C. 1974. *Pattern Recognition Principles*. Reading, MA: Addison-Wesley.

Tenenbaum, J.M. & Barrow, H.G. 1976. Experiments in interpretation-guided segmentation. *Stanford Research Institute Technical Report 123*.

Thomson, D.W. & Mundy, J.L. 1987. Three dimensional model matching from an unconstrained viewpoint. *Proceedings of the IEEE International Conference on Robotics and Automation*, 208-220.

Thorpe, S.J., Celebrinin, S., Trotter, & Imbert, M. 1991. Dynamics of stereo processing in area V1 of the awake primate. *Supplement No. 4 to the European Journal of Neuroscience*, 83.

Tononi, G., Sporns, O. & Edelman, G.M. 1992. Reentry and the problem of integrating multiple cortical areas: simulation of dynamic integration in the visual system. *Cerebral Cortex*, 2, 310-335.

Treisman, A. 1977. Focused attention in the perception and retrieval of multidimensional stimuli. *Perception & Psychophysics*, 22, 1-11.

Treisman, A. 1982. Perceptual grouping and attention in visual search for features and for objects. *Journal of Experimental Psychology, Human Perception & Performance*, 8, 194-214.

Treisman, A. & Gelade, G. 1980. A feature integration theory of attention. *Cognitive Psychology 12*, 97-136.

Tsal, Y. 1983. Movements of attention across the visual field. *Journal of Experimental Psychology, Human Perception & Performance*, 9, 523-530.

Tsotsos, J. 1990. Complexity level analysis of vision. *Behavioral and Brain Sciences*, 13(3), 423-455.

Turk, M. & Pentland, A. 1991. Eigenfaces for recognition. *Journal of Cognitive Neuroscience*, 3, 71-86.

Tversky, A. Features of similarity. *Psychological Review*, 84, 327-352.

Ullman, S. 1979. *The Interpretation of Visual Motion*. Cambridge, MA: MIT Press.

Ullman, S. 1980. Against direct perception. *The Behavioral and Brain Sciences*, 3(3), 373-415.

Ullman, S. 1983. Recent computational studies in the interpretation of structure from motion. In: A. Rosenfeld & J. Beck (eds.), *Human and Machine Vision*, New York: Academic Press.

Ullman, S. 1984. Visual routines. *Cognition, 18*, 97-159.

Ullman S. 1989. Aligning pictorial descriptions: an approach to object recognition. *Cognition*, 32(3), 193-254.

Ullman, S. & Basri, R. 1991. Recognition by linear combinations of models. *IEEE Transactions on Pattern Analysis and Machine Intelligence*, 13(10), 992-1006.

Ullman, S. 1995. Sequence seeking and counter streams: a model for bidirectional information flow in the visual cortex. *Cerebral Cortex*, 5(1), 1-11.

Ungerleider, L.G. & Haxby, J.V. 1994. 'What' and 'where' in the human brain. *Current Opinion in Neurobiology*, 4, 157-165.

Ungerleider, L.G. & Mishkin, M. 1982. Two cortical visual systems. In: D.J. Ingle, M.A. Goodale, & R.J.W. Mansfield (eds.), *Analysis of Visual Behavior*, Cambridge, MA: MIT Press.

Valliant, R. & Faugeras, O.D. 1989. Using occluding contours for recovering shape properties of objects. *IEEE workshop on Interpretation of 3D scenes*, 26-32.

Van Essen, D.C. 1985. Functional organization of primate visual cortex. In: A. Peters & E.J. Jones (eds.), *Cerebral Cortex*, 3, New York: Plenum Press.

Van Essen, D.C. & Maunsell, J.H.R. 1983. Hierarchical organization and functional streams in the visual cortex. *Trends in Neuroscience*, 6, 370-375.

Van Voorhis, S. & Hillyard, S.A. 1977. Visual evoked potentials and selective attention to points in space. *Perception & Psychophysics*, 22(1), 54-62.

Varanese, J. 1983. Abstracting spatial relations from the visual world. *Bs.C. Thesis in Neurobiology and Psychology, Harvard University.*

Vaughan, W., Jr. & Greene, S.L. 1984. Pigeon visual memory capacity. *Journal of Experimental Psychology: Animal Behavior Processes*, 10, 256-271.

Vetter, T., Poggio, T. & Bülthoff, H. 1994. The importance of symmetry and virtual views in three dimensional object recognition. *Current Biology*, 4, 18-23.

von der Heydt, R., Peterhans, E. & Baumgartner, G. 1984. Illusory contours and cortical neuron responses. *Science*, 224, 1260-1262.

Walters, D. 1986. Selection and use of image features for segmentation of boundary images. *Proceedings of IEEE Conference on Computer Vision and Pattern Recognition*, 319-324.

Warrington, E.K. & Taylor, A.M. 1978. Two categorical stages of object recognition. *Perception*, 7, 152-164.

Warrington, E.K. & James, M. 1986. Visual object recognition in patients with right-hemisphere lesions: Axes or features? *Perception*, 15, 355-366.

Weiskrantz, L. 1990. Visual prototypes, memory, and the inferotemporal lobe. In: E. Iwai & M. Mishkin (eds.), *Vision, Memory and the Temporal Lobe*, New York: Elsvier Chapter 2, p. 13-28.

White, E.L. 1989. *Cortical Circuits.* Boston: Birkhäuser.

Willshaw, D.J., Buneman, O.P. & Longuet-Higgins, H.C. 1969. Non-holographic associative memory. *Nature*, 222, 960-962.

Wilson, C.J. 1995. Dynamic modification of dendritic cable properties and synaptic transmission by voltage-gated potasstiom channels. *Journal of Computational Neuroscience*, 2, 91-115.

Winston, P.H. 1970. Learning structural descriptions from examples. *Ph.D. Thesis, MIT, Cambridge, MA.* Also in P.H. Winston (ed.), *The Psychology of Computer Vision*, 1975, N.Y.: McGraw-Hill.

Winston, P.H. 1977. *Artificial Intelligence.* Reading, MA: Addison-Wesley.

Winston, P.H. 1992. *Artificial Intelligence.* Reading, MA: Edison Wesley.

Witkin, A.P. 1985. Scale-space filtering. *Proceedings Int. Joint Conference on Artificial Intelligence*, 1019-1021.

Witkin, A.P. & Tenenbaum, J.M. 1983. On the role of structure in vision. In: J. Beck, B. Hope & A. Rosenfeld (eds.), *Human and Machine Vision*, 481-453, New York, Academic Press.

Woodham, R.J. 1984. Photometric method for determining shape from shading. In: S. Ullman & W. Richards, (eds.), *Image Understanding 1984*, 97-125, Norwood NJ: Ablex Publishing Corp.

Wurtz, R.H., Goldberg, M.E & Robinson D.L. 1982. Brain mechanisms of visual attention. *Scientific American*, 246(6), 124-135.

Wurtz, R.H. & Mohler, C.W. 1976a. Organization of monkey superior colliculus: enhanced visual response of superficial layer cells. *Journal of Neurophysiology*, 39(4), 745-765.

Wurtz, R.H. & Mohler, C.W. 1976b. Enhancement of visual response in monkey striate cortex and frontal eye fields. *Journal of Neurophysiology*, 39(4), 766-772.

Yolles, Y. 1989. Finding natural units of analysis in images. *Ms.C. Thesis, Department of Applied Math. and Computer Science, The Weizmann Institute of Science, Rehovot, Israel*.

Yolles, Y. 1996. *Ph.D. thesis in progress, Department of Applied Math. & Computer Science, The Weizmann Institute of Science, Israel*.

Young, M.P. & Yamane, S. 1992. Sparse population coding of faces in inferotemporal cortex. *Science*, 256, 1327-1331.

Yuille, A.L., Cohen, D.S. & Hallinan, P.W. 1989. Feature extraction from faces using deformable templates. *Proceedings of IEEE Conference on Computer Vision and Pattern Recognition*, 104-109.

Yuille, A. & Hallinan, P. 1992. Deformable templates. In: A. Blake and A. Yuille (eds.), *Active Vision*, Cambridge: MIT Press.

Zeki, S. & Shipp, S. 1988. The functional logic of cortical connections. *Nature*, 335, 311-317.

Zeki, S. 1993. *A Vision of the Brain*. Oxford: Blackwell Scientific Pub.

Zipser, D. & Rumelhart, D.E. 1990. The neurobiological significance of the new learning models. In: E.L. Schwartz, (ed.), *Computational Neuroscience*, Cambridge: MIT Press. Ch. 15, 192-200.

Zipser, K, Lee, T.S., Lamme, V.A.F. & Schiller, P.H. 1994. Spatial extent of extra-rf mechanisms in macaque. *Society of Neuroscience Abstracts*, 20, 1477.

Zucker, S.W. 1987. The diversity of perceptual grouping. In: M.A. Arbib & A.R. Hanson (eds.), *Vision, Brain and Cooperative Computation*, Cambridge, MA: MIT Press, 231-262.

Zucker, S.W., Dobbins, A. & Iverson, L. 1989. Two stages of curve detection suggest two styles of visual computation. *Neural Computation*, 1(1), 68-81.

Index

W